D0927484

"*Introduction to Church Administration* is a comprehensive volume on the various aspects of doing church. Dr. Welch uses his military experience, his church leadership experience, and his teaching experience to describe what he feels is necessary for an effective church operation.

"The chapters which deal with the organizational structure of the church are inclusive and well written. The chapters which relate to administering the activities and programs of the church provide suggestions which will help the church meet its responsibilities and remove itself from legal or tax complications.

"Overall, the book provides guidance for anyone seeking to give leadership to the church for its organization and for conducting its business in a logical and effective manner."

William G. Caldwell
Distinguished Professor in Administration
Southwestern Baptist Theological Seminary

"Robert Welch has written a valuable resource for today's church leader. The information in Church Administration addresses basic administrative issues all church leaders face. The book is practical, insightful, and clear. It certainly will be the text of choice in Christian Education and Pastoral Ministry. This book is a necessary addition to every church leader's library."

Carroll Marr, Senior Pastor
Southcliff Baptist Church
Fort Worth Texas

"Dr. Welch has created a comprehensive book on church administration in his user-friendly, easy-to-understand style. This work is an excellent companion to his previously published work with NACBA Press, *The Church Organization Manual,* and provides helpful assistance to those persons responsible for conducting the business affairs for a local congregation."

Simeon May, CAE, CPA, FCBA
Chief Executive Officer
National Association of Church Business Administration

"For many, church administration may be a cross to bear, but it is nonetheless a necessary concomitant to successful churchmanship. Dr. Bob Welch has brought to his monograph *Church Administration* the wealth of his observations gleaned from many years of doing church administration and teaching church administration. The chapter on Administering Personnel Resources alone is worth the price of the book, and his discernment in administering the programs of church ministry is priceless. I commend the book to all who approach this task."

Paige Patterson, President
Southwestern Baptist Theological Seminary

"For the layperson, administrator, or student who is seeking to guide and direct the administration of the church, Bob's wisdom is vital. He has been there and done it.

"His practical insights and experience will guide you every step of the way...."

Robert Vaughan, Administrator,
First Baptist Church
Fort Smith, Arkansas

CHURCH

ADMINISTRATION

CHURCH
ADMINISTRATION

Creating Efficiency for
Effective Ministry

ROBERT H. WELCH

NASHVILLE, TENNESSEE

Copyright © 2005
by Robert Welch

All rights reserved
Printed in the United States of America

ISBN: 978-0-8054-3164-3

Published by B&H Publishing Group
Nashville, Tennessee

Dewey Decimal Classification: 254
Subject Heading: CHURCH ADMINISTRATION

Unless otherwise noted, Scripture quotations marked HCSB have been
taken from the Holman Christian Standard Bible® Copyright © 1999, 2000,
2002, 2004 by Holman Bible Publishers. Used by permission. Verses marked
TLB are taken from *The Living Bible.* Copyright Tyndale House Publishers,
Wheaton, Illinois, © 1971. Used by permission. Scripture quotations marked
NLT are taken from the Holy Bible, New Living Translation, copyright ©
1996. Used by permission of Tyndale House Publishers, Inc.,
Wheaton, Illinois 60189. All rights reserved.

10 11 12 13 14 15   14 13 12 11 10

Contents

Preface

Evolving from a military background of over twenty years that saw administrative duties woven into nearly every fiber of the fabric of responsibilities to a church ministry position that included simultaneous seminary studies was an interesting life transition for me. Where before I commanded activity and expected it to be accomplished, I now had to request a volunteer to carry out a needed activity. Church volunteers are different, I discovered, from a subordinate sailor. As I began my seminary studies in the Christian Education School, however, I soon found that the basics of administration and leadership taught there were no different from what I had carried out in the military. Churches or religious nonprofits still had to plan, an organization was needed to accomplish the task, leadership had to train and motivate workers, and evaluation and follow-up were necessary elements of ensuring progress.

Through my concentrated studies during the doctorate in church administration, an interesting phenomenon became apparent to me; most church leaders do not carry out their administrative duties very well. For my dissertation studies I focused on a large cross section of the ministers that make up the largest Protestant denomination in America. I studied their job satisfaction based upon the model of intrinsic satisfiers and extrinsic dissatisfiers that had been postulated by other researchers. In my study, 89 percent of the staff members were college graduates, 75 percent held master degrees, 62 percent were graduates of seminaries, and 72 individuals held doctorates—50 of which were pastors. Of the intrinsic satisfaction factors noted, receiving praise and recognition for work, performing creative work, and growth in skill were the highest predictors of satisfaction.

The extrinsic factors that tended to cause job dissatisfaction included absence of adequate salary, job security, interpersonal relationships with supervisor, and meeting family needs. When the position of senior pastor was separated from the other 579 individuals in the study, these 91 pastors who identified themselves as senior pastors of churches were the only group in the study that identified all of the extrinsic dissatisfaction factors as significant in playing a role in their satisfaction. These significant predictors included such factors as relationships with peers, supervisory personnel, and the techniques of supervision of subordinates. Working conditions and the presence (or absence) of policies and procedures also played a significant role.

The review of literature that spawned my dissertation research as well as many investigations and review of other research has caused me to come to the conclusion that the wounds which ministers receive attempting to manage their church or parish are self-inflicted, the result of a poor preparation for ministry by the institutions that were charged to provide competent leaders to the church. This failure to prepare church leaders by seminaries could be attributed, I surmised, to the tenuous balance between a seminary providing a legitimate graduate-level theological education as demanded by accreditation agencies and the need for a practical education as demanded by the local parishioner.

In the early 1990s I had a research class I was teaching conduct a walking survey of several hundred ministers attending a large Bible conference held in the eastern states. The students were to ascertain the ministry position of the individual and then ask two quick questions: If you could choose only one minister from a list of associate pastor, minister of education, minister of music, minister of youth, minister of children, and church administrator, which would you choose first, then second, and third? The second question was: If you could have any one minister with a combination of skills, what would that combination be? The results of the survey were interesting. Most of the respondents were senior pastors. The single most chosen individual was youth minister (apparently pastors want someone else to handle the youth), followed by minister of music, and then the education minister. When a combination was chosen, the most frequent combination individual was music and youth. But when we looked at the dual roles that included the administrator, the administrative dual position was sought significantly higher than any other combination. In other words, whatever the second person on the staff was, it needed to combine the administration of the church.

In the July/August 1996 issue of *Your Church* magazine published by Christianity Today International, I wrote an article about the lack of administrative acumen of individuals who have been called and placed by churches as the leaders of their congregations.[1] Admittedly, some of the article was based on a hunch—but a hunch founded in the dialogue and conversations I had with numerous church leaders. And some of the article was based on the interaction I had with colleagues in the seminary I serve whose philosophy for preparation was to fill the student to the brim with Greek, Hebrew, and the Scriptures, and they will learn how to pastor/lead the church by the school of hard knocks.

When one reads the mission and purpose statements of institutions that prepare ministers for the local church, one encounters words like *graduate education, theological and doctrinal expertise, evangelical zeal, church growth, forward-thinking, mission-minded, parish/church leadership.* A problem exists with such statements in that the creators of these lofty academic goals are usually not the developers of the curriculum that prepares the seminarian for pastoral or ministerial service. Those individuals are the professors of Greek, Hebrew, New and Old Testament, Church History, Ethics, Missiology—traditionalists who think their subjects are the most important for a good education. Often lost, as an oh-by-the-way, is the practical ministry of administration.

Too often when seminary alumnae offices seek to find their graduates, they discover them in occupations other than in church leadership. Studies have been conducted through the years that have indicated that between one-third and one-half of a seminary's graduates are not in church leadership positions a decade after graduation. One of the reasons given is that ministers did not feel that the administrative hassles of the job were what they were called into ministry to do.

In 1997 a nonscientific but comprehensive survey was conducted that asked alumnae of Southwestern Baptist Theological Seminary, "What was it that you wish we had taught you that we didn't teach you?" Over 85 percent stated they needed administrative skills to conduct their ministry. Almost an equal percentile asked for skills to develop relationships with the people they lead.

To prepare for this book, I felt that I should research my hunch to see if my presupposition that pastors are generally inept at administration because they are not instructed in those facets of the ministerial responsibility by the institutions that have been established to prepare them for ministry. The research involved going to the Web sites of about two hundred institutions that are accredited by the Association of Theological Schools (ATS) and the Transnational Association of Christian Colleges and Schools (TRACS). The research developed a listing of 176 institutions that had a Web site that could be scanned to reveal whether they offered a primary degree in pastoral ministry training (the M.Div. was used in all but three institutions); and, whether the Web site provided information that listed the content and discussion of the degree requirements.

Twenty-six of the institutions reviewed were Roman Catholic seminaries, and two were Greek Orthodox institutions. Of these twenty-eight schools only one required a church administration course, one required a leadership course, and two offered leadership as an elective option. Lack of training in this tradition is understandable when one considers the church is a hierarchy with appointed business leaders servicing the diocese. Priests are not expected to provide administrative leadership.

When these 28 Roman Catholic/Greek Orthodox seminaries are removed from the survey analysis, then the results of the remaining 148 institutions are modified:

- Twenty-one institutions required a church administration course.
- Thirty-one institutions required a leadership course that had little to do with administration skills development.
- Four institutions required both an administration and a leadership course.
- Nine schools required an elective that could have included an administration course.
- Two schools require an elective that could have included a leadership course.
- Fourteen institutions offer a church administration course that could be taken as a free elective if the M.Div. student chose.

The average semester-hour requirement of the M.Div. is 94.5 with 90 hours as the mode. Using the 90-hour degree as a standard, these 148 institutions will require of their students about 13,320 hours of academic preparation (90 x 148). Yet only twenty-five institutions will require an administration course (0.563 percent of the course load assuming a three-hour administration course) and only thirty-five will require a leadership course (0.788 percent of the course load for a three-hour course). Another way of reporting the findings is that 84 percent of the institutions (25/148) will have no requirement for administration training, and 77 percent (35/148) will not require leadership as a portion of their academic curriculum. Only 2.7 percent (4/148) of the schools will require both leadership and administration of their M.Div. graduates.

The bottom line is that seminarians attending these 148 seminaries in preparation for pastoral ministry will spend slightly over 1 percent (1.351 percent) of their total academic course preparation in study for the administrative or leadership responsibilities of the church; and up to three-fourths of the others will receive none. This is an interesting balance of preparation requirements given that studies have demonstrated that a pastor spends 50 to 75 percent of his time in administrative and leadership responsibilities in the church.

In a study conducted by Christianity Today International and the Gallup Poll association and reported in *Your Church* magazine, it was found that the average pastor had a workweek of sixty-five hours. In that workweek an average of twenty-four hours was spent in administrative activities, six hours in meetings, and seven hours in miscellaneous activities that did not relate directly to pastoral duties. Only ten hours a week were spent in sermon or teaching preparation, six hours in pastoral care, five hours in counseling, six hours in personal devotions, and one hour in evangelism. In other words, about 57 percent of their ministry was tied up in strictly nonpastoral administrative duties.[2]

One general statement can be drawn from the Web site analysis and the CTI studies: the more liturgical the institution, the less emphasis on administration or leadership. No particular denomination or group of institutions seems to provide a consistent pattern for instruction. Nor does size of the institution seem to affect whether administration is a part of the curriculum. Most institutions that prepare individuals for ministry focus on theological acumen and not on pastoral leadership. Another way of stating this conclusion is that these institutions spend 97 percent of their academic preparation equipping an individual to do about 40 percent of his job and about 3 percent of the training in preparation for about 60 percent of his responsibilities.

In the year 2000, the executive board of the largest Protestant denomination in America reported that nearly one thousand (987) ministers were considered as "forced terminations" from their positions. The reasons often given were issues about who will run the church, poor people skills, pastoral leadership style perceived as too strong, the church's resistance to change, and the church was already conflicted when the pastor arrived. The sad part of the report was the comment that of the 987 forced terminations, 444 (45 percent) did not return to ministry.[3] The seminaries and training schools did a wonderful job of equipping the minister theologically, since these factors were not mentioned as reasons for termination. But they apparently did a poor job of preparing them for pastoral leadership because these were the factors mentioned. And the outcome was that 444 individuals hung it up and said "no more" to their calling. While that may appear as a weakness in the ministerial call, it could also be perceived as poor stewardship of the calling on the part of the leadership that was responsible to ensure this didn't happen.

In the pages that follow I will attempt to assist the reader in becoming a leader, a manager, and an administrator. Perhaps you are in seminary or in ministerial preparation in a college setting; this text will assist you in becoming familiar with the dynamics of administration as they relate to the church or religious not-for-profit organization. If you are in a position of leadership already, the objective of the text will be to become a resource tool you can use to assist you in conducting your business. Whether you are in academic preparation or on the field, the objective of the text is the same. If you understand the tenets of general administration and the techniques of ministerial leadership, your job will be made significantly easier. With leaders prepared to carry out the mundane and often tiresome activities of administration, they can focus on the primary elements of their call to ministry. Pastors can shepherd the flock, counselors can aid in healing the hurting, educators can disciple, musicians can conduct praise and worship, and the church or organization can move forward in accomplishing its vision.

Though this is an academic text, the author has attempted to interject examples and personal experience where appropriate to place the topics discussed in a real-life context. Additionally, scriptural reference has been made to emphasize the biblical mandate for Christian leadership by individuals who fill positions of ministry and service in the local church, diocese or denominational office, or religious nonprofit organization.

An Introduction
to Administration

But you should select from all the people able men, God fearing, trustworthy and hating bribes. Place them over the people as officials of thousands, hundreds, fifties, and tens . . . they can bring you every important case but judge every minor case themselves. In this way you will lighten your load and they will bear it with you.
EXODUS 18: 21–23

One day Jethro, Moses' father-in-law, came up over a sand dune and looked down on a long line of people. It was an interesting group, and it was apparent that all were not happy wanderers. *Fights, arguments, discord* and *disenchantment* would be good words to describe this group of Israelites. Every once in a while a person would just get discouraged and leave the line.

Jethro noted that at the head of the line was his son-in-law, sitting under a tent listening to the various people who made their way to him. So he went down to see what was going on. "Mo," he said, "what's going on here?"

"Well, honored father-in-law," Moses responded, "God made me these people's leader. They have disputes, and I am here to listen to them and settle the problems. I sit here day in and day out listening to all these gripes, solving personal and marital problems, and trying to explain theological issues."

Jethro was astonished. Had not Moses read Drucker during his years in the Pharaoh's palace? In the kind words of a father-in-law, Jethro responded; "You're crazy!" Having expressed his true sentiment, he went on to explain, "If you keep this up, you are going to experience burnout in ministry. What will become of my daughter if you go over the deep end? But worse yet, what will become of the people? God has made you their leader. If you are not able to lead because of fatigue, then they will suffer, and God's purpose for them will not be achieved."

Now Jethro was a Midianite priest, which made him a leader. Good leaders know you do not pose a problem without providing a resolution. So he told

Moses, "Select some men who are prominent in the nation. Look for quality men who are moral in character and righteous in virtue. Place them in charge of portions of the nation. Don't overwhelm them. Assign the most capable person to groups of one thousand, then give them two lieutenants who can lead five hundred each of that group. Keep dividing the group into smaller units with leaders of each subgroup of one hundred, fifty, ten, or whatever. Now each subgroup leader is to be responsible to the leader above him. Let these various leaders solve problems at their level. If they can't solve the problem, then they have someone over them whom they can take it to. That way you can reserve your decision-making responsibilities for the biggies—responding only to the issues that the leaders of the thousands bring to you or issues to which God directs you. Now if you listen to my sage advice, not only will it be easier for you, but you will develop some leaders as well."

If you will excuse my transliteration of Exodus 18 above, some interesting facts may be drawn from the passage:

- God appoints leaders.
- God expects those leaders to function effectively.
- No leader can do the entire job alone.
- Leaders who try to do the job alone either burn themselves out or wear out the followers.
- God often provides advisors to assist us in leadership.
- By delegating portions of the job, a leader can focus on the main issues.
- Delegation does not relieve leaders of responsibility, but it does keep them from carrying out the mundane and routine issues.
- Individuals who are delegated tasks must be qualified to do the job.
- Individuals who are delegated tasks must be given responsibilities at their level of ability—the more qualified, the higher the responsibility.

In the letter to the church at Corinth, Paul wrote about how the conduct of the affairs of the body should be carried out: "How is it then, brothers? Whenever you come together, each one has a psalm, a teaching, a revelation, another language, or an interpretation. All things must be done for edification" (1 Cor. 14:26). Then Paul addressed the confusion that follows whenever all of these are being done at the same time, or whenever there is no order to the activities: "God is not a God of disorder but of peace" (1 Cor. 14:33).

Vines in his *Complete Dictionary of New Testament Words* says that the word that has been translated "peace"—*eirene* in the Greek—means quietness, a harmonized relationship, a sense of rest and contentment.[1]

Paul continued his instructions in this fourteenth chapter of 1 Corinthians to speak to other issues that disrupt the orderliness and function of the church. While he encouraged a variety of forms of Christian expression, he cautioned in verse 40 "Everything must be done decently and in order." The New International Version translates this phrase, "Everything should be done in a fitting and orderly way." *The Living Bible* says, "Done properly in a good and orderly way." The New Living Translation renders it, "Be sure that everything is done properly and in order."

What Paul is saying is that when we "do church," we are to do it in a proper and fitting manner. There should be order, not chaos. There should be sensibility, not insensitivity. There should be consistency, not discord. There should be guidance, not irresponsibility.

In the development of two major organizations of the Bible—the nation of Israel beyond the era of the patriarchal fathers from Abraham and the local church beyond the era of the ministry of Christ—God chose significant leaders who were prepared for the task of leadership and organization. Moses, though born a Hebrew, was brought up in the household of the pharaoh of Egypt. At the time of Moses, Egypt was the ruler of the world. Thus, in his development in the court of the pharaoh, Moses had access to the literature, history, and languages of virtually the known world of his day. Egypt was a highly organized society with sophisticated systems of commerce, transportation, and government. Its military was next to none. Moses was taught all this as part of his preparations for leadership.

Paul (known before his conversion as Saul), like Moses also had a dual citizenship. Paul was a Hebrew, but he was also a Roman citizen. Saul was from Tarsus, the capital of the Roman province of Cilicia and home to a significant Roman university and school of philosophy. The Roman culture in the time of Paul was highly organized, much as Egypt was in the time of Moses. The Romans revered knowledge, skill, and craft. They embraced the academia of Greece, the science of the Mesopotamians and the Egyptians, and the art of their own culture. As Rome conquered the world, they absorbed the best of each culture and organized it around Roman philosophy. It is obvious from his writing and later experiences that Paul received a significant education from the University of Tarsus.

Both Moses and Paul received divinely appointed calls from God to carry out his mission of leadership. Moses, from the burning bush, was called by God to lead the Israelites from Egypt to the promised land. Paul, from the blinding call by Christ on the Damascus Road, was called to form the *ekklesia* into the body called the church. Both received significant preparatory religious education—Moses from Jethro, a Midianite priest; and Paul from Gamaliel, one of the most important Jewish rabbis at the time.

And both were ordained of God to record God's instructions in written form. Moses, drawing on his access to vast historical context and revelation; and Paul from his research, eyewitness account, and revelation. The documents written by these men provided the foundation for the order and operation of the priesthood and the sacrificial worship system of the Old Testament as well as the organization of the church and the integration of the ministries (gifts) of the body of Christ in the New Testament.

In 1 Corinthians 12:28 we read, "And God has placed these in the church: first apostles, second prophets, third teachers, next, miracles, then gifts of healing, helping, managing, various kinds of languages." Many other translations render the word *managing* as "administrations." It comes from the Greek *kubernētēs,* which has as its root the context of a helmsman steering a ship. *Kubernētēs* is used uniquely in 1 Corinthians 12 and in Romans 12 in the listing of spiritual gifts.

Consider a sailing vessel. It is a hollow object with buoyancy which allows it to carry a cargo. It has a keel on the bottom that gives it stability. Sails give it mobility and power. Yet for the vessel to be functional, it needs a rudder to give it direction. The rudder is useless, though, without a helmsman moving it to provide direction and steering the ship to the desired objective. But the helmsman does not take the ship where he wants it to go; there is direction given by someone over him, the captain of the ship. The captain receives his direction from some superior authority who tells him that this is the strategic position that his ship will play in the overall objective of the fleet. The commanding officer of the ship consults his officers and directs the helmsman to move the rudder left and right to take the ship on course to meet the objectives set before them.

With this ship metaphor, as we consider the church, we see that the use of the term *kubernētēs* is appropriate for the context. The leadership of the church (the pastor) receives sailing orders from God through the Holy Spirit and Scripture. Pastors consult others in the leadership of the church and then direct certain individuals whom the Holy Spirit has empowered to carry out the mission and objectives of the church. All are not helmsmen, but each has unique responsibilities in meeting the goals set before the church.

In the New Testament significant passages relate to this description of administration in the church:

1. Administration is not practical versus spiritual (2 Cor. 9:12–15).
2. Administration is about the minister's total task (Titus 1:5–9).
3. Administration is brought about by scholarly study (2 Tim. 2:15).
4. Administration is an art to be practiced (James 2:14–18).
5. Administration is concerned primarily with persons, not processes (1 Cor. 12:18–28).
6. Administration is the means to an end, the process that leads to a product (Phil. 3:13–17).
7. Administration is an orderly process (1 Cor. 14:40).

8. Administration is a preserver of peace, not a producer of conflict (1 Cor. 8:7–13).
9. Administration is a source of fellowship (Acts 2:42).

Throughout this text additional passages of Scripture will be given for every topic introduced to demonstrate that the role of administrative leadership is found throughout the Bible. The objective is to validate from Scripture certain activities that ensure the viability of the New Testament church organization. Essential to this is an understanding by leadership of the administrative responsibilities of the church:

1. To define and set forth the purposes, aims, objectives, and goals of the church.
2. To lay down a broad plan for structuring the church organization.
3. To organize and recruit the executive staff outlined in the plan.
4. To provide clear delegation and allocation of authority and responsibility.
5. To provide standardization of all activities and programs in order to ensure that goals and objectives are uniformly met.
6. To make provisions for committees, councils, and ministry teams to achieve good coordination between all facets of the ministry.
7. To provide for evaluation and look ahead to ways of improving church programs, activities, and ministry.[2]

Historical Philosophy of Administration

"Be careful that no one takes you captive through philosophy and empty deceit based on human tradition, based on the elemental forces of the world, and not based on Christ" (Col. 2:8).

When man began to organize his society and to order the culture is difficult to pinpoint. We know the history of mankind recorded in Genesis demonstrates numerous activities that indicate an intelligent and organized society. They had governments, they built cities, and they formed armies and carried out commerce and trade.

Prior to Abram (Abraham) leaving Paddan-Aram, first into Aram, and then the promised land, we know that the cultures of his home country of Mesopotamia were very sophisticated. In an ancient library found in Nippur of Babylonia, hundreds of clay writing tablets recorded a civilization of history, poetry, commerce, taxes, and religion. Management systems were designed by the Sumerian priests to maintain and hold their vast tax system and to record and inventory loans and personal accounts.

In Genesis 41 we find Joseph conducting a refined and extensive business in the house of the Egyptian pharaoh. In fact Genesis 11–50 describes a civilization of refined organization and structure. Archeological evidence demonstrates that at the time of the pharaohs, Hammurabi in Babylonia developed a code that addressed minimum wages, control of buying and selling, and management (leadership) responsibility. Over a thousand years later, records indicate that King Nebuchadnezzar of Babylonia instituted an inventory control system and an incentive wage system based on worker production.

While other historical and archaeological evidence seems to point to structured cultures in Greece, India, China, and Southern Europe, organization and management philosophy seemed to remain a conceptual design of the dominant leader and had no fixed structure. Thus, while management and organization did exist, it was nebulous and not well articulated. The principles used were derived out of necessity and functioned for the time of the leader.

In summary, three important models for organization existed:

1. The military with its generals and admirals who led armies and fleets into battle. There was a hierarchy of leadership, and this hierarchy was strictly (and often cruelly) enforced. Success was attributed to the brilliance of the winner, and failure was a function of poor leadership, poor equipment, or numbers of followers. Success was highly sought after since it meant living to fight another day.

2. The government with its emperors, kings, potentates, and rulers. Successful governments lead the people. The consideration of the individual that made up the populace was usually not even made. Governments existed because the leaders had some type of "power" over others—whether military, taxation, ownership, or mystical.

3. The religions of the world with their priests and a hierarchal chain of command that flowed through a series of ecclesiastical and clerical levels. Often the organization calls upon the follower to ascribe to some tenet of belief, ritual, sacrifice, or other type of commitment.

Organized management philosophy of the workplace is a latter-day arrival. Prior to the industrial revolution, much of society was built around self-reliance. You planted your fields and harvested what you needed. You traded or bartered away the excess to fulfill a need that you did not have the capacity to fulfill. Fishermen traded the daily catch for lumber to build or repair their boats. Farmers traded the produce of the field to the tanner for leather to make implements. You built your own equipment, your own wagon, your own house.

In time, however, craftspeople came on the scene who could do something better than other people. Their craft and skill became a sought-after item. In this context business management theory began to develop. It flowed out of the evolution of the craft trades and the master craftsmen who flourished in them. It was not until the late nineteenth century and through the twentieth century that administrative philosophy came to fruition.

Four major philosophies of management thought have evolved in the past century.

The Scientific School

This philosophy best embodies the concept of task management by administrators. It was most clearly expressed by the engineer Frederick Taylor in his book, *The Principles of Scientific Management.*[3] Four principles are given.

1. *Discover the best way to accomplish a task.* This relied upon the master craftsman to analyze tasks in time-and-motion studies. How best to produce the product efficiently. How could equipment and resources be better used? Every stick of wood, every swing of the saw, every fastener used was accounted for.

2. *Discover the best worker to accomplish the task.* This expanded the apprentice and journeyman concept of the craft age to encompass the recruitment and coordination of others in the task. The wagon master would recruit the blacksmith to make the wheels, brackets, and fasteners. The tanner would provide the harness and cushions. Inherent in this discovery process was the training and development a worker would receive that provided him opportunity for increased salary.

3. *Provide incentives for the workers.* Up to this point salary was nonexistent. Individuals worked because of indentured responsibility, family responsibility, or the desire to learn a skill at the expense of remuneration for work accomplished. Taylor said that increased incentives would increase productivity, which would in turn result in higher production and profit.

4. *Provide close supervision by the manager.* Perhaps the most significant result of the Scientific School was the definition and demarcation between labor and management. Managers knew best how to do the job; workers did it. The worker had little say in how the task was to be accomplished. Management planned the work, provided the resources and tools, and management was responsible for marketing the products.

While the Scientific School was not truly "scientific," its Victorian moniker does illustrate that for the first time man was beginning to think about how he did his work and carried out business. Benefits to this philosophy were significant for the company because it meant increased productivity and profits. On the other hand, the scientific approach was a significant demoralizer for the common worker. The worker became a tool, a tool that could be manipulated and used. Managers assumed that the worker worked to earn money and that an inherent desire for identity or personal pride in a job well done were cast aside. The inhumane application of this approach would lead to the study of the worker and the second philosophy of management.

The Human Behavior School

This management philosophy came out of a growing need by organizations to create an environment for their personnel to have greater productivity. Most management scholars point to the 1927 Hawthorne studies conducted by Elton Mayo at the Western Electric Plant in Cicero, Illinois, as the basis for the theory. In his book *The Human Problems of an Industrial Civilization,* Mayo describes his studies of variance of light intensity and the effect that it had on production in the assembly areas. The basic question was, What level of light intensity was necessary to ensure maximum productivity? The basis of the study was the desire by the company to save the costs of electrical lighting in the production area while at the same time ensuring maximum output.[4]

Mayo used a typical research study format of a control group that got no variance of light intensity and an experimental group whose light intensity changed every day. The objective was to lower lights until the production rate significantly decreased below the standard set by the control group.

What Mayo discovered in his results had nothing to do with light intensity; it had everything to do with human nature. He found it made no difference whether the lighting was poor or good; productivity in the experimental group increased. What impressed the researcher and the company was that when the control group discovered that the other segment of the production crew was being tested, they increased productivity—possibly out of fear of losing their jobs because they might be perceived as producing less.

Mayo discovered that neither issues of physical fatigue, monotony, nor an environmental issue such as lighting affected production. The important factors of increased productivity were the perception of the worker that management was paying attention to them and the pride of the worker by being placed in a special group, and conversely, the pride in workmanship despite being placed in a special category by the control group. It all focused on the individual, the worker—not the work.

The results of this experiment have been termed the Hawthorne Effect and have caused management to reconsider their attitude of a worker as merely a tool but as a social and psychological being who has needs, desires, and motivation that are intrinsic to their personal psyche.

One of the problems that emerged out of this theory and the desire for management to make application is that it is not as well defined as the Scientific School with its procedural-driven methodology. Douglas McGregor introduced in his book, *The Human Side of Enterprise,* the theory X and theory Y worker.[5] McGregor's thesis was that management must change the attitude and perception of the worker, assessing workers for what their capabilities are and how best to address those issues. His theory X worker is a passive, low-risk taker who prefers job security. McGregor says that this worker needs to be administered with policies, rules, and close supervision. His theory Y person, on the other hand, is an individual who works best in a creative and reward-focused, incentive atmosphere. Their potential and capability needs to be considered; they require less supervision. Mayo's and McGregor's work has brought into tension the age-old question by management—when do we focus on the job, and when do we focus on the worker doing the job?

The Management Process School

While American and European businesses were scurrying to make application of the Scientific School to their organization in hopes for greater productivity (and profits), a French mining director began to consider how the theory could best be applied. Henri Fayol began as a mining engineer and worked his way through the organization to the directorship. Often considered as classical management theory, Fayol postulated that there existed a difference between the role that management played and that of the administrative supervisor—giving management a higher status.

Fayol divided business operations into six segments:
1. *Technical*—producing and manufacturing products
2. *Commercial*—buying raw materials and selling products
3. *Financial*—acquiring and using capital
4. *Security*—protecting employees and property
5. *Accounting*—taking stock of profit and costs
6. *Managing*—the functions of guiding the organization

Thus, Fayol defined management as something someone did, not a title or a position. In his book, *General and Industrial Management,* Fayol described five functions of a manager:
1. *Planning*—examining the future and drawing up a plan of action
2. *Organizing*—building up a dual structure of human resources and materials to achieve an undertaking
3. *Commanding*—maintaining activity among the personnel of the organization
4. *Coordinating*—binding together, unifying, and harmonizing all activity and effort
5. *Controlling*—seeing that everything was accomplished in conformity with the established plan

Fayol then set about to define fourteen principles that describe how these functions could be carried out: division of labor, authority, discipline, unity of command, unity of direction, subordination of individual interest to the common good, remuneration, centralization, hierarchy, order, equity, stability of staff, initiative, and esprit de corps.

Fayol stated these are skills that can be learned and that management can become a vocation as a scientific discipline. For him, with these learned skills and with an understanding of the scheme as outlined in his five functions, the process could be applied in any organizational situation.[6]

The Quantitative School

In the last half of the twentieth century, management concepts became processes of technology. With the advent of the modern computer, calculations, including analyses, became less burdensome and more accurately derived. Capitalizing on statistical analysis, management processes became functions of an operations analysis network rather than a group of managers sitting in a conference room surrounded by charts and production estimates. The Quantitative School takes the problems faced by management and calls on experts from various disciplines to solve the problems using mathematical models. It takes advantage of the systematic approaches of Taylor and Fayol and adds to it the tools of modern qualitative analysis.

The school had as its birth the advent of the nuclear age and the U.S. Navy's desire to produce a nuclear-powered submarine. From start to finish, how long would it take to design, gather the resources, build, man with qualified personnel, and provide an operational weapon of war? Starting with lumps of iron ore, unprocessed uranium, and technologies yet to be developed, operations analysis explored every eventuality of the process and created a time line for completion.

The process took the utilization of specialists from physical science, engineering, accounting, human resources, economists, government, and industry. This group followed a six-step process:

1. *Formulate the problem.*—Address both the consumer's problem and the researcher's problems.
2. *Construct a mathematical model.*—Develop a formula that will represent the system under study. Express the effectiveness of the system as a function of a set of variables with at least one of them being able to control. These variables may fluctuate and may even be under the control of a competitor.
3. *Derive a solution.*—From the model find the values of control that maximize the system's effectiveness.
4. *Test the model and solution.*—Evaluate the variables, checking the model's predictions against reality and comparing actual to forecasted results.
5. *Establish controls over the solution.*—Develop tools for determining when significant changes occur in the variables and functions on

which the solution depends. Determine how to modify the solution in light of changes.

6. *Put the solution to work.*—Implement and evaluate actual results.

One significant advantage of the Quantitative School was that it brought management to the point that problems must be considered in a holistic sense, whereas other theories looked at the work, the worker, or the process. This system addressed all these factors.[7]

Historical Foundations for Administrative Theory

Modern management theory continues to evolve with the introduction of numerous new theories or applications. Three are worthy of mention:

The Systems Approach

This approach of Koontz and O'Donnell and others describes management as a synergy whose whole is greater than the sum of its parts and operates in either an open (interacts with the environment) or closed (no environmental interaction) system. The Systems Approach encourages the manager to combine the concern for task, people, process, and problems in an approach that calls for a manager to integrate his style of management to fit the situation.[8]

The Contingency Approach

This approach describes a system that varies with the situation or circumstances that are present. It allows the manager to ask the question, "Given the task to be accomplished and the individuals that I have to complete the task, the time constraints, and other environmental issues, how best should the situation be managed?" The contingency approach would have managers draw from the foundational theories described above and select the theory or combination of theories described above and select that which best applies in the particular situation. This approach is best exampled in the work of Paul Hersey's *The Situational Leader*[9] and in Blanchard and Johnson's *The One Minute Manager.*[10] In both of these models, the manager is called upon to evaluate the context and content of the task and merge that with his assessment of the individual's capability and motivation to accomplish an assigned task.

The Total Quality Management Approach

This method describes a systematic and structured approach to continuous improvement. The system had its birth with the work of Walter Shewhart prior to World War II with the utilization of control charts and sampling methods and the development of the philosophy of quality assurance. TQM is best associated with the work of W. Edwards Deming, who used the model to revive the Japanese economy after World War II. There are five principles associated with TQM:

1. *Customer focused*—what does the customer want?
2. *Systems thinking*—consider the activity from beginning to end.
3. *Leadership*—remain focused to the service or product.
4. *Continuous improvement*—give attention at every phase of the operation.
5. *Shared decision-making*—implement at all level, worker to manager, in the organization.

These three facets of the model—quality control, the participative work environment, and customer-driven products—form the basis for management decisions.[11]

Administration Defined

To understand how modern administration is carried out in the local church or nonprofit organization, it is necessary to define the terms *management* and *administration*. Many authors will use these terms synonymously, often making no differentiation between the focus of each. As has already been discussed in this chapter, early managers were in fact both decision-makers and supervisors of the work. But as management theory evolved, a definite demarcation developed between the manager, decision maker, and the individual or individuals who actually accomplished the work.

In a modern corporation today, you will find that differentiation. There will be a group we will call the owners of the company. They have provided the capital and impetus to form an organization. This ownership may be vested in a few individuals or many people, such as stockholders. This group of owners selects from among themselves individuals who will give leadership to the company. We will call them the board. This board selects from among themselves officers and a treasurer and reports to the Securities and Exchange Commission (SEC) the formation of their company and obtains legal status for their company and product. It is not the intent of the board to become the individuals who produce the products, so they hire a chief executive officer (the president) to run the business. The CEO is given the authority to employ other individuals who will supervise or actually produce the product.

Management is a technical term that describes the leadership given to an organization and the process for providing the personnel, physical, and fiscal resources to meet defined goals. *Administration* is described as the process of utilization of the personnel, physical, and fiscal resources in order to meet the organization's objectives and goals. Managers tell you what to do; administrators tell you how to do it. Managers see that the right work is done; administrators see to it that the work is done right. Managers provide leadership in identifying the objectives of the organization and setting goals to reach them; administrators supervise in getting the work done to meet those goals.

Administration is thus defined as *the art and science of planning, organizing, leading, and controlling the work of others to achieve defined objectives and goals.*[12]

- Administration is an art because it calls upon the individual to develop and nurture through learning, experience, and training the abilities necessary to accomplish the work.
- Administration is a science because it calls for process, analysis, decision, evaluation, and report. It is pragmatic in its focus.
- Planning considers the futurity of circumstances and the course of actions necessary to achieve set objectives.
- Organizing draws together the human, physical, and fiscal resources into a cohesive element.
- Leading becomes the direction given to accomplish the goals. It is the necessary training, motivation, and coordination of activities.
- Controlling is the evaluation of the process to ensure the goals were met and the organization is moving toward established objectives.
- Work of others identifies the understanding that administration processes involve the integration of supervisor and worker to accomplish a task.
- Objectives are the overarching statements of mission of the organization.
- Goals become the elements established to meet the objectives of the organization.

Thus, managers provide leadership; administrators supervise the work.

Interpretations of Administration in the Local Church

How this philosophy relates to the local church is found in several passages in the New Testament. This comes about with an understanding of the term *church.* The church is a living organism.

- In 1 Corinthians 3:16 and 6:19, the believers are the sanctuary or temple in which the Holy Spirit dwells and the sanctuary of the living God in 2 Corinthians 6:16.
- In 1 Peter 2:5 the believer is the priest of that temple.
- The church is described as a building with Christ as the cornerstone in Ephesians 2:20.

The church is also an organized organism.

- In Romans 12:3–8 and in 1 Corinthians 12:4–11, all individuals who make up the body of Christ (the church) have spiritual gifts.
- In 1 Corinthians 12:12–26 the body parts are interdependent; and in Romans 12:4, they have different functions.

- In Ephesians 4:11–12, 1 Corinthians 12:27–28, and Romans 12:6–8 certain gifted individuals are to take leadership roles in the church.
- Paul identifies certain titled individuals in 1 Timothy 3 who are to carry out the role function of providing leadership to the church.

This division of responsibility in the church is probably best seen in the situation of Acts 6. In this passage of Scripture, we find the church faced a problem. Some widows were not being ministered to adequately. The church leaders (the apostles) became aware of this and provided a solution whereby the church selected individuals from among themselves to minister to the widows. The key verses are found in the middle of the paragraph: "It would not be right for us to give up preaching about God to wait on tables. . . . We will devote ourselves to prayer and to the preaching ministry" (6:2, 4). The role responsibility of the apostles was to provide leadership to the early church, but they were essential in the formation of a solution by directing the provision of the personnel resources from among the body to accomplish the task.

Most church historians give credit to Clement of Rome for the first use of the term *layman*. Clement (circa A.D. 95) implies in 1 Clement 40.5 that the layman was a full participant in the life and work of the church, including the liturgy, and was not just an observer. Early records of the church indicate that baptism came to mean ordination into the royal priesthood in which every person so baptized was set apart with the people of God to be a witness to the Christian faith. It was not considered out of order for any professing baptized Christian to perform any of the liturgical rites of the Christian community.

Through the second century and well into the third century, even though certain persons were being set aside as leaders of the congregation to perform leadership roles, Tertullian (A.D. 160–230) reported that it was not uncommon for laypersons to fulfill those roles in their absence.

In the early church, it was taught that the Christian priest was not a replacement of the Old Testament Jewish priest but a designate who was totally different. Christ came as the completion of the old dispensation priest, paying once for all the sacrifice for sin. The priesthood of the Christian was one of worship and service. Ministry in the early church was the recognition of ability and appointment by the Holy Spirit. The local congregation selected from their own membership individuals they felt endowed for ministry and prepared to lead them. The recognition of this was an affirmation by symbolic ordination (laying on of hands).

As these local bodies became larger, it became the custom for the church to begin to support or pay their leaders. Paul had addressed this topic in 1 Timothy 5:17. Soon, however, the terms of deacon, elder, and bishop, which in the early church related only to the local body leadership, began to take on a hierarchical significance.

Clement of Rome draws the analogy of the Jewish ministry of high priests, priests, and Levites to illustrate the orderly differentiation in the church between the order of the ministry and the laity in general. Ignatius states that it was the privilege of the membership to share the communion of the Eucharist, but it was the bishop who represented Christ in that celebration.

Tertullian asserted that the Christian church, with its orders, succeeded the Jewish priesthood when Christ was crucified by the Jews. The bishop was the high priest and the Christian community in general was a royal priesthood with direct access to God. But Tertullian was clear in his assertion that there was in the Christian community a separate ministry and a priestly discipline that was charged with the priestly functions of the church.

Probably no one influenced the concept of church organization from the late third century onward as did the lawyer Cyprian. He began to interpret the church in light of civil government and the clergy in light of civil authority. For him the bishop was head of the congregation and held authority over lesser clergy. Through ordination the bishop was empowered with power to absolve sins and exact penance. Cyprian felt that the bishop had the right to select lesser clergy. He saw the clergy as a mediator between God and man and the example by the layman of true repentance for sin as demonstrated in some decreed penance.

With Cyprian the idea of apostolic succession became a fixed doctrine of the Western church. For Cyprian, bishops were apostles in the same sense as the first-century apostles; they represented Christ. The bishop became the authority over the church; wherever there was a bishop, there was a church. The lesser clergy, the deacons and elders, became assistants to the bishop. Cyprian set off the clergy from the laity with authority of office. He gave them an official dress to signify their office. These individuals of authority were given an official residence and official functionaries to assist them in their work. Thus, by the end of the third century, the monarchical episcopate had become the universally recognized system of church government.

Thus, as the church moved into the Dark Ages, the separation between the laity and clergy widened as the church sought to expand its hierarchical orders with minor categories of leadership as subdeacon, acolytes, doorkeepers, exorcists, readers, etc. The deacon was no longer an administrator of the church—the local body—but an administrator for the church—the church catholic.

Through the Middle Ages until about A.D. 1200, the concept had been that authority rested with the clergy. The role of the layperson was to protect the feudal society the church had established about itself and to keep silent. The poor were prevented from any association with the church.

In the early thirteenth century, Francis of Assisi launched a lay movement of witness and service to their neighbors. Though the papacy insisted that

Francis be ordained a deacon and many of his friars also ordained, the Third Order of the Franciscans maintained a historic lay movement model. In the late fourteenth century, Gerald Groot formed the Brethren of the Common Life, a lay order dedicated to preaching to the poor and conducting charitable work among the poor and downtrodden. This group focused on education of their adherents. Among significant individuals who attended their schools were Erasmus of Rotterdam and Martin Luther.

During the period of the Renaissance, the authority of the church came into deep question. With the scientific discoveries and humanistic—love of man—philosophy that ensued, the church found its power over the laity eroding. No movement attacked the schism that existed between them like the Reformation that followed. Out of the sixteenth-century Reformation came three distinct groups of laymen who helped form the changes that would occur in the church: the lawyers, the merchants, and the scholars. Martin Luther and Calvin fell into this latter category.

Out of the Reformation came Luther's basic concepts of the church and the laity:

1. Before God all Christians have the same standing, a priesthood which they enter by baptism and through faith.
2. As a comrade and brother of Christ, each Christian is a priest and needs no mediator except Christ. He has access to the Word of God.
3. Each Christian is a priest and has an office of sacrifice, not of the Mass, but the dedication of himself to the praise and obedience of God and to bearing the cross.
4. Each Christian has a duty to hand on to others the gospel which he has received.

One group that emerged out of the Reformation that is of interest to us is that which is often called the radical reformers. This group reconstituted their church offices much as those of the first-century church. Offices were functional in character and held no authority. In fact, the entire church body was subjected to discipline, to the enforcement of all rules, and to witness. Littell states that "it has sometimes been wrongly said that the Anabaptists, Baptists, Quakers, Mennonites, Brethren and like groups have no true doctrine of ordination and frequently no clergy at all. A more perceptive over-simplification would be to say not that they have no clergy but that they have no laity."[13]

In the United States it is interesting that new denominations usually come into being generally as the result of a doctrinal emphasis or an emphasis on some form of church polity. Marvin Judy in *The Multiple Staff Ministry* points out an interesting life cycle of such groups:

- They usually start with an "unordained" clergy.
- Ordination, when done, is local and simple.

- Schools and institutions are created to produce individuals who are capable of ordination.
- The group develops a formal requirement for a trained clergy with increasing emphasis upon ordination.[14]

In discussing the response to trained clergy, we need to redefine what the "employed" staff means. We are familiar with the terms *senior pastor, associate pastor, minister of music, minister of education, youth pastor/director, children's/preschool director, hostess, building supervisor,* and *janitor.* Special talents and professional training make for different positions in the church staff.

The word *professional* is the key to differences of positions in the church. This word comes from the root *professed,* which originally described one "that has taken a vow of the religious order." By 1675 the word had been secularized to mean "the occupation which one professed to be skilled in and to follow . . . a vocation in which professed knowledge of some branch of learning is used in its application to the affairs of others, or in the practice of an art based upon it." In the seventeenth century it applied to the military, law, medicine, and the clergy. A professional professes to know better than others certain facets or matters relating to a vocational exercise.

Historically, the profession was practiced after some degree of demonstrated skill and examination and was duly licensed. Around these professions came guilds or unions. For instance, the guild of the educator was the university; the guild of the doctor was the medus (medical school); and the guild of the theologian was the seminary. These guilds began to develop fundamental philosophies concerning their practice, the requirements for acceptance, standards for practice, and ultimately a constitution and bylaws. The professional stood in judgment of his or her fellow professionals. Today the AMA (American Medical Association) dictates who is qualified to practice medicine, the criteria for continued licensure, and appropriate discipline for errant members. Similar societies or guilds do the same.

The professional clergy also comes under some type of scrutiny. This is usually exercised in the denomination in mainline Protestant churches and the Catholic Church and by the local body in other democratic polity bodies. Regardless of the source of establishment of professional status, three basic criteria usually underlie the preparation for becoming a recognized minister in a given denomination or church:

1. A genuine sense of calling on the part of the candidate, a feeling of purpose.
2. Formal training. This varies from a few courses by correspondence, attendance at a Bible school, to the attendance and/or completion of graduate seminary training.

3. Some type of in-service training or internship in which the candidate demonstrates his gifts, graces, and potential as a useful minister.

As we have seen with other professions, the ministry has also become diversified in the past few decades. Beginning with a minister of education at First Baptist Church in Dallas, Texas, in the 1950s, today most churches that have a regular attendance of two hundred or more on a Sunday will have some form of additional staff that assists the senior pastor in equipping the church for ministry.

As these new professional ministry needs have developed, seminaries have instituted curriculum schemes to prepare these individuals for competent service. In some instances, new ministerial organizations have come into existence. For example, the National Association of Church Business Administration, the American Theological Society, the National Association of Professional Christian Educators, the National Association of Pastoral Counselors, the Religious Education Association, and the Southern Baptist Religious Education Association.

Thus, the church staff has evolved as a group of professional persons, presumably competent in their respective fields, who blend their services together to perform a ministry as a whole to the congregation. Each may have definite functional roles for ministry leadership, but each works together to help the individual Christian fulfill his or her responsibility in worship, nurture, and work.

In the fourth century Jerome wrote in his *Dialogus contra Luciferianos* that "there can be no church community without a leader or a team of leaders." At the risk of comparing the church to a secular organization, consider these analogies to the company organization discussed earlier in this chapter.

*   Christ owns (is head of) the church and provides direction via the Holy Spirit to leaders in the church.
*   Those identified leaders are the "bishops, presbyters, elders, pastor-teachers, deacons" or whatever term a specific church chooses to use.
*   This board of leaders provides the management decisions that lead the church in accomplishing the objectives and goals (mission) of the church.
*   These leaders designate a particular "senior minister" through which the organization (the church) functions to carry out the mission of the church. This individual acts like a CEO/president but is in fact a chief staff officer (CSO) and is usually given the title *senior pastor.*
*   The other professional clergy and paid and lay leadership become the "staff" that assist the CSO in carrying out the mission of the church.

- Church members become the workers (ministers) who carry out the "work of ministry" of Ephesians 4:12 to meet the objectives and goals of the church.

Chapter Review

For administration to work in the local church or any religious nonprofit organization, misconceptions must be dealt with. From the information developed in this chapter, formulate a response to the following objections to administration in the church:

- The church is a spiritual environment and should not have a business atmosphere.
- Administration is an unspiritual activity and has little to do with the processes and ministry of the church.
- Administration takes a minister (or any leader) out of his primary role and places him in a position where he becomes a "desk jockey" or has his ministry controlled by a group of boards or committees.
- The church is fit together by the Holy Spirit and needs no human help or intervention. All members of the body will "naturally" sense their call and become active elements of the function of the church without administration or leadership.

While these objections to effective administration in the church seem weak or inappropriate, they are valid misconceptions held by both clergy and laity and must be dealt with by the leadership of the church. The material in the following chapters will validate the scriptural necessity of efficient church administration and provide church leaders with effective tools to meet the mission and purpose of their church or organization.

Basics
for Administration

Two are better than one because they have a good reward for their efforts. For if either falls, his companion can lift him up; but pity the one who falls without another to lift him up. Also, if two lie down together, they can keep warm; but how can one person alone keep warm? And if somebody overpowers one person, two can resist him. A cord of three strands is not easily broken.
ECCLESIASTES 4:9–12

This passage of Scripture came to life for me several years ago as I was completing my qualifications using underwater breathing equipment (SCUBA) in the Navy. The final qualification was a deep ocean dive that occurred off the coast of Jamaica. There, deep fresh-water wells boiled up from the ocean bottom fed from island rivers that had gone underground only to surface several hundred yards off shore. Similar to sinkholes, these depressions had unusually clear water. The marine life was unique. My diving instructor chose a dive of about 150 feet.

As we entered the water and began our descent, I noted the beautiful marine growth on the walls of the well. Because of the clarity of the water, the colors of the growth remained vivid for several feet down. I noted that at the bottom of the well were several sharks. There was no concern because they looked to be only a few feet in length—far smaller than the many sharks I had dived with off the coast of Florida. As we continued our descent, I put the sharks out of my mind. At about 110 feet down, I again looked, and the sharks had gotten bigger! About that time a shark swam by a metal chair that had sunk to the bottom of the hole. Judging from the size of the chair, the shark was about ten to twelve feet long. And he had many equally large friends.

One of the sharks looked up and took note of the four tempting legs hooked to two bodies dangling down like a meal. And they began to circle up toward us. My diving instructor tapped me on the head and pointed to his writing pad with this message: "Place your back to mine and clank your diving tank on mine as we go up." I liked the "go up" part but didn't understand the clanking part. The body must acclimate to changes in pressure as the diver rises. At every thirty-two feet you must stop and wait. We would have four stops on the way up.

The trip to the surface was long and agonizing. We pushed off the sharks every once in a while with our probe sticks. And of course we clanked. The last pressure stop seemed like an eternity, but just as soon as I could do so safely, I popped out of the water in one motion and into our rubber raft. After getting my composure back, I was able to relive the adventure with my diving instructor. "That was a good idea banging our tanks to scare them off," I said.

"That clanking noise probably made them mad," he replied. "The reason I had you clank your tank against mine was to let me know you were still there looking after my backside. If you had stopped clanking, I would have assumed you had gotten eaten, and I would have gone to plan B."

As in every venue of ministry, there must exist some semblance of organization—a plan A and a plan B—in order to move forward. Ministers are called to minister. But this is difficult to achieve without an understanding of how to go about carrying out that ministry. Church leaders do not function in isolation; they are surrounded by boards, committees, councils, teams, deacons, and other staff members. Effective and efficient ministry requires the institution to develop some principles of administrative organization.

Dynamics of Administration

For years managers, administrators, and supervisors have rallied around a process for getting the job done. For discussion, we will call this process the modern process of administration. It involves a consideration of four principal functions: planning, organizing, leading, and controlling. In each of those four functions certain activities will take place as the task is accomplished.[1]

A word of discussion before the modern process of administration is presented. What is described below is a process. It is not a series of steps that require the leader to move slavishly from room one to room two. It must be viewed holistically. It is like a hamster on a four-colored tread wheel that has nineteen rungs to step on. As the wheel spins around, the hamster steps on the rungs of each of the four quadrants several times. Sometimes the rungs are bypassed because the wheel is in motion and that rung no longer represents a critical stepping stone. As the wheel moves faster, the functional areas seem to blur into a uniform color. In the process of administration, each of the functions and their activities must be considered.

Administrative Planning

"For which of you, wanting to build a tower, doesn't first sit down and calculate the cost to see if he has enough to complete it? Otherwise, after he has laid the foundation and cannot finish it, all the onlookers will begin to make fun of him, saying, 'This man started to build and wasn't able to finish'" (Luke 14:28–30).

Planning is the work we do to predetermine a course of action. Planning is concerned with the futurity of present decisions—that is, what will happen in the future with the decisions we make now. This means three things to the church planner:

1. What alternative courses of action are open?
2. What will be the cause and effect chain of events resulting from certain decisions?
3. What activities and actions will be required to implement that choice?

Planning is reasoning about how a church or organization will get where it wants to go. A basic task of comprehensive planning is to visualize the mission as the pastor and other leaders envision it and to see the church moving in the future. When we consider planning, we must remember three important facets:

*   It is a process.
*   It takes time.
*   It involves people.

There are seven administrative activities that leaders must consider as they move through the planning process:

1. *Estimate the future.* This is the work we do to anticipate what tomorrow will be like. The smart administrator will constantly consider the future and its eventualities. Futurists tell us that the rate of change in the world is rapid and dramatic. Demographic characteristics of the culture change daily. There was a time when we could look to a future of five to ten years with some degree of accuracy and reasonableness. This is not the case today. Astute administrators will constantly correlate the historicity of the church or organization with the present events and draw some estimate of what the future will look like within the next few years and what type of organization it will take to move the church there. Forecasting the future is not planning for the future; it is only providing a database to make those plans.

2. *Establish objectives.* This is the work we do to determine goals or targets. Based upon how the administrator foresees the future as it relates to the organization, decisions should be brought forward to address those issues. This is the time when brainstorming and prayerful discussion seeks to discover just exactly how the organization should address what should be accomplished. These objectives then become the focus for administrative efforts and resource allocation. Objectives are statements of ultimate end toward which the church or organization aims its activities. This is often called the vision of the church and is expressed in mission statements and master plans. From

these objectives will be developed goals and strategies for accomplishment. For example, your church may set as a mission objective to evangelize your community for the Lord. A goal in attaining that objective would be to start an apartment outreach in a section of town near the church.

The development of objectives is an important step and must be made in consideration of several factors:

- The mission and purpose of the church or organization
- The specific results expected
- Who will be expected to accomplish the objective
- The where, when, and how it is to be done

3. *Develop policies.* A policy is a command decision from top management to perform in a specified manner. It establishes definite limits of authority. Policies do not spell out the end itself but specify a means to accomplish the end described in the objective. In every organization certain concepts of management must be established to reduce confusion and ensure uniformity:

- What is meant by policy?
- Who will formulate and recommend policy?
- How will the policy be made known to those it affects?
- How will we measure performance against the policy?
- How do we go about changing policy?

The greatest threat to effective policy making is the failure to keep policies current, applicable, and legally defensible. Policies state how the church or organization will function. We will address the development of policy and procedures in the next chapter.

4. *Develop implementing procedures.* Procedures are plans that implement the policies of the church or organization. They become guides to action rather than guides to thinking. They detail the exact manner a certain activity will be carried out—a chronological listing of what must be done and by whom. Procedures are best developed by the individuals who must implement the policies regulating action.

A simplistic example might be: *It is the policy of the church that the hall carpets be always kept clean.* The procedures for vacuuming the hall carpets might be:

- Every Monday, Wednesday, and Friday the carpets will be vacuumed by the custodians.
- The carpets will be vacuumed at 9:00 a.m. on Monday and Wednesday and after working hours on Friday.
- The carpets will be vacuumed with the upright floor vacuum.

The church administrator determined the policy, and the lead janitor developed the procedures to ensure the policy was met.

5. *Program.* This involves establishing the priority and sequence of activities for the accomplishment of the objectives and goals. Programming is setting up a sequence of events that will lead to objective completion. Often programming is interrelated with the development of procedures. It is part of the process, however, because it determines major steps to accomplishment, establishes priorities for accomplishment, and then determines the overall time frame in which the objective will be met.

6. *Schedule.* This administrative activity involves putting a time factor on the program and inserting into the church or organization calendar the program with dates, hours, and minutes. Scheduling gives a beginning date. In programming we developed a time frame for accomplishment. From that estimate of time to completion, we can establish an ending date.

7. *Budget.* This activity is the application of all your resources. This calls for a determination of how much manpower, finances, and facilities will be utilized to achieve the objective. Budgets are frequently expressed in dollars and cents. And, sadly, they become the driving force that determines the extent of completion of the objective. On the other hand, in reality, budgets include a variety of resources—human, fiscal, and property. Budgeting becomes an easier task if an administrator has effectively prioritized the objectives because it then becomes a simple matter of allocating resources to accomplish the activities. Effective fiscal management will be discussed in the chapter on church finances.

Administrative Organizing

"You should select from all the people able men, God-fearing, trustworthy, and hating bribes. Place them over the people as officials of thousands, hundreds, fifties, and tens. They should judge the people at all times. Then they can bring you every important case but judge every minor case themselves. In this way you will lighten your load, and they will bear it with you" (Exod. 18:21–22).

Administrative organizing is the work of grouping people and resources so the work can best be performed. We have noted that the elements of planning are conceptual in nature and in practice are not discrete functions but pervade the entire fabric of administration. So too, the concepts of organization cannot be separated out as sequential activities that must precede or succeed any other of the steps in the administrative process.

It is obvious that as a person plans, the organization to accomplish that plan is foremost in the mind of the administrator.

- The facet of estimating the future is organization driven—what kinds and who will be the people who will be integral to the ministry.
- In the church one cannot set objectives and goals without first considering the people (organization) they will affect in carrying out the mission.

- Programs require people.
- Policies and procedures must be considered and made with the individuals involved in mind.
- Budgets provide the resources to build the facilities, pay the salaries, and facilitate the programs that people use.

As we consider the three elements of administrative organization—the structure, the process of delegation, and relationships—it is obvious that the conceptualization of the church organization will be fluid. In a later section of this book we will address the factors necessary to establish an intentional structure that will define personnel goals and roles. We will assume that the planning phase has provided a clear outline of the activities that will implement the objectives and goals of the church.

1. *Organizational Structure.* Structure is the blueprint or pattern in which we will relate people roles to one another. It is the framework for getting the job done. Its purpose is to create an environment for human performance. Consider the building of a skyscraper and the metal framework that forms the structure on which the building is built. Depending upon the characteristics of administrative philosophy of the individuals that are used in building the structure, the organization can take on several forms. One of the first tasks that must be considered is to determine the philosophy for organization of the church or institution. In a later section of this book, specific formats for church organization will be discussed.

2. *Delegation.* This means the assigning of things (work or a task) to individuals. Jethro told Moses to delegate the lesser tasks so he could focus on the major issues of leading the nation of Israel to the promised land. Delegation involves three important elements:

1. Clearly assigning the *responsibility* the individual is entrusted with
2. Granting the necessary *authority* and *ability* to accomplish the task assigned
3. Holding the person *accountable* for the completion of the assigned task

Delegation is not giving an unpleasant task to someone, nor is it getting rid of work to make your workday less than responsible. It is, however:

- Sharing the work with individuals who have the capability so you may concentrate on more challenging or more difficult assignments.
- Providing a format whereby an individual can mature and learn through on-the-job work.
- Encouraging others to become part of the organization by participative task accomplishment.
- Allowing the individual to exercise his or her special gifts and abilities.

An important element of the organizational structure of the church is the granting of authority to accomplish the task. Authority is the right to invoke compliance by subordinates on the basis of the formal position in the organizational structure and upon the controls that are placed upon that position by the formal organization. Authority is linked to the position, not the person. Authority is derived in various ways:

- Position
- Reputation
- Experience
- Expertise

Authority and responsibility are directly linked. When you give someone responsibility for a task, the individual should be given the ability to see to it that the task is accomplished. Responsibility and accountability are also directly linked. If the individual is given the responsibility for a task as well the authority to see to its accomplishment, it is the manager or administrator's responsibility to hold the individual accountable to complete the task in the manner assigned and planned. Elements of describing the use of organizational authority include:

1. The use of an *organizational chart* that establishes the chain of command.
2. The use of *functional authority,* assigning to individuals in other elements of the organization the authority to administer and control elements of the organization outside their own.
3. Defining *span of control,* defining within the task assignment specifically what elements of the organization the individual has authority over.

3. *Relationships.* As leaders of the church or organization, we are developers of people. While it often appears we are managing "things," we are in truth managing the people who get the things done. The establishment of effective relationships with the people involved in accomplishing a task is difficult and becomes impossible without a thoroughly thought-through philosophy of leadership. It demands a sensitivity to the individuals in the process. Effective relationships do not break down the differentiation of leaders and workers; they build it up.

In recent years management styles that have embraced the worker have become popular. As mentioned earlier, TQM or the Japanese model invites the worker to participate with leaders. This is best exemplified by a TV commercial by a major automotive company that depicts an assembly line worker reaching up to pull a lever to stop the entire production line. He did this because he had discovered something in the process that could be improved. The commercial shows his fellow workers as well as management congratulating him for his contribution to a more effective car. He was given the responsibility to produce an effective car and the authority to exercise his skills and abilities in building that car. Leadership, whether in the church or other type of organization, needs to be sensitive to the desire to contribute to the process and completion of objectives set.

Administrative Leading

Paul, speaking to his young student Timothy, exemplifies leadership in these words: "Timothy, my child, I am giving you this instruction in keeping with the prophecies previously made about you, so that by them you may strongly engage in battle, having faith and a good conscience . . . First of all, then, I urge that petitions, prayers, intercessions, and thanksgivings be made for everyone" (1 Tim. 1:18–19; 2:1).

And again in 1 Timothy 4:12b–16a Paul says, "You should be an example to the believers in speech, in conduct, in love, in faith, in purity. Until I come, give your attention to public reading, exhortation, and teaching. Do not neglect the gift that is in you. . . . Practice these things; be committed to them, so that your progress may be evident to all. Be conscientious about yourself and your teaching."

Administrative leading is the work we do to inspire and to impel people to take specific action. Note in the passage above that Paul, having selected Timothy to represent him to the newly formed Christian churches, praises, motivates, and instructs Timothy.

Administrative leading is frequently called *directing* by some management writers. We choose to use the term *leading* since it best describes a shepherd leader who moves ahead of the flock rather than driving them from behind. As we have noted in administrative planning and organizing above, these activities do not stand alone. We will also note that leading permeates all the process of modern administration.

The concept of administrative leading can be compared to a symphony conductor. It is the responsibility of the conductor to know the music, the instruments, and the capability of the instrumentalists. His role is to blend together the work of the orchestra members to produce the symphony that the writer of the music envisioned. At the appropriate time the conductor calls into play the instruments that are needed for correct interpretation of the piece of music. He directs the intensity, volume, and meter.

Thus, it can be said that leading is not simply or solely directing. It is, instead, a planned and organized communication to create an environment conducive to participative action. Unplanned, disorganized activities are meaningless; thus, as administrators, we should orchestrate our leadership toward the end of productive output.

The administrative function of leading has five basic administrative activities: decision-making, communication, motivation, selecting people, and training or developing people.

1. *Decision making.* Decision making is problem identification and problem solving. Decision-making is a process that involves a situation that demands, or seems to demand, action. It usually has a compressed time frame and the requirement to investigate and gather data, and there exists the strong likelihood that some consequences will result based upon the decision that is made.

Wise decision-makers do not solve nonproblems! They discover the real problem and work on it. Decision-making is the art of identifying alternatives and selecting the best solution. It also means that a contingency course of action should be held in the event the initial response requires modification or restructuring.

In the administrative environment two types of decisions are made nearly every day: (1) Programmed decisions are decisions that are routine and are usually answered by some set of established procedures and criteria for operation. No new process is required, only the decision to do it or not. (2) nonprogrammed decisions are nonroutine decisions that must be made based on a unique or new situation. In these processes the individual must decide a course of action.

Good administrators focus on the important nonprogrammed decisions. When a situation arises, they will ask:
1. Is this a problem, and if so, can it be dealt with?
2. Might the problem resolve itself?
3. Is this my decision to make?

There is a close relationship between the problem-solving process and the decision-making process. A simple five-step strategy for decision-making includes:
1. Identify and describe the situation, specifically the problem and cause.
2. Gather alternative solutions. How could this problem be solved?
3. Compare the various alternatives. What solutions seem best to address the problem?
4. Calculate the risk for each alternative. What are the cause and effect of each solution?
5. Select the best alternative and implement it. Which solution best addresses the problem while remaining within the parameters of church polity and policy?

Remember the old adage, "If there is a possibility of anything going wrong, it probably will." What may have seemed a good decision at the time it was made may turn into a can of worms later. Some considerations that might prevent this include:
1. The timing of the announced decision. Are all details worked out?
2. The manner in which the announcement was made, from the pulpit or through a memorandum.

3. The individuals to whom you made the announcement. Have all important individuals been involved or informed?
4. Planning that will be required to implement the decision. How much more work is involved?

2. *Communication.* Communication is the work in which we engage to arrive at an understanding between ourselves and other people about mutual needs and goals. It is the interchange of thought or information to bring about mutual understanding in confidence or good human relations. It is words, letters, symbols, or messages. It is facts, ideas, opinions, or emotions. In many instances the informal communication—the body language, emotions, and context of the communication—will speak more powerfully than formal communication.

Communication involves: (1) the exchange of facts and information, (2) the expression of attitudes and values, and (3) the provision of warmth, acceptance, and support of others. Principles for effective communication include:

- Clarity. Communicate in commonly understood language.
- Attention. Give full attention to transmitting *and* receiving information and data.
- Integrity. Make communication a means to effective administration, never the end.
- Strategic use of the informal organization. This involves plugging into the grapevine. It is ensuring the rumor mill is accurate and supports the organization's goals and objectives. Administrators will learn a wealth of information from member and parishioners. It doesn't take a committee to discover a problem.

As was seen in the decision-making process above, effective leadership requires a broad-based communication process.

3. *Motivation.* Motivation is the work we do to cause people to want to do what needs to be done. Effective motivation comes from within. It frequently stems from personal needs that outweigh other, even more attractive, modes.

A synthesis of research has indicated that people do things because of three general reasons:

1. External reasons. They do work because they are told to do it by an authority figure or there is an external, tangible reward.
2. Social reasons. They accomplish objectives because of social, moral, or peer pressure.
3. Internal reasons. They have an internal self-motivation to do a task. They *want* to do it.

The same research also indicates that the most effective motivation is that internally driven desire to do something worthwhile or that satisfies an inner

longing. A Christian administrator's role is to build a climate in which a person can fulfill his or her needs in a way that brings internal satisfaction and joy. This environment for motivating work can be established in numerous ways:
- The administrator can create an organization that fosters participation and teamwork.
- Policies, procedures, and organizational goals need to be clear and well communicated.
- Work should be organized to create a challenge while at the same time provide a sense of satisfaction in success.
- Leaders should give affirmation and support. Respond when asked, but allow the individual autonomy in the work.

4. *Selecting People.* Selecting people consists of appraising people's God-given capacities and the opportunities to use them in working environments. Selecting people is an attempt to predict somebody's job performance on the basis of standards of previous work history, test scores, interview impressions, or other standards.

When selecting people:
- Define exactly what you are looking for.
- Do some comparative shopping.
- Allow sufficient time before selection.
- Check for quality.

Selecting personnel for a task is a process that should be carefully considered. In a later chapter we will discuss personnel issues that relate to effective human resource processes.

5. *Developing People.* Developing people is the work we do to upgrade the capacities for work and service that have been provided. Smart management teams are in a constant state of growth. The prime job of the administrator is to create a work climate that encourages individuals to develop and broaden their fullest capacities and at the same time to shoulder their individual responsibility for achieving the objectives of the organization.

The administrator can call upon three basic activities to assist in the process of developing people:
1. Performance Appraisal—evaluating the performance and capabilities of the individual supervisor and the individuals who work with him. Actual on-the-job evaluation should be made based upon definitive job expectations.
2. Performance Counseling—the actual discussion of the supervisor's evaluation of task performance, allowing the individual to be a participant in resolving weaknesses.

3. Performance Development Activities—helping the individual to develop his or her potential as well as to meet job expectations. This can be done through a variety of activities:
   - Example—letting them see the proper way by doing it
   - Coaching—on-the-job training
   - Job rotation—finding the best position in the organization
   - Training courses and seminars—continuing education

Administrative Controlling (Evaluation)

"Do you not know that the runners in a stadium all race, but only one receives the prize? Run in such a way that you may win. Now everyone who competes exercises self-control in everything. However, they do it to receive a perishable crown, but we an imperishable one. Therefore I do not run like one who runs aimlessly, or box like one who beats the air. Instead, I discipline my body and bring it under strict control, so that after preaching to others, I myself will not be disqualified" (1 Cor. 9:24–27).

Paul would write later to his young associate, Timothy, "I have fought the good fight, I have finished the race, I have kept the faith. In the future, there is reserved for me the crown of righteousness, which the Lord, the righteous Judge, will give me on that day" (2 Tim. 4:7–8a).

While the management world uses the term *control,* we will substitute the term *evaluation* since it better describes the activities that are carried out in administrative control in the church or Christian organization.

Administrative evaluation is the work we do to ensure that results conform to plans. It is focusing events to contribute to preconceived plans. Remember when we considered the *planning* phase of administration we looked at the elements of developing policies, programming, establishing procedures, scheduling, and budgets. These are all elements of an evaluation to come. When we considered the *organization* phase, we developed a structure that gave control over positions, the use of delegation that called for responsibility and accountability. Then we considered *leading* and noted that in the elements of decision-making, communicating clearly, and scheduling activities that provided developmental opportunities were the essentials of administrative evaluation.

It becomes obvious, as in the three previous elements of administration, that administrative evaluation is not a discrete operation but one that must be considered throughout the entire administrative process.

Several years ago George Odiorne introduced in *Management by Objectives* a philosophy which became an important statement of how organizations should be run. There should be a reason for doing what you are doing.[2] The success of Odiorne's MBO process was phenomenal. Soon leaders were looking at ways of integrating the aspects of MBO into the nonprofit organization. In the church venue it was met with little success, not because of any fallacy in the concept of administration but in the negative connotation that *control* implies—authority and constraint. Free-spirited church leaders did not want to set goals and then be held accountable for achieving them. Nor did they want to become the agents of management that directed others to meet goals and objectives. Formal business controls, they contended, required first of all a dedicated set of employees. Everybody knows that a church is a volunteer organization, and you cannot control volunteers. Controls also call for measuring the results based on management objectives. Christians should not be placing themselves as judges over people.

Through the years, however, Christian administrators have taken the precepts of the MBO process and have cast them into terminology that is acceptable to the church. Thus, when we talk about controls, we are not talking about the autocratic principles of monitoring work but establishing evaluation processes to ensure the job is done. All evaluation systems have four common elements:

1. Measurable characteristics for which standards are known
2. Means of measuring these characteristics
3. A methodology for comparing actual results to the standards
4. A process for effecting changes to adjust the characteristics

Administratively we can divide the evaluation process into four activities:

1. ***Establishing Performance Standards.*** Establishing performance standards means that we agree with the person or persons working with us about what quality of work should be accomplished before it is begun. Standards establish criteria against which performance (outcome) can be measured. Without standards:

- Individuals have no way of knowing what is expected of them in a task assignment.
- They have no way of knowing if what they are doing is what is desired.
- Supervisors have no way of knowing if their employees are progressing toward goal/objective accomplishment.
- Unreasonable demands can be made on the individual who has received the task assignment.
- How will you know when you are finished?

Our modern society calls for us to compare ourselves to preconceived standards. Women should be beautiful, and men should be macho, etc. It is often called peer or culture pressure. In the church environment it is necessary for administrators to create both effective and fair standards. Certain criteria will help the Christian administrator in establishing effective and fair standards:

1. Standards should be developed that present a challenge to the worker.
2. Standards that are competitive in nature are effective motivators.

3. Standards should consider both the task and individual goals and needs.
4. Standards should be simple and straightforward.
5. Standards should be clearly communicated.
6. Standards should have a measurable, quantitative outcome.
7. Standards should be perceived as fair.

2. *Performance Measuring.* Performance measuring means that someone is measuring the work. To be effective, performance measuring requires quantitative as well as qualitative standards. How can you measure a nebulous or unknown objective? Performance measuring is most effective when the process includes:

- Standards based upon mutually agreed-upon expectations.
- Standards for beginning the work or phases of the work.
- Standards for monitoring the work, guideposts of accomplishment.
- A statement of termination/completion.
- A process for predicting problems or future outcome.

Some common performance measuring techniques include budgets, time-completion charts, audits, reports, inspections and inventories, questionnaires, and numerical evaluations.

3. *Performance Assessment.* Performance assessment is appraising the work. It involves establishing the degree of success of an individual's work in light of established standards and the techniques used to measure those standards. It is also evaluating completion toward the total goal of the church or organization.

The evaluator asks, "Based upon what has been accomplished, has the goal that was established in the plan been met?" Performance assessment calls for the evaluator not only to determine whether goals have been met, but if they have not been met, how far off the mark has the work been done. An important aspect of assessment is to know the degree of tolerance allowed to declare the goal as having been met. Throughout this text, various schemes will be introduced to allow the administrator to assess that facet of ministry through reports, audits, and inspections.

4. *Performance Correcting.* Performance correcting involves not only correcting mistakes that have been made but also coaching, providing the person(s) the "how" to bring performance in line with the planned standards. Methods for carrying out performance correcting include:

1. Identify the real problem. What really caused the unsatisfactory performance?
2. Establish clear criteria that any solution must satisfy. Frequently the planned goal was not clearly stated, and thus it may have been misunderstood by the performer. Sometimes the planners themselves

misunderstood the objectives and thus the goals that would lead to accomplishment of those objectives.

3. Arrive at alternatives to accomplishment. Maybe the goal was not achieved because the method was not able to produce success. How else could this be accomplished? The wise administrator will involve the individuals who made the first attempt to participate in determining alternative methods.

4. Select an alternative. Choose the best response to the completion of the task. Build in implementation. Having chosen an alternative way to go, implement it. This more than likely will involve redirection, retraining, reworking, and reevaluation. Smart administrators should be prepared to participate in the activity of restructure.

5. Evaluate the decision. If the action corrects the problem, great. If not, reevaluate or start over again.

As a summary and review of the process of administration, let's look at a practical application. The pastor of Church-in-the-Town has noted a growing problem that has surfaced since the church replaced its sanctuary last year after fire destroyed the historic old wooden structure. Before, the pastor was involved with maybe two or three weddings a year, mostly by church members. Now many people in the community want their weddings to be performed in the new, and more "lovely" sanctuary. The pastor and the church don't seem to mind. Lately, however, the pastor feels that he has lost control of groups that are not members of the church. Deacon Jones, the chairman of the building committee, thinks a policy is needed on this sort of thing. The pastor feels that a wedding policy and procedure manual is in order since he does not *foresee* a change in the desire of community residents to use the building for weddings. The *objective* then is to describe how both church members and nonmembers can use the church for weddings.

In reviewing existing church policy, the church discovers that its ministry statement is that they will be a lighthouse to the entire community. The building committee decides to take to the church a *policy* statement that says the church can be opened to the community given certain stipulations: that the pastor or someone appointed by the pastor be present during use of the building and also that only the church janitor can arrange for and clean up after the wedding.

One other stipulation is that the bride must pay the janitor's salary for the setup and cleanup costs. The pastor, his wife (since she is good at wedding planning), and the janitor meet and write out a set of *procedures* for meeting this policy decision by the church. The wedding manual begins to take form as they describe the sequence of events (*programming*) that a bride must go through in the planning process. They determine that weddings can take place at any time there is not a regularly scheduled church service (*scheduling*). Since the church provides the building free, the pastor suggests to the stewardship committee that maybe they should increase the heating and cooling *budget* to take care of the additional use of the building.

The pastor determines that he will spend an inordinate amount of time in this wedding planning process, so he asks the associate pastor/counselor to add to his *organizational* responsibilities the monitoring of the wedding manual and process. Internally, the associate pastor will work with the bride and the pastor's wife in planning the wedding and doing marriage counseling. The church secretary will schedule the wedding, and the janitor will set up for it. Having set an organization that *delegates* certain responsibilities to individuals to carry out the wedding manual provisions, the pastor then decides that each wedding will require a meeting (*relationship* building) with the staff, his wife the wedding planner, and the bride and groom to ensure that all plans are understood and that the wedding goes off without a hitch.

The pastor is now satisfied that the wedding manual will become a routine standardized *decision-maker* for him, hopefully *communicating* answers to all the questions a bride may have. Only in unusual circumstances will he have to make decisions, and the meeting with the team will ensure everybody knows what is happening. As the wedding manual comes into being, individuals involved become excited (*motivated*) that the church will have a way of ministering effectively to the community, at the same time preserving the new sanctuary. In the future the pastor may want to add to (*select*) the individuals involved in premarital counseling, but for right now the church counselor can handle that. He realizes that when that time comes, they will have to *develop* a training program for premarital counseling that teaches biblical concepts of marriage.

As the first proof of the manual comes from the printer, the pastor and other members of the group (associate pastor, the wedding planner, the janitor, and the secretary) look it over. "Does the manual meet our objectives (*standards*)?" is asked. Are the steps set forth workable? How do we determine when changes are needed? It is decided that annually the implementation group will meet with the building committee and discuss the wedding manual and question (*measure*) how it is working. This *assessment* will involve discussions with the pastor, associate pastor, wedding planner, secretary, and janitor as well as committees that relate to finance and building. They may even ask a bride or two how their wedding went and if changes would be suggested. Unless something urgent comes up, the group decided that changes (*corrections*) to the procedures of the wedding manual would only come out during the annual church business meeting in January.

And there you have the wedding hamster on a treadmill. Notice that some rungs needed a pause and work, while others the hamster just bounded right over.

Dynamics of Leadership

This saying is trustworthy: "If anyone aspires to be an overseer, he desires a noble work. An overseer, therefore, must be above reproach, the husband of one wife, self-controlled, sensible, respectable, hospitable, an able teacher, not addicted to wine, not a bully but gentle, not quarrelsome, not greedy—one who manages his own household competently, having his children under control with all dignity. (If anyone does not know how to manage his own household, how will he take care of God's church?) He must not be a new convert, or he might become conceited and fall into the condemnation of the Devil. Furthermore, he must have a good reputation among outsiders, so that he does not fall into disgrace and the Devil's trap" (1 Tim. 3:1–7).

I exhort the elders among you: shepherd God's flock among you, not overseeing out of compulsion but freely, according to God's will; not for the money but eagerly; not lording it over those entrusted to you, but being examples to the flock (1 Pet. 5:1b–3).

The word translated as overseer in the 1 Timothy passage above is *episkopoi* and relates to those "bishops" of the early church. Vine's *Dictionary of New Testament Words* identifies these individuals as "those who, being raised up and qualified by the work of the Holy Spirit, were appointed to have the spiritual care of, and to exercise oversight over, the churches." The related term *presbuteroi,* translated "elder" in the 1 Peter passage, indicates the nature of their work as having mature spiritual experience. In the Peterine passage above, the *presbuteros* (elder) is linked to shepherds (*poimen*) who pastor the flock (church).[3]

Elder, bishop, presbyter, overseer, pastor—all are terms that relate to the individual who is God called and Spirit empowered to lead the church. A study of Scripture leaves little doubt that God had a plan for leadership in the church through called-out leaders. This call to leadership is clearly defined. The character of the leader is also clearly defined.

Christ is the model leader:
- He was a servant leader (Luke 22:27).
- Followership is a function of service (John 12:26).
- We follow Christ as little children (Matt. 18:1–5).
- Leading is not lording over (Mark 10:42–45).
- We are to follow Christ's example in our leadership (1 Cor. 11:1).
- We are to be servants of Christ (2 Cor. 4:5).
- Our leadership considers those above us as well as the admonition for work (Titus 2:15–3:1).
- Leaders are to set an example for others (1 Pet. 5:2–5).

In *Leadership: Strategy for Taking Charge*, Bennis and Nanus state, "Leadership is what gives an organization its vision and its ability to translate that vision into reality. Without this translation, a transaction between leaders and followers, there is no organizational heartbeat."[4]

Kotter in *What Leaders Really Do* states that leadership is the "development of vision and strategies, the alignment of relevant people behind those strategies, and the empowerment of individuals to make the vision happen, despite obstacles."[5]

Remember, management:

- Involves devising new systems as well as keeping the current system operating through the functions of planning, organizing, leading, and evaluation.
- Usually works through a hierarchy and in-place system.
- Brings about order and consistency.
- Attempts to provide as much as possible a fail-safe and risk-free environment.

Managers are leaders. They provide leadership by:

- Influencing, guiding in direction, course of action, and opinion.
- Introducing change; creating and coping with change.
- Translating vision into an organization that produces activity and production.
- Motivating, inspiring, and developing relationships.

Christian leaders are vision catchers and vision casters. By remaining attuned to the Holy Spirit and through Scripture, leaders receive direction about the vision that should be implanted in the church.

In Joel 2:28–29 we read, "After this I will pour out My Spirit on all humanity; then your sons and your daughters will prophesy, your old men will have dreams, and your young men will see visions. I will even pour out My Spirit on the male and female slaves in those days." Luke recorded in the book of Acts the beginning of Peter's sermon at Pentecost by citing this passage as a fulfillment of the prophecy.

The King James Version of Scripture translates Proverbs 29:18: "Where there is no vision the people perish: but he that keepeth the law, happy is he." The New International Version renders the same passage as, "Where there is no revelation, the people cast off restraint; but blessed is he who keeps the law." And the New Living Translation gives, "When people do not accept divine guidance, they run wild. But whoever obeys the law is happy."

Vision is God-inspired guidance—a God-thing. It is a mystical happening dreamed in the hearts of God's servants by the Holy Spirit. For leaders to be receptive to vision from God, they must consider vision as a three-dimensional concept:

- An upward dimension. An insight of who God is and that he alone is the provider of the vision.
- An inward dimension. A realization that human frailty prevents us from doing a God-sized job.
- An outward dimension. An understanding that vision is to be played out in ministry.[6]

Leaders have two roles in leading the church with regard to the vision: (1) To translate and interpret the vision of God in the hearts and minds of the church and (2) to equip the people to carry out the vision through the mission of the church. Mission is the planned activities that are made to carry out the vision. It is vision instituted and leader directed.

Theories of Leadership

The approaches to the study of leadership have taken three specific patterns.

Trait Theories

These theories focus on key traits that separate leaders from followers and successful leaders from unsuccessful leaders. Frequently termed "the Great Man Theory," this concept of leadership espouses that leaders are born not made.

Five general characteristics identify these leaders:

1. Intelligence and scholarship. Trait leaders are somewhat more intelligent, perform better at academic tasks, and possess superior judgment and decision-making ability.
2. Personality. These leaders are self-confident, honest, creative, and have high levels of integrity and initiative.
3. Social status and experience. Leaders appear to possess good personal interaction skills and are able to inspire and motivate team effort.
4. Task orientation. Trait leaders assume responsibility and provide self-initiated direction to accomplish tasks. They are highly motivated individuals who set challenging goals.
5. Physical prowess. Trait leaders are usually more attractive and healthier.

Studies have indicated that these characteristics are not consistent. Yet their presence makes for development of the creation of characteristics that may contribute to leadership potential.

Situational Theories

These theories depend upon the relationship that exists between the organizational situation, the leader's style, and the follower's motivation and ability to follow. The goal of a situational leader is to predict the most effective style of leadership under varying circumstances.

The theory states that the most effective leadership style should vary with the maturity (later termed development level) level of the subordinate.[7] In this model the leader gains intimate knowledge of the follower's needs, abilities, and task aptitude and then modifies his leadership style to meet those requirements. Subordinate development level is a function of the assessment of the leader's ability to accomplish a task and his commitment (motivation) to do it.

DEVELOPMENT LEVEL	LEADERSHIP STYLE
D-1 The individual has limited ability to accomplish the task. While initially motivated to do the work, commitment will wane as the magnitude of the task reveals itself.	DIRECTOR. The leader must take the responsibility for providing the information that will accomplish the task. Little effort is given at this point to establishing a working relationship until the subordinate begins to develop some of the basic skills to accomplish the task.
D-2 The worker has developed competence enough to begin to understand the task and the magnitude of the work. His skill ability has improved enough to allow him to participate in determining how a task might be accomplished	COACH. The leader, while still directing the activities that lead to task accomplishment, begins to establish dialogue that will increase the confidence in the subordinate that the task is achievable. More often than not the leader's style will allow him to begin to relinquish more of the task through delegation.
D-3 The worker has competence and ability to complete the task but lacks the motivation to continue. This is often the situation with individuals who are burned out in ministry or who lost interest in the work.	SUPPORTER. The leader no longer has to provide instruction and direction since the subordinate has most of the requisite skills to complete the task. What is needed is a higher level of interaction and motivation. The leader allows the subordinate to become the primary source of task resolvement and becomes a supporter and advisor to his actions.
D-4 The subordinate has both the ability and commitment to accomplish the task.	DELEGATOR. The leader delegates the task to the subordinate. Remembering that delegation calls upon the delegator to remain in charge, the leadership that will be called for will be that of monitoring, providing assistance only when needed, and motivating through praise, recognition, and granting of higher levels of authority and responsibility.

Behavioral Theories

These theories focus on a set of divergent leadership styles: those focused on the subordinate and those focused on the task. These theories take as their tenet that successful leadership is oriented on an employee-centered axis. Four important research projects picture this model:

1. McGregors's Theory X—Theory Y in which the Theory X subordinate is considered naturally lazy and the leadership style that must be used is one of direction and controlled coercion. The Theory Y individual desires to be effective and efficient in the task accomplishment, and therefore leadership will have to exert little effort in getting the job done.[8]

2. Lewin's Leader Continium identifies three types of leaders: autocrat, democrat, and laissez-faire. Both the autocrat and laissez-faire are deemed as poor leaders. The democratic leader will share in decision-making responsibilities and maintains open communication lines with the subordinate.[9]

3. Blake and Mouton's Managerial Grid identifies five leadership tendencies that an individual possesses, based upon learned and environmental circumstances. The model calls for the best leader to be one who will take into consideration both the organizational task to be accomplished and the goals and needs of the individual who is to accomplish the task.[10]

4. Likert's Four Systems identifies the most effective leaders as those who focus their primary attention on the human aspect of their subordinate's problems and on endeavoring to build effective work groups with high performance goals. In order of least effective to most effective, these leaders are termed as follows:

- Expletive-authoritative has an autocratic task orientation.
- Benevolent-authoritative uses rewards instead of fear as a motivation tool.
- Consultative leaders maintain control at the top, but goals are discussed with the subordinate.
- Participative leader's motivation comes from ego and group involvement. Extensive interaction and involvement of the subordinate occurs.[11]

The tension between being the leader God wants you to be and the leader the people want you to be is often voided by our actions. Paul concludes his first letter to the church at Thessalonica with an interesting exhortation:

> Now we ask you, brothers, to give recognition to those who labor among you and lead you in the Lord and admonish you, and to esteem them very highly in love because of their work. . . . Warn those who are lazy, comfort the discouraged, help the weak, be patient with everyone. . . . Rejoice always! Pray constantly. Give thanks in everything, for this is God's will for you in Christ Jesus.

Don't stifle the Spirit. Don't despise prophecies, but test all things.
Hold on to what is good. Stay away from every form of evil
(1 Thess. 5:12, 14, 16–22).

If a minister does not accept the adulation and respect shown as a leader with the humility of servanthood that God expects, then problems will arise.

McIntosh and Rima in *Overcoming the Dark Side of Leadership*[12] and Shawchuck and Heuser in *Leading the Congregation*[13] discuss the consequences of a leader's personality and motivation when less than effective leadership mannerisms are projected upon the congregation. They, as well as other researchers of leadership style, have identified five dysfunctional styles of leadership that must be analyzed and overcome by the leader. They describe a narcissistic/dramatic, a paranoid/suspicious, a detached/codependent, a depressive/ passive-aggressive, and a compulsive leader whose leadership mannerisms are projected on the congregation causes a dysfunctional organization.

Applying the concept that poor leadership mannerisms will affect the church or religious nonprofit organization's ability to function and carry out its mission, we will discuss four dysfunctional styles that are prevalent in the church today.

The Showman

1. These individuals often have an inflated view of their leadership position and ability. They tend to focus on their own needs without consideration of the individuals they are leading. They perceive themselves as "God's appointed man for the hour." Everything they do must be larger than life, grandiose. Their egotism and self-centeredness drives them to fail to consider the church or organizational entity.

2. Churches/institutions led by these individuals tend to outgrow their structure. Plateau and decline often follow the charismatic growth the Showman brings to the entity. If for some reason the leader is not there, the church or organization flounders because of the total reliance they have placed on the Showman-leader.

3. These leaders are macromanagers, involving themselves in the routine matters of the organization—not so much because they have the answer to all of life's questions but because they must be the center of all activity. They insert themselves through spontaneous, unstructured leadership. Some may take on a CEO mentality, expecting everyone to accept their decisions without question.

4. Members of these churches tend to be hero worshippers, whether it is with the present leader or not. They exhibit a strong need dependency formation.

5. In these organizations the leadership is totally the leaders' ideas, intuitive impressions, and impetuous ventures. Decision-making does not include the staff of the organization. Members are not consulted for opinion or desires.

The Doubting Thomas

1. This leader has not developed the ability to rely upon the individuals they lead. Often they appear to followers as uncaring and detached. This type of leader will demand proof of loyalty of those they lead. They garner as much data as they can and often conceal this information from others in the organization for fear they may lose authority. They are highly suspicious of anyone who questions them.

2. Churches and institutions with this type of leader will position all power at the top—the leader. These leaders often find themselves reacting to situations and eventualities rather than creating a plan of ministry that looks to the future. Since these leaders must involve themselves in all that happens in the organization, they often become bogged down in details. When this happens both the leader and the church or organization frequently forgets the mission or the goals set to accomplish that vision.

3. Members/workers tend to be boss-pleasers. The work environment is one of uncertainty, hostility, insecurity, and distrust. Significant effort is expended in determining what the leader has in mind and then developing a response that appears to meet that interpretation.

4. Within the organization much effort is spent around the time-consuming assignment of data gathering to satisfy the information needs of the leader. Since the Doubting Thomas must make all decisions, action is often delayed for fear of making a mistake.

The Monk

1. This type of leader is an individualist. He prefers to function in his leadership role with little or no interaction with other individuals in the church or organization. In many respects these are nonleaders because they would rather isolate themselves from the structure and allow the institution to function without their input. They often do not establish working relationships with the individuals they lead.

2. This leader may have had some event occur in his ministry that causes him to withdraw from the leadership role. It may be burnout or an unfortunate hurtful situation that causes this detachment.

3. Leadership in the church or organization is often expressed at the next levels of control within the organization. Because of this, political infighting and position-taking occur. Members tend to take sides, and the competing forces often cause disruption.

4. It is not uncommon in a church or organization with a Monk leader to have subordinate groups formed and developing power within themselves. Without centralized leadership these groups may dominate elements of the church or organization such as budget, meeting times, and calendaring. If these groups do not form, often the church or organization will lapse into the status quo.

5. When the Monk does vest authority in others to act in his behalf, it will be to a few trusted individuals who they feel can accomplish the job without the necessity of involving the leader.

The Control Freak

1. This leadership style is often characterized by a strong, dominant leader. This individual differs from the other dysfunctional leaders discussed so far in that these leaders are know-it-alls, or at least they think they have all the answers.

2. The Control Freak creates an organization that centers him at the top and in a hierarchical system of delegated responsibility will ensure the organization functions exactly as the leader dictates. To ensure this the leader will establish a series of formal rules, controls, and regulations that ensure all the internal operations follow an exact pattern that he has either created or approved.

3. The staff and membership of the church become functionaries of the leader, clones or robots of the system that he has established.

4. Since in this church or organization the leader has established himself as the controlling source of expertise, innovation, and creativity, the subordinates and members alike lose a sense of creativity and innovation for ministry. Little effort is given to learn new and better methods of ministry.

Every leader, administrator, and minister must assess their own tendencies for leadership and develop a philosophy for accomplishing the task through people. In *The Power of Ethical Management,* Kenneth Blanchard and Norman Vincent Peale suggest individuals evaluate their motives for leading by asking three important questions:

1. Is this legal? Will I be violating civil law or church polity?
2. Is this balanced? Is it fair? Does it promote a win-win relationship?
3. How will I feel about myself? Will I be proud? What if the decision was widely known?[14]

To these three questions Shawchuck and Heuser in *Leading the Congregation* add:

4. Is this suitable material for prayer? Can I talk to God about this?
5. Does this support my ordination vows? How would it reflect on my ministerial colleagues?[15]

Because most ministers are both leaders and supervisors of the administrative process, it is important for them to develop sensitivity to and knowledge of appropriate processes that will combine their personal skills with the needs to express the spiritual gifts of the parishioners they serve. This philosophy of "doing church" is best expressed in a written document. We have a manual for our religious expression; it is called the Bible. In Exodus 24:3–5 we find these words: "Moses came and told the people all the commands of the LORD and all the ordinances. Then all the people responded with a single voice, 'We will do everything that the LORD has commanded.' And Moses wrote down all the words of the LORD."

Chapter Review

This chapter has introduced two important dynamics that form the basics for effective administration in the local church or nonprofit organization—administrative processes and leadership principles. While the material is conceptual in design, the application will meet nearly every practical need in the church or institution. The reader should be able to respond to the following:

1. The process of administration is comprised of four basic functions with attendant administrative activities that define and describe the elements of that function. Describe how a minister might go about instituting a program of outreach through a Vacation Bible School in a church that has never had a VBS by identifying each functional area and activities involved in developing that program.

2. Christian leaders are expected to provide guidance in the affairs of the church. This guidance includes both spiritual guidance as provided through the Holy Spirit and practical guidance that comes about through the application of the principles of dynamic leadership. Describe how the minister wears the hat of leader in providing spiritual management of the mission of the church while at the same time integrates principles of effective administrative leadership in accomplishing that mission.

3. Evaluate your tendency for leadership. What are your strengths and weaknesses? Are you described in any of the failed forms of leadership cited in this chapter? What would be a proper form of leadership that would meet the biblical role of an administrator in a Christian institution?

Documents
for Administration

CHAPTER
3

Now the first covenant also had regulations for ministry and an earthly sanctuary. For a tabernacle was set up; and in the first room, which is called "the holy place," were the lampstand, the table, and the presentation loaves. Behind the second curtain, the tabernacle was called "the holy of holies." It contained the gold altar of incense and the ark of the covenant, covered with gold on all sides, in which there was a gold jar containing the manna, Aaron's rod that budded, and the tablets of the covenant. The cherubim of glory were above it overshadowing the mercy seat ... These things having been set up this way, the priests enter the first room repeatedly, performing their ministry. But the high priest alone enters the second room, and that only once a year, and never without blood, which he offers for himself and for the sins of the people committed in ignorance ... They are physical regulations and only deal with food, drink, and various washings imposed until the time of restoration. Now the Messiah has appeared, high priest of the good things that have come.
HEBREWS 9:1–11

The Church Organization Manual

In 1977 the Navy took me to the University of Oklahoma as the executive officer of the NROTC unit there. My family and I joined a small (about 250 in attendance on a good Sunday) Baptist church. The church had a pastor—who was preparing to retire after twenty years—a minister of education, and a minister of music and youth. In the next five years, under the direction of a new, young pastor, the church grew both spiritually and numerically. At one point the church was one of the fastest-growing churches in that denomination. Along with growth came new ministries and new staff members to provide leadership. In 1982 I retired from the Navy and joined several other individuals who made up the ministry staff.

From 1977 until 1982, I functioned in a variety of volunteer roles: deacon, member of committees, chairperson of other committees, teacher, and council member. One of the issues that plagued the church in the early 1980s was the fact that there seemed to be no coordinated effort or response to what we were doing. Having discovered (after much searching) an ancient copy of the constitution and bylaws that was written in 1934 and modified in 1956, we noted that how we were doing business was not how our constituting documents said we should be going about ministry. A task force was formed to rewrite that constitution and bylaws.

This process of defining what the church was and was to become was lengthy, spiritual, and visionary. After over a year the group brought to the church a philosophy for doing church that was a reflection of how the task group interpreted Scripture and how that church should practically adopt those tenets. Since the task group had been formed from a broad base, encompassing nearly every facet of the membership; and also, since the task force constantly communicated to the church what was learned about how the church should be scripturally constituted and operated, adoption of the new constitution and bylaws was a celebration of renewal.

Having a focused mission and purpose statement to build policy about, the various groups of leadership in the church set about to formulate documents that expressed "doing church." As the newly called church administrator, I was involved with many of the groups writing their policy documents, and then working with staff members in helping them create procedures to respond appropriately. I was involved directly with the personnel, finance, and the properties committees.

In one particular staff meeting, I was complaining about the difficulty of collecting all these developing ministry and functional policies and procedures and suggested that it was now time to create a policy and procedure manual for the church. "Well, Bob," the pastor said, "you are a doctoral student studying church administration; you write a manual for us." I was at first honored and humbled that my pastor and colleagues would think me capable of such an endeavor. Then I came to my senses. If I wrote that manual, it would be Welch's manual, not the church's. Now mind you, I could have written a good manual. By that time I had enough experience in churchmanship to do it. With my Navy background I had written a zillion regulation manuals. So I could have done it. But why, when our new constitution and bylaws charged the various organizations of the church (ministries, committees, and councils) to create their own policies and procedures for doing church.

Rather than becoming the writer of the church organization manual, my role became the compiler of the information that went into the book, editing the work to make it consistent in format. When the church organization manual[1] was finally given to the church, it had dozens of writers. The associate pastor, counselors, chaplains, and benevolence ministry team developed the pastoral sections. The minister of education, age group ministers, education curriculum council, age group councils, etc. developed the education portions. And so forth. The CBA office assisted in developing personnel, financial, and property sections.

In the Scripture passage that ended the last chapter, the covenant between the nation of Israel was established; God had Moses write it down. And having given the whole body of what we call the Law, God reminds Moses in Exodus 34:27, "Write down these words, for I have made a covenant with you and with Israel based on these words."

In the Old Testament, history was written down. An example would be Moses recording in Exodus 17:14 Joshua's defeat of Amalek. "Write this down on a scroll as a reminder and recite it to Joshua." How to worship was given direction: "Write down this song for yourselves and teach it to the Israelites; have them recite it, so that this song may be a witness for Me against the Israelites" (Deut. 31:19). Important events and criteria for obedient living are recorded. Note Joshua in the renewal of the Law at Shechem: "Joshua recorded these things in the book of the law of God" (Josh. 24:26). Samuel reiterates the law after Saul is chosen King: "Samuel proclaimed to the people the rights of kingship. He wrote them on a scroll, which he placed in the presence of the LORD" (1 Sam. 10:25).

Luke introduces his accounts of the gospel of Christ and the growth of the early church by telling Theophilus, "Many have undertaken to compile a narrative about the events that have been fulfilled among us, just as the original eyewitnesses and servants of the word handed them down to us. It also seemed good to me, since I have carefully investigated everything from the very first, to write to you in orderly sequence, most honorable Theophilus, so that you may know the certainty of the things about which you have been instructed" (Luke 1:1–4). Paul, John, Peter, and James wrote boldly to the churches to instruct and encourage them to correct behavior and appropriate ministry.

Writing down the way we do church is useful for several reasons:

1. Written instructions inform church members how their church operates and how they should operate in it.
2. The written material benefits staff communication, since specific responsibilities and duties are spelled out.
3. Written material assists individuals in acclimating to the new church or job.
4. When decisions and ways of operation are recorded, it is important to record those actions so that the same problem will not be solved again,

or worse yet, a way of doing things is modified/changed without consideration of an established format.

In studies cited in the preface of this book, it has been determined that senior pastors feel a tremendous uneasiness with their responsibilities as administrators. Some, in fact, have left the ministry because they felt that if they could not be studying Scripture and preaching full-time, they were not fulfilling God's call. They reasoned that if being a pastor was all this administrative hassle, they didn't want any part of it. Others ministers have been fired because of administrative ineptitude or for other administrative problems.

Effective organization and administrative processes can reduce the degree of confusion and uncertainty that exists when no specific guidance is provided for the operation of the church. Policies and procedures will have a definite impact on the working and personal relationships of the individuals in the church or organization. If one is to consider the church a "team" involved in the mission of the church, then every member must work together in a coordinated effort.

Consider a football team. When I was with the faculty at Oklahoma University, I got to work closely with some of the football team members. I noted that everywhere they went they had this large red notebook they guarded closely. They were constantly studying it—much to my chagrin since I wanted them to study the math class I was tutoring them for. They had what is called the "Play Book" which describes exactly what each player is suppose to do to make each play a success. When the quarterback calls a play, every member of the team has an assignment, and they know what to do to carry out that assignment. Even the substitutes on the sidelines knew exactly what was supposed to be happening on the field on each play.

A church is somewhat like that football team. All members have assignments; some wait, others play, but all know what the team is supposed to be doing. We might call the church playbook the *church organization manual*.

As can be seen from the discussions so far and from the Scripture we have considered, a church organization manual can be divided into three basic areas:

1.   What the church is called by the Holy Spirit to do
2.   How they are organized to do it
3.   What methods or techniques will need to be employ to do it

A suggested organization for the manual, dividing it into three major sections, might be:

1. Authority
   • Church charter or articles of incorporation
   • Constitution and bylaws (which includes mission statement)
   • History

2. Organization
   - Organizational chart
   - Ministries
   - Committees
   - Personnel (staff and lay leadership position descriptions)
   - Personnel policies
   - Salary plan
3. Administration
   - Fiscal policies
   - Physical policies
   - Office policies
   - Ministry policies (day care, volunteers, revival, education, counseling, etc.)

This chapter will deal with the first division of the book—*authority*. In the next chapter church *organization* is developed, and the following chapter will deal with personnel manual issues. The remainder of the book will discuss the various topics under the third major area—*administration*.

The Constitution and Bylaws

Moses went up the mountain to God, and the Lord called to him from the mountain: "This is what you must say to the house of Jacob, and explain to the Israelites: You have seen what I did to the Egyptians and how I carried you on eagles' wings and brought you to Me. Now if you will listen to Me and carefully keep My covenant, you will be My own possession out of all the peoples, although all the earth is Mine, and you will be My kingdom of priests and My holy nation. These are the words that you are to say to the Israelites." After Moses came back, He summoned the elders of the people, and put before them all these words that the Lord had commanded him. Then all the people responded together, "We will do all that the Lord has spoken" (Exod. 19:3–8).

Any organization needs documents that define what it is and its mission and purpose, the structure by which it will do business, and the process that directs activity. Documents such as a constitution and bylaws serve several purposes:

1. They state who you are and why you exist as a church or religious not-for-profit organization.
2. They describe and define the theology, doctrine, polity, and philosophy of your church or organization.
3. They describe the membership of your church, how one becomes a member and how one leaves membership.

4. They define who are the leaders of the membership.
5. They spell out how the church will carry out its business and operation.
6. They spell out the decision-making responsibilities of major groups in the church and the process they use to make those decisions.
7. They identify the legally constituted authority that exists in the church or organization.

Constitution and Bylaws Defined

Constitution: A definitive statement of the name, location, doctrinal purpose, and rules of conduct of the church. It is the way the organization is structured. It includes basic beliefs, dogma, and polity. It describes the covenant under which the membership operates. *Bylaws*: From the old English loosely translated "village law." Bylaws focus on the rights and privileges of the members, the responsibilities and powers of church officers and how they become officers as well as how long they will serve. Included in the bylaws are rules for doing business and conducting meetings, who will moderate meetings, and the parameters for quorum. Committees and other polity organizations of the body are identified. How finances are received and used is defined.

Both documents must describe how they come into existence, how they may be modified, and what becomes of the assets of the organization in the event of cessation of existence. The management of both documents must be assigned to a polity organization of the church for review, evaluation, and recommendation to the church for revision, correction, or deletion.

In the case study that introduced this chapter, one of the major problems that existed in the church was that we didn't know what the constitution and bylaws said because we didn't have a copy of it. I admit that I became the church administrator without even looking at the "rules for doing church." I discovered I wasn't alone. It took me several weeks to discover a copy of the constitution. The version I found was a 1956 revision of the original 1934 creation. Once we read the document through, we discovered we were doing many things in violation of the constitution and bylaws. One was that there was no provision for the paid position of church administrator; I was not legally employed!

There are many practical reasons the church should periodically review the constitution and bylaws:

1. There is a biblical precedent for orderly conduct in the church. For example, Paul wrote letters to Timothy to help him instruct the leadership of the church in understanding their leadership role and conduct.

2. Inappropriate direction may exist:
   - Outdated policy
   - Unwritten rules to be added
   - Traditions and processes to be formalized
   - Inflexible and narrow guidance needs to be evaluated
   - Unethical or illegal practices
3. It is good to review the documents after a lengthy pastorate. Many items in a written set of documents may have been set aside or granted by consensus as the congregation yielded more authority to a pastor. These relaxed conditions may not be allowed for new leadership.
4. Several unofficial and official documents may exist in the church because of various decisions at business meetings that need to be incorporated into a formalized document.
5. How the church does business (meetings, committees, programs, etc.) needs to be reviewed periodically. Eliminate redundant direction, clarify communication, and consolidate similar decisions.
6. Periodic review establishes an attitude among the church body that the leadership is sensitive to the desires of the congregation.

Writing Constitution and Bylaws Documents

Development of a constitution and bylaws should be a spiritual odyssey. The leadership of the church should lead the church in discovering the vision that the Holy Spirit has placed in their midst and then create a mission statement that describes how the church or organization will act out that vision. Vision is a God-inspired direction that the church or organization should inculcate. Mission consists of the plans that are made to carry out the vision.

Here are the practical procedures to follow when developing and writing a constitution and bylaws:

1. The pastor must provide the leadership. The pastor creates a positive attitude toward "doing church" properly. The pastor (and other spiritual leaders of the church) leads the church in formulating its vision and mission statements.
2. Establish a committee if that assignment has not already been made by other documents in the church.
3. Conduct research:
   - Consider any present documents of polity and policy—existing constitution and bylaws documents, existing policy and procedures, church business minutes, minutes of committees or other policy-making groups in the church.
   - Consider examples from denominational resources, other churches, and professional literature.

- Review all reports of business meetings or meetings where churchwide decisions were made.
4. Determine if there exists any federal, state, or local government regulations that are applicable to the church and need to be included in the documents.
5. Keep the congregation informed and involved.
6. Adopt the documents by a churchwide vote.
7. Publish the document and make it available to all staff, leaders, and organizational groups in the church.

Because of recent court decisions as well as enacted law, there are certain elements that should be carefully considered whenever the constitution and bylaws are crafted.

The church or organization should:

- Specifically identify itself as a "religious, not-for-profit" entity.
- Identify the theological and doctrinal stance taken by the church or institution.
- Identify any dogma or doctrinal position that separates the church from secular or other religious institutions. (For example, the church may choose to ordain only male clergy. That exclusion should be stated and justified from the theological documents to which the church or organization subscribes.)
- Describe the methodology for dealing with errant or inappropriate behavior by leaders and members alike. Included should be factors and conditions for termination of relationship.
- While most states will require the identification of officers and trustees by name in the incorporating documents (covered next), the church should make clear that these are not lifetime assignments and that a process for the frequent or infrequent replacement of the individuals is provided.
- Identify what a quorum is. For example, is the "total membership" to be considered, only those who are considered "active" members, or "those members present and voting." What number represents a quorum—simple majority, two-thirds, three-fourths, a percentile?
- Identify what form of parliamentary procedure will be adopted. Usually *Robert's Rules of Order* will be used.
- State upon what conditions meetings will be closed to the public or membership.

It is strongly recommended that the church not encumber the constitution and bylaws with details of doing business. The appropriate place for that is in a policies-and-procedures manual. The principle reason is that to change the constitution or bylaws takes a quorum vote in a special, formal meeting of the church. To change a policy takes only a majority vote in a business meeting, and to change a procedure can be done by the group assigned responsibility for administration of the policy without a vote at all.

INCORPORATION

Historically in America churches or not-for-profit religious bodies functioned under a society or unincorporated format. They were individuals who formed a loose association based upon a theological, doctrinal, familial, or other cooperative reason. Many churches and nonprofit organizations in America today remain in this unincorporated status. In the past half century, however, the attractiveness—and quiet honestly the necessity—of forming an incorporated not-for-profit religious organization is becoming apparent. Whereas before the church was considered a sacrosanct institution that was immune from litigation, now the church is named as a defendant in court just like any other element of society.

All states and territories of the United States have provisions for nonprofit organizations to incorporate as a corporate entity, enjoying the privileges—as well as the responsibilities—that any corporation may have. The processes for and provisions of the incorporation vary from state to state but usually includes: (1) the filing of an application that identifies the institution, place of meeting, its officers and incorporators; (2) a filing fee; and (3) some provisions for reporting proof to the state that the organization is operating as chartered—as a nonprofit, religious organization. Some states will require a copy of a constitution and bylaws; others will require the institution be registered as an Internal Revenue Code 501(c)(3) tax-exempt organization.

Significant advantages exist for incorporating a church or nonprofit organization:

1. It creates a legal entity. The church or organization becomes a registered corporation with the state, and a charter is issued that identifies this legal status.
2. Only corporate assets may be garnished in the event of litigation. The personal assets of members, trustees, and leaders are protected from any litigation or garnishment. Only the assets of the corporation are liable.
3. Most financial institutions and other commercial ventures will deal only with legal entities. Banks and other lending agencies as well as trust and land developers want the assurance of a legally identified and insurance-protected entity.
4. It protects (copyrights) the church name. A charter is issued that gives sole recognition to the church identification.
5. Perpetual legal presence will exist even if leadership changes.

6. It becomes a forum for review and update of ways the church does business. In states that require annual reports and filing, the process will encourage a comprehensive review of church conduct.
7. Many states will require annual evaluations and reports of expenditures and funds which will prompt appropriate and legal financial operations.

Most disadvantages to incorporation relate to the reluctance of the church or organization to become entangled in government oversight. Some, not all, states will require reports that will necessitate a detailed assessment and evaluation of the church's financial activities. Some states will require the church or institution to abide by any state laws that have been written that relate to chartered, not-for-profit organizations. In summary, disadvantages include:

1. It will bring the church under state nonprofit regulations and statutes.
2. It will require legal counsel to develop and maintain the charter application.

While some churches and organizations choose not to get involved in the hassles of incorporation, Proverbs 27:12 reminds wise leaders that "the sensible see danger and take cover; the foolish keep going and are punished." Church leaders should consider carefully the potential for disaster that might befall them and the members of the church if they fail to think about the protection incorporation affords.

The Process for Filing Incorporation Documents

The procedures to follow in developing the documents to file for incorporation should be developed in the context of an existing committee or a specially formed committee to create the application. The following process should be considered:

1. Request an information packet from the state attorney general's office. Most states issue incorporation from the attorney general's office or secretary of state. Local denominational leaders can provide assistance in determining the agency from which the church should request application forms.

2. Retain legal counsel to draw up the formal document. In most states the filing of the church constitution and bylaws will be required. If that document has not been produced, then the church needs to take this step first. While the constitution and bylaws is a document of the statement of faith of the church and the philosophy for doctrine and dogma, the lawyer may be asked to review the document for legal requirements since he or she may have to defend the church in litigation matters relating to the church's statement of operation.

3. Select incorporators—the individuals named in the document who will draw up the articles of incorporation. In most states these must be the trustees elected by the church as well as the identification of a president and treasurer.

4. Review requirements for incorporation.

5. Identify what other not-for-profit organization will receive the assets of the church or organization in the eventuality of dissolvement of the church or organization. By law this must be another IRS 501(c)(3) organization.

6. File the articles of incorporation with the appropriate authority.

7. Hold the initial meeting of the incorporated church or organization.

8. Legally transfer all assets of the unincorporated church or organization to the new incorporated, nonprofit, religious organization.

9. Prepare and record the dissolution of the unincorporated church.

10. Modify bylaws or policy and procedures documents to ensure any requirements of review or reporting are developed and implemented.

Policy and Procedures

No other church provides more instructions for "doing church" than the Corinthian church. For example in chapter 11 of 1 Corinthians, Paul begins the section by talking about social customs and worship. Numerous topics are discussed—covering the head, long hair, women-men relationships, prayer, and so forth. Beginning with verse 17, he chides them about their poor practices relating to the common meal and the Lord's Supper—the failure to share, gluttony, and drunkenness. He then goes on to describe in detail how the supper should be observed. He concludes the section with the statement in verse 34, "I will give instructions about the other matters whenever I come."

I moved to a church business administrator position in a local church directly out of the U.S. Navy. Having served twenty-two years as an active duty naval officer, I was "oriented" to do things by the book. For those of you who have served in governmental agencies or offices, you are well aware of what I am about to say. Everything we did in the military was by the "regs"—the regulations. We had regulations for how to do every facet of our responsibilities. Having been sent to a six-month school to become one of these "regulation writers," I knew full well the research, evaluation, and detail that went into every regulation. There was a practical reason for doing Navy by the book. As an individual went from command to command, the way things were done was "standardized." You could fit in quickly because administration, operation, and activity was the same everywhere. We all did business the same regardless of the type of ship or shore station to which we were assigned.

Policies and Procedures Defined

Policy: A policy is a general statement that relates the church's position on a particular subject. It is an expression of a course of action that directs a church or organization in attaining its stated mission and objectives. A policy is a managerial decision that defines the church's attitude on a particular matter. Policies respond to the routine operations of the church. Policies are statements of church or institution polity and therefore should be approved formally by the membership.

Procedures: While the policies are the broad statements of principle that chart a course of action, procedures are the oars in the water. They describe the how by which the church or organization will implement the policy. They become administrative decisions that define how the policy will be effectively carried out and administrative guidelines used by those who carry out the policy. They are never written without some clear and definite policy statement by the institution. Procedures are developed by administrators. These administrators may be a pastor, business administrator, the building supervisor, a committee, or any other individual or group. Procedures do not require the vote of the church. They should be developed, however, with sensitivity to the desires of the church as voiced in the policy statement.

Advantages of Policy and Procedures

Policy and procedure statements offer significant assistance in the management and administration of the church or organization. Some advantages of policies and procedures are:

1. Policies and procedures organize the efforts of the church or organization in attaining its objectives and goals. They become the road markers by which the leaders of the church can assess accomplishment or nonaccomplishment of an expressed direction toward which the church wants to move. They are the concrete expressions that move the church from the *what* and *why* to the *who, when,* and *how.*

2. Policies and procedures present to both those in the church and those outside an atmosphere of order, business, and sense of purpose. Church-designed policies and efficiently administered procedures develop a sense of satisfaction and fairness by the membership in the functioning of the church. Established, formal procedures convey to those who deal with the administrators of the church a sense of confidence and business rapport.

3. Formalized, written policies and procedures become guides for operation. They communicate methods of doing business. They become information instruments for the general church body. They are the training curricula for new staff, committee members, or employees.

4. Policies and procedures convert recurring problems to routine processes. They direct response and resolution to the lowest level of administration possible. They free higher levels of administration and management of the church to focus on significant or unique problem areas of the ministry of the church.

5. Policies and procedures aid in the formulation of church objectives and goals. They provide a meter to measure accomplishment. They focus on areas that require revision or modification. They highlight functional areas that require addressing to move the church in accomplishing its mission.

Disadvantages of Policies and Procedures

The disadvantages that surround policies and procedures lie not so much in their use but in their misuse and abuse.

1. Policies and procedures tend to become legal documents. The church becomes an organization by the book, and that book is not the Bible. Policies and procedures are not designed to harass the congregation but to facilitate their service.

2. Policy and procedure statements are legal documents. In some instances where church groups have had to respond to legal situations, courts have held that organization manuals, personnel manuals, policy and procedure manuals become legal contracts or binding expressions by the church. Policies and procedures must be constituted in legally defensible terms.

3. Policy and procedure statements when unequally applied become vehicles for contention and conflict. What's good for the goose has to be good for the gander. While exceptions can occur, they should be few and far between. The grantor of the exception should be on solid ground and would be wise to consult the designers of the procedures that are being violated.

4. Out of date, unnecessary, or unmodified policy and procedure documents become hindrances to efficient operation. When a policy needs to be changed, change it. When procedures no longer apply, modify or eliminate them. Policy and procedure documents should be evaluated constantly for effectiveness. All documents should be reviewed by the body which constituted them at least annually. This means that an organization which represents the church body should review the policy statement at least annually. The administrative body which produced the procedure guidelines in support of that policy should also review those steps for applicability and efficiency.

Developing Policy and Procedures

This is not the time to hire a lawyer. Policy statements should be stated in terminology that is understood by the church member who will acknowledge, approve, and function by it. It is best to use the language that addresses the issue while at the same time allows for the expansion of the statement to embrace future contingencies.

- Effective policy statements should be a few short sentences in length; they should be concise but complete.

- They should address a few related topics in each statement. If several policy statements would best address the topic, then present each policy with its implementing procedures.
- They should be broad in scope. Policy statements should focus on the desire of the church or organization but leave latitude for creativity, innovation, and application in the implementing procedures.
- They should assign responsibility for implementation and review to some group or polity organization in the church or institution.
- They should be written in a positive rather than punitive context.
- They should not be unnecessarily restrictive. Policies become guidelines that address a wide variety of topics in the church. Overly burdensome policies become demotivators for ministry rather than motivators.
- They should be enforceable and legally defensible. Policies should be developed within the context of the church or organization's constitution and bylaws and within the parameters of any local, state, or federal statutes.
- They should be developed with the assistance of the individuals or groups who must implement and use the policy. Who best to ensure the policy is carried out to the intent of the church or organization than the people who will have to live with it and explain it to others?

A record of the policy should be entered into the formal, historical documents of the church or organization. Usually policies are presented by committees or other polity organizations of the church or organization during a formal business session. Many churches or organizations will adopt a standardized format for presenting such business. Presented on a one-page document, the policy should be stated as the committee or group recommends, the date of such presentation, a space for any approved amendments or modifications, and the date of formal adoption. The final wording of the policy is to be entered prior to filing.

The policy, when approved, becomes a permanent record in the records secretary's, church historian, or other permanent file location. A serial sequence code and the recommending and implementing groups would be useful for retrieving the document for future review.

Implementing Procedures

Once the church has approved the policy, the necessary procedures to implement it will be developed by that group assigned to administer the policy.

- Effectively written procedures will address the policy that has been written. Policy statements become limits for operational statements. Don't rewrite the policy.

- They should be written in the language of the individual or individuals who will use the procedures. If it is a maintenance policy, use maintenance terms; if it applies to use of the facility by individuals outside the church, use language they can understand.

- Procedures should use a step-by-step, sequential format. An outline format lends itself well to procedure statements. Limit subtopic items under each procedural step to those necessary for clarity of that particular step.

- Procedures should allow for creativity and innovation in the implementation of some of the steps. Managers do not have all the answers. Allow for the expertise of the individuals who use procedures to amplify and make the procedures more efficient.

- Procedures should avoid any ambiguous or unclear statements. The objective is to develop procedures that will be applied in all situations by all persons in a uniform and consistent manner. Even the part-time or volunteer secretary should be able to determine how a member goes about checking out a video projector for a class activity.

- Procedures should be conscious of the paperwork mill. Many procedures will call for the development of forms, ledgers, check-offs, diagrams, or other associated documents. In developing procedures, limit these items. Consolidate or revise existing forms. Develop new forms with multiple use in mind.

- Provide policies with the implementing procedures in a written form to the church. While formal approval is not usually undertaken, the church must understand the procedures that implement the policy. This is effectively accomplished in the publication of a church organization manual. If published in loose-leaf form, additions and modifications are easily made. Available in various locations throughout the church (church office, library, division offices), the manual becomes a sourcebook of church operation. Reviewed routinely and periodically, the manual becomes a current source of efficient administration.

Manuals of Operation

As can be seen in the discussion so far in this chapter, a church organization manual is a compilation of many separately produced documents. The remainder of this book will be devoted to developing policy statements about various elements of church or institutional organization. For example, the next chapter will focus on developing an organization. Job descriptions, committees, and other small-group charters come into existence via several modes—personnel committees, committee-on-committees, and staff development. In the following chapter will be presented the personnel operations of the church or organization. These are often termed personnel policy manuals in many organizations. Later we will develop financial policies and property polices, which will in effect be finance manuals and property manuals.

Other manuals that will lend themselves to separate presentations are documents such as wedding procedures manuals, kitchen operations manuals, office procedure manuals, family life and recreation manuals, youth mission project manuals, benevolence procedures manuals, and so forth.[2]

Significant advantage exists for creating the church organization manual in this format.

- A specific office, committee, or polity group is identified as the manager.
- Processes for review are easier to identify.
- It is easier to create changes and modifications to the policies and procedures in a compartmentalized version of the manual.
- Publication of the smaller manual may target specific users. For example, a bride is given a copy of the wedding procedures manual section of the church property manual.

Developing specific manuals for operation should always be done in the context of the legal documents (constitution, bylaws, and articles of incorporation) of the church or organization. Policies should be reviewed and developed by the assigned polity manager (staff, committee, council, etc.). Procedures should be reviewed and developed by both a representative of the policy manager and the group that will implement the policy. A scheme for developing an office procedure manual might follow this pattern:

- The church administrator meets with personnel, finance, property, and other polity groups to ascertain if policy has been developed that would impact church office procedures.
- The administrator meets with current staff personnel to develop a consensus of how they view the church office will support their particular element of ministry or responsibility.
- The administrator meets with other program and ministry leaders to ascertain how they view the church office in helping them to meet the requirements of their particular area of responsibility.
- Existing procedures are reviewed to develop a consensus of how business is now being conducted.
- Research and a review of publications and other example church office manuals is conducted to develop a potential format for the document.
- A review of any regulatory documents such as the U.S. Postal Service, the IRS/Social Security, and state and federal employment commissions is made for legal requirements.

- A listing of all topics deemed appropriate for the church or organization is made and analyzed.
- A rough draft of the manual is completed and is circulated to assess understandability, readability, and legal defensibility.
- A final document is created, published, and distributed.

Each of the subsequent chapters of this book will provide the basis for the development of most of the documents that any church or not-for-profit religious organization will ever need.

A word or warning early in this book: since this is a textbook of church administration, it is necessary to present the complex, complete version of a church organization manual rather than an incomplete, sketchy version. Church or organization leaders must consider the totality of the material provided herein and select that which will be appropriate for their institutions. Not everything will be needed or desired.

Chapter Review

Professionalism will require the church or nonprofit organization to present itself in a formal, yet understandable manner to both the constituency it serves and the general public it encounters. This is often best accomplished through the documents that define and state the function and operation of the organization.

- The reader should be able to define the terms *constitution, bylaws, incorporation,* and *policies and procedures* and describe how each interrelates in the church or nonprofit organization.
- The term *legal defensibility* was used in the chapter. What does this term mean in the context of the documents described in the chapter?
- Be able to describe procedures an administrator should follow to develop any of the documents discussed in the chapter.

Organizing the Church

Now there are different gifts, but the same Spirit. There are different ministries, but the same Lord. And there are different activities, but the same God is active in everyone and everything. A manifestation of the Spirit is given to each person to produce what is beneficial. . . . For as the body is one and has many parts, and all the parts of that body, though many, are one body—so also is Christ. . . . Instead, God has put the body together, giving greater honor to the less honorable, so that there would be no division in the body, but that the members would have the same concern for each other. . . . Now you are the body of Christ, and individual members of it. And God has placed these in the church: first apostles, second prophets, third teachers, next, miracles, then gifts of healing, helping, managing, various kinds of languages. Are all apostles? Are all prophets? Are all teachers? Do all do miracles? Do all have gifts of healing? Do all speak in languages? Do all interpret?
1 Corinthians 12:4–7, 25, 27–30

Now as we have many parts in one body, and all the parts do not have the same function, in the same way we who are many are one body in Christ and individually members of one another.
Romans 12:4–5

And He personally gave some to be apostles, some prophets, some evangelists, some pastors and teachers, for the training of the saints in the work of ministry, to build up the body of Christ, until we all reach unity in the faith and in the knowledge of God's Son, growing into a mature man with a stature measured by Christ's fullness. . . . From Him the whole body, fitted and knit together by every supporting ligament, promotes the growth of the body for building up itself in love by the proper working of each individual part.
Ephesians 4:11–13, 16

From these passages of Scripture, it is evident that God, speaking through the Holy Spirit and the writer Paul, created the church about a specific philosophy and concept of organization. From this we discover that:

- All members have a "gifted" responsibility.
- The distribution of the responsibilities made a complete, functioning body.
- There were objectives set for the ministry.
- There were individuals whose role was to provide leadership.

Types of Polity

The *New American Heritage Dictionary* defines *polity* as the "form of government of a nation, state, church, or organization." Polity describes an organization's philosophy for conducting business, carrying out commerce, or relating to the public.[1]

With regard to religious organizations, polity may be categorized as a monarchial system, an episcopate, a loose hierarchy, or congregational in format.

Monarchial

Within the monarchial system there exists a strict hierarchy. An example might be the Roman Catholic Church with the pope as the head. The pope's decrees are authoritative and must be followed by all Catholic entities worldwide. He will exercise control of the church through a group of appointed cardinals and bishops who, through delegated responsibilities, carry out the functions of the church in a particular area.

Episcopalian

Within the episcopalian system there exists a loose hierarchy scheme. The decisions of the church as made by its leader will be observed throughout the total denominational structure. An example of this form might be the United Methodist Church with its diocese organization and operation. Leaders of the local church and region are responsible to the denominational hierarchy for the conduct of the church.

Presbyterian

In the presbyterian form of church polity, authority is vested in a regional hierarchy. While denominational guidance may be provided, each appointed/elected presbytery is responsible for interpretation and implementation. The Presbyterian Church USA is an example of this form of regionalized hierarchy with church-elected presbyters conducting the business and church affairs of the presbytery.

Congregational

The congregational form of polity is best illustrated by the Baptist denomination and its democratic autonomy from any denominational governance or hierarchy. In this polity structure, the local church or organization executes its own rules of conduct and appoints or elects its own leaders, who act for or in behalf of the church. While allegiance to or cooperation with other like-minded bodies may exist, and even if a denominational structure is in place, the church or organization acts independently of any outside influence.

Good administrative leaders know the polity within which they function. In hierarchical church organizations, leaders must lead because the congregation will expect them to provide the form and function for what they do. However, in a congregational polity setting, the church or organization expresses a democratic philosophy for doing church and will rebel at any attempt by a denomination- or leader-imposed hierarchy. Does this mean that leaders cannot effect change? No, but administrators must become change agents rather than directors of change.

The crafters of the philosophy for change agency such as Towns, Anderson, and Maxwell all state in one sense or the other that leaders "effect" change. They do not necessarily change the masses; they change the people who can cause the change to occur.

Several years ago in a small church my family and I joined, a new pastor was called. The church was of moderate size (250 or so) and had been led for the past twenty years by a beloved pastor. He retired and the new, younger pastor showed up. When he arrived, he said that the church needed to know he was a church growth advocate. We really didn't understand that. Naturally we thought it meant that the church would grow in numbers. And it did, but that was not what he was talking about. What he meant was the church was to mature spiritually. If we grew spiritually, then all the rest would fall into place. He began a men's Bible study program on a Saturday morning and invited us to learn how to read and study the Bible. The women were also invited to participate in a spiritual development program. Within a few years the church doubled, tripled, quadrupled, and so forth. Many of the individuals who participated in the spiritual growth studies led by the pastor became the leadership of the church.

In time, that pastor led the church to study what the church was to be about, to reestablish its mission and purpose. Concurrent to that study was a review of the constitution and bylaws as well as the church policy and procedures documents. Significant changes occurred in that church because the congregation, for the most part, had been changed. It was no longer the little church of 250 but a church of 1,250 and more with many more ministries and leaders in those ministry areas. The change was not without some problems.

Many of the group of the earlier 250-member church did not like the way the church was moving with regard to polity—especially with the deacon ministry. They viewed the deacons as the elders of the church who made all the decisions and rules for conduct. The new philosophy for deacon ministry called for the deacons to set aside decision-making and begin to conduct ministries of pastoral help.

Why do churches or organizations change? They change when the present polity, policy, or procedure hurt, when stagnation or status quo will not satisfy the needs of the church or organization. They also change when they learn a better way of doing what needs to be done. Smart administrators are capable of evaluating the situation, determining where detriment is occurring, and going about effecting change by working with the individuals who are responsible for the area, informing them how to go about correcting the problem. While the old adage of "don't fix a problem that doesn't exist" is a wise admonition, moving along at the status quo is not sufficient. Change agent administrators can:

- Evaluate a situation and determine the causes of problems.
- Select one or two individuals who can assist them in solving the problem.
- Lead those "change effectors" in understanding the problem and allow them to participate with the administrator in determining a change.
- Release the change effectors to cause the change to occur within the organization.
- Evaluate and redefine change when it needs to be done.

Smart administrators understand the polity within which they work. If this is a family-led small church, then find the matriarch or patriarch of the family and change them if you want to effect change. When the church is called to a vote, then you want Grandma Hunter to raise her hand if you want all the other Hunters in the church to vote.

Developing an Organizational Scheme for the Church

A Philosophy for Developing Organizational Structure

Notice in the example of development of the church organization manual in the previous chapter, at some point the leadership of the church had determined that it was necessary to create defining documents called the constitution and bylaws. Why was that necessary? Remember that the constitution is, among other things, a statement of the theology that describes how the church interprets Scripture for their vision and mission for being a church. And the bylaws describe the organization they form for doing church. Thus they are documents that say, "This is what we believe, and this is how we are going about doing what we believe." These statements become the standard by which all activities of the church are measured. It is the major policy statement by which all procedures, programs, budgets, organizations, selecting and training, evaluation, and so forth occur.

The mission and purpose statement of a church or organization is usually a preamble to the larger document, the constitution and bylaws, and describes how that group envisions its existence. The development of a mission and purpose statement, the constitution and bylaws that implement that statement, and the incorporation as a religious and/or not-for-profit organization are important steps in the organizational development of a church. These documents should be developed by the church or organization with sensitivity to the spiritual direction provided to the leadership.

Organization by Style

Responding to a report of an unruly situation in the church at Corinth, Paul wrote the church and admonished them in 1 Corinthians 14:33, "God is not a God of disorder but of peace." *The Living Bible* states it like this, "God is not one who likes things to be disorderly and upset. He likes harmony, and he finds it in all the other churches." The New King James Version translates it, "For God is not the author of confusion but of peace, as in all the churches of the saints." In an earlier section that discussed the process of administration, one of the principal functions was the development of an organization to carry out the work. In any group of people who come together to complete a task, two general forms of organization will exist:

Formal. A pattern of formal relationships as defined in a hierarchy of interactions. It is mechanistic in its approach, rule-oriented with defined work policies and procedures, and has well-established control mechanisms to monitor effectiveness.

Informal. A pattern of spontaneous relationships, often the result of activities or participant interaction. It derives from social, vocational, interest, prestige, or informal recognition of leadership lines. Leadership is loose and voluntary.

In Scripture we find three basic types of organization:

1. *A Centralized Organization.* Often termed a centric organization, this is the structure that Jethro found Moses using in the account recorded in Exodus 18. There Jethro found Moses trying to do all the work himself because he was "God's appointed leader." Jethro warned Moses of the potential of burnout; the result of which would cause the nation to be without a leader. In this style of organization, all staff authority is vested in the office of the chief administrator. This type is often referred to as the authoritarian/dictator approach.

In the centralized organization there is little or no participation on the part of other staff or workers. Imposed goals and methods exist for achieving them. There is little relativity, initiative, and interest in the job under this approach. This type of organization often is rigid and resistive to change. And as Jethro pointed out, it could lead to burnout!

This type of organization is found in many churches and religious organizations today. At the upper level the pastor or director has all staff and committees reporting to him. This type of organization often becomes controlling and repressive. These types of leaders were described in chapter 2 as Showmen, Doubting Thomases, and Control Freaks, hoarding all authority and power.

This type of organization often appears in the mission or new, small church plant where there has been little time to develop a sense of disbursed leadership. Often this small church expects the pastor to be the leader. However, the wise pastor/administrator will quickly develop a sense of distributed leadership to prevent the mind-set by the congregants that "the pastor will do all the work, and we don't have to do anything."

2. *A Nonorganization* is one in which there is no one central line of authority or responsibility. This organizational approach is often classified as the "collegial" or "noncentralized" form since each staff member relates to the other equally. Paul admonished the church at Corinth and then reminded them in 1 Corinthians 12 that the Holy Spirit had given every believer a responsibility in the church, and some of those responsible persons were to act as the leaders of the body.

A church that has this style of organization will have the senior staff member (the senior pastor possibly) as an advisor to the other members, but he will not exercise any direct authority over them. They each do their own thing. This organization approach is ripe for miscommunication, poor relationships, duplication of effort, and wasting of resources. Frequently it becomes a dog-eat-dog work environment where the strongest survive. In chapter 2 we introduced the dysfunctional leadership style of the Monk, used by those who remove themselves from the role of leader.

3. *The Line or Participative Organization* is one in which there is a leader, but this leadership is delegated downward through the organizational matrix through lines of authority. Thus, it is often called the "line" or "matrix" organization. While leadership remains established, a portion of the responsibility resides at a variety of sublevels in the organization. Charles Tidwell in his book *The Educational Ministries of a Church* reports that when A. T. Robertson looked at the lists that Scripture gave of the apostles, there appeared three distinct groups of apostles, each headed by Simon Peter, Philip, and James the son of Alpheus, respectively (compare Matt. 10:2–4, Mark 3:16–19, Luke 6:14–16, and Acts 1:13).[2] Whether Jesus intentionally organized his apostles, the listing given in Scripture apparently indicates an implied organization.

This is the organizational approach that Jethro suggested to Moses in Exodus 18. The line organization was the suggested format that Jethro gave Moses to prevent his burnout in carrying out his assigned responsibility. There were groups of people headed by leaders of thousands, then groups headed by leaders of hundreds and so forth to the smallest group. This approach to an organization encourages worker initiative and creativity in task accomplishment. It fosters a sense of ownership in decisions made and accomplishment of the organization's mission and purpose. Its structure identifies needs and eliminates duplication of effort. While it is rigid in structure, it is flexible in that within the matrix there is the utilization of skills and abilities at all junctures of the organization.

We have seen that the first two types of organization do not lend themselves well to effective and efficient utilization of personnel or resources. Let us then consider that the third, the line or matrix format of organization is best suited to the church or religious institution. Several advantages can be identified by using this type of organizational structure:

- Administrative decisions are pushed downward to supervisory levels.
- Management remains focused on the "big" picture.
- Line structures use the resources of the organization effectively and efficiently.
- As decision-making is pushed downward through the matrix, flexibility in large and complex organizations is restored.
- Because more people are decision-makers, the concept of the team is more prevalent.

Most pastors and other ministry leaders have a difficult time letting go and delegating work to subordinates in the organization. Usually it is not that they want to do all the work themselves; they just do not know how to delegate. Failure to delegate, however, will lead to burnout in ministry. But more importantly, failure to delegate violates a principle role of the leader—to equip the body to do the work of ministry.

The church organizational structure should continue to pattern itself after the traditional matrix or line format. People need policies and procedures with a defined work flow. Personnel should be directed through their work by job descriptions not only for accountability but also for responsibility. The alert church administrator must always be mindful of the informal structure that exists in the church and take advantage of it when possible. As will be noted later in this chapter, projects, special assignments, and study groups become excellent avenues for the informal organization in the church.

Organizing by Size

A few years ago I received a frantic call from a former student. He began by asking me if I remembered the allegory I used in class about not considering all the alternatives and finding yourself neckhigh in water surrounded by alligators, remembering that your initial objective was to drain the swamp. He stated that he was nose high in the swamp and about to be eaten alive by alligators. He said that he wished he had paid attention to my administration lecture about organizing for the future. He explained that he left seminary and began a church plant. Things went well, and soon his church was a storefront church, and now it was about to become a church in a real building. Things had moved too fast, and he had not planned for the growth. His question was, "What do I do now?"

While most churches in America today are either stagnant or declining, many are growing and moving forward with the Great Commission mandate. When I am asked, "How large should your church be before you call another staff member?" or "What type of staff member should I lead the church to call first?" I usually respond, "It depends." How a church or institution is organized is a function of several variables.

1. Pioneer or mission churches function best without a cumbersome hierarchy. In most cases a group of thirty to fifty people can be effectively led by a single person. This does not mean that the individual will be expected to do all the work, but it does imply that decisions can be made collectively and problems shared throughout the group.

2. Churches or groups above fifty people should consider some form of organizational structure. Initially that may be the development of one or two committees that will assist in research and decision-making. Usually a group this size would have considered ministry-assistant deacons to assist the pastor in pastoral and other ministry responsibilities. The larger the church becomes and the more activities that are carried out, the larger the lay organization will become. Committees can assist in decision-making with regard to elements of church operation like finances, personnel, and facility management. Councils can advise the pastor in issues of age-group programming and education and curriculum without the need for a paid minister. (Committees, councils, and ministry teams will be discussed later in this chapter.)

3. Whenever a church approaches two hundred active members, the consideration of additional paid staff may become an issue. But a caution flag needs to be raised. Often churches will call additional staff without first considering why they are calling that staff. Visionary leaders will look at the present situation as well as the future potential. The criteria by which an organization develops should be that form (the organizational structure) follows function (what the church or organization envisions itself to be doing in their community).

4. Organizational structure should be developed to enhance strengths of the church and to propel or continue whatever has caused the church to grow. These decisions should come about after demographic and historical research, inquiry of the body about the needs of the church, and prayerful consideration of the needs of the community to which the church is ministering.

Organization by Function

Gene Mims defines the functions of the New Testament church in his *Kingdom Principles for Church Growth* as worship, discipleship, fellowship, evangelism, and ministry.[3] Paul would describe the church, using the metaphor of the human body in 1 Corinthians 12:12–26, as being made up of many parts, each interrelated and reliant upon the other, each carrying out a particular function, yet all working together to accomplish the mission of Christ through the church. Contemporary church organization models frequently reflect how a church interprets their function and then develops a staff structure about that interpretation. For example, a church may have a minister of outreach and evangelism or a minister of discipleship. Frequently the minister of music has been retitled as the worship leader. Deacon groups are often organized about a ministry focus of the church.

Regardless of the activity or segment within the church organization, four distinct functional groupings can be identified: pastoral, education/discipleship, music/worship, and support. Using this fourfold nomenclature for describing the general functions of the church, programs, activities, and ministries may be placed. Expressing this functional organization in the terms of leadership positions, a typical organizational chart for a moderate-sized church might look like this:

SENIOR PASTOR			
PASTORAL (Associate Pastor)	EDUCATION (Minister of Education)	MUSIC (Minister of Music)	SUPPORT (Church Administrator)
Deacon Ministry Nursing Home Ministry Hospital and Jail Chaplains Counseling Ministry Mission Organizations	Sunday School Discipleship Training Age-Group Ministries Media Ministry	Adult Choir Program Graded Choir Program Organist Pianist	Office Secretaries Finance Records Clerk Custodians

Note the similarity to the line or matrix organization discussed earlier.

Where would a minister of outreach and evangelism fit into this organizational scheme? Anywhere you want it. One church might envision outreach and evangelism as a function of education/discipleship, since Sunday school is its outreach program and evangelism visitation is carried out by them. Another church will see the function as best being carried out by the pastor in the pastoral ministries section. The beauty of a line organization is its matrix flexibility.

Suppose your church chooses to have the minister of outreach and evangelism fall under education for administrative management. When the music ministry of the church plans an Easter pageant and wants to involve evangelism, the person in the position of minister of outreach and evangelism moves across lines to work with the minister of music in developing a plan for evangelism for the production. When the mission council of the pastoral section wants to include a neighborhood VBS as part of their mission program for the year, they will cross matrix lines and work with the outreach and evangelism minister as well as the preschool and children's minister to help facilitate the activity. The line matrix allows the flexibility for cross utilization of the skills and abilities of the organizational structure while at the same time retains the lines of responsibility and authority necessary for management control.

The Church Staff Plan

Were the apostles a staff to Christ? We know that he chose the twelve apostles from a larger group that was called his disciples. We also know that he frequently would use them to carry out ministry functions: to prepare people to receive a meal, to arrange for a Passover meal, to find a donkey, to go on mission trips, and so forth. Scripture identifies some of the apostles as possibly heads of groups as A. T. Robertson noted in his *A Harmony of the Gospels for the Students of the Life of Christ*. We know that one of the group, Judas Iscariot, was the treasurer. Three of the apostles (Peter, James, and John) seemed to have a closer relationship to Christ than the others. And one was entrusted with the "keys to the kingdom" while another was given the personal responsibility for caring for Christ's earthly mother.[4]

But were they a staff? Turning to the dictionary, we find *staff* defined as "a group of personnel who carry out a designated function or activity of the institution or organization under the direct leadership of the director or head." The word comes from the same root that also describes a measuring stick or metered device. In a military connotation a staff is a group of advisors who provide research and information to a commander in his decision-making responsibility. Jesus was definitely the head of the group. The apostles provided information ("Who do people say that the Son of Man is?"—Matt. 16:13) and research ("The apostles gathered around Jesus and reported to Him all that they had done and taught"—Mark 6:30). Did they facilitate his ministry? Scripture describes them providing for and serving at least two recorded feedings of thousands, and their arranging for the last supper meal during the Passover. They provided transportation and arranged for sleeping accommodations.

Earlier we defined organization as the work that is done to group people and resources so that work can be efficiently and effectively accomplished. One of those significant groups we will call the "staff." While most of our discussion in this section of the chapter will center on the church staff—that group of ministers and workers under the leadership of a pastor—a staff occurs anytime leaders gather individuals about them to conduct work or accomplish a task. Therefore, the concepts and actions outlined below will be applicable to the formation of any staff unit—the senior pastor forming a ministerial staff, the church administrator forming a support staff, or the children's minister forming a children's ministry organization. The process will apply, whether forming a staff of professional ministers or lay volunteers.

Philosophy for a Staff

The development of a philosophy for creating a staff organization must flow out of the constituting documents that describe the church—its theology, doctrine, and statement of beliefs. Institutions create organizational structures for a variety of reasons:

- Organizations provide a format for establishing lines of authority and accountability.
- Staff structures ensure work is delegated based on appropriate skill and ability.
- Staff organizations provide a forum for dialogue, discussion, and shared decision-making responsibility.
- Reviews of staff organizational responsibilities ensure all facets of an institution's mission are being addressed.
- Duplication of effort is more easily identified in a formal organization.
- Structured organizations, with attendant rules of operation, provide to the client and church member alike a sense of professionalism and adroitness to responsibility.
- Development of a staff structure identifies who leads whom as well as what supervisory responsibilities exist in the organization.

The formation of a church staff will be evolutionary in nature. That is, it will develop over time. A mission church will begin with a single ministerial leader. Later the church will begin to add structure through committees and lay volunteers who take on leadership roles. In time the church will decide that the need for a particular area would best be served by a professional minister, either full-time or part-time. As the church continues to grow, new decisions are made about when and what ministerial and support staff are added. The wise church will begin to think about the potential for an organized church long before the need for that organization arises.

In order to develop this philosophy for an organizational staff, let's review what we have learned so far in this book:

- Christ has assigned to the church, through the leadership of the Holy Spirit, the work of ministry in the world today.
- All individuals in the church have been given some gift by the Holy Spirit that they are to use to develop and build up the body as it accomplishes the work of ministry.
- Certain individuals have been assigned the responsibility of equipping the believers and facilitating their work of ministry.

In developing a philosophy of organizing individuals to do the work of ministry, the church needs to:

- Determine what mission and role it will play in ministry as defined by God through the Holy Spirit.
- Determine what organizational leadership structure would best respond to that task.
- Help individuals identify where their gift of service fits into the structure.
- Determine what elements of the structure require professional or staffed facilitation.

Process for Developing a Staff Organization

As a church matures, one of the earliest organizational entities that should come into existence is a group we will identify later in this chapter as the personnel committee. A variety of titles exist for this group; in some organizations they might be termed the human resources management office or some other similar term. The title may differ, but the function is the same—to organize for, recruit, and provide the personnel resources to accomplish a task. Good personnel management calls for clear, effective, and legally defensible guidelines for activities relating to the human resources of the organization. The remainder of this chapter and the next chapter will deal with these issues.

The astute personnel manager will have a clearly articulated *staff plan*. This staff plan outlines the steps taken to assess the need for processes for recruitment and employment of personnel and the supervisory and management activities to ensure effective use and production of these resources. In its rawest sense the staff plan asks "why?" In its practical sense the staff plan outlines a format for consideration whenever a group creates an organizational scheme for doing business. The staff plan is visionary, evolutionary, and fluid. That is, it looks to the future needs of the organization with regard to personnel resources. It develops over time with each element building upon the other. It must remain flexible to meet the changing needs of the church or institution.

1. Review the philosophy of the church for the development of a staff. What is the theological basis for ministry and support personnel? How are lay and professional leaders integrated to accomplish the work of the church? What are the functional areas of the church within which the staff will serve? Church or organizational staff members are not the people who do the work of ministry; they are the leaders who equip the ministers in carrying out the functions of the church. While some will have active, functional roles (such as a secretary, pianist, department director), most will be responsible for task accomplishment in working with groups of individuals.

2. Review the organizational philosophy of the church or organization. What lines of authority are established? Are there clear lines of supervisory responsibility? Religious organizational dynamics depend heavily upon spiritual direction. Healthy organizations are those whose members understand and participate in the entity within which they function. For example, a Sunday school teacher should know her responsibility, who she is accountable to for the accomplishment of her job, who she can rely on to provide adequate supervision to complete the job, and how the outcome of her work will contribute to the overall mission of the organization.

3. Create a leadership profile of the organization. What leadership activities must be considered to accomplish the task? Is there an organizational chart that defines lines of responsibility? In what priority will leadership and other staff positions be considered? What type of skill or expertise should a person have in order to fill this position? Will leadership positions be filled from outside the organization, or will they be taken from the resources of the church or organizational entity?

Organizations must be cautious to explore thoroughly the rationale for a leadership organization before actively recruiting for the position. One critical issue that must be faced is the level of expertise expected of an incumbent. Will that person be expected to function immediately at all levels of the position, or will he be brought into the position through a process of indoctrination and training. Often the Holy Spirit will direct a church to move into a new ministry arena via a gifted individual within the church or organization. That is why an organizational structure should remain fluid; as it matures, the Holy Spirit will give it more to do.

4. Are the mechanisms for bringing staff personnel in place? Is there a current job description written for the position? Is there a salary plan and a budget to support that plan? Does the church have office and support space? Are personnel policies and procedures in place to ensure fair and legal recruiting and employment? Do documents exist that define the ministry, program, or activity

the individual will be expected to accomplish? Current human resource laws and guidelines demand that the church or organization carry out personnel actions in a fair and legal manner. Potential employees and leaders will approach the process with a legitimate expectation of professionalism on the part of the church.

5. Reevaluate the personnel requirement. Frequently churches rush out and "buy one of them" because their neighboring church has one and it seems to work for them. They fail to determine; "If we buy one, can we support it." It is like my brother and his St. Bernard. She was cute as a puppy, but she grew up! Religious organizations must think beyond the immediate and assess the long term. "Can we really support one of those?" is a real and immediate question that needs to be evaluated. Questions like these should be asked: "Is this task something an already existing position should be accomplishing?" "Are there qualified personnel within our laity that could accomplish this?" "Are there qualified personnel who can be employed to accomplish the task?"

6. Put in place a process for continual assessment and improvement. The staff plan is the beginning document of the process of human resource administration in the church or organization. It establishes the philosophy and underpinning for all actions that follow. It is the responsibility of some polity organization of the church to evaluate and modify the provisions systematically to ensure an effective and efficient organization.

In summary, the staff plan becomes the philosophical foundation through which the church or institution creates its leadership and ministry support organization. The plan should be revisited periodically, but especially on two important occasions: the replacement of an existing position, and whenever a new position is recommended. Some important reconsiderations for each are:

1. When replacement of a vacated position occurs, ask questions relating to the staff plan:

- Do we need the same type of work done, or has the job changed?
- Have demographics altered the justification for the position?
- Will the criteria for qualifications be the same, or has the need for expertise or education level changed?
- Are lines of supervisory authority the same, or have they changed?
- Has this position contributed to the mission and purpose of the church or organization?
- Have the requirements that this position called the incumbent to perform changed and need to be modified, deleted, or added to?
- Have financial and budgetary considerations that were in place for this position changed, and are there modifications that will be required?

When the creation of a new position is recommended, ask questions relating to the staff plan:

- Will this position meet the most critical need the church or organization has at this moment as well as in the future?
- Have the mechanics of the position such as job description, salary plan development, supervisory responsibility, and physical location including resources been provided?
- Are people with the qualifications available, and how will we go about identifying, recruiting, and employing/placing these personnel?
- Has an indoctrination and introduction process been developed by the supervisor that will ensure the incumbent will be adequately acclimated to the specific responsibility and the church or organization in general?

The presence of a support staff has been alluded to several times in the discussion thus far. Let's take a moment and focus on that group since they are integral to the total staff organization of a church or institution. When we speak of support staff, the positions of secretary, ministry assistant, clerk, office manager, receptionist, custodian, janitor, cook, hostess, and so forth come to mind. These individuals are what we will later term as hourly wage personnel because their compensation is based generally on the hours they work. In the next chapter we will discover that they are so termed because of legal ramifications about their employment.

Whether the church determines that these positions will be paid personnel or will be filled by lay volunteers, they must be considered in the comprehensive plan known as the *staff plan*. How many ministry assistant secretaries does a church need? Again the answer is, "It depends." It depends on the philosophy of the church with regard to providing clerical support to the ministry personnel. Do they assign a secretary to each minister or pool resources among the staff under the leadership of an office manager? It depends on the technology available to the program or ministry director. Some people prefer to carry out their own word processing rather than have someone else produce it. And it depends on the organizational structure the church has deemed best for it to do effectively what God has called it to do.

It is essential, therefore, for the church or organization to integrate plans for support staff in the comprehensive staff plan for the church. To give you a broad plan for where we are going with this structure, let's return to the organizational chart developed by function and integrate some support staff positions. Described in the table on the next page is an organizational structure that integrates both lay and paid professional leadership positions. The advantage of developing such a chart and the attendant staff plan philosophy is that it causes the leaders of the church to think through the plan for implementing the mission and purpose of the church through the efficient and effective use of human resources.

SENIOR MINISTER (Senior Pastor)			
PASTORAL (Associate Pastor)	EDUCATIONAL (Minister of Education)	MUSIC (Minister of Music)	SUPPORT (Church Business Administrator)
Deacon Ministry	Sunday School Director	Adult Choir Program Director	Office Manager
Hospital Chaplain	Discipleship Training Director	Senior Adult Choir Program Director	Receptionists
Nursing Home Chaplain	Senior Adult Minister	Graded Choir Program Director	Secretary Ministry Assistant(s)
Jail Chaplain	Adult Program Minister		Financial Record Clerk
Family Life Center Counseling Program Director	Single Adult Program Minister	Ensemble Director	Records and Data Management Clerk
Crisis Counseling Ministry	Student Ministry Program Director	Organist	Building Supervisor
Mission Program Organizations	Preschool and Children's Program Minister	Pianist(s)	Custodian(s)
Benevolence Program	Evangelism and Discipleship Program Director	Orchestra Director	Church Hostess
	Activities Program Director	Worship Media Program Director	Cook(s) and Food Service Workers
	Recreation Intern(s)		

Job Descriptions

"Select from all the people able men, God-fearing, trustworthy, and hating bribes. Place them over the people as officials of thousands, hundreds, fifties, and tens" (Exod. 18:21).

"Appoint judges and officials for your tribes in all your towns the LORD your God is giving you. They are to judge the people with righteous judgment. Do not deny justice or show partiality to anyone. Do not accept a bribe. . . . Pursue justice and justice alone" (Deut. 16:18–20).

"Select from among you seven men of good reputation, full of the Spirit and wisdom, whom we can appoint to this duty" (Acts 6:3).

"An overseer, therefore, must be above reproach, the husband of one wife, self-controlled, sensible, respectable, hospitable, an able teacher, not addicted to wine, not a bully but gentle, not quarrelsome, not greedy" (1 Tim. 3:2–3).

"Deacons, likewise, should be worthy of respect, not hypocritical, not drinking a lot of wine, not greedy for money, holding the mystery of the faith with a clear conscience" (1 Tim. 3:8–9).

In these passages of Scripture that describe the appointment or selection of leaders, criteria or qualifications for that position are given. It was as if God was saying; "This is a job description for a pastor, for a benevolence minister, for an elder, for a deacon." In fact, a tenet of Scripture appears to be that whenever God calls, appoints, directs, or assigns a responsibility, there is a clear definition of what it is and the qualifications for doing it. In other words, God gives us job descriptions for doing church!

Job descriptions are valuable documents for any organization because they:

- Outline the overall concept for the position.
- Describe how elements of the organization fit together to accomplish the task.
- Identify unique facets or elements of a position.
- List necessary qualifications, skills, and experience a person must possess to function in the position.
- Define supervisory lines of responsibility and accountability.
- Give to the supervisor a format for evaluating job performance.

Job descriptions are sometimes called position descriptions. They have been defined in a variety of ways, but one of the best definitions provided is that by Cliff Elkins, former minister of education at University Baptist Church in Fort Worth, Texas. Writing in *Church Administration* magazine in 1977, he defined a *job description* as "a systematic outline of the information obtained from a job analysis. It describes the job title, the principal function, including the person to whom the employee is responsible. Responsibilities include a description of the work performed, the skills or training required, and the relationships with other jobs and personnel."[5] That definition has been repeated in numerous other publications and monographs through the years and forms the basic premise for the job description format that is presented in this book.

While job descriptions are commonplace in the secular environment, research by organizations like the National Association of Church Business Administration, Christianity Today International, and private research by this author indicates that few churches provide an adequate job description for their ministerial or support staff. In fact, one study by this author found that less than half the churches surveyed had job descriptions for their professional staff and only one church had job descriptions for the lay leaders in the church.

Not only is this a poor business practice, but it provides an opportunity for the church and individual to develop significant misinterpretations about the responsibilities the individual is held accountable for. It is like inviting an individual to become the minister to whatever. The organization is saying to the person, "You go out and do whatever you think you should be doing, and we will tell you when you are not doing what we think you ought to be doing." What a terrible disservice to the program that expects professional leadership as well as the person who perceives that he is performing in an appropriate manner, only to be told that he is a failure because he was not doing what the supervisor (or church as a whole) thought he should be doing.

Who should have job descriptions? Everyone who has a leadership position in the organization. Everyone that would make up an organizational chart like the example in the previous section should have written job descriptions. Many organizations will write job descriptions for their lay workers, especially if these people have responsibilities that call for them to be accountable for some significant portion of the church or institution or to supervise some element of the program ministry or activity. Other institutions will have job descriptions for individuals who perform tasks that are commonly accomplished by a group of individuals and the organization wants that task to be accomplished in a standardized manner.

Elements of an Effective Job Description

A job description arises out of the assessment of the church or organization of its perceived mission statement and a definition of the leadership required to accomplish that purpose. Once the need for the position has been validated and an organizational chart developed to establish the format for relating the responsibilities one to another, the process for writing the job description begins.

1. Ascertain where the position will fit into the administrative functional organization.
2. Determine who will supervise this position.
3. Determine the qualifications of expertise, experience, education, and skill that will be required of the incumbent to fill the position satisfactorily.
4. In cooperation with the prospective supervisor and/or the ministry function head, detail the expectations of the job—the specific responsibilities the individual will be held accountable for accomplishing.
5. Write the job description and evaluate it for completeness and clarity.

Every job description should answer six questions:
1. What is the title of the position?
2. What are the general expectations of the position?
3. What are the qualifications for the position?
4. Who supervises the incumbent?
5. Who does the incumbent supervise?
6. What are the specific detailed duties and responsibilities?

A job description responding to the six questions above is shown below. Note that it follows the format of title, principal function, qualifications, and responsibilities.

MINISTER OF EDUCATION

PRINCIPAL FUNCTION: The minister of education is responsible to the senior pastor for directing the educational organizations of the church in planning, conducting, and evaluating of comprehensive program of Christian education and training.

QUALIFICATIONS FOR THE POSITION: The incumbent will possess significant knowledge of the Christian education and training programs, systems, and resources. A degree in Christian religious education or equivalent experience in the church setting is required.

REQUIREMENTS OF THE POSITION:

1. Lead in planning, conducting, and evaluating a comprehensive program of Christian education, discipleship, and training.
2. Serve as educational resource person and advisor to programs, services, and committee and ministry team organizations as assigned.
3. Supervise leaders of assigned programs, services, and committee and ministry organizations.
4. Develop special education and training projects and programs such as retreats, study sessions, seminars, colloquiums as well as ongoing training opportunities for new and existing education leaders and workers.
5. Remain aware of current trends in Christian education and ensure that individuals who lead programs under his or her direction are informed of such new opportunities.
6. Lead in the evaluation and selection of Christian education curriculum.
7. Guide in the designation, enlistment, and training of new lay workers.
8. Develop and supervise a program of churchwide visitation.
9. Develop, coordinate, and manage an annual budget to meet the educational needs of the programs assigned.
10. Act as staff advisor to other program and ministry function leaders with regard to facets of Christian education that will assist the minister in accomplishing his or her assigned responsibilities.

Note the title of the position—minister of education. Also note in the principal function section this person is supervised (responsible to) by the senior pastor, and that the incumbent supervises other educational leaders of the church. (The people they supervise are easily seen in the organization chart.) The qualifications an individual must possess calls for a formal education in Christian education or equivalent experience. What is "equivalent" experience? The church or institution must preestablish what they would consider equivalent experience. For example, one church might say six years of full-time experience would suffice. Another church might say that serving as a minister of education of a church of similar size would constitute equivalent experience. The church should decide before the process begins what "experience level" will equate to an education degree.

In the requirements of the positions section, the church defines the specific expectations that have been established for this position. Note the supervisory responsibilities assigned in items 3 and 8. While job duties and position responsibilities have similarities that exist from church to church or institution to institution, the requirements portion of the job description must be an expression of the assessment by the organization of what it wants that particular job to actually do. Examples abound in numerous books and other publications. Gleaning ideas for responsibilities from other churches or organization's job descriptions is another source of information about what a position should do.[6]

Process for Developing Job Descriptions

Now that we know what a job description looks like, we move on to the processes an administrator will use in developing such a document. This process will be considered for three possibilities: creating a job description when one does not exist and no incumbent exists, creating a job description when one does not exist but there is an incumbent acting in the position, and finally, creating a job description by partitioning off a portion of a multilevel responsibility position.

1. Writing a job description when no one is filling this position:
   - Begin with a reevaluation of the need for the position.
   - Research the position; do other churches/organizations have this position? Is it described or used elsewhere?
   - List tasks the incumbent would be expected to accomplish.
   - Define the supervisor and level within the organizational structure.
   - Determine education, skill, expertise, or experience levels required.
   - Create a rough of the position description and compare it to other examples or models.
   - Evaluate the position description; ask individuals within the organization if the position description is clearly stated, the qualifications are adequately considered, and the responsibilities are completely described.

- Have the supervisor or administration entity evaluate the position description to see if it meets their requirements and whether they would feel comfortable delegating the assigned duties to an incumbent with these qualifications.
- Write the final version and publish the job description.

2. Writing a job description when an incumbent already exists in the position:

- This process will require the developing office to exercise sensitivity in creating this document with the cooperation and participation of the incumbent. A high level of communication to establishing a strong trust level is essential.
- Have the incumbent conduct a time-analysis survey. This will involve creating a log that describes what the incumbent does from hour to hour and how long he spends on this task. This analysis should be of sufficient length to establish a daily/weekly routine.
- Group the elements of the time analysis into common job responsibilities.
- Ask the incumbent to review the grouped job responsibilities and add those tasks that he is responsible for that do not occur on this analysis. For example, infrequent, monthly, or annual activities.
- Ask the incumbent to describe the expertise level required to do this job, the equipment he works with, skills required, and unique requirements for the job.
- Create a rough draft of the job description and ask the incumbent if it accurately describes the position.
- Ask the supervisor or administration entity to evaluate the job description for accuracy, completeness, and effectiveness.
- Write the final version and publish the job description.

3. Creating two job descriptions when an incumbent is performing the duties of each position:

1. This process will also require the development of rapport with the incumbent to establish trust, openness, and creativity. Sensitivity must be ensured since an incumbent will have elements of the job he has been performing which he deems more desirable than other duties. The supervisor or administrative manager must create the job descriptions based on the needs of the organization and not the desires of the individual.
2. Determine the principal function of each of the two positions.

3. Have the incumbent assess his present job structure and divide those tasks into the two partitions that have been established with the new organizational structure.
4. Determine the supervisory lines and the qualifications for both positions.
5. The supervisor or administrative manager will evaluate the two sets of data to ensure that there is equity of work, that the assignments of responsibility are appropriate for the function of the job, and that the qualifications delineated are appropriate to ensure quality job performance.
6. Write and evaluate the job description the incumbent will fill first.
7. Write and evaluate the new position.
8. Publish new positions.

In this last example of job description development, a position that had been a dual-role ministry position was divided into two separate positions. The creation of a dual-role position is a natural and logical decision as a church matures and grows and develops a professional staff that meets the needs of its growth. A church or an organization may approach this dual-role position in one of several ways. The two most often used are:

1. Create both job descriptions, describing the position as though a single individual who devotes full time to the position will fill each. Then, after the two job descriptions have been described, assess the single position that will be filled by selecting the critical or necessary elements of both positions and combining them into one position description. Caution must be taken using this procedure to make sure that the single job description does not describe a position that only a superman could fill. Expectations should be reasonable.

2. Consider the most important of the two positions that the church or organization wants to be filled. Then seek a person who can fill that position as well as other elements of the second position. Then negotiate with the person the elements of both job descriptions that will be accomplished. This method relies upon the ability of the prospective incumbent to determine what responsibilities he can effectively accomplish. It presumes that some of the elements of the primary job description will be replaced by elements of the second job description. If a church or organization plans to use this approach, then in fairness to the future incumbent, those important elements of a secondary job description which it feels are critical should be stated during the job recruitment process.

With both of these approaches to dual-role position assignment, when the time comes to create two positions out of one, then the original job descriptions will already exist and will only require the administrator to review them for completeness.

The job description is a critical element for effective and efficient personnel management. It becomes the vehicle for recruitment as well as the basis for performance evaluation. Some element in the church or organization must be assigned the responsibility to ensure these documents remain viable, fair, and provide the caliber of personnel necessary to accomplish the mission of the church or organization. In the next section and the next chapter, it will be suggested that the personnel committee is the best group to accomplish this task.

Committees, Councils, and Ministry Teams

An interesting event occurred in the early church as recorded by Luke in Acts 6:1–6:

> In those days, as the number of the disciples was multiplying, there arose a complaint by the Hellenistic Jews against the Hebraic Jews that their widows were being overlooked in the daily distribution. Then the Twelve summoned the whole company of the disciples and said, "It would not be right for us to give up preaching about God to wait on tables. Therefore, brothers, select from among you seven men of good reputation, full of the Spirit and wisdom, whom we can appoint to this duty. But we will devote ourselves to prayer and to the preaching ministry." The proposal pleased the whole company. So they chose Stephen, a man full of faith and the Holy Spirit, and Philip, Prochorus, Nicanor, Timon, Parmenas, and Nicolaus, a proselyte from Antioch. They had them stand before the apostles, who prayed and laid their hands on them.

Let's look at some of the issues from this passage that we can consider administratively. First, a church conflict arose. The Aramaic Jews who followed strictly the tradition of the Law were taking care of the widows (and assumably the orphans) just as the Torah in passages like Exodus 22:22; Deuteronomy 14:29; 24:19–21; 26:12; and 27:19 had required. The widows of the Greek-speaking Jews were not being cared for in the same manner by having food provided for them. Note the respect for the Torah which the apostles had. They recognized a duty to minister to the needs of the widows, but that was not their role. They were assigned a preaching and prayer responsibility. And to take care of waiting on tables would detract from their primary leadership responsibility.

Four keys of church organization administration exist in this passage: (1) the church has the responsibility for ministry; (2) the church is to select (literally *elect* from the Greek) the people to do the job; (3) these individuals must meet certain job description qualifications; and (4) the leaders of the church appoint the individuals. Literally, the laying on of hands signified a prayer of blessing for the beginning of the new ministry.

What a powerful passage. Leadership role responsibilities were identified and respected. Ministry responsibility was placed in the church body where it should be. Individuals of qualification were literally elected by the church. And the group was empowered—given blessing by the apostles—to do their job.

Look back at Acts 6 at what happened when the church followed the guidance given: "So the preaching about God flourished, the number of the disciples in Jerusalem multiplied greatly, and a large group of priests became obedient to the faith" (Acts 6:7). God blessed them.

Ecclesiastes 4:9–12 says, "Two are better than one because they have a good reward for their efforts. For if either falls, his companion can lift him up; but pity the one who falls without another to lift him up. Also, if two lie down together, they can keep warm; but how can one person alone keep warm? And if somebody overpowers one person, two can resist him. A cord of three strands is not easily broken."

Throughout Scripture we find examples where an organization best accomplishes the task at hand. Consider:

- Organization and delegation (Exod. 18).
- Development of the priesthood under Aaron and his sons (Exod. 28).
- Call and commission of the leaders of the nation of Israel (Deut. 31–34).
- The usefulness of numbers (Eccles. 4:9–13).
- The wisdom of seeking counsel (Prov. 15:22).
- Christ calls the apostles (Matt. 3:16–19).
- How multiple activities coordinate to produce results (John 4:37).
- How the church grew because of community effort (Acts 2:42–47).
- The selection of the first benevolence ministry team (Acts 6:1–7).
- How the leadership team put down heresies in the church (Acts 15).
- Cooperative nature of the church (Rom. 12:4–8).
- Interrelationship of the functions of the church (1 Cor. 12:4–27).
- The functions of the church body (Eph. 4:11–12).

Churches and ministry organizations thrive in an atmosphere of collective groups which perform specific tasks with a single mission and are led by individuals who focus their efforts in strengthening those ministry units. For years I have told students the hardest task they will have in ministry is to convince the church or organization they serve that they (the students) are not the ministers of the church. Their role is to equip the ministers of the church—the body of believers. Successful ministers (leaders) will know how to organize their followers to "do the work of ministry." Three important elements of group organization exist that can be used to advantage by the leader: committees, councils, and ministry teams.

Committees

In the *Church Officer and Committee Guidebook,* Sheffield and Holcomb define a committee as a group of persons assigned specific tasks by the congregation to assist the church in planning its program, managing its resources, and governing its life and work.[7] In *Robert's Rules of Order,* a committee is a polity body of an organization that may act in behalf of the whole assembly or conduct preliminary work to be presented to the entire body for their decision.[8] They derive their authority to act in a constituted charter that is approved by the church or organization. When an issue comes before the church from a committee for the vote of a church, the moderator will say "This comes as a motion from a committee and needs no second." The reason is that under *Robert's Rules of Order,* the committee representatives of the church made a motion, seconded it, and voted on it in their small group and now bring it to the larger body for a full vote.

Committees are essential to most organizations because they:

- Provide a forum through which research and report can assist the congregation or organization as a whole in making decisions.
- Delegate to a legally constituted subdivision of the entire organization certain activities that may be carried out in behalf of the entire body.
- Offer opportunities for individuals with gifts, abilities, qualifications, and skills to provide discussion, input, guidance, creativity, and innovation, whenever that capacity does not exist in the whole.
- Provide the opportunity for individuals to mature and grow in their service to the church or organization.

There are two basic types of committees, the standing committee and the special or select committee.

1. **Standing committees** are groups that are formed to respond to an ongoing assignment of responsibility. These are generally permanent committees of the church or organization and exist because of some polity statement such as being named in the bylaws of the organization. Standing committees have an elected or appointed chairman and a membership that is elected by the church or appointed by institution leaders. Membership in a standing committee will be sufficient in size to carry out the responsibilities assigned, which may include the formation of subcommittees that report back to the principal committee about matters of research, investigation, or analysis.

All standing committees should have an appointed staff liaison member. This individual may be an ex officio—assigned by virtue of position—member and may or may not be granted voting privileges. Membership in committees is usually tenure-restricted with a formula often created for replacement that ensures a major portion of the group remains each year to ensure consistency of operation. Standing committees are usually required to appoint a recording clerk to provide a record of their minutes and actions and to report their activities to the whole assembly periodically.

2. *Special committees* are temporary groups that are organized to resolve a specific problem or to investigate an assigned issue. Often called an ad hoc committee, they are given authority by the church or organization to focus on a particular issue. Usually this type of committee is given little latitude in obligating the church; rather, they are directed to investigate and report to the body so the matter may be resolved by agreement of the whole assembly. Since they are a polity organization of the church, they are appointed and given authority to act by the church. The group will function with a chairman leader and other officers usually found in the committee. The principal difference is that the membership is usually permanent and will function until the task is complete. As with standing committees, the activities of the special committee will be recorded and reports made to the complete body.

Every church or organization that has become large enough will find that administration of the activities of the body is best managed by the formation of committees. Have standing committees chartered in at least three areas of operation: personnel, finances, and property. Most state government offices that monitor the constituting or incorporating of nonprofits will require that group to identify in the articles of incorporation who in the organization has the authority to carry out the above three functions. To facilitate this requirement, most churches and organizations will identify these three committees in some terminology the church has adopted.

Because of the nature of the organization of a church body, a fourth standing committee might be recommended—the committee on committees. This is an entity that assigns membership in group organizations, evaluates their performance, and coordinates the activities of subgroups of the church or organization. From time to time, temporary or ad hoc committees may need to be formed that will act in matters of polity for the church. Examples are a pastor search committee, a constitution and bylaws rewrite committee, or a building program committee. The committee on committees becomes the administrator of such groups.

Councils

By definition a council is an advisory groups. They assist leaders in doing their work. A presidential advisory council on math education may be made up of math educators who report to the president how math should be taught in school. They are on the council because of their expertise, experience, and interest.

A senior pastor who has a large group of singles in the church may want assistance in ministering to this group. He has two options: to call a professional minister to singles or to appoint an advisory group to assist him in that ministry.

Typical councils in the church are a preschool/children's, youth, single adult, senior adult, recreation, education, media council, etc. These councils are made up of people who have interest, expertise, and willingness to function in the group. They become advisors to the professional ministry administrator. For example, for several years XYZ Church has functioned with only a senior pastor who has carried out his program organization management with advisory councils. When the church calls a part-time youth minister, that individual continues the youth council, but now that council advises the youth minister in his or her ministry.

Councils are formed by interest. Members should be allowed to serve as long as their interest and effectiveness last. Councils may elect their own leader or designate that leadership role to a professional minister. Councils should be chartered by the church. All the provisions of records of meetings and actions taken in the ministry, as well as the report of such actions, should be the same as committees.

A council each pastor should consider is an organization comprised of all the principal leaders of the church. Sometimes called a church council or church leadership council, this group represents all the major elements of the program and polity organizations of the church. They become a vital link for the pastor to feel the pulse of the church while at the same time creating an avenue for dialogue and dispersion of his vision and leadership desires for the church. This advisory group should be comprised of all the professional staff, the ministry and program directors, chairpersons of critical committees such as personnel/finances/property, the chairman of the deacons, and chairpersons of other significant ministry teams or councils. Meeting at least once a month under the leadership of the pastor, this group becomes the primary vehicle for assessment, discussion, coordination, and evaluation. This council will become the forum the pastor will use to evaluate the vision and mission of the church as well as the long-range plan to achieve that vision and to recommend direction and strategies to accomplish that vision.

If used properly by the leaders of a church or organization, councils become effective ways that individual members of the church or organization can express their interest and perceived spiritual gifts, while at the same time offering a fertile ground for the development and maturing of the future direction of the church.

Ministry Teams

Not all committees in a church act in matters of polity. For instance, what policy does the usher's committee make? Or the flower committee or baptismal committee? What about the youth committee or the benevolence committee? In reality, these organizations are actually groups that do the ministry of the church or carry out the programs of the church. They are task-oriented as opposed to polity-oriented groups. So a better nomenclature might be appropriate. In the secular/corporate world, terms such as task force, ad hoc committee, or research and development group have been used. An excellent term to use for these groups in the church or Christian organization is *ministry team.*

In the passage of Scripture cited earlier in this chapter, a problem was recognized by the members of the church. The leaders of the church said, "Solve it among yourselves." Note that the leaders gave qualifications for these individuals to be selected, and it was the leaders who granted them power to do the work. The leaders didn't get involved in the nitty-gritty of doing the work. The individuals selected were people who had an interest and people whom the church selected to do the work.

Ministry in the church is done by ministers. Ministers by definition of Ephesians 4:11 are the people who make up the body of believers—the church. In recognition of that, a trend has developed in the last few years with regard to the use and equipping of the ministers to do the work of the church. In many churches committees are now being transformed into ministry teams. Parking lot and worship center greeters, flower arrangement, welcoming greeters and ushers, benevolence groups, offering counting, grounds and landscape, missions, recreation, etc. are examples of groups that were formerly known as committees but are now called ministry teams.

Ministry teams are being formed by members who feel the Holy Spirit has empowered them to express their ministry in this area. They elect their own leaders and work out the ministry. They are usually given a budget to work from and will have some church leader to act as liaison to other leaders and organizations of the church. They follow similar guidelines of committees and councils in that they make record of their activity and are obligated to report to the church or organization their ministry actions and budget expenditures. While they carry out polity already developed, they are authorized to suggest to the leadership (usually through an organization like a committee on committees) suggested policy change.

Administration of Groups

Whether you are forming a committee, a council, or a ministry team, each of these groups discussed should be organized with a charter. A charter is a formal document that gives a title, defines the principal function, grants the group authority to act, details the duties they will perform, and holds the group accountable with reports to the church. The elements of a charter are:

1. *Name.* This should give a general description of the committee, counsel, or team.

2. *Constitution.* This is a statement of the purpose of the group. It will outline the principal duties, the authority it has to act, the staff or professional coordinator, and who the group is responsible to for their work.

3. *Membership.* The numbers and membership will vary between groups. This statement should indicate how the group members are selected; who the chairman is and how he or she is selected, the number of members and how long they serve, and provisions for additional members—ad hoc, temporary, replacement.

4. *Responsibilities.* What exactly the group is to accomplish in the work that has been assigned to it.

5. *Reports.* To whom and how often should the group report progress or action that they have taken.

Here's an example of a charter for a committee:

BENEVOLENCE COMMITTEE

CONSTITUTION: The benevolence committee is a standing committee that functions as an integral part of the pastoral ministries organization of the church and is responsible to the associate pastor for the study of church family and community needs and the design and administration of a plan to meet those needs.

MEMBERSHIP: Six to nine individuals will be appointed to membership as determined necessary by the committee on committees. One-third of the members will be renewed annually. No member may serve more than two consecutive terms. The committee will elect annually a chairman, vice chairman, and recording secretary. Ministry chaplains in the pastoral ministry division will serve as continuous liaison members. The associate pastor will serve as professional staff support member with no voting privileges.

RESPONSIBILITIES: The benevolence committee will be responsible for the following activities:

1. Develop, recommend, and administer policies and procedures that define the church and committee's response to needs by both the church family and community members.

2. Make a thorough study of all needs for assistance in the church membership and in the community. Develop strategies for meeting those needs.

3. Serve as clearinghouse or coordinating group for all benevolence actions carried out by the program and ministry groups of the church.

4. Serve as the church liaison with the community for meeting selected community needs.

5. Determine, organize, and administrate a ministry of compassion that will assist church members in times of particular need such as death, sickness, or extreme distress.
6. Recommend and coordinate budget funding and special funding provisions for the administration of all benevolence actions.
7. Conduct programs of awareness, training, and sensitivity to the needs of the church and community. Attempt to involve as many church members in the benevolence program as possible.

REPORTS: Submit quarterly reports of activities accomplished and resources expended. Submit an annual summary report of all benevolence activities, involvement by the church, and fiscal and physical resources expended.

If the church determined that the benevolence committee was not really a polity body but one of the ministry elements of the church, the charter could be rewritten as a ministry team and might look like this example:

BENEVOLENCE MINISTRY TEAM

CONSTITUTION: The benevolence ministry team functions as an integral part of the pastoral ministries organization of the church and is responsible to the associate pastor for the study of church family and community needs and the design and administration of a plan to meet those needs.

MEMBERSHIP: Individuals who sense their spiritual giftedness and desire to express that call to ministry or help may be members of the ministry team. There is no fixed number of members or limit of tenure. Members will elect their own ministry team chairman and other officers as they deem appropriate. Ministry chaplains in the pastoral ministry division will serve as continuous liaison members. The associate pastor will serve as professional staff support member with no voting privileges.

RESPONSIBILITIES: The benevolence ministry team will be responsible for the following activities:

1. Develop, recommend, and administer policies and procedures that define the church and team's response to needs by both the church family and community members.
2. Make a thorough study of all needs for assistance in the church membership and in the community. Develop strategies for meeting those needs.
3. Serve as a clearinghouse or a coordinating group for all benevolence actions carried out by program and ministry groups of the church.
4. Serve as the church liaison with the community for meeting selected community needs.

5. Determine, organize, and administrate a ministry of compassion that will assist church members in times of particular need such as death, sickness, or extreme distress.
6. Recommend and coordinate budget funding and special funding provisions for the administration of all benevolence actions.
7. Conduct programs of awareness, training, and sensitivity to the needs of the church and community. Attempt to involve as many church members in the benevolence program as possible.

REPORTS: Submit quarterly reports of activities accomplished and resources expended. Submit an annual summary report of all benevolence activities, involvement by the church, and fiscal and physical resources expended.

It is not improbable to suggest that a senior pastor who does not have an associate pastor on the staff might even form a benevolence council made up of people who would advise him in the direction of a ministry of benevolence for the church. To avoid confusion, however, the church or organization should choose one or the other of these types of internal, lay-structured groups. The church or organization may have either a benevolence committee, a benevolence council, or a benevolence ministry team but not all three, or even two.

Every committee, council, or ministry team should have some professional staff member who will provide administrative assistance when needed. That person may be designated a staff liaison (voting or nonvoting) advisory member or may be assigned only a staff support role. The size of the organization will vary, depending on the job to be accomplished. If it is a complex job such as a building committee for a major building program, it may be advisable to have a large committee with several subcommittees. On the other hand, in most standing committees a relatively small number can get the job done. Five to seven members are usually appropriate with a top number of nine for larger churches. Councils and ministry teams are as large or as small as needed to get the job done.

Church committees, councils, and ministry teams are living, vital elements of the church or organization that does the work of the ministry. They are administrative elements that research and make decisions for the church or present those options for church vote. They carry out the directives of their charter. Membership dynamics all members should possess include the following:

• *Spiritual Sensitivity.* The members of the group must be able to sense the leading of the Holy Spirit in their actions. While some churches will allow new Christians to be part of ministry teams, expressing their perceived spiritual gift, individuals who are part of councils and committees should possess spiritual maturity.

- *Relational Skills.* Individuals in these groups must understand that they are one of a part of a group of individuals. They must be "team players." They must understand the dynamics of group interplay; be honest, patient, and stable. They must be open and candid, yet maintain a sense of decorum and confidentiality. They must sense the needs of the people they serve.

- *Leadership Ability.* The members of the groups must be able to share dreams, conduct research, solve problems, make decisions, and then build a supportive, team atmosphere as they report to the church or organization.

- *Communication Skills.* Communication must occur within the group as well as outside to the organization or church. The group must be sensitive to the expressed communication of the body they serve as well as the nonverbal or sensed communication of the church. The effective use of formal methods of communication as well as informal communication must be used. The bottom line is that the members must be able to converse one with another as well as with the church body.

- *Technical Expertise.* One of the reasons an individual is selected or becomes part of the group is that he has some expertise or spiritual calling in the area that the group addresses. Good organizational administration takes advantage of the innate ability or skill of the members, but at the same time uses the small leadership group to develop and mature the persons who serve in those groups.

Each year in a church where I was a member, we had an interesting event. It was held in the fall about the time the church budget was approved and the new church calendar was adopted. All the committees, ministry programs, and advisory councils came together for a meal and time of orientation. We were asked to sit with our future ministry assignment personnel. I was part of the personnel committee. The three members of the committee who were rotating off also sat with us for the first part of the dinner. At the conclusion of the meal, the pastor spoke to the group. He told us of the achievements the church had accomplished in the last program year and then shared the vision the church council had developed for the next program year. Afterwards, we met with our new assignment.

We listened to a critique from the members who were rotating off and then they left; sometimes they went to another assignment or just went home. The group then elected new committee leaders for the coming year and then discussed how the personnel committee could help implement the goals of the leaders. The minister of education had prepared a project that directed us in our deliberations. One of the major elements of that training was reviewing the charter for the personnel committee and the operating principles we were to use—the personnel manual. We had the church administrator with us because she was our staff support person for our deliberations.

Good administration states that you organize to conduct your business. Leaders delegate to those individuals who are selected and tasked to carry out the work. The person who delegates the work must provide the individual or group assigned a task the necessary authority to accomplish the task. Earlier in this book we redefined *authority* as the ability to accomplish the task. An individual may have the ability to accomplish the task, and all that is needed is the statement of formal authority—for example, the charter. But most individuals or groups are growing and maturing, and that authority must be translated into the ability achieved through training and experience. Thus, a tenet of good administration with groups such as committees, councils, and ministry teams is the provision of training to have the ability to accomplish their work. This training is essential for:

- Helping individuals and groups understand their purpose and what specifically they are to accomplish.
- Helping the groups to understand how their organization fits into the overall purpose of the church.
- Providing them the tools (ability) to accomplish their job, to develop skills of relationship and leadership, and to achieve the ultimate goals of the church.
- Establishing a sense of responsibility and accountability.

Chapter Review

Professional administrators will know within what bounds of polity they are to operate. In the church or religious not-for-profit organization, the product as well as the process is people. The development of an organizational scheme was suggested that focused on the line organization divided by functional areas. Given that organizational philosophy, the chapter then addressed the plan the church or organization should follow as it seeks to establish how the organizational scheme would be implemented to meet the tenets of the mission and purpose of the institution. Job descriptions defined how each element of leadership would form a matrix to meet goals of the organization. And finally, the creation of subgroups within the matrix that carry out elements of polity, ministry, or action were suggested. With these skills the reader should be able to:

1. Create an organizational structure from a real or hypothetical organization that would meet stated goals of the mission and purpose. Think of a

church or organization you are familiar with. Can you create the organizational chart? Can you evaluate that organization with a view to suggesting a more appropriate matrix?

2. Develop a plan that would lead a church or organization through the complexities of developing a philosophy for staff organization and how that plan would be implemented.

3. Write job descriptions for leadership and support ministry positions, using the scheme of title, main responsibility, qualifications, and responsibilities.

4. Create a charter that would describe a lay leadership organization of the church such as a committee, a council, or a ministry team. Be able to define how the professional support and ministry staff integrate and participate in such organizations.

Administering Personnel Resources

For the kingdom of heaven is like a landowner who went out early in the morning to hire workers for his vineyard. After agreeing with the workers on one denarius for the day, he sent them into his vineyard. When he went out about nine in the morning, he saw others standing in the marketplace doing nothing. To those men he said "You also go into my vineyard, and I'll give you whatever is right." So off they went.

MATTHEW 20:1–4

Upon first reading this parable, one would think the employer is unfair. But when the passage is taken in the context of all that Jesus was speaking of in describing the kingdom of God, it is understood differently. The parable continues with the landowner employing more workers at noon, at three in the afternoon, and finally at five, just an hour before quitting time. Picking up the story in verse 8, we continue to read:

> When evening came, the owner of the vineyard told his foreman, "Call the workers and give them their pay, starting with the last and ending with the first." When those who were hired about five came, they each received one denarius. So when the first ones came, they assumed they would get more, but they also received a denarius each. When they received it, they began to complain to the landowner: "These last men put in one hour, and you made them equal to us who bore the burden of the day and the burning heat!" He replied to one of them, "Friend, I'm doing you no wrong. Didn't you agree with me on a denarius? Take what's yours and go. I want to give this last man the same as I gave you. Don't I have the right to do what I want with my business? Are you jealous because I'm generous?"

Here was a landowner who had a vineyard that needed to be harvested. He hired what he could at first, and then upon assessment during the day he hired more. The job needed to be done, and he needed workers to do it. When Jesus was telling the parable, a denarius was a small silver coin that represented about a day's wage for a common laborer. It was the contention of the landowner that he had acted fairly. He had paid the wage he had promised.

Personnel management in most secular organizations is highly bureaucratic, structured, and rules oriented. For twenty-two years I had operated under that philosophy in the Navy. Now I was a church administrator. I began my seminary studies while serving as a church administrator. Early in that seminary period, one of my administration professors admonished me, "Bob, churches are horrible employers. Do your best to break the mold and be a good personnel administrator." At the time I really didn't know what my professor was talking about, but through the years I have come to understand the reality of that statement. Churches, for the most part, are lousy employers.

There are exceptions, to be sure, but they exist usually only in the larger churches that have employed qualified church administrators or in churches that have been poor personnel managers and have had to pay the costs for their poor management either through tort action in civil courts or legal action by state or federal employment agencies. Poor personnel management by churches may be explained in some instances by churches that have operated for many years under the concept that churches are not bound by employment laws. Other explanations might include that while laws might be applicable to large churches, they wouldn't apply to that particular church because they are too small to matter. While both of these explanations are basically ignorance of the law, there are other instances of churches who are abusers simply because they routinely mistreat ministerial and support staff.

In one of the studies cited in the preface of this book that was conducted by Christianity Today International, some evangelical churches that routinely terminated their ministerial staff were identified. This happened usually at the unction of only a handful of individuals in the church who had made the decision for the entire church that the individual's employment was no longer desired.

It would be desirable if churches could be counted as the most conscientious, honest, and valid employers in the nation. As an educator, I also wish that all churches had all the tools available to them to ensure that personnel management is carried out fairly, openly, and within the bounds of appropriate personnel management. Through the years as a seminary professor, as a fellow in the National Association of Church Business Administration, and as a church administration practitioner, I have come to realize that this desire is often wishful thinking. This chapter is designed not only for the student of church administration but also for the pastor and church and/or organizational leaders as they carry out the functions of personnel management.

Conceptual Philosophy for Personnel Management: The Personnel Committee

In the previous chapter it was strongly recommended that one of the first organizational entities that a church or institution should have is a personnel committee. Remember that a committee is a polity entity of the church capable of making decisions for the church. This committee provides the research and evaluation necessary to conduct the personnel affairs of the church or organization. In larger organizations much of that responsibility is vested in a professional church business administrator or in a not-for-profit organization in a human resource manager.

Let's create a charter for a personnel committee to explore the extent of its responsibilities.

PERSONNEL COMMITTEE

CONSTITUTION: The personnel committee functions as a standing committee of the church responsible for the proper and appropriate management of the personnel actions of the church. In carrying out the administrative functions, they will be responsible for the recruitment, hiring, and administration of adequate and skilled personnel with craft or training to efficiently and effectively carry out the ministries and programs of the church.

MEMBERSHIP: The personnel committee will be comprised of seven to nine individuals who are nominated by the committee on committees and elected by the church in business session. One-third of the membership will be replaced annually. No member may serve more than two consecutive, three-year terms. Each year the committee will select a chairperson, a vice chairperson, and a recorder/secretary. The senior pastor will serve as a liaison committee member. The church business administrator will serve as the professional support member to the group.

RESPONSIBILITIES:

1. Establish and maintain appropriate personnel policies that will provide for an effective professional ministry and support staff.
2. Investigate, evaluate, and develop an organization diagram that will address the leadership needs of the church to implement the mission and purpose of the church. Develop and maintain current position descriptions for all leadership, ministry, and staff support positions.
3. Review at least annually the efficiency and effectiveness of personnel and the organization within which they function.
4. Recruit, interview, and hire necessary support personnel to effectively and efficiently administer the church.

5. When directed by the church, recruit, interview, and recommend to the church professional ministry personnel to effectively and efficiently administer the ministries and programs of the church.
6. Develop and maintain a church salary plan for the provision of adequate pay and benefits for the employees of the church.
7. Investigate and select appropriate insurance for the protection of liability, hazard, and professional function as well as the health and welfare of the staff of the church.
8. Coordinate with other committees and organizations of the church the personnel requirements to meet the mission and purpose of the church.

REPORTS: The personnel committee will provide a monthly report of all personnel actions. A summary annual report will be provided to the church that details all personnel actions for the year. Included in this report will be a summary of all personnel by name and their current disposition. A summary report will be made detailing expenses in the categories of salary and benefits as outlined in the current salary plan.

As can be seen from this charter, the personnel committee is a vital element of the organization of the church. While its primary purpose can be summarized as that of personnel management, the committee does significantly more. It becomes the research venue for discovering the legal aspects of personnel management as it pertains to the church or not-for-profit organization. It is an advocate for the employees, representing them before the church or institution in matters of salary, benefits, and performance. Members of this committee are the ethicists of the church with regard to the proper and legal conduct of employees and those who interact with the employees. And they are stewards of the church resources. This last obligation becomes critical when it is realized that studies of church budget allocations for the past several years have consistently indicated that churches will designate between 45 and 55 percent of their annual budget in direct and indirect personnel costs.

Who should be members of the personnel committee? As we have discovered in previous chapters, when individuals were assigned a responsibility in the Scripture, qualifications often accompanied that assignment. While we cannot specifically identify a personnel committee in the Bible, we can intelligently outline some qualifications that would support an individual's selection to the committee. The following qualifications should be considered in selecting members:

- Individuals who are spiritually mature and who understand the mission and function of the local church.
- Individuals who will accept the responsibility for being an advocate for the employees of the church while at the same time recognizing they represent the church body.

- Individuals who know and understand group dynamics such as communication, discussion, interaction, confidence, give-and-take, and decision making.
- Individuals who are willing to work to understand the intricacies of personnel management, tax and employment law, and appropriate practices of human resource management.

Return to the committee charter above and look at the responsibilities listed there. Note the responsibilities:

- They research, establish, and administer personnel policies and evaluate procedures that implement those policies. This includes being aware of appropriate legal issues with regard to employment.
- They create the organizational structure for personnel accomplishing the mission and purpose of the church.
- They research and write job descriptions which ensure that qualified personnel are assigned the tasks of the church.
- They evaluate personnel performance as well as ensuring proper decorum and ethics are maintained.
- When assigned, they become the recruitment and hiring organization of the church or organization for the employed personnel resources to accomplish the church's mission.
- They are the salary administrators of the church. They are responsible for researching and providing for a fair and equitable compensation for the employee contingent upon position and expertise.
- They provide for the protection of and sustenance of the employee through appropriate insurance and safeguards.
- They integrate their activities with other entities of the church or organization. They become the clearing house for evaluation of personnel needs in each of the ministry and support areas of the church or institution.
- They keep the church informed of their actions, providing periodic reports of the activities and bring to the floor for action those issues that impact the body or which is beyond their assigned level of authority.

Thus, the personnel committee becomes the human resource manager of the church. For some institutions whose number of employees is large enough to require professional expertise, a church or business administrator may be employed. It is the contention of this author that even though a church or institution employs such a professional manager, the presence of a personnel committee or personnel board provides positive impact on the quality of human resource management. The eyes, ears, and minds of several people are a valuable asset in any decision-making responsibility.

The Personnel Manual

In chapter 3 the concept of a church organization manual was presented. This comprehensive document describes the philosophical and practical organization of a church or institution. In many respects it is a document made up of several smaller elements which address many facets of church organization and administration. One of those important elements relates to the personnel issues of the church or organization—the personnel manual.

The personnel manual accomplishes several important functions;

1. It becomes the standard by which personnel employment actions are carried out. It not only becomes the guide for the procedures to be followed during employment but also becomes the basis for ensuring that legally defensible processes are used.

2. The manual describes the salary plan used by the church or organization in compensating its employees. It not only describes the process for developing salary and the administration of salary, but it discusses issues like employment benefits and reimbursable business expenses.

3. It becomes a tool to be used in recruitment and orientation of employees. The manual describes the expectations for employment.

4. The manual becomes a handbook for employment activity. It describes items such as periods of work, vacations, planned and unplanned absences, manner and demeanor of the work environment, and other appropriate employment expectations.

5. It will discuss and outline the format for evaluation of performance, including the award for meritorious performance and a discussion for dealing with unsatisfactory or improper performance.

One of the most significant advantages of having a well-written, legally defensible, comprehensive personnel manual is that it becomes a modus operandi that describes to the employee and member alike the expectations for carrying out personnel actions in the church or organization. The manual avoids confusion, defuses conflict, and establishes a standardized method for dealing with the personnel of the church. A great disservice is done to an employee whenever a nebulous work environment is established—one in which there are no rules, bounds, or guidelines. Human nature craves for a standardized, comfortable work situation where expectations are fairly and openly established.

The elements of a personnel manual will vary from organization to organization, church to church, but it seems to focus on these areas:

- The philosophy of the church or organization with regard to personnel resources including a diagram of relationships of authority and accountability.

- The process by which an individual becomes a paid employee of the church or organization.
- The expectations of the employer with regard to the work environment.
- Salary administration and benefits.
- Work performance evaluation, grievance, and termination.

Chapter 3 addressed the philosophy and organization of the church's personnel resources. The remainder of this chapter will address the remaining four issues of the personnel manual: employment, conduct, salary, performance.

Employment

Employment practices of any organization—church, nonprofit, or secular—should be standardized, fair, and legal. For many years churches have carried out personnel practices that were outside of or in direct violation of mandated employment law. Often this was because of ignorance of the requirement; sometimes it was based upon the misguided assumption that churches were not required to comply with secular employment law. Not only have churches and nonprofit organizations been included in recent laws written relating to employment; other federal, state, and local government regulations and laws that previously appeared not to apply to churches or nonprofits have been interpreted to require the church and nonprofit to comply. Churches, considering themselves to be religious institutions, have assumed they have the ability to discriminate in employment. While allowance for religious discrimination may exist, it is narrowly defined and must be theologically justified.

Of all institutions in the world, one would think that ethical employment would be foremost in the mind of religious organizations. Through the years, because some employers were not ethical, employment laws had to be written by federal, state, and sometimes regional governments to protect the rights and privileges of the worker. When some religious and nonprofit organizations were found to be in noncompliance with this standardized employment ethic, subsequent laws were written that specifically included all employers—including churches and nonprofits. Then when other activities of these institutions violated laws that had not specifically included religious institutions, tort action and judicial decision included churches and nonprofits under their provisions.

Employment is process driven. We speak of the hiring process, the salary process, the evaluation process, and the termination process. What this means is that the employer has developed a scheme that will carry out these functions. While it is employer developed, it is process driven. That is, if you have a scheme for hiring a person for a support position in the church, you must follow it. The reason is that the courts have determined that processes described in documents such as a personnel policy and procedure manual become legal contracts for employment. If you have them, you must follow them. So if you have a personnel manual, you have to follow it. If you don't have such a manual, then you are open to interpretation for conducting your business by some judge or bureaucrat. So the obvious answer is to do it right. Let's learn some things to make sure it is done right.

Employment begins with the *hiring process*. This process will have several facets: the review of the staff plan, invitation or application process, evaluation of the applicants, contract for employment, and orientation.

1. ***Review of the Staff Plan.*** Return to the staff plan that was developed in chapter 4. What six steps made up that staff plan? Do you remember that the staff plan was an expression of the church with regard to how the leadership of the church would come together to carry out the mission of the church? Note in step 3 we asked:

- What lines of authority exist for the position?
- What is the priority for this position?
- What skill or expertise will the position require?
- How will this position be filled?

In step 4 additional questions were asked:

- Is there a job description?
- Is there a salary plan and budget allocation?
- Are there support facilities?

And in step 5 the critical questions were:

- Is this position accurately defined to meet the needs of the church?
- Are there qualified persons who can be employed?

Before any hiring process begins, these and other questions must be satisfied. Several years ago I was involved with a calling committee that did not take this first step. Our church had operated for a year or so with a recreation minister. He was actually a college student who was a sports major whom the church initially hired as an intern. We had a new recreation facility at the church—all the bells and whistles that included a gym, weight room, raquetball courts, craft rooms, and game rooms. When the recreation intern graduated, we were left without leadership in that area. Immediately the cry went up that we needed to replace him. Our search committee did its job in a professional manner. We visited other churches with recreation ministers, got job descriptions, discussed the job with other professionals, and then collected resumes. Eventually we hired a qualified recreation minister.

Several months later that recreation minister complained to the pastor that the church really didn't need a recreation minister; the recreation part could take care of itself without a paid professional. What the church really needed was a senior adult minister. What our search committee failed to discover in our zeal to get a recreation minister replacement was that over the months before the previous minister left, he began to focus on the senior adults. He developed craft sessions, took them on trips, formed Bible study groups, took them shopping, he and his wife even taught their Sunday School class, and so forth. Our new minister didn't focus on that aspect. In fact, we didn't even have it in his job description. But that was where the ministry was needed in our church. We should have been looking for a senior adult minister. Do your homework. Review the staff plan.

2. *Application Process.* Where does your church acquire its future employees? Are they to be drawn from a pool of qualified applicants from any venue or are they only to be selected from the local membership? Do they have to be Christian? Do they have to be or become members of your church? These are important and significant questions that must be addressed before the employment process. And the results of this determination must be a matter of record in policies and procedures.

The hiring of ecclesiastical/ministerial personnel in an organization is hand's-off with regard to an employment challenge. In other words, a church can say that it will only hire twenty-seven-year-old, male, red-haired ordained youth ministers and get away with it. But what about secretaries, janitors, and the interns that support the ministries? Not so easy. I attended a staff training conference conducted at a large church in California a couple of decades ago. There I discovered an interesting phenomenon; all the church employees were either ministers or deacons. When I asked why, the answer was to make sure that all employees were Christian. To accomplish this, the church in its constitution and bylaws declared that it viewed all persons who were employees of the church to be servants of the church. Thus you were either a minister if you led a program or ministry, or you were a deacon if you were a secretary, janitor, or whatever.

Today many churches state that all employees of the church will be members of the church, will be members of evangelical or designated denominational churches, or some such designation. Like the church in California, they will cite an ecclesiastical need for all employees to be Christian. Because of the nature and potential for employment problems with non-Christian employees, many churches will solve the problem by simply stating that all employment will come from within its membership. If you want a job at our church as a secretary, join it.

The employment of only Christian individuals is only one of several general qualifications that a church or nonprofit organization must determine before beginning the hiring process. Other questions that must be answered are:

- Will the church employ spouses of employees?
- Can relatives work at the church or agency?
- Will you employ individuals who are divorced or separated?

- Could an individual who has a prior criminal record or drug addiction be employed?
- Will the church or organization make accommodations for handicapped persons?
- Can an individual who has been terminated be reemployed?

Every one of these questions should be addressed in the personnel policy and procedures manual. If they are not, then the church or organization is opening itself to interpretation and possibly charges of fraudulent hiring practices.

An example policy statement might read:

It is the policy of XYZ Church to employ in paid positions those ministers and ministry support staff as designated by the constitution and bylaws of XYZ Church and other positions deemed appropriate by agreement of the church, personnel committee, and ministerial staff. All employees will be professing Christians and active members of evangelical Christian churches. It is the policy of this church to seek employment of personnel who are members of this congregation. All full-time and part-time ministry and professional director personnel will be or become members of XYZ Church.

By establishing the criteria by which an individual will be considered for employment in the church or organization, several key issues of contention are eliminated;

- The guidelines set the parameters by which applicants will be sought. If policy prevents employment of relatives, then applications from relatives will be rejected.
- Guidelines establish the format for seeking appropriate applicants. If the general policy requires membership in a church, then the question becomes a valid discriminator in the application process.
- Preestablished guidelines inform the applicant of his potential for employment. While he may meet the specific qualifications of a job description, he may not meet the general qualifications that govern the employment of all employees.
- General and specific employment criteria aid in ensuring only qualified individuals are employed by the church or organization.
- A set of well-established, legally defensible guidelines promotes a sense of fairness, openness, and professionalism.

Probably the best way to formalize a legitimate application process is through the use of an application form. While many organizations today become interested in a future employee through a resume prepared by the individual, when the process for screening for employment begins, most will require the submission of an organization-prepared application. The principle purpose of the application form is to standardize the questions about a potential employee

APPLICATION FOR EMPLOYMENT
XYZ CHURCH

Position applied for _____ Full Name _____

How may we contact you? (telephone, e-mail, etc.) | Identification number (Driver license, INS No., SSN)

Are you legally eligible for employment in this country? _____ Yes _____ No
Federal law requires employers to verify whether applicants may be employed and will require proof of citizenship or immigration status upon employment.

Employment History

Current or Last Employer
Name _____ Mailing address _____
Dates of employment _____ Position held _____
Describe your responsibilities:

Reason for leaving_____
May we contact them? ___ Yes ___ No
Previous Employer
Name _____ Mailing address _____
Dates of employment _____ Position held _____
Describe your responsibilities:

Reason for leaving_____
May we contact them? ___ Yes ___ No

Qualifications

Education and Training
High School _____ Date graduated
College/University _____ Degree _____ Date _____
Graduate School _____ Degree _____ Date _____
Other training _____

References

Because of the nature of the positions and ministries of this church, the verification of the character of employees is a necessity. If you cannot respond to any of the questions below, please provide an explanation.
Do you have any medical or health problem that will affect the accomplishment of the work being applied for?
XYZ Church is an ADA equal opportunity employer and will make reasonable accommodation for employment.
_____ No _____ Yes If yes; please explain.
Do you have any personal responsibilities or problems that may affect your daily work attendance? *Work schedules are established in the Personnel Policy and Procedure Manual.*
_____ No _____ Yes If yes; please explain.
Have you participated in a drug or substance abuse program? *Employees must acknowledge restrictions to the use of any drug or substance abuse as terms of employment.*
_____ No _____ Yes If yes; please explain.
Have you ever been convicted of child molestation or any other felony regarding child abuse or have been ordered by a court or law enforcement agency to register as an offender? *Since all employees will have access to children under age 18, a police record check will be completed as part of the routine for employment.*
_____ No _____ Yes If yes; please explain.
Provide the names and contact information for at least two individuals who will attest to your Christian character:
Name _____ Telephone/Address_____
Name _____ Telephone/Address_____
Name of current church membership:
All employees of XYZ Church will be or become members of this church or a church approved by the personnel committee

I understand that this application may be withdrawn or my employment terminated if I have made any misrepresentation on this form.
I authorize the church to contact all references (unless otherwise noted) to seek available information about me. This may include former employers, character references, police files, court records, and credit files. I release the church and all other persons or organizations from liability for furnishing this information

_____ _____ _____
Name   Date   Witness to the application

that the employer wants answered. It becomes a standardized format for evaluating all applicants because the same questions are asked of each one of the individuals. But more importantly, certain specific information is needed to ensure the individual is legally employable, is qualified to occupy the position, and meets the character and other related personal mannerism characteristics the job requires. An example application form is given here.

Application forms must be sensitive to privacy and confidentiality issues. For example, you may ask for a means to contact the person, but you cannot demand a telephone number. Similarly, since you will have to conduct records checks on the individual, you must ask for some form of valid identification. But you cannot ask for the Social Security number. Law prevents you from asking that until employment activities have started.

With regard to references, many employers are now taking a "neutral" reference policy. That is, they will acknowledge that a person worked at that place and the dates, but they will not give you any other information. This reluctance has been brought about by the many tort actions in recent years, both because a former employer failed to give damaging information and also because an employer biased an employment decision by giving less than a glowing recommendation. An application form solicits information about employment as well as character reference and by signature of the individual authorizes the organization to validate those references. Even in the presence of a neutral reference policy, most former employers will answer the question, Would you reemploy this individual? And character references will almost always answer the question, Is this the type of person you would want to teach your child's Sunday school class? or some other Christian character statement, without going into detail.

Note the questions about health, lifestyle, substance abuse, and character toward children. Current laws restrict employers from asking questions that may bias the decision for employment. For example, the employer cannot say to a person in a wheelchair, "How can someone in a wheelchair possibly do janitorial work?" without biasing the decision for employment based upon perceived inability to do the work of a janitor. What can be done is to write into the job description the qualification to be able to move heavy objects. Then every applicant for a janitorial position is asked to set up a classroom with tables and chairs. If the person in a wheelchair cannot perform that action, and the church is not willing to make a reasonable accommodation to allow that person to do other types of janitorial work, then the individual disqualifies himself by not being able to do the expectations of the job description, not because he is handicapped.

The same employment philosophy is taken with issues of character. Most states have a mandatory substance abuse program. All states and territories now have laws relating to background checks for individuals who work with minors (usually defined as children under eighteen years of age). In an application you ask the individual to reveal that private (and sometimes public record) information, and then when required, you validate that through legal reference checks. If the person says he has no criminal record and you find that he does, then he has terminated himself because of falsifying the application.

3. *Evaluation of Applicants.* Once applications have been received for an announced job opening, screening must take place as the employer moves toward hiring the desirable applicant. The evaluation process has three basic phases: screening of applicants, review of qualified applicants, and selection of the desirable applicant.

Screening occurs in two steps: when the application is received, a designated agent of the church or organization reviews the application at the time it is submitted. This initial screening is to ensure all sections of the form are completed and to ask questions to clarify entries. The second step occurs when the application is validated to see if the applicant meets the general and specific qualifications of the position being applied for. If the initial screening was done properly, two categories of applicants are then made: those who meet the qualifications of the position and those who do not.

A review of the qualified applicants then begins. This process will vary from organization to organization but will follow these general steps: (1) validating qualification, (2) prioritizing desirability based on level of competence, (3) confirming the capacity and capability of the individual to do the job, and (4) designating a limited number of applicants for interview. While that took only four lines to relate to you, in practicality it probably will take four weeks to accomplish.

I once served as chairman of a search committee. When we got to this point in our process, I admonished the group that we needed to make sure that we would select the person whom God had already selected for us. I then announced to the surprise of the group: "I am going to toss the stack of applications up in the air and the person God wants he will grab and hand to us." I tossed them up and they all came back down on the table. Then I said to the group, "God has chosen to allow us to prayerfully seek his will for this position. We have our work cut out for us. It will certainly be easier if we are of one accord in prayer." We then divided the applications up among the group and took them home with the task of praying over them, reading them, and learning as much as possible about each person, calling at least one reference that was allowed. Then we would come back and in the next meeting give our impressions about the applicants.

At the next meeting the applicants were presented, and the group began to prioritize desirability based on the applicant's qualifications, experience, and potential for the position. Ultimately three were selected to validate in full their qualifications, and from that limited evaluation one individual was finally selected to be interviewed by the committee. Notice the process:

- The information on the application form was the basis for initial decisions.
- We recognized that God fits together the workers of the church—paid and lay—and prayer is an important ingredient.
- Validation of the qualifications occurred. Sometimes this is carried out by an entire committee; other times this is relegated to a staff member.
- Selection focused on the person whom the evaluation group felt was best qualified to do the work. In-depth discussions ensued with one individual, not every applicant.

If the selection group determines this is the person for the position, then the next phase of the hiring process occurs—contracting for employment.

4. *Contract for Employment.* One day a soon-to-graduate student stopped by my office for advice. She said that she had been dealing with a church as their children's minister. She said they told her that if she could get there by June 1, then she could have the job. I asked her if she had visited the church. She had not. Did she have a job description? Her answer was no. Since she was filling a position they didn't have, she was supposed to write the job description when she got there. She had not read the church policy manuals yet; they told her they were still working on some of them. And then she said they had offered a salary lump sum which she was to divide up as needed. My advice was not to go. She went. A year later she had left the church position to teach in a public elementary school.

Executing a contract for employment is far more than a handshake and a gentleman's agreement. It must be a carefully thought-out, comprehensive, legal process. It involves an affirmation of the qualifications to hold the position, mutual agreement of the expectations of the position, establishment of provisions of pay and benefits, and the notation of any variance mutually agreed upon by the employee and employer.

Probation and at-will employment. It is strongly recommended that every new employee (senior pastor to janitor) be employed in a probationary status at least as long as it will take to finalize all reference, record, and credit research. If, during this probation period, information is developed that would question the advisability for continued employment, then current employment law allows the employer to release the employee without recourse. It is not uncommon for churches or organizations to place support staff in a probation period of one year. Ministerial and professional staff personnel are usually in probation employment in a shorter duration. If termination is pursued outside a probation period, then employment-at-will law requires the employer to state the cause.

While most states allow employment-at-will to prevail, the organization must state in its employment practices (personnel manual) that it subscribes to that philosophy as a warning to employees. Termination using the at-will clause allows an employer to release an employee in situations other than disciplinary reasons. For example, the church can no longer afford the level of staff employment because of failure of funds to pay salaries. The reason cited for termination at will is financial.

Establishing job standards. By this time in the employment process, the individual will have been introduced to the job description that outlines the requirements for the job. The prospective employee will also have been introduced to the church organization manual, or at least the personnel section. This step of the contracting process calls for the individual to understand fully the job which he will be expected to perform and the expectations that supervisory personnel will have of him. In a subsequent step the individual will be asked to subscribe to those documents as a condition of employment. The prospective employee should acknowledge that the guidelines of the church will be followed. It should also be stated what the supervisor expects from the prospective employee with regard to satisfactory performance. In this step it is strongly recommended that the supervisor of the prospective employee go through every responsibility of the job description and establish what expected performance will be. These mutually agreed upon performance standards will be the criteria that will be used in future assessment to evaluate competent performance on the part of the employee.

For example, if a job description item for a children's minister says that the incumbent will conduct teacher training, the minister of education supervisor of that children's minister might establish a standard of at least two training programs a year for acceptable performance. When that is written down as a set of performance standards of job acceptance, then both the supervisor and employee have a fair and legal definition of teacher training.

The next step in the contracting phase is agreement about salary and benefits. It is necessary to establish in this phase of the hiring process that fully agreed upon salary and benefit provisions be made. If there is any variance in the established salary plan, then these modifications will be part of the contract for employment. This protects both the prospective employee and the employer.

The final step in the contract phase is to create a written document that confirms the agreements for employment. While the form and format of such a document varies with different organizations and churches, the basic elements are standardized:

- The employer and employee are identified by name.
- The position which the employee will fill is identified.

- The employee acknowledges that employment falls under the provisions of the church's legally constituted documents—the constitution and bylaws and all policies and procedures in effect or that will come in effect by action of the church/organization.
- The employee reaffirms significant qualifying criteria that was stated in the application—church membership, substance abuse, health issues, and so forth.
- The employee acknowledges any provision for probation and the realization that the church is an at-will employer.
- The employee acknowledges that he or she understands the job description and the performance expectation of that job as well as any general employment expectations of all employees of the church or organization.
- The employee agrees to the provisions of pay and benefits stated in the contract.
- Any mutually agreed upon exceptions to pay, benefits, or job expectation should be stated in writing.

This document is then signed and dated by the employee, the employer, and is acknowledged by an officer or designated group of the church or organization (for example, the chairman of the personnel committee). The contract becomes part of the permanent personnel file of the employee.

5. *Orientation.* Probably one of the greatest contributors to failure in a ministry or support position in a church or organization is the failure by the employer to orient the individual to the job. Formal and informal research has indicated that a major contributor to poor job performance is the absence of a designed orientation period. In secular organizations or large church and nonprofit groups that have numerous personnel with a frequent turnover, this is not a problem. In most churches it becomes a problem because it is an infrequent event since employment turnover does not happen often. But it does not have to be a problem. The orientation process occurs in three basic phases: the moving phase, the first week on the job, and follow-up.

The *moving phase* will involve the actions to get the prospective employee to the church or organization. This could be as simple as saying "show up" to someone who lives in the city or as complex as a cross-country move. This phase will require certain actions on the part of the church or organization and is usually carried out by an office assigned these responsibilities such as the church administrator or personnel committee:

- Make arrangements for the move. This should be negotiated and part of any salary and benefits portion of the contract. The church may make arrangements for the move or provide assistance to the future employee who arranges for their own move.

- Provide for assistance in residence relocation. One of the first items would be a real estate brochure of the area. Most churches or organizations have at least one member who is an agent and could easily provide this help.
- Arrange for temporary living accommodations if needed.
- Complete arrangements for office and ministry support.
- Gather relevant documents and equipment to assist the person in the performance of his duties.

The *first week on the job* may not be the first week in the area for the future employee. Nevertheless, orientation events that should be planned by the new employee's supervisor and occurring early in the arrival of a new employee should include the following:

- Arrange for the employee to meet not only coworkers but also significant elements of the church or organization with whom they will work.
- Arrange for a general introduction to the entire church or institution. Be sure to include family members in this introduction.
- Conduct acclimation tours: the facility, the neighborhood, the community. Show the new employee common places to shop. Provide maps and other brochures and information to introduce him to the area.
- If the individual is a ministerial or directorate person, introduce him or her to other professionals in the local area.
- Spend time ensuring the person is familiar with operations such as work periods, office procedures, staff meetings, group expectations such as the Sunday morning service, and other work-related "rules."
- Acclimate the individual to the information technology equipment and resources of the church or organization.

Follow-up orientation occurs in the first several months of employment. While arranged by the supervisor, other elements of the organization continue the acclimation of the new employee to the position. Some of these activities should include:

- A discussion of the historicity of the church, its polity and philosophy of ministry.
- An introduction to the church membership; active, resident, and nonresident.
- An introduction by every program ministry and group that carries out the functions of the church or organization.
- A discussion of financial operations, budget processes, reimbursement plans, use of benefits, and purchasing procedures.

- An introduction of the various security provisions and measures as well as codes, keys, and disaster reaction plans.
- A discussion of the records, record systems, and filing processes.
- Schemes for personnel evaluation and development.
- Communication media and methods.
- Cooperative ministries.

The Work Environment

In the early part of the twentieth century, a researcher named Herzberg developed a theory relating the motivation of workers to their work. Building on formative research that indicated humans did certain things based on needs they perceived as essential for them, Herzberg stated that those needs could be grouped into two categories. The first category he termed hygiene and related these needs to the environment or context of the workplace. They were identified as such things as the work space, the supervisor, their peers, a title or status, salary, and considerations for security and well-being. A second set of motivational factors he termed intrinsic and related them to the psyche of the individual. He noted that content items relating to the work such as a challenge, rewarding work, being able to think creatively, and carrying out several important activities related to the satisfaction of work. The bottom line of his research was that it was the intrinsic factors that really motivated a person to excellence in the workplace.

But a key element of this research was that the hygiene, the extrinsic/context environmental factors, really didn't motivate persons to work when they were present. But when these extrinsic factors were not satisfied, employees became dissatisfied with their work. Do you want your employees to work on the intrinsic motivational factors and be satisfied in the workplace? Then solve and neutralize the extrinsic factors so they will not become detractors to the work. Practically, if an administrator wants the employee to think creatively, then provide a comfortable work space. If you want employees to take on challenging work, then pay them an adequate salary. Warm rooms and salary won't motivate them to heights of grandeur, but the absence of things like this will demotivate them if they are not present.[1]

This section of the chapter will not be an exhaustive analysis of the context of a successful work environment. In fact, factors that relate to appropriate working environments will be discussed in several of the following chapters. It is appropriate, however, to discuss several work-related issues, including periods of work, absences, and demeanor.

Periods of work. In a study conducted by Christianity Today International, it was discovered that less than one-fourth of ministers surveyed spent less than fifty hours a week on the job. Another quarter spent fifty to fifty-five hours; and nearly another quarter spent sixty-five or more hours on the job. About forty hours a week were spent in administrative details, meetings, and other office "stuff."[2]

A few years ago I asked one of my classes to attend a large state pastor's conference and conduct some research. One of the questions the students asked the participants was how many employees they had in their church. My students were prompted to help the pastors accurately determine what an employee was. After counting up all the professional ministers and program directors, office personnel, day care workers and Christian academy workers and such, if the number totaled fifteen or more employees, the student was to ask the pastor; "Do you have to pay overtime to your secretary if she works more than forty hours a week or could you tell her to take comp time off the next week to make up for the extra hours worked." The vast majority stated that they could allow the secretary time off next week to make up for the overtime. Then the student asked whether the church fell under the guidelines of the Fair Labor Standards Act. All said no—either because they didn't know what the law said, or because they thought churches are exempt from employment law, or because the law didn't apply to their employees. The problem is that churches are bound by the Fair Labor Standards Act, either legally or morally. Since much of what will be stated in this section requires an understanding of employment law, let's review some of the important laws.

Laws that Include Churches and Nonprofits in Their Context

Tax Reform Act of 1986. Provides for ministerial conscientious objectors to opt out of Social Security upon ordination. Allows ministerial personnel to claim both housing allowance and housing interest. Requires churches which offer benefit plans to one category of personnel who work 17.6 or more hours per week to make the benefit available to all employees of that category.

Immigration Reform and Control Act of 1986. Requires employers who have three or more employees to verify the citizenship of the employee. The completion of Form I-9 must be made within seventy-two hours of employment. I-9 forms must become part of employee records.

Americans with Disabilities Act of 1988. Requires churches to make an application process available to the handicapped. Requires churches to make reasonable accommodations for employment. Requires churches to make public areas available to the handicapped.

Welfare Reform Act of 1996. Requires all employers of three or more employees to report new employees' Social Security numbers. Requires all states to establish an agency to monitor and correlate information nationwide.

Various State and Local Laws. Some states require background checks for employees who work with minors. Some states have laws relating to drug-free working environments and drug and substance abuse program requirements. Some states have more stringent laws relating to handicap access/ accommodation.

Laws That May Be Applicable to Churches

Most laws listed below require a certain number of employees for applicability. That number is usually fifteen individuals who work twenty or more hours per week. Additionally, the church or organization must be engaged in interstate commerce to be applicable. This may include the use of long-distance telephone out of state, the purchase of products and goods from out of state, or the mailing of church-produced products out of state. Even the use of an e-mail service with an out-of-state server may cause the church to be held in compliance.

Fair Labor Standards Act of 1938. Outlines wage and hour rules with regard to nonexempt (hourly-wage) employees. Ministerial employees are considered exempt employees and provisions do not apply. Requires minimum wage to be paid hourly to nonexempt employees. Requires overtime of time and half to be paid for greater than forty hours per week. Prohibits the use of comp time (compensatory time off) in lieu of overtime pay for nonexempt employees. Prevents child labor. Always applicable to schools or similar educational institutions.

Equal Pay Act of 1963. Prevents differential pay based on gender.

Civil Rights Act of 1964. Prevents consideration for hiring or promotion based on race, color, creed, sex, religion, etc. The act allows churches to discriminate based on founded sectarian, doctrinal, or theological basis for ALL employees. Prevents the sexual harassment, actual or perceived, of employees.

Age Discrimination in Employment Act of 1967. Prevents consideration in hiring, promotion, or termination based on age.

OSHA Act of 1970. Requires employers to provide a safe and hazard-free work environment. Requires employers to provide the necessary training for safe working.

Veterans Readjustment Assistance Act of 1974 and Soldiers and Sailors Relief Act. Prevents employers from discrimination against veterans. Requires employers to allow military reserve personnel time off for required obligations without penalty or loss of employment.

Privacy Act of 1974. Restricts the types of questions you may ask of an applicant. Restricts the use and inspection of an employee record. Restricts the disclosure of certain information about employees/individuals without their approval. Opens the employee record for the employee's inspection.

Jury Systems Improvement Act of 1978. Prohibits employers from discouraging, threatening or discharging, intimidating or coercing employees because of their jury duty.

Family Medical Leave Act of 1993. Requires the employer to grant up to twelve weeks of unpaid leave during a twelve-month period. May be because of serious illness of the individual, family, or close relative.

Churches have been brought into compliance with these laws, not necessarily by the organization or administering body charged with ensuring compliance but through the civil courts. In other words, a family who lost a husband/father who was a janitor sued a church for not providing a safe work environment when the man (a janitor) was overcome from fumes in a janitorial closet. Or the case of a seventy-year-old associate pastor who was terminated because he was "too old" to do the job. Whenever civil courts become sympathetic toward the plaintiff, then the law is rewritten, and churches are drawn in by court precedence.

Throughout this text reference will be made from time to time to regulations or laws that require churches or nonprofit organizations to comply. Even when compliance is not dictated, religious institutions should, out of a Christian ethic, seek to comply with the legitimate provisions of the law. Paul wrote to the church at Rome (Rom. 13:5–6) that we are to submit to authorities because governments are ordained by God. He admonished his associates Timothy (1 Tim. 2:2) and Titus (Titus 3:1) that Christians should respect civil authority.

Returning to our discussion of an appropriate work environment, what are some issues that will make for the conditions of work an inducement to motivated employees?

1. *Define work hours.* It was mentioned in this section that most ministers worked far longer than a forty-hour week. As discussed above, the nonexempt employee must have a forty-hour week. Well-administered churches or organizations will establish how those are determined.

Ministerial and director personnel who would be considered exempt or executive employees should have their work periods defined by their immediate supervisor. Obviously these hours would be contingent upon the scope and program organization of the job. A word of warning: The parishioner will determine a minister is not at work unless he is behind his desk. Smart administrators will educate the parishioner/client that a youth minister is actually at work even though he or she is meeting some teens after school at a local gathering place. Supervisors must use sensitivity and tact when developing working hours for ministers.

Program personnel such as school or academy, day care or nursery, bookstore or media center, or recreation center, should have their hours designated by the supervisor of the program. Some form of time allocation and record process is mandated to ensure the employee remains within the guidelines of a legitimate workweek.

Office hours will dictate when most nonexempt employees will work and when ministerial or director personnel will be at their desks. While these hours may be flexible, for the sake of the public the church or organization serves, they should be well established and fixed. When variance occurs, managers or supervisors must monitor hours worked to ensure the employee remains within the guidelines of a legitimate workweek. Incidentally, I learned the hard way that Sunday is the *first* day of the week. If you schedule a secretary or ministry assistant to be in the church office on a Sunday, then those hours count toward the upcoming week.

2. *Holidays.* Employees should be granted certain days off with pay for secular and religious holidays. The church or organization must determine which holidays will be granted. Usually the equivalent of one workweek (five events) is deemed appropriate for holidays, but the organization may choose to allow more.

3. *Absences.* Absences usually relate to periods employees are away from their normal work environment and usually will occur in two venues—planned and unplanned absences.

Planned absences include days off for personal business, extended absence in a leave-of-absence status such as military obligation or assignment; organization granted sabbatical leave; church business that may include conferences, meetings, or training; and of course vacation. These contingencies must be stated in writing, explaining when the provision is applicable, who grants the absence, and any restrictions or limits to the absence. For vacation it is strongly suggested that a formula for granting vacation time be established along with rules that relate to the granting of vacation. For example, can an employee with previous ministerial tenure come into the organization at the same level and be granted vacation commensurate with the total time in ministry, or does it apply only to tenure at the current position? Another problem that requires resolving early is whether a minister can take more than two consecutive Sundays off during a planned absence.

Unplanned absences include sickness of either the employee or member of the household, legal responsibility such as jury duty, death of a family member, and inclement weather. As with planned absences, specific guidelines should be established that designate who can grant the absence, the term or length of the absence, and any provisions for validation of the absence. As you probably noted in the many employment laws above, much of this has been addressed in the various regulations that many churches must abide by. For example, the church may be responsible to comply with the Family Medical Leave Act and grant up to twelve weeks a year for an employee's absence because of his or her personal illness or the illness of a family member.

In both of the situations of absence above, the church or organization must specify when the absence may be taken with the provision of continuance of pay and when pay will be suspended during the absence. For example, most vacation, business days off, and a designated number of sick days will include pay. Most organizations also include jury duty, two weeks for military duty, bereavement in the death of a family member, and so forth. But when an individual exceeds those established limitations, then statements must be made about how pay will be reflected. In the case of illness, the Family Medical Leave Act allows the institution first to require the employee to use all paid vacation and sick leave before being placed in a nonpay status. The administrator of the church or organization must weigh the two tensions of cost of employment and the benevolent nature of the employer. It would be nice if churches and nonprofits were financially able to allow for extended paid absences while at the same time employing a part-time person to fulfill that absent employee's workstation. But such is not generally the case.

4. **Conduct and Demeanor.** Administrators must be sensitive to the expectations of the parishioner and community about the regulations established for an employee's personal conduct and their actions in the work environment. While employee activities outside the secular work environment are not reflected upon the employer, the situation with a church employee is different.

Personal conduct relates to the appearance that is perceived by an individual or group of individuals. If the organization is to require a dress code on premises, then that should be stated clearly. If certain activities, memberships, or participation in certain events is considered inappropriate, then they should be stated. If you have employed a person with Christian characteristics, then those should be the general expectations. But the administrator must remember a person can be a Christian and wear blue jeans to work. Or could be a Christian and attend a rock concert. If the church or organization views certain elements of an individual's lifestyle, then the wise administrator must ask, "Is this conduct influencing the witness of the church or organization in the community and is it something that should be generally addressed in conduct regulations?" Paul admonished the church at Corinth in 1 Corinthians 8:9 and 10:30–33 not to do that which would be a stumbling block for the sake of the ministry.

There should be only one official spokesperson for the church or organization. Public relations is a critical issue in today's society in which an apology of the Christian principle is demanded at every turn. The senior minister or similar organizational leader should be the only official source of public information and comment for the church or institution. In some larger organizations, that may be vested in an officer specifically designated as the public relations officer. Paul warned the church at Corinth (2 Cor. 12:20) that rumor, gossip, slander, and arrogance are acts of disorder and thus sin. Administrators should state their policy, announce the expectations, and then require compliance.

It has been a tenet of this text that the use of drugs and substance abuse is not accepted behavior for Christian leaders or functionaries in churches or religious not-for-profit organizations. Admittedly, this philosophy comes from a rather conservative Baptist perspective. And it is recognized that not all religions and religious groups take the same view. What the administrator must recognize, however, is that there are certain employment laws that require employers to address this issue. So the caveat for this paragraph is that the administrator must be aware of state laws that control certain activities in the presence of minors. In many states the employer must have in place a substance-abuse assistance program. The strong suggestion is not to allow drugs, including alcohol, as part of the demeanor of your employees. If you do allow it, then you must make statements that address how it is to be managed in your organization.

Unfortunately sexual harassment is commonplace in the work environment today. Sexual harassment is defined as any unwelcome advance of a personal nature by another person. It can take the form of inappropriate requests, statements or comments, physical contact, the display of inappropriate items or pictures, or body language that demeans or threatens an individual. Institutions must establish policy about this activity and designate an appropriate method of reporting, investigating, and dealing with the activity. It is strongly suggested that this activity be vested in a single officer (pastor or church administrator) or group like the personnel committee.

Sexual harassment does not necessarily mean that one of your employees is the perpetrator. I once had to investigate a complaint of sexual harassment toward one of our employees by an individual who made routine deliveries to the church for a company the church did business with. I had to go to the company and say, "This is the problem, I have observed it in action, you deal with your employee to stop the action, or we will cease to do business with you." Sexual harassment can occur between genders and within genders. The church or organization must make a policy statement, establish a methodology for investigating the complaint, and then define a process for correcting the activity. Serious legal ramifications can result if the church or nonprofit organization does not deal with this issue.

Remember, the role of the administrator is to establish a work environment that satisfies the extrinsic or context conditions that would cause employees not to be able to focus on their intrinsic motivation for satisfying and challenging work.

The Salary Plan

Several years ago I began a study to determine the job satisfaction of employees in Southern Baptist churches. My initial study was to be comprehensive in that it involved all different types of employees in the church, both ministerial and support, but the study, because of the cost involved, focused on a statistical sample. The SBC's Sunday School Board became interested in the study and offered to fund it with the provision that the study be one of broad range and extensive in assessment.

Using the Herzberg model of job satisfaction based on the neutralization of context/extrinsic factors and focusing satisfaction based on the motivation for work from the intrinsic principles, the research made several interesting discoveries among Southern Baptist church staffs. What motivated a church employee for job satisfaction varied by type of employee studied. But one solitary factor seemed to concern eleven of the thirteen groups of staff and employees studied—salary. Only the senior minister and custodian were not concerned with salary, and thus it was not considered a demotivater for job satisfaction on their part. Statistical significance was found with all other ministerial and support staff positions indicating that the lack of an adequate salary or salary-related items such as benefits detracted from their ability to become engaged in the intrinsic factors of motivation that lead to job satisfaction.

It is doubtful if much has changed in the decade or so since that study. Numerous salary surveys indicate that the "professional" staff member is rarely paid a compensation commensurate with other types of professional employees. Churches seemed to have the attitude, "How cheaply can we pay this person and still get the work done?" Unfortunately, altruistic individuals who sense their employment a calling of God on their life have allowed this situation of poor salary practice to prevail. This is an important issue in churches and religious organizations. Scripture has much to say about stewardship and particularly salary.

> Now we ask you, brothers, to give recognition to those who labor among you and lead you in the Lord and admonish you, and to esteem them very highly in love because of their work (1 Thess. 5:12–13).
>
> You yourselves know how you must imitate us: we were not irresponsible among you; we did not eat anyone's bread free of charge; instead, we labored and toiled, working night and day, so that we would not be a burden to any of you. It is not that we don't have the right to support, but we did it to make ourselves an example to you so that you would imitate us. If fact, when we were with you, this is

what we commanded you: "If anyone isn't willing to work, he should not eat" (2 Thess. 3:7–10).

My defense to those who examine me is this: Don't we have the right to eat and drink? Don't we have the right to be accompanied by a Christian wife, like the other apostles, the Lord's brothers, and Cephas? Or is it only Barnabas and I who have no right to refrain from working? Who ever goes to war at his own expense? Who plants a vineyard and does not eat its fruit? Or who shepherds a flock and does not drink the milk from the flock? Am I saying this from a human perspective? Doesn't the law also say the same thing? For it is written in the law of Moses, Do not muzzle an ox while it treads out the grain. Is God really concerned with oxen? Or isn't He really saying it for us? Yes, this is written for us, because he who plows ought to plow in hope, and he who threshes should do so in hope of sharing the crop. If we have sown spiritual things for you, is it too much if we reap material things from you? (1 Cor. 9:3–11).

Jesus sent out these 12 after giving them instructions: . . . Don't take along gold, silver, or copper for your money-belts. Don't take a traveling bag for the road, or an extra shirt, sandals, or a walking stick, for the worker is worthy of his food (Matt. 10:5,9–10).

The elders who are good leaders should be considered worthy of an ample honorarium, especially those who work hard at preaching and teaching. For the Scripture says: You must not muzzle an ox that is threshing grain, and, the laborer is worthy of his wages (1 Tim. 5:17–18).

From these passages we can make some important statements:

- Pastors (ministers) should expect support for their ecclesial actions.
- Providing support to these individuals is the church's responsibility.
- Supporting the pastor is a good deal for members because it frees the minister up to do his work full-time.
- Ministers are cautioned to ensure priorities are placed correctly and not put their support before spreading the gospel.

Compensation

The word *compensation* is an administrative term that describes the costs to a church (or other organization) for the employment of an individual. It is best exampled by describing it as the total cost for having a pastor (or other staff member or employee) serve in a paid position in the church. It is the expenses the church will have to bear for that individual. Usually compensation is computed on an annual basis and becomes part of the annual church budget.

Compensation is when the personnel committee and the finance commit-tee come together with church leaders and count the costs. It includes the salary paid the individual; any fringe benefits the church will provide such as a medical insurance plan; the expenses paid out for certain business expenses like transportation, education, book/computer allowances, etc.; the cost for support personnel such as a secretary; and the costs for physical operations like provid-ing an office space.

Salary is the take-home pay. It is the portion of compensation that the employee will pay taxes on. Later we will discover that an ordained minister may declare a portion of the salary as a housing allowance from which he will not have to pay federal income taxes.

Benefits are termed "fringe benefits" in the secular business world and are the inducements provided by an employer to attract and retain top-quality employees. Since these are business expenses of the employer, they are not part of the taxable salary paid the employee. And since churches are tax-exempt entities, no taxes—either federal income or social security—will be paid by the church. We will discover that very strict rules apply for churches to follow. Nevertheless, benefits provided by the church are good opportunities to reward employees above their salaries.

Reimbursements are basically that; you spend your own money for a busi-ness expense, and we pay you back after you give us a receipt for it. These are church expenses you have obligated your money to buy. Reimbursement plans require receipts.

Developing the Salary Plan

As a portion of every personnel manual, the church should develop a salary plan that describes how it will conduct operations with regard to salary and ben-efits of the personnel it employs. The salary plan preestablishes the rules (poli-cies and procedures) for financial management of personnel resources. Later we will discuss some issues the church should consider in creating this plan.

There are eight steps in developing the salary plan.

1. Determine the mission and purpose of the church.
2. Create a leadership organization to meet that mission.
3. Write job descriptions for all leadership or employee positions.
4. Determine the relative worth of each job description.
5. Determine the categories and limits of a scale of salaries to be paid.
6. Establish policies and procedures relating to the administration of pay.
7. Determine benefits that will be provided.
8. Determine reimbursable business expenses offered.

We have accomplished steps 1 through 3 in previous chapters. Be cautioned, however, without first establishing what the church is to do and a determination of what human resources will be required to accomplish this mission, the remainder of the salary plan will not be spiritually based. We will continue by looking at steps 4–8.

4. *Determine the relative worth of each job description.* Worth is translated as level of importance. The best way to determine worth is to look at the organizational chart developed in chapter 4. From the organizational chart determine who supervises whom. We have suggested four basic ministry areas: pastoral, education, music, and support. And the biblical analogy of "the leaders of thousands" of Exodus 18 would become the associate pastor, the minister of education, the minister of music, and the church administrator. Each of these ministry areas will have other leaders. For instance, in education you will have age group (adult, youth, children, preschool) leaders; in administration you will have office and housekeeping employees, and so forth.

An indicator of relative worth placed upon an employee is the summary of wages given to the various types of positions in the church. Probably the best such summary is produced biannually by the National Association of Church Business Administration. Their survey gives a summary of nearly every paid position in a church. Summary information is provided for all churches, for Protestant churches, for churches of selected denominations, for churches of selected size, for churches of selected budget, and for churches within five geographic regional areas of the U.S. Other surveys are available from denominational and state convention agencies.

What tables such as these salary surveys do to assist the administrator is to provide an estimate of an average salary and other compensation issues for a particular type of minister. An example may help:

Suppose your church has a senior pastor, minister of education, minister of music, youth minister, church administrator, part-time children's minister, three secretaries, a youth intern, an organist/pianist, and three custodians. Set up a survey chart that looks something like this:

POSITION	SALARY	INSURANCE	RETIREMENT	REIMBURSEMENTS	OTHER	TOTAL COMP
Sr Pastor	65,368	8,008	5,971	5,362	5,573	90,282
Min Educ	46,463	6,151	3,967	2,126	4,204	62,911
Min Music	47,355	6,882	4,245	2,124	3,021	63,627
Youth Min	37,498	4,719	3,137	2,271	3,193	50,818
ChildrenMin	34,699	4,698	2,881	2,089	3,678	48,045
CBA	44,203	4,411	3,742	2,524	3,541	58,421
Secretary	22,410	3,100	2,006	850	233	28,599
Custodian	20,174	3,359	450	0	0	23,983
Y Intern	18,023	6,408	0	348	0	24,779
Organist	6,965	0	0	0	1,069	8,034

It becomes easy to then visualize how the $459,519 in total compensation for the employees of the church will be distributed. And it confirms the organization plan you have established that creates levels of relative importance. We

STEPS	CATEGORY 1	CATEGORY 2	CATEGORY 3
76,000			
74			
72			
70			
68			
66			
64			
62			
60			
58			
56			
55			
54			
52			
50			
48			
46			
44			
42			
40			
38			
36			
34			
32			
30			
28			
26			
24			
22			
20			
18			
16			
14			
12			
10			
8			
6			

then can visualize three general levels of relative worth: upper executive made up of the pastor, ministers of music and education, and the church administrator; a middle level of program staff made up of the youth and children's minister; and a third level of support comprised of the secretaries, custodians, organist, and interns.

5. *Determine the categories and limits of a scale of salaries to be paid.* The next task is to establish some format for the salary plan. This is best visualized in a diagram that establishes the categories of salary groups and the levels within each group. An example of such a diagram is shown here. In the example, we are developing in this section, there are three categories of salary. Category 1 in this example, for instance, might be all the support personnel: the secretaries,

janitors, organists, interns, and other lower-paid salaried personnel who would be added at a later date.

In category 2 might be the age group directors (youth and children) and other nonexecutive ministry personnel that might be added at a later date such as a singles minister, a recreation and outreach minister. In the category 3 column would be the executive ministers: senior pastor, ministers of music and education, and church administrator. Another category might be established that will describe how the church or organization pays part-time employees.

In the left column are the steps that would be included in each category. A sufficient number of steps should be present to ensure the potential growth and tenure of the employee. For example, the church may decide and write into the elements of a salary policy and procedures section of the personnel manual that a minister will get a step increase for every two years of employment. If the church administrator started at the bottom of category 3 with a beginning salary of $42,000, then it would be thirty years before the limits of that category will be reached. If a pastor was brought in at the average salary for a senior pastor at $65,000, then he would have six steps or a possible tenure of twelve years before the limit of the scale is reached.

The lower limit of the scale is developed by looking at the salaries that make up the scale. For example, in category 3, made up of the senior pastor, the ministers of music and education, and the church administrator, you will note that the national average for the church administrator is about $44,000. While most salary surveys will report an average salary for a ministerial position, the administrator must be aware that this average is based on a range of salaries and only the average is reported. If the church or any other religious organization desires to attract a quality individual to a position, they will have to offer at least the average salary for individuals of their category and classification.

When establishing your chart, the first step increment would be one step below the minimum of the lowest individual that makes up that category to allow for an instance where employment may occur at a lesser level. For example, the church decides to call a minister of education who is finishing seminary. The church may state in the contract that initial salary designation will be the first step; but upon completion of the degree, the individual would be moved to the step that indicates where the average minister of education would be paid.

The upper limit of the chart is established by taking the highest paid individual's salary and then extending it to the desired number of tenured steps. In the example above, the average pastor's salary is $65,000. Thus a salary plan to $74,000 will ensure twelve years of tenure with a step increase every two years before the limit is reached.

In summary:

- Establish the number of categories of personnel.
- Establish who will be in each category.
- Set the lower limit by finding the average salary of the least paid employee of the category.
- Set an upper limit by determining the average salary of the highest paid individual of the category and then extending it up to the tenure/steps you desire.

6. ***Establish policies and procedures relating to the administration of pay.*** In establishing the salary plan, the church or organization needs to develop certain rules and regulations about issues relating to pay. Example polices and procedures can be found in numerous publications. But the same caveat is given that was given for job descriptions: do not blindly adopt or copy without assessing applicability to the church or organization you are developing them for. Most policy and procedures statements will include the following:

Classification of workers. We have already discussed the category of exempt and nonexempt employees as this nomenclature relates to the Fair Labor Standards Act. Another useful classification is whether the employee is a full-time or part-time worker. And another subcategory within that classification would be whether the individual is a professional or support person. For example:

- The pastor would be a full-time professional exempt employee (FTP).
- The church secretary would be a full-time support nonexempt employee (FTS).
- The children's minister would be a part-time professional exempt employee (PTP).
- The organist would be a part-time support nonexempt employee (PTS).

Compensation of part-time workers. The easiest way to pay part-time workers is to give them a percentage of the pay they would receive if they were a full-time employee. This means you must have a job description and evaluate that position for worth. For example, a thirty-hours-per-week janitor would be a category 1 employee and would receive a $20,000 per year ($9.60/hour) total salary if full-time. Since he works only 75 percent of that time, he would receive an annual salary of $15,000. Part-time employees usually do not receive fringe benefits. The church/organization must remember that they may be under the guidelines of the wage and hour employee laws of the Fair Labor Standards Act relating to minimum wage and hours worked.

Credit for experience. The church or organization may grant credit for experience. This comes about in two venues. (1) As employees continue employment, they may be granted step increases based on tenure. Most churches or organizations will establish a step increase with every two years of employment. (2) When a person is hired, the church may choose to reward the person for experience he has gained prior to his employment. If the job description calls for an experienced applicant, then the personnel committee must determine how many years is considered necessary. If future employees have more years of experience than this base, then they may be rewarded for this additional experience. Usually one step increase for each additional five years of experience is given.

Credit for education. The church or organization may grant credit for education or training. Like experience, this may come about in two venues. (1) Education or training completed while an employee. A formula for awarding step increases for continuing education units (CEU) or degrees should be established. For example, for every ten CEUs the person will receive a step increase. (2) The second place where education reward may occur is in the hiring process. If the position description calls for a seminary degree, that usually means a master's degree. What if the person has a doctorate? Then a formula should be developed for recognizing that additional training. Usually one step increase for every degree above the minimum is appropriate.

Process for moving up steps. Already discussed are step increases for tenure and for additional education. A mechanism should be in place for rewarding merit or outstanding employees through a step increase. This is an especially useful process for retaining top employees. Merit increases should be the result of evaluation and general recognition for exceptional performance.

Cost-of-living increases. Unless the church or organization has some method for providing an automatic adjustment in salary each year for cost-of-living increases, the employee will, in effect, be required to incur a pay reduction. A simple way to accomplish this is to adjust automatically the value of each step in a salary-plan profile. For example, for category 3, step one ($42,000), this figure will change to $43,260 to reflect a 3 percent cost-of-living increase from the previous year. Cost-of-living indexes are provided for the nation as well as by region and state. The adjustment of steps and salaries is a simple mathematical computation for a financial secretary if the church has established a policy dictating the automatic adjustment to maintain salary level. Every four to six years the chart can be revised and updated to reflect current salary-range steps.

Housing. As the result of the Tax Reform Act of 1986 and as explained in IRS Code, Section 107, employees who are ordained ministers may declare a portion of their salary as "housing allowance." This declaration must occur within a brief period of time after ordination, of employment, or by December 31 of each year. The minister designates how much of the salary he wishes to declare as housing allowance; the church approves the designation. Churches should not dictate housing allowance. This is a tax matter between the ordained minister and tax officials. In past years significant confusion has existed about housing allowance. It is available only to ordained, commissioned, or licensed ministers who perform sacerdotal duties in a church or religious organization and are recognized as religious leaders by their church or denomination.

Because of the confusion of interpretation, most denominational groups have prepared excellent documents to assist ministers in determining whether they qualify for housing allowance. For example, Southern Baptists would use the Web site www.GuideStone.org to obtain current interpretations of this and similar tax matters for clergy and churches. Housing allowance allows an individual to remove from federal tax requirements any reasonable expenses for rent, utilities, furnishings, and other household expenses. A provision exists for a minister to add to the provision of a parsonage to cover additional household expenses.

Social Security. Social Security taxes must be paid for and by all employees. The church or organization must have policies and procedures in place to cover the varieties of situations that will be present with the combination of ministerial and nonministerial employees.

In all cases of nonministerial employees, the church is responsible for 50 percent of the Social Security and Medicare tax and employees have deducted from their salaries the remaining 50 percent. This is the FICA/Medicare tax. These payments are made on a monthly basis through a deposit system by the church or nonprofit organization. Some of the more important IRS publications to assist in determining tax responsibility are:

334 *Tax Guide for Small Businesses*
517 *Social Security for Members of the Clergy and Religious Workers*
525 *Taxable and Nontaxable Income*
571 *Tax Sheltered Annuity Programs for Employees of Tax Exempt Organizations*
937 *Business Reporting (Employment Taxes, Information Returns) Circular E Employer's Tax Guide*

These publications may be ordered online via www.irs.ustreas.gov/prod /forms_pubs or by calling 1-800-TAX-FORM.

Ordained ministers are responsible for their own Social Security and Medicare taxes. This tax is called the self-employment tax (SECA) and has caused significant confusion in churches that do not know employment tax law. While the ordained minister is considered an "employee" of the church for *federal income tax purposes,* the ordained minister is "self-employed" with regard to Social Security. This dual status as an ordained minister has caused confusion in the past, and, in some instances cause for tax problems with authorities.

Ordained ministers are responsible for filing their own taxes. This is usually accomplished by filing quarterly estimated taxes. Ministers may choose to allow the church to withhold federal income taxes and to pay those taxes on a monthly basis for them. Pastors may choose to allow the church to compute and withhold Social Security and Medicare taxes, but they are responsible for filing these taxes themselves. Ordained ministers will pay federal income tax only on that portion of salary that is not declared by them and approved beforehand by the church as "housing allowance." The minister will pay self-employment (SECA) taxes on *all* salary, including the portion declared as housing allowance.

7. *Determine benefits that will be provided.* Through the years students have come to me for advice about "salary packages" churches have offered them as they move from seminary to employment. Sometimes a church will say to a prospective staff member, "Here are so many dollars. You divide it among salary, insurance, and transportation allowance like you want." There are two problems with this reasoning. The first is a legal problem. Rulings and determinations by IRS have stated that if the individual has any decision in the process of remuneration for their services, then the entire amount may become taxable income. Thus, if the employee says, "I choose to have this portion as salary, this portion as housing, this portion as medical insurance, this amount for retirement, this amount for convention and education, and this portion as transportation allowance," he will be taxed on the whole mess—federal income and Social Security.

The second problem with this philosophy is that it negates the concept of "fringe benefits." *Fringe* means "outside of" or "in addition to." With regard to the employee, it would mean "in addition to salary." It would be ridiculous to tell a pastor, "Here are X thousands of dollars. You designate part for salary, housing, insurance, etc., *and* you pay your secretary's salary, you give us X hundreds of dollars each month for rental of your office, *and* you are responsible for X percent of the utility bills." A pastor's secretary, office, and work environment are normal givens; why not insurance, medical care, retirement, and other business expenses?

It's like telling a soldier, "You come fight for me, but you have to bring your own weapons and provide your own armament. In addition to that, if you get injured, we won't provide medical assistance. If you get killed, we won't provide for your family. If you spend a lifetime fighting for us and have to retire, you better sock away money for living because we won't provide you a retirement." I spent twenty-two years in the Navy. I am retired and now receive a lifetime pension. I received medical benefits in the Navy then and now. I have an insurance policy for my family provided by the Navy. A smart general will provide for his soldiers. A trained fighter is hard to find and keep. So is a quality minister or church employee!

A *little exercise:* Ordained minister, which would you rather have: $45,000 and you provide all your own benefits. Or $35,000 with the church providing medical and insurance benefits and establish a reimbursable business expense limit?

With $45,000

Housing $16,000	Salary $16,000	Medical and life insurance $7,000	Business Expenses $5,000	Retirement $1,000

⟵————————————————————————————————⟶
You pay Social Security taxes on this amount.

⟵——————————————————————————⟶
You pay federal income tax on this amount.

Spendable income of the salary portion:

$16,000

Less taxes   -8,000   Based on Social Security taxes on $45K and income taxes on $29K

$8,000

With $35,000 plus benefits provided by the church

Housing $17,500	Salary $17,500

⟵————————————————————————————————⟶
You pay Social Security taxes on this amount.

⟵——————————————————————————⟶
You pay federal income tax on this amount.

Spendable income of the salary portion:

$17,500

Less taxes   -6,300   Based on Social Security taxes on $35K and income taxes for $17.5K

$11,200

That's $3,200 *more* spendable income. You might even be able to buy a new car!

Benefits should be considered inducements for employment. They are tax-free fringe benefits because the *church* pays for the expenses and because a church is a tax-exempt, nonprofit religious organization. Benefits are legal ways to maximize the dollar spent for such services.

Some of the benefits usually provided employees are:
- Up to $50,000 accidental death/dismemberment life insurance policy.
- Medical insurance for the member and/or member and family.
- Contributions to a retirement plan.

One additional word about benefit plans for the church or nonprofit employees: While the church or organization does not have to fund the benefit at the same level, the Tax Reform Act of 1986 requires that if a church provides a benefit plan to one category of employee, the plan must be available to all other individuals in that same category. Translated: as part of the salary plan, the church may tell a senior pastor, "We will provide you full medical coverage for you *and* your family." To the minister of education, however, his or her salary plan may say, "We will provide medical coverage for you. If you want to pay for the coverage of your dependents, then we will deduct that from your pay, and you can buy into our tax-exempt group-rated plan." Incidentally, tax courts have begun to extend that requirement of availability to other than executive staff. This means that benefit plans for the pastor's secretary will have to be available to all secretaries, but not funded equally based on the church's salary plan.

8. ***Determine reimbursable business expenses offered.*** A church may say to a minister, "Here is $2,000 for you to spend for transportation, convention, or education expenses, or so forth. You don't have to account to us how you spend that money." Sounds good; no paperwork or strings attached. Some ministers like this idea—no red tape. Trouble is, they will have to pay taxes on that $2,000, income and Social Security. Sure, if they itemize their taxes, they can declare it as a business expense, but then they will get only about 3 percent of it back.

What if there was a way to provide a minister an allowance for travel he or she does on behalf of the church, a way of paying for expenses like convention, educational materials and courses, books, and a variety of other business-related expenses? There is if the church will establish an *accountable,* reimbursable, business-expense plan. Key features of the plan must include:

1. A description of the limits that will be reimbursed upon receipt:
   - Transportation allowance up to the limit established by the IRS. Note: commuting from home to work is not an allowable expense.
   - Transportation, lodging, and meals on business trips away from home.
   - Attendance expenses for conferences, symposia, meetings, or other professional gatherings.
   - Education or professional development expenses.
   - Professional books, literature, or other ministry-related materials.
   - Hospitality expenses for direct ministry-related activities.
2. Time limits for submission. Receipts or invoices must be within sixty days of incurring expense.
3. Time limit for return of advances beyond actual expenses. Must be returned within 120 days.

Churches and organizations may set limits for each category. They may also discriminate between the various categories of personnel who will receive the benefit. For instance; the pastor may get a transportation allowance of $2,000, a conference/meeting allowance of $1,000, and an education allowance of $1,000. The minister of music, on the other hand, may be limited to a transportation allowance of $1,000, a conference allowance of $1,000, and an education allowance of $500. These various limits should be spelled out in the accountable reimbursement plan policy. They should not be linked to the individual's salary plan except to say that they will have certain accountable business expenses available to them.

Let's close this section of the chapter with an extension of the last sentence of the paragraph above. Salary plans for employees of the church should *define* the salary they will receive and *describe* the benefits and reimbursements they have available to them. Salary is taxable income; benefits and reimbursements are not taxable if treated as business expenses of the church. It is strongly suggested that separation be as apparent as possible to avoid any hint of linkage. An appropriate contract discussing the salary and benefits portion might read this way:

> As the minister of education, you will be category 3, regular full-time professional employee of XYZ Church. In recognition of your previous experience and training, you will be employed at step 3 of that category with a beginning salary of $46,000 per year. You will be provided the following benefits: medical insurance for you and your family, an accidental death/dismemberment life insurance policy to the limit established by law, and a contribution equal to 2 percent of your annual salary to an authorized church retirement plan. The church will provide reimbursement upon proof for legitimate business expenses incurred by you and as defined in the accountable reimbursement plan policy and as developed annually by the personnel committee.

Note that you don't give a value or dollar amount to the benefits or reimbursement plan elements. Since these will change over the years, you just *describe* them! It is strongly advised to have business expense items become part of the church administrative budget line items. (These will be discussed in the next chapter on the financial operations of the church.) Include insurance and retirement costs in the administrative budget as opposed to the personnel budget because they are legitimate church business expenses, not personnel salary items.

The objective of a church salary plan is to provide an adequate salary and offer inducement benefits to obtain and retain qualified, professional employees.

By following certain guidelines, churches can provide fair salaries as well as legal benefits for employment.

Performance of Work

In this final section of the chapter relating to personnel issues, we need to discuss a topic that Jesus spoke about more than any other issue in the Gospels—our stewardship. While many will focus this topic on the management of financial resources, this was not necessarily the thrust of Jesus' teaching. From his early teaching in Matthew 13 about the expected production of the sowers, to the final teachings of the alertness of the ten virgins and adroitness to invest a master's talents in Matthew 25, Jesus taught that we should be productive, fruitful workers. He, as does all of Scripture, rails against slothfulness, laziness, and poor workmanship.

Several years ago my mentor, Dr. Bill Caldwell, set out during a sabbatical leave from Southwestern Baptist Seminary to discover how churches evaluated their personnel. His objective was to collect information to write a book on evaluation processes in the local church. He never wrote the book but not because of lack of interest on his part; he just couldn't find enough churches that evaluated their personnel to merit a book. One wonders why that is. Think about it; in almost every area of life we are evaluated. In school we take tests and perform experiments. When I was in the Navy, I was evaluated every six months to assess my competence to continue service. In business and industry work performance evaluation is commonplace, often the basis for promotion and pay raises. Then why not the church?

Evaluation is an important element of the administrative process. Without evaluation how can a leader determine whether the organization has achieved what it set out to do in its plans? Without evaluation how does a supervisor assess the process by which an individual is doing the work, to ensure the work is being done not only correctly but efficiently? We can ascribe certain benefits to a process of evaluation both to the individual and to the church or organization:

- It is a methodology for relating church/organizational goals to the personal goals of the individual.
- It is a process by which an assessment is made of the progress toward meeting the organization's mission.
- It informs both the worker and supervisor of the tasks they are supposed to accomplish.
- It becomes a communication vehicle to relate perspectives of how a job is to be accomplished.
- When areas of weakness are noted, it identifies needs for training, development, or increased supervisory involvement.

- It provides a format for evaluating the administrative processes and the leaders and supervisors of those processes.
- It is a scheme for recognizing exceptional performance.

In summary, a well-founded philosophy for constructive evaluation will be based on decisions the church or organization will establish to measure performance, communicate the analysis, and connect it to the continued development of the individual. As the result of this evaluation process, the church or organization will have a mechanism to ensure greater productivity and effectiveness while at the same time a process to deal with negative situations of job performance. This final section will address three issues: how to develop an evaluation process, how to develop personnel when needed, and how to deal with disciplinary problems, including the termination of an individual.

Developing a Personnel Evaluation System

There are six steps to developing an evaluation system in the church or nonprofit organization: (1) develop a job description that outlines responsibilities and establishes who the supervisor of the employee is, (2) establish performance standards for each of the job description items so that both the supervisor and the employee know the expectations for average performance, (3) create an instrument that will assist the supervisor in measuring job performance, (4) establish a process that will routinely evaluate job performance, (5) discuss the evaluation, both from the supervisor's perspective and from the employee's, and (6) design a process for recognizing meritorious performance or for correcting less-than-desirable or unsatisfactory performance. So far in this text we have discussed and provided ample guidance for steps 1 and 2. We need to look at the final four elements.

3. *Use evaluation instruments.* These instruments have many formats, from the interview of the *One-Minute Manager* philosophy that has evaluation in an ongoing scheme, to the formal, written document that evaluates numerous areas of job performance. When developing an instrument for evaluating an employee, the administrator should pay attention to several facets of the process:

- Will there be an opportunity for the employee to provide a self-report?
- How will each element of the job requirements of the job description be assessed?
- What will be the foundation for establishing "satisfactory" performance?
- How will general requirements for personal and work demeanor be assessed?
- Is the instrument chosen comprehensive, yet concise enough that it is easily administered?

Evaluation instruments take on elements of two dynamics, a written section and an interview section. A brief description of the various forms found in personnel management include the following.

(1) An essay evaluation is one in which the supervisor writes out his or her evaluation of the job performance of the employee and then discusses that evaluation with the employee to ensure understanding. This is a laborious process and often is not comprehensive.

(2) A critical-incident evaluation is one in which the supervisor keeps a "little black book" of the individual's job performance and then periodically discusses the issues, both good and bad, that have been noted. This scheme tends to focus on the "bad things." Additionally, it fails to correct poor performance as it is happening.

(3) A dimensional rating system will take a job element and then evaluate it on some sort of scale. For example: Prepares correspondence—excellent, good, average, poor, unsatisfactory. This scheme works as long as everyone who evaluates employees understands the scale and applies it equally. It also works only if the supervisor has an understanding of what "average" performance is.

(4) A behaviorally anchored system is similar to the dimensional rating system. However, it gives a narrative of what each of the criteria are. For example:

PROGRAM LEADER TRAINS LEADERSHIP	___ Excellent.	Conducts a variety as well as numerous training events each quarter. Program leaders demonstrate exceptional growth
	___ Good	Conducts more than one type of training program each quarter. Workers demonstrate growth.
	___ Average	Conducts at least one training program each quarter. Acceptable worker development.
	___ Poor	Frequently fails to conduct training.
	___ Unsatisfactory	Does not conduct worker training. Workers demonstrate no growth.

Average performance in this scheme is the performance standard (step 2) that was the mutually agreed-upon indicator in the job description for competent worker performance.

(5) A management-by-objectives rating system has received popular acceptance in many church and religious nonprofit organizations. The scheme focuses on mutually agreed upon goals for a forthcoming rating period and then the evaluation of accomplishment toward those goals. Five basic elements of the process include: the goal, present level of performance, desired level of performance, time frame for accomplishment, and method to achieve the objective. While the MBO process provides a thorough assessment of specific

performance, it often fails to look at all the job responsibilities assigned to an individual.

4. **Evaluate the employee.** Two philosophies exist in this step of the process. One says that employee evaluation should be an ongoing process and that a good supervisor would congratulate good performance when it occurs, and correct poor performance when it is noted. Such is the *One-Minute Manager* philosophy and one that every competent supervisor should take. But the second philosophy, which states that the supervisor and employee should sit down periodically and conduct a comprehensive review of job performance, needs to be seriously considered. We have a job description, we have established what we agree are standards of acceptable performance for those job description elements, and we have established a philosophy by which we measure those elements; it is now time to actually do that.

Remember, you are evaluating the *work* of the employee, not the employee. Unless character and demeanor are part of the normal job expectations and those expectations have been transmitted, then they are not part of job assessment. The periodicity of evaluation should fit the needs of the church or organization. In most instances an annual evaluation is all that will be required. In situations where there is a new employee, or when a supervisor is working to develop the skills of an under-performing employee, more frequent evaluation may occur.

5. **Discuss the evaluation.** It is useless to evaluate the performance of an employee without discussing the results of that evaluation with the person. Throughout the life cycle of the work environment, the administrator will conduct several types of evaluations of work:

- Daily analysis appraisal as part of the routine as supervisor.
- Clarification discussions to allow two-way dialogue for clearing up confusing or difficult elements of a task.
- Developmental interviews, often called on-the-job-training (OJT), that allow the supervisor to develop the skills and capability of the employee.
- Directive discussions, sometimes called a "chewing out," that targets inappropriate or poor performance and direct corrective or appropriate action on the part of the employee.

A performance discussion should be conducted in such a manner that there is a mutual understanding on the part of both the evaluator and the employee that the purpose of the evaluation is the enhancement and improvement of the work performance of the person. While some would suggest that this should be a formal time in the life of the employee, it is recommended that formality be reserved for those times when a more strict approach must be taken, such as corrective or disciplinary action. Begin by allowing the employee to state any self-evaluation of his job performance. The supervisor then presents his or her evaluation. Discussion ensues that will clarify any questions. And then a set of mutually agreed upon goals or actions will be established to ensure the performance of the employee continues or corrects itself if need be.

6. *Correct or reward performance.* It is recommended that meritorious pay, step increases, banquets, and what have you not be part of the direct outcome of the job performance evaluation. While these have a place in the development of the morale and a strategy to retain quality personnel, the rewards should be granted based on criteria that include numerous factors—with the annual job evaluation being only one part of the scheme. Many institutions will choose times like an annual recognition banquet, on the anniversary of the employee, or some other designated time that pays attention to excellence in performance.

Correcting poor or unsatisfactory performance occurs in three supervisory venues: (1) Providing feedback. The day-to-day dialogue that instructs and informs the employee of progress. (2) Providing training. It is the responsibility of the supervisor to arrange for or provide the necessary training for improvement. (3) Providing coaching. Coaching is the day-to-day dialogue that takes the form of providing needed assistance and allowing the employee to take the lead in the process of correction.

Before we move to the next topic that discusses developing personnel, it would be well to point out an important facet of an evaluation system that has not been discussed in this text: Create a paper trail in case you have to justify your personnel actions. Research by business organizations indicates that about 90 to 95 percent of all employees are at least competent and motivated to do their job. Only a handful of the employees will have to be dealt with about unsatisfactory performance. Not surprising, however, is the fact that a vast amount of time, money, and heartache will be spent in relating to those individuals. Evaluation schemes should always be conducted with the intent of recognizing appropriate behavior; but in the back of the mind of every administrator must be the recognition that you may be dealing with that 5 to 10 percent whom you might have to terminate in the future.

Employee Development

During the discussion above about the outcome of an evaluation system, we have already established the fact that development of personnel in the organization is the responsibility of the organization. The role of the administrator is to create the environment that will cause the individual to see the need for development and be motivated to want to improve and have a successful ministry. Large corporations have training programs that develop or create employees that meld to their philosophy. Churches and most nonprofit organizations do not have the luxury of such a long development time. When we employ a secretary, we expect that person to be able to do the job within a short period of orientation. The same is true for the ministerial staff. When we call a youth minister, we expect him to begin immediately to lead youth.

Churches and nonprofit organizations will have to view employment in a different way. Three actions are suggested: Employ only qualified persons, immediately correct unsatisfactory performance, and finally, remove persons who cannot meet the standards of performance expectations.

Everything this text has discussed up until this time has emphasized diligence to the employment process. If these tenets are followed, qualified, motivated, God-selected persons will fill your employment rolls. The bottom line is, don't hire a future problem employee.

The second action calls for the supervisor to deal redemptively with personnel who are not performing adequately. The evaluation process described above is an excellent way to identify marginal or unsatisfactory performance and then develop a means of correcting that failed performance. The keys to this action are (1) a mutual recognition of failed performance, (2) a mutually agreed-upon course of action that will correct the weakness, and (3) supervisory follow-up to ensure the correction is made.

The final action requiring discussion is one which most ministerial administrators do not relish—having to terminate a poor performer. It is the altruistic attitude of most religious leaders that there is good in everyone and that we should not be the judge to call a person a failure—let's give him another chance. Let's face it, if you are working at McDonald's and you keep failing to put the secret sauce on the Big Mac, or worse yet you tell the customers that Burger King makes a better burger, you are going to get fired. You have breached the terms of your contract for employment. You were supposed to make Big Macs like management said, and you were supposed to have allegiance to the company.

Every once in a while an employee of the church will have to be terminated. Since it is something we do not want to do, a methodology needs to be established so we do not have to fire them; they should fire themselves. This methodology can be linked to the redemptive attitude we established in the second action. Here is how it might go:

1. During an annual evaluation you note the financial secretary has made several errors that were noted on the annual audit. You discuss this with her and you set goals for the next audit not to have errors.

2. During the next audit, errors have occurred again. In a developmental interview you discuss the secretary's failures again and then make arrangements for the person to attend a weeklong training program by the church management software provider.

3. At the next evaluation period, you note that errors are still occurring and that it is now time to take directive action. You issue a letter of warning which states that absolute accuracy is the expected norm. You ask the person to outline what she will do to ensure that accuracy is achieved.

4. Upon the occasion of the next error, you engage in a directive discussion in which you place several things the incumbent must accomplish to ensure accuracy. This discussion is reported in a final letter of reprimand, and the person is cautioned that if the necessary actions that lead to accurate records are not taken, then termination could be a consideration.

5. The next time the employee fails to make accuracy part of the normative procedures for the financial records, you send her home on suspension with the proviso, "You think about whether you want to continue working in this job that demands accurate records. If you come back in two days, you are stating that all records will be accurate."

The administrator has taken actions to correct deficient performance that first included the individual but later became directive in nature. When the individual continues to have inaccuracies in the financial records, then the final warning of termination is executed. The financial secretary cannot say, "You didn't tell me you were unhappy with my poor records," nor could she say, "You didn't do anything to help me meet your expectations." She has fired herself. Note, however, the redemptive intent as well as the paper trail that may lead to the final termination action.

RULE VIOLATION	OCCURRENCE OCCASION				
	1ST	2ND	3RD	4TH	5TH
ASSAULT	TERMINATION				
MOLESTATION	TERMINATION				
INSUBORDINATION	UNPAID SUSPENSION	TERMINATION			
DRUG ABUSE	UNPAID SUSPENSION	TERMINATION			
SEXUAL HARASSMENT	UNPAID SUSPENSION	TERMINATION			
UNCHRISTIAN LANGUAGE	PAID SUSPENSION	UNPAID SUSPENSION	TERMINATION		
UNCHRISTIAN BEHAVIOR	PAID SUSPENSION	UNPAID SUSPENSION	TERMINATION		
SAFETY VIOLATION	WRITTEN WARNING	WRITTEN REPRIMAND	UNPAID SUSPENSION	TERMINATION	
EXCESSIVE ABSENTEES	WRITTEN WARNING	WRITTEN REPRIMAND	UNPAID SUSPENSION	TERMINATION	
MARGINAL WORK	VERBAL WARNING	WRITTEN WARNING	WRITTEN REPRIMAND	UNPAID SUSPENSION	TERMINATION

Because of the many problems that could occur because of termination, many employers will establish a format for disciplinary action. A simple example might look like this:

Charts like this are useful to demonstrate that the church or organization is redemptive in the context of disciplinary actions. The problem with such schemes is that courts and employment administrators have deemed them as legal processes and must be followed. An appropriate statement in the church or organization's policy statement might be to allow steps to the process to become accelerated whenever multiple disciplinary events occur. For instance, the church administrator comes in drunk and curses out the pastor—you go straight to termination. Otherwise, the church would have to follow the course of action for correction it has established for the problem.

If and when the time comes for termination, a formal process must be established. This process should include these concepts:

Questions the church and/or recommending staff/committee should ask before the process begins include:

1. Does the person *need* to be terminated?
   - Is this person's ineffectiveness, poor example, or poor leadership actually blocking the progress of the ministry? What actual harm is being done?
   - What if the position goes vacant for a while? Is that worse than the current affairs?
   - What standards are being used to measure job performance? Are they fair?
2. Who else believes the person needs to be replaced?
3. What will be the basis for dismissal?
   - Relational
   - Moral
   - Theological
   - Inability/performance
4. Should a second (or third or more) chance be given?
5. What is God through the Holy Spirit directing the church to do?

Once the decision to terminate an individual has been made—including any approval process—a face-to-face termination interview should be held between the responsible hiring/firing leader and the person involved. This is a formal procedure. It should be held in the presence of the final employment authority in the church—personnel committee, church administrator, or pastor. It should be held in an office setting and have witnesses. If the church has retained legal counsel, that person should be present. Considerations of a termination interview should include:

1. Establish the proper environment.
   - This should be in a formal setting.
   - Put the person at ease if possible.
   - Show no malice, anger, or bitterness.
   - Make the interview personal even if others are present.
2. State the facts that lead to termination.
   - Be consistent, consecutive, and comprehensive.
   - Relate failure to mutually agreed upon goals.

- Have documentation available and ready for review.

3. Be discriminating and considerate.

- Show Christian concern.
- But do not allow the person to talk you into an extension or change of decision.

4. Explain terms of termination.

- Discuss separation benefits if any. You may be legally responsible for payment of any unused vacation or sick leave and also in some instances obligated for continued medical or other benefits.
- Relate the church's position for reemployment assistance. State whether your church will provide reference to any future employer.
- Discuss the logistics in/during transition.
- Make a record of all transactions, agreements, and terms for termination. This record becomes part of the permanent personnel file of the individual. A copy is also placed in the permanent historical record of the church or organization.

5. Close off responsibilities quickly.

It is recommended that termination for cause will require the individual to leave the premises immediately upon removing his personal effects. You must be sensitive to the fact that the former employee will need to have time to close off relations and move on. However "pity parties" and "lame-duck" periods are not useful or healthy for the church or organization.

Often the employee, when faced with the prospect of forced termination, will state that he wants to resign. The church or organization must realize that this may be a legal possibility, especially if the personnel manual allows an individual to resign. There are advantages and disadvantages to both the individual and church in this situation. For the church, some legal responsibilities with regard to pay and continued benefits are removed as well as having to deal with the future questions of reference to another potential employer. For the individual the stigma of being fired is removed. But the individual may give up certain unemployment benefits and rights.

Whether the individual is terminated for cause or resigns his or her position by choice, the church or organization must keep accurate records of all actions and transactions related to the cessation of employment.

Chapter Review

Personnel administration in the church or nonprofit organization is a critical area that requires the administrator to be a knowledgeable and skillful manager of the human resources of the institution. In the past personnel administration was considered the domain of the church or organization and generally was left alone by outside influences. Not so in this modern age. Not only are the parishioners more aware of the criteria by which employees are brought into the organization, but their interest is joined by outside influences such as state and federal employment agencies that require the church or non-profit to abide by employment criteria. Effective personnel administration will require the individual to:

- Define the criteria by which policies and procedures are created that outline effective personnel administration.
- Describe a process for legally and efficiently employing an individual.
- Describe a process for integrating a new employee into the church or organizational structure.
- Define the elements of a salary plan and develop a scheme for fairly and legally providing for the fiscal and fringe benefit needs of the employee.
- Outline a process for evaluating an individual's performance and describe the steps to be taken to ensure that expected performance is provided.

Administering
Financial Resources

CHAPTER
6

*Bring the full 10 percent into the storehouse
so that there may be food in My house.*
MALACHI 3:10

What is the tithe? And where did it come to mean a tenth? Vine's *Dictionary of Old and New Testament Words* states that the word *tithe* comes from the root *dekatos,* which means a tenth.[1] So when one pays a tithe, one is paying a tenth. But where did that come from? In Genesis 14 we find Abram the Hebrew saving his nephew Lot from a group of marauding kings. After defeating his enemies and recovering Lot and all his possessions, he returned through Salem. Picking up the story in verses 18–20: "Then Melchizedek, king of Salem, brought out bread and wine; he was a priest to God Most High. He blessed him and said: 'Abram is blessed by God Most High, Creator of heaven and earth, and give praise to God Most High who has handed over your enemies to you.' And Abram gave him a tenth of everything."

For centuries the Hebrew culture functioned within the philosophy of religious obedience to God of offering sacrifices to him and bringing the tithes and offerings into the storehouse. It was an act not only of obedience, but in the passage of Scripture cited above from Malachi, failure to do so was an act of robbery against God. By the time of Jesus, the vast Hebrew temple system had levied a temple tax. Remember the incident recorded in Matthew 17:24–27:

> When they came to Capernaum, those who collected the double-drachma tax approached Peter and said, "Doesn't your Teacher pay the double-drachma tax?" "Yes" he said. When he went into the house, Jesus spoke to him first, "What do you think Simon? Who do earthly kings collect tariffs or taxes from? From their sons or from strangers?" "From strangers," he said. "Then the sons are free," Jesus told him. "But, so we won't offend them, go to the sea, cast in a fishhook, and catch the first fish that comes up. When you open its mouth you'll find a coin. Take it and give it to them for Me and you."

At that time, the double-drachma could purchase two sheep. The temple tax Peter paid for him and Jesus was that half-shekel which was called for in Exodus 30:11–16 for all Jewish men to support the temple.

Developing a Theology for Financial Management in the Church

Luke records another incident in chapter 20 where Jesus was challenged by some religious leaders about taxation. The story begins in verse 20:

> They watched closely and sent spies who pretended to be righteous, so they could catch Him in what He said, to hand Him over to the governor's rule and authority. They questioned Him, "Teacher, we know that You speak and teach correctly, and You don't show partiality, but teach the way of God. Is it lawful for us to pay taxes to Caesar or not?" But detecting their craftiness, He said to them, "Show me a denarius. Whose image and inscription does it have?" "Caesar's," they said. "Well then," He told them, "give back to Caesar the things that are Caesar's and to God the things that are God's" (Luke 20:20–25).

In Jesus' day there were two coinage systems in Jerusalem. One was the Roman coin that was the official monetary system of commerce. In other words, if you wanted to buy a loaf of bread or a jug of oil, then you used the Roman *denarius*—a coin that represented about a day's wage for an ordinary labor of that era. This coin is frequently translated by the KJV as a "penny." It was a silver coin that was slightly smaller than our nickel. The denarius, like most Roman coins of the era, had an image of the current emperor of the Roman Empire on it.

A second coin that is often mentioned in Scripture is the Hebrew coin, the shekel. Both coins were familiar to the Jewish community. The coins differed in appearance and use. The shekel was used for temple functions. The Jewish worshipper bought sacrifices from the temple vendors and paid the temple tax with this silver coin. The shekel bore no image or likeness of God on it, only Hebrew inscriptions, since the Torah forbid "graven images." Remember when Jesus cleared the temple of the "money changers"? (see Matt. 21:12). It was this conversion of Roman coinage to temple coinage that Jesus railed against. Apparently the money changers were making a profit on the operation. The Hebrew of Jerusalem would conduct business in the marketplace and pay taxes to the government with the official coin of the realm, the silver *denarius,* thus rendering to Caesar. He would conduct temple business with the coin recognized by the religious community, the temple shekel, thus rendering to God.

In Romans 13:1 Paul discusses the Christian's responsibilities to governing authorities: "Everyone must submit to the governing authorities, for there is no authority except from God, and those that exist are instituted by God. So then, the one who resists the authority is opposing God's command, and those who oppose it will bring judgment on themselves." Then in verse 6 he concludes the admonition about civic responsibility by stating, "And for this reason you pay taxes, since the authorities are God's public servants, continually attending to these tasks. Pay your obligations to everyone: taxes to those you owe taxes, tolls to those you owe tolls, respect to those you owe respect, and honor to those you owe honor."

Fiscal responsibility in nonprofit and church organizations has made news in recent years. From the financial clerk who embezzled hundreds of thousands of dollars to "give to the needy" to the national denominational president who purchased elaborate houses for himself and his female aide, media takes every opportunity to attack or embarrass Christian organizations which do not live up to the standards of Scripture. In this day and age when every church has a target drawn on it, the arrow of fiscal irresponsibility is a very easy one to shoot and hit the mark.

There are three important reasons for the church or religious nonprofit organization to develop a philosophy of financial operations that are to be conducted professionally and in good order:

1. *It is a Christian principal.* Jesus speaks often of the faithful steward, and stewardship of ministry is addressed frequently in the New Testament. From the folly of placing too much reliance on material things to the stewardship expected of the worker, Jesus made clear that we are to be responsible in the resources—spiritual and practical—that we have been given. The New Testament teaches that Christians should always conduct themselves in prudent and resourceful ways.

2. *The people of the church expect it.* More church problems have come about through poor money management techniques than any other administrative difficulty. Not that individuals were dishonest; they just did not exercise good accountability principles. Some common errors include:

- Poor accounting principles
- Double obligations
- Failure to have two individuals involved
- Failure to make reports to the church

Below is an excerpt of a memorandum from a pastor to his staff:

MEMO TO STAFF AND ALL PERSONNEL

Wednesday night, December 14, I was put in a very awkward position—that of trying to justify several things in the realm of our finances, two of which were overexpenditures in our budget and the lack of financial accountability.

A great deal of this has been my fault for a lack of strict accountability and ardent attention to all our budget areas. I do not want us to be put in this position again.

The following financial guidelines will be put into effect January 1. There will be no exceptions.

1. Quarterly financial statements will be printed and presented to the church by the third Sunday following the close of the quarter.

2. Every staff member will work within the confines of the budget. Any deviations from allocations must be approved first by the pastor and then the finance committee.

3. A purchase order system will be instituted. All staff and program personnel must operate in this system. No payments of any kind will be made that do not have a preapproved purchase order. This includes check requests.

4. The finance committee will be responsible for maintaining accountability and balance. They will meet at least monthly on the Wednesday following the first Sunday. Monthly financial statements will be prepared and presented to the committee by the administrator.

5. The new budget will be prepared and adopted by November 1 of each calendar year. The fiscal year will be the same as the calendar year.

6. The finance committee will be elected in December and commence functioning January 1 of each year.

Our proposed budget for this year is the most challenging in our church history. Any expenditures, even though they may be budgeted, must be scrutinized for viability and contribution to the mission of the church. As our church grows and the staff increases, greater accountability will be required, and we will have it!

Interestingly, this church did not have someone stealing from them; they had just gone $35,000 in the hole because of poor money management principles. Fortunately, today's modern computerized church management systems will often detect problems in fund allocation and obligation and draw to the attention of administrators poor or improper fiscal management.

3. *Poor money management can be a violation of federal, state, or local law.* The church and nonprofit organization has certain obligations for personnel financial records with regard to federal tax and Social Security laws as well as an obligation to handle properly charitable contributions to the organizations. Many states now require church and nonprofit organizations to submit annual financial statements that detail receipts and disbursements for the year. Both

federal and state laws require the disclosure of property and noncash assets. And more and more, local governments are requiring not-for-profit, tax-exempt organizations to disclose not only value but organizational use of funds that would prove the charitable or religious nature of the organization.

Financial management requires attention by administrators to three key elements:

1. Organization
   - Organization provides for policies and procedures that ensure fiscal operations are carried out appropriately and efficiently.
   - Organization identifies individuals who will be responsible for the proper administration of the fiscal resources of the institution.
   - Financial management systems must be organized in such a way that recording is easy and retrieving information is quick.
   - Financial systems must be organized to facilitate reporting requirements.
   - Organization will also allow nonfamiliar personnel to use the system with greater ease.
2. Simplicity
   - Financial policies and procedures should not be so excessively complex as to confound the individuals who must work with them. The system must be understandable and useful.
   - Simple systems will prevent excessive time requirements on the personnel who must maintain them.
   - Systems that are established with clear, consistent guidelines for operation have a tendency to have less opportunity for error or fault.
3. Accuracy
   - Accurate financial records free ministry staff to concentrate on ministry, preaching, etc.
   - Accuracy also allows leaders to effectively carry out the programs of the church by knowing when budget/funding limitations occur.
   - Accuracy also allows the leadership of the church to pinpoint excessive spending, deficits, and to prepare for large expenditures, and set contingencies for lean months.
   - Accurate records and accounting develop a strong sense of confidence on the part of the congregation or supporter.

Organizing for Fiscal Management—the Finance Manual

With literally hundreds of thousands of churches and religious nonprofits conducting fiscal operations each week, it is essential that an established set of guidelines be provided to ensure legal, safe, and responsible management.

These churches and organizations range from a small community church whose offering barely meets its needs to the complex megachurch whose weekly offerings total multiple thousands. It is apparent that fiscal operations will vary depending on size and structure. However, for purposes of this text, it will be easier to describe an idealized administrative system for a large organization. With this broad process established, then facets of this fiscal organization can be adapted and adopted by the local church or organization to fit its needs. This organizational concept we will term the finance manual. Most manuals will have at least four sections: personnel, budget/stewardship, policies and procedures relating to fund management, and special fiscal operations.

Overview of Leadership Activities Relating to Fiscal Operations

It will be the responsibility of the leaders of the church or organization to develop policies and procedures that will ensure legal, secure, and manageable handling of the fiscal resources of the church. Certain basic actions must be included to develop a strong fiscal management philosophy. These actions will translate into comprehensive policies and then detailed procedures to implement those policies.

General management philosophy considerations:

- Develop a stewardship program for the church.
- Conduct reviews of giving and spending as well as projections for giving.
- Create a budget that will adequately provide for the church ministry programs and activities.
- Coordinate budget requirements with committees and other budget units of the church.
- Ensure that gifts and funds are properly receipted and accounted for.
- Monitor spending against budget.
- Conduct periodic audits of resources and independent annual reviews of records and procedures.
- Write and promulgate policy and procedures for efficient fiscal operations.
- Ensure compliance with federal, state, and local laws relating to fiscal operations.
- Report to the church and leaders the status of funds and accounts.

Through the years many authors have suggested contents of fiscal manuals. In this text we will discuss some, but not all, of the suggestions by the National Association of Church Business Administration:[2]

- Budget processes—development, approval, modification, etc.
- Receipt of funds and gifts
- Counting money
- Depositing money

- Recording contributions
- Accounting processes
- Purchase processes
- Disbursement processes
- Reporting fiscal status
- Special offerings—mission, love, benevolence, etc.
- Receiving stocks, bonds, securities, property
- Fund-raising events
- Designated gifts
- Benevolence operations
- Investing church funds
- Payment priority
- Excess funds
- Petty cash funds
- Bonding and security of personnel
- Security of records and accounts/funds
- Charge and credit cards
- Government fiscal responsibilities
- Tax and Social Security issues
- Personnel and financial records
- Salary and expense line items
- Recording gifts and time of volunteers

Fiscal Personnel

Not every church or nonprofit organization will need every one of the fiscal managers listed below, but all must have the function accomplished by someone.

1. *Church Business Administrator.* Every church will have a church business administrator—the pastor, maybe the minister of education, a formal church administrator. In some churches the role of the CBA is carried out by a deacon, group of deacons, elders, or some other designated group or individual. In some cases the church treasurer is the church financial officer. To this individual falls the responsibility of ensuring the policies and procedures, the functions of budget administration, and competent fund management are carried out. To this individual the integrity of the church is entrusted. He is accountant and paymaster. He produces reports to the corporate church as well as maintains for the individual church members a record of fiscal transactions.

2. *Committees.* Most churches will manage their financial operations through church-appointed or church-elected committees. Though most churches will function with only one finance committee, depending upon the size of the church, other committees may be appointed:

- Stewardship or planning. Addresses broad aspects of church finances and obligations.
- Giving or pledge. Charged with raising the money for the budget.
- Budget. In coordination with the budget units of the church, composes the annual budget.
- Audit. Ensures the security of fiscal operations conforms to policy.
- Building program. A special committee for managing a building project.

Committees should be formulated with a committee charter as discussed in chapter 4. Below is an example charter for a finance committee.

FINANCE COMMITTEE

CONSTITUTION. The finance committee functions as the administrative managers of all church-related finance operations. The finance committee is a standing committee responsible for coordinating the preparation, submission, and administering the annual church budget. To carry out the administrative functions of providing support to the professional staff, the finance committee will ensure adequate salary and benefits are provided.

MEMBERSHIP. Two of the positions of the finance committee will be assigned by title: the senior minister and church business administrator. Five to seven other members at large will be nominated by the committee on committees and elected by the church. One-third of the at-large members will be replaced annually. At-large committee members may serve only two successive three-year terms. The finance committee will elect a chairman, vice chairman, and recording secretary. The church business administrator will serve as professional staff liaison. Neither the pastor nor church business administrator will have voting privileges with regard to salary or benefit issues that directly relate to themselves.

RESPONSIBILITIES

1. Coordinate the submission of program needs and prepare the annual church budget.
2. Establish and maintain appropriate fiscal policies and procedures to ensure:
   a. Proper receipt and disbursement of all funds.
   b. Adequate accounting of special funds and monies.
   c. Adequate controls for the use of purchase orders.
   d. Balanced and appropriate expenditures of funds for each program organization.
   e. Internal controls for impress, change, and cash funds and for the sales of items and material by the church.
   f. Annual and periodic audits and examinations.
   g. Monthly, quarterly, and annual fiscal reports.

4. Coordinate fiscal and personnel activities with other program organizations and standing and temporary committees.
5. Provide input to the personnel committee in matters of the salary plan of the church.
6. Assist in the coordination of the insurance requirements of the church.
7. Establish subcommittees as needed for the effective and efficient management of the church's fiscal resources.
8. Nominate to the church a church treasurer to coordinate monetary procedures.

REPORTS. The finance committee will provide a monthly report of all receipts and disbursements in the format of the church budget. Quarterly, the finance committee will provide a formal report of all fiscal activities. The finance committee will cause an audit to be taken annually. The report of the audit will comprise a portion of the annual church report by the committee. An annual accounting of all fiscal operations and fund accounts will be made at the time of the annual church report.

3. *Budget Unit Managers.* Budget units are defined as those elements of the church which have been given authority to request expenditure of funds from the church budget. Moreover, they are also charged with assisting in the development of the annual budget by providing information to the budget committee with regard to needs and planned expenditures. Budget units may be staff personnel, program leaders, ministry team leaders, committee chair, or other designated individuals.

4. *Purchasing Authority/Agent.* The church purchasing agent is that (those) individual(s) who has been given authority to authorize the obligation of funds for the purchase of requests from budget units. The fewer number of purchasing agents the church or organization will have the better; however, do not restrict authorization so severely as to inhibit the function of the church.

5. *Church Treasurer.* An individual identified by the church that has the responsibility for the safe and efficient management of the church funds and accounts. The treasurer is usually the individual assigned formal money management of the church or organization. The treasurer should *never* be the purchasing agent for the church. Most states will require the designation of a treasurer in the incorporation documents and will be the individual who formally responds to money management queries by authorities.

6. *Financial Secretary or Clerk.* An employee of the church or organization who is responsible for recording receipts and disbursements of all financial transactions approved by the church and its leaders and other clerical operations that relate to fiscal operations. The church financial secretary should

never hold simultaneous positions of responsibility as a budget unit, purchasing agent, or check signer.

Job descriptions should be written for each of the above positions and any other positions that the church or organization creates for effective fiscal administration. In chapter 4 we introduced a format for job descriptions. Let's look at an example job description for two of the above positions:

CHURCH BUSINESS ADMINISTRATOR

PRINCIPAL FUNCTION. Responsible to the senior pastor for the business and administrative affairs of the church. Provides leadership and supervision to support staff personnel. Provides administrative and physical support to staff and program directors.

QUALIFICATIONS. The church business administrator must have adequate education or equivalent training to manage business and fiscal affairs, supervise personnel, direct facility maintenance activities, and supervise food service operations. Familiarity with typical Christian church program activities would be a sought-for attribute.

REQUIREMENTS OF THE POSITION.

1. Assist the senior minister in administering all facets of the operation of the church.
2. Lead the church in planning, conducting, and evaluating a comprehensive plan of business operations for the church.
3. Give direction to the weekday operation of the church office; supervise secretarial and clerical workers assigned to this function.
4. Provide administrative support for all personnel activities; administer church salary plan.
5. Direct the maintenance program of the church; work with the church properties committee to establish and direct a maintenance and housekeeping schedule.
6. Act as safety and security officer of the church; periodically review insurance requirements; inspect the church to ensure a safe and secure habitat.
7. Maintain an inventory of all church property; annually verify presence and condition; establish a schedule of replacement, upgrade, or addition of plant-account equipment.
8. Act as transportation officer for the church; plan for and coordinate transportation requirements for program activities; maintain transportation assets; make recommendations for major repair or replacements.
9. Direct the food service program of the church; supervise the hostess and food service personnel.

10. Work with professional ministry staff, program leaders, and other church activity leaders to assign classroom or church facility space and equipment for regular and special needs.
11. Coordinate the preparation of the annual budget; establish a financial records systems for the church and direct its operation; direct the receipt and expenditure of all church funds; act as purchasing agent for the church.
12. Coordinate all general church publicity, literature distribution, and media production.
13. Coordinate and provide administrative leadership to assigned committees and program and ministry organizations.
14. Perform other duties as assigned by the senior minister.

FINANCIAL SECRETARY

PRINCIPAL FUNCTION. Responsible to the church business administrator for maintaining the church financial records, for receipt and disbursement of church funds, and for preparing periodical financial reports.

QUALIFICATIONS. Demonstrate competent secretarial skills. Computer literate. Demonstrate familiarity with general ledger and bookkeeping procedures either through formal training or equivalent experience. Must be able to be bonded; a certified notary of the state.

REQUIREMENTS OF THE POSITION.
1. Receive, count, and deposit all church offerings according to church policy.
2. Post receipts and disbursements of all accounts according to church financial procedures.
3. Post offerings weekly to individual accounts; file envelopes.
4. Prepare bank reconciliation statements monthly.
5. Prepare monthly, quarterly, and annual budget financial reports for the administrative committee.
6. Receive and answer queries about financial matters from authorized staff and committee personnel; maintain a file of invoices, correspondence, and reports.
7. Check and total all invoices when approved; inform responsible persons of their budget status.
8. Prepare and issue checks in accordance with church policy.
9. Check and compute weekly time cards of hourly paid workers; issue checks; issue checks to salaried full-time and part-time employees according to church policy.

The introduction of this chapter has spelled out the strong biblical admonition for competence in fiscal and stewardship matters. The selection of personnel to fill these roles should be carried out with equal concern and spiritual direction. The instructions to Timothy by Paul about leaders in 1 Timothy 3 indicate that individuals who are self-controlled, sensible, respectable, not greedy, managers of their household, persons with a good reputation in their community, faithful and tested in their faith are those who are to be placed in leadership positions. I tell my students that Judas was the first church administrator, and he hanged himself because of a financial indiscretion. It is hard to be in charge of the resources, even if you are an apostle! Managing fiscal resources requires vigilance, competence, and trustworthiness.

What are some considerations in selecting these persons? First, the individual should have a strong sense of spiritual direction. Second, the individual should be someone who is known by the congregation. Third, regardless of how well known, all persons who handle the disbursement of money should have both background and credit checks. Fourth, the individuals who have access to the funds and resources should be bondable as defined by the church or organization's insurance agency. And finally, do not allow familial relationships (husband-wife, brothers, etc.) to exist where one verifies what the other does.

Budget Operations

We began this chapter by considering the words of the prophet in Malachi 3. Let's continue our Scripture review by looking at verses 7–10:

"Since the days of your fathers, you have turned from My statutes; you have not kept them. Return to Me and I will return to you," says the LORD of Hosts.

But you ask: "How can we return?" "Will a man rob God? Yet you are robbing Me!" You ask: "How do we rob You?" "By not making the payments of 10 percent and the contributions. You are suffering under a curse, yet you—the whole nation—are still robbing Me. Bring the full 10 percent into the storehouse so that there may be food in My house. Test Me in this way," says the LORD of Hosts. "See if I will not open the floodgates of heaven and pour out a blessing for you without measure."

Note the promise of Jesus in Luke 6:38: "Give, and it will be given to you; a good measure—pressed down, shaken together, and running over—will be poured into your lap. For with the measure you use, it will be measured back to you." Jesus was not advocating a prosperity theology but reminding us that the rewards of our stewardship are measured in terms of the liberality of our gifts.

When we discussed the administrative function of planning, the administrative activity of budget was listed last of the seven elements that made up the process of planning. I explained that this is the rightful place for budgeting. If planners seek the mind of God in establishing their objectives and the parameters which they will follow to achieve those objectives—including the personnel resources the Spirit has empowered to accomplish the goals—money will not be a problem. God will empower that which he wants done in the church or religious organization.

Almost every entity operates within some boundary—a budget of resources. Several years ago when I went through survival school as a military officer, we were taught that once we had secured our safety, one of the first things we should do was to inventory our resources—find out what we had to work with. Once we did that, we were to allocate those resources in such a manner that the worst case scenario would be met. Poorly used or squandered resources could be life-threatening. We had to budget what we had in order to survive.

In many respects today churches and nonprofit organizations are having to seriously consider their allocations. Many demographers state that the altruistic individual is going away with the death of the survivor generation (those alive in the 1930–1950 era). Other demographers state that the society in which we live is the most affluent in the history of this nation and will be willing to give to "worthy" causes. My mother, who is in her nineties, religiously places her tithe in the offering plate every Sunday. My wife and I tithe on a monthly basis. When I served as a church administrator, I noted that the last week of December was the largest giving month of the year. I discovered that most baby boomers and baby busters would wait until the end of the year to assess their total annual income and then write one big check for their gift to the church to ensure their tax break that year.

What is the bottom line of these stories? Several admonitions can be offered:

- Budget does not begin the planning process; it culminates it.
- Plans should support the mission—the objectives and goals of the church.
- Budgets should be created to support the Holy Spirit-directed objectives and goals.
- Wise administrators carefully evaluate their resource pool.
- Budget schemes must take into account different types and forms of giving on the part of the church member/program supporter.

Traditionally, churches have created their budgets using one of two commonly accepted business systems:

Zero-Based Budget. The zero-based budget is similar to the philosophy of the executive branch of our government. That is, all budget allocations begin at zero each budget year. Funds budgeted and not used are recouped and/or lost. New budget submissions, even if they represent ongoing expenditure needs, must be justified with adequate documentation. An advantage of a zero-based budget system is that it forces the budget units to review annually their resource needs. Questions related to whether the need still exists, whether funding has been adequate in the past or have the requirement levels increased, and what additional budget requirements will need to be considered are made during the budget development process. Weak programs are either strengthened after review or eliminated. A significant disadvantage of this type of budget system is that to create such a budget takes a great amount of time and personnel resources.

Line-Item Budget. The line-item budget can be compared to that used by the legislative branch of our federal government. In this format, items are sustained year-after-year once the appropriation is initially justified. A significant advantage to this budget system is that once an expenditure is justified, only minor modifications need to be made through the years. This advantage is also a weakness of the system. Once a program has been established, review and evaluation tends to cease. Dead or dying programs are often sustained when the funds could be better used in other ministries.

Administrators of line-item budgets also have a tendency to treat the budget as a whole and fluctuations to one element must be applied to all. Therefore, if budget receipts fall behind by 10 percent, then generally all programs and budget items are reduced by 10 percent. While this proportional mind-set exists in both these types of budgets, one can readily see that the lack of critical evaluation, the possibility of mid-budget modifications, and the danger of underfunding a significant ministry through generalized reductions in allocation are all possible.

Ministry Action Budget. To solve the problems that line-item budgets bring with odious work in preparation, and the problem of underfunding a critical ministry through a line-item reduction, many churches have adopted a system of budgeting called the ministry action budget. This system of budgeting is taught in seminaries and training centers nationwide. The ministry action budget (sometimes referred to as a *mission* action budget in SBC denominational literature) takes advantage of the good features of the two traditional systems (zero-based and line-item) while at the same time reducing or eliminating their unfavorable attributes. It is similar to the zero-based budget in that it requires each budget unit to evaluate their program or ministry expenditure each year and either sustain, modify, or eliminate the activity. Like the line-item budget, the ministry action budget allows some consistent, recurring budget items to be brought forward into the new budget year without significant review. Thus, items such as debt, utilities, salary, and insurance are carried forward as required portions of the budget with little or no modification each year.

The activity that makes the ministry action budget ministry-based is the step that calls for leadership to establish a priority for expenditures for each item in the budget. This priority statement is derived from the principal mission or missions of the church or organization. Thus, this priority is a statement of the importance of the budget item in carrying out the mission of the church. It is a determination made by the congregation of what is the most important programs, ministries, activities, etc. The significant advantage of ministry action budgeting is that priority ministries—those deemed most significant—are fully funded to ensure success. Thus, when adjustments are required for budget shortfalls, items of lesser priority are reduced or eliminated and the critical, ministry items are sustained. Additionally, when budget surpluses are achieved, lesser important budget submission items that may have been intentionally underfunded or even eliminated can be reevaluated and funded.

The process for developing a budget varies from church to church and organization to organization. Generally a historical review of funding needs is made. From this basic audit, elements of the church submit anticipated requirements. Then the "number crunchers" attack this submission and arbitrarily pick and choose—at least to the budget requestor it seems that the decisions are capricious and arbitrary—what areas will be funded and at what level.

The ministry action budget calls for a different scheme:
- Leadership reviews the mission and purpose of the church. Long-term objectives and short-term goals to meet these objectives are reviewed to see if the church is accomplishing what is envisioned.
- Programs and ministries are reviewed to assess their contribution to meeting the objectives of the church (mission). Goals are evaluated and either redefined, carried forward, or eliminated. During this step new program goals are also created.
- Program and ministry leaders evaluate resource requirements to meet the goals that have been established for the coming budget year. While this evaluation will consider all elements of resources—personnel, physical as well as fiscal—for purposes of the budget preparation only the fiscal cost of the items will be addressed.
- Program and ministry leaders then prioritize items in the funding request—what is critical, necessary, or what could be dropped.
- A budget formation group consolidates requests and develops a preliminary budget.
- The preliminary budget is reviewed by the budget units. A sequential scheme for priority is established for the entire budget.
- The budget is submitted to the church for approval.

Let's return to the bullet that speaks of the budget unit program and ministry leader prioritizing their requests. This is an important step for two reasons: (1) This is where the budget unit administrator communicates the importance of each budget request item to the group that will develop the final churchwide budget, and (2) this step is also important because it causes the program or ministry administrator to evaluate what they do and then establish a contingency plan in the event items of lesser priority are eliminated or receive reduced funding.

Budget prioritization may take on whatever form the church or organization wishes; however, three basic blocks of budget request items exist:

1. *Ongoing budget items that will require funding regardless.* These usually include items such as loan payments, utility bills, personnel tax payments, and salary and benefits. Since these items are "gotta-pay" items, they are usually not assigned a sequential priority item by the organization-wide budget development group.

2. *Ministry actions that describe the resource needs for the various programs and ministries of the church or organization.* These items are assigned a priority number. Some churches will sequentially list all the budget items; others will form groups of priorities. In general, the scheme might look like:

- Numbers 1–20. High priority items that are critical for the program to exist.
- Numbers 21–40. High priority items that are very important for the ministry or program to continue in its present form.
- Numbers 41–60. Items that are important but could be modified in one form or the other.
- Numbers 61–80. Items that are desirable and would enhance the program if provided.

3. *Ministry budget challenge items.* These are items that appear in the budget on an as-funds-are-available status. They represent two types of funds: (1) Ministry action items that did not make the final budget bottom-line cut, but because the budget unit submitted them, are listed to be funded if budget receipts exceed expectations. (2) Contingency or accumulating funds. For example, the church may have a contingency fund for major repairs. Their desire is to place at least $5,000 per year in the pool of money if it becomes available. And they want the money that has been placed in the account to remain until the contingency calls for its use.

A word now about the challenge item budget requests. In a few paragraphs we will discuss types of funds, and I will make a case for not having "designated" funds—funds in which the giver specifies how the money or gift is to be used. By having challenge items in the budget, if an individual wants to provide a serendipity gift above his tithe, then the administrator could direct him to a challenge item he could direct his gift toward while at the same time meeting a need that the leadership of the church has identified.

Church Fiscal Operations

Several verses in Luke 12 follow Jesus' teaching about money and possessions in verses 22–33 and about his second coming in verses 35–40. Beginning with verse 42, he speaks to the adroitness of a manager: "The Lord said; 'Who then is the faithful and sensible manager his master will put in charge of his household servants to give them their allotted food at the proper time? That slave whose master finds him working when he comes will be rewarded. I tell you the truth: he will put him in charge of all his possessions.'" The passage continues with Jesus describing the punishment of a slave who squanders the responsibility of the master. Jesus ends this teaching with an interesting admonition in verse 48: "Much will be required of everyone who has been given much. And even more will be expected of the one who has been entrusted with more."

The Greek word for *servant* used in this passage is *oikonomos*. In Vine's *Complete Expository Dictionary* he defines this as one who manages for another, usually in the context of a household or estate.[3] While all of God's children are stewards of the manifold riches of the Lord, certain leaders have been entrusted with the earthly riches of the church. We are expected to be good stewards of this responsibility. Certain operations are critical for effective fiscal management and administration in the local church.

Types of Fund Accounts. In most churches fund accounts exist in two formats: (1) a general fund for basic operations of the church, and (2) special designated funds for specified expenditure requirements. When one speaks of fund accounting, this entails the posting of authorized funds to the account, obligations (expenditures) against that account, and the management of fund utilization until the end product is received.

1. *Designated funds* are those funds that are either collected for a specific church-authorized activity or designated by a donor to an authorized special giving account.

- Examples of church-designated accounts are building funds, scholarships, love offerings.
- Examples of individual designated accounts are mission, benevolence, and special focus purchases of a church-approved need (carpet, roof, etc.).
- Designated funds require special handling. By federal law, the fund must be used as the giver designates. Depending upon the value and type of gift, there will also be special reporting requirements for designated gifts. By federal and most state laws, the funds must be separated from general fund accounts. The church is given the latitude of a general bank account, but within that account must be separate fund accounting for each fund at the bank level. Generally, these funds are

set up with either a separate checking account number or as a savings account to take advantage of potential interest earned.

Let me tell you two stories about designated funds. One is about a church that has thousands of dollars in the bank, has replaced carpet, organs, grand pianos, etc. The church also barely pays its bills and salaries. People through the years have specified how the church could spend their gifts, and often these gifts have languished in the bank.

The other story is about a church that also had thousands of dollars in the bank in designated accounts, but its administrator—me—helped the church to understand that the biblical model was for the leaders to determine needs and the congregation's role was to bring the tithes and offerings into the storehouse. So how did we legally move the money from a designated account?

I had good advice; the IRS area coordinator was a member of our church and a member of the finance committee. He told me the only way the money could be transferred would be upon agreement of the persons who gave the gifts. So the finance committee recommended to the church that only one designated fund exist—a building fund—and the church adopted this as policy. Then I sent letters to all the individuals who had given over the years to these designated accounts, informing them of the decision of the church and requesting permission to move the money to the general fund. All but one agreed. The leverage was that in the letter I had to tell the people that if they did not give me permission to move their gifts, I had been directed by the church to return their gifts and report to the IRS the return of the gifts so the givers would have to refile taxes for that giving year.

While I am off on this subject, let me continue the story. Several years earlier dear friends of my wife and me, who were members of the church, had started a memorial fund for their daughter who had disappeared. Faithfully this deacon and his wife contributed to a fund that would ultimately provide a new organ for the worship center. At the time the decision was made to eliminate the designated fund accounts, the organ fund had thousands of dollars in it but far from enough to purchase a memorial organ.

What the finance committee did was to establish a ministry challenge item in the regular budget—budgeting from church receipts to the level of $5,000 per year. Since it was a budget contingency item, the accumulated balance was allowed to carry over from one budget year to the next. And since the church was receiving more funds than the budget needs called for, the organ fund grew much faster than it could have grown if our friends had continued their routine giving level. In fact, other gift donors helped ensure that this $5,000 item was reached each year.

Most all the designated gift areas were translated to ministry challenge items. These included media, library, benevolence, scholarships, and the like.

Generous givers who wanted to give beyond the tithe were directed to these needs that the budget would not have otherwise provided. Thus, when a family said they would like to make a contribution to the church in honor of their recently departed loved one, I had several ministry challenge items available that they could choose to fund. And when the item was funded, we acknowledged that fact in the church newsletter; "The family of Mrs. Loved One has generously funded the new play equipment in the children's area in honor of her many years of service and love to the church."

2. *General Funds* are those funds that operate the general budget of the church—that pay the bills. The strength of a general ledger account is that funds remain fluid within the bank account and can be used for the purpose of fulfilling the church budget needs. There are several considerations for use of general funds:

- Expenditures from the general account are easier since they are budget driven; that is, the church has already authorized the expenditure when the budget was adopted.
- Expenditures from the general account not in the budget will require approval by the church or the group the church authorizes to make revisions to the budget (finance committee, for example). Thus, all expenditures of the church will be those the church is aware of and has approved.
- By having all funds—including the ongoing contingency fund allocations and accumulations—in the general fund account, more money is available to the fund administrator to carry out the operations of the church.
- Expenditures from the general fund account should always be made through a purchase order or some other form of tracking process for the authorization of the expenditure.

Let's return to bullet three above. Remember the story of the church I mentioned earlier that had thousands of dollars in the bank but couldn't pay their bills? What if all that money was in a general account that the administrator could gain access to in order to carry out the routine functions of the church. Here's a quick example of what I am talking about. The church has adopted a realistic budget, one in which the church will undoubtedly collect all the funds through the year required to carry it out. Early in the budget cycle the singles minister has planned a ski trip to the mountains. The $5,000 for the ski trip has not yet been collected by offerings in February when the trip is planned. The administrator knows that it more than likely will be collected by December of the budget year, but it is not available right now. What are the options? Delay the trip until the funds are collected, cancel the trip, or tell the singles that they can go if they pay their own way. What if the administrator had funds available in the general account that included various contingency funds that could be used until the offerings do come in to fund the trip? That is the beauty of having fluid funds in a general account. This flexibility will require the administrator to be very cautious and to work harder for the following reasons:

1. You are borrowing money that is a contingency item that must be replaced. That is, you are not robbing Peter to pay Paul.

2. The administrator must be keenly aware of budget dynamics. If funds are not being received through the budget year in the anticipated manner into the general fund, you cannot continue to borrow from contingency accounts. You must revise the budget to reflect the giving level. Lower priority items must be reduced or eliminated altogether so that you can replace the transferred contingency accumulations to their original level.

3. The administrator must be keenly aware of the dynamics of all line items of the budget to develop an understanding of the responses required for each budget action.

The wise church administrator will first establish how funds and resources will be categorized as an initial step for developing policies and procedures that will describe the accountability of the funds.

The Two-Person Rule. In 2 Corinthians 8 we read of Paul reporting the delivery of the gift from the Macedonian churches to the Jerusalem church. In verse 6 Titus is identified as the delivery messenger. In verse 18 another brother is identified, selected by the churches, to accompany Titus. In verses 20–21 Paul states why the two individuals: We are taking this precaution so no one can find fault with us concerning this large sum administered by us. For we are making provision for what is honorable, not only before the Lord but also before men.

From the moment an offering, tithe, or gift leaves the hands of the donor, the money should have the two-person rule applied. This includes receipt, counting, recording, request for expenditure, authorization for expenditure, purchase, payment, and audit of the transaction. Policies and procedures for handling the fund resources of the church or organization should be developed with the philosophy of the double check that the two-man rule calls for.

1. *Ushers.* In the church, receipt of tithes and offerings usually begins with a group of ushers collecting the offering for the service. In other organizations receipt may take different forms. Regardless of how funds are received, from the moment a person places the offering in the worship offering plate, Sunday school records basket, or places a check in an envelope for mailing, the money should be under constant supervision.

- The ideal is to take the money immediately and count the receipts.
- If the offering is held and consolidated with other receipts for the day, two persons should always watch it.

- It is not suggested that the offering be placed "at the front" during the service. This invites a robbery.
- If funds are to be received during the week or at times other than in a community or congregational setting, specific guidance should be given to establish who in the church or organization can legitimately receive such contributions. Usually that is delegated to a church finance officer or clerk. In such cases, either establish a policy where two individuals in the organization acknowledge the receipt, or if only one person receives the money, then a written receipt for the gift is provided to the donor.

2. *Counting groups.* A designated counting ministry team should be established. The function of this group is to count and validate the gifts and offerings and to make a record of such actions. Most counting groups will also be assigned the responsibility for delivering the money and gifts to a secure location after they have validated the receipts. Some suggestions for this group include:

- There should be a rotation of individuals serving as counters. Do not let the same individuals always count funds. Establish a pool of about five to seven so they can rotate.
- You may appoint a leader, usually the church treasurer, who will organize and coordinate the activities of the team.
- Do not let family members serve together on the same counting team.
- The counting process should occur in a secure location. Provide a lock and peep hole.
- Provide all necessary equipment and materials necessary to do the work. Don't have them running out every other minute to "get something."

Remember: while you as an administrator will want to ensure there is no theft or loss, the principle purpose of these processes is to guarantee the integrity of the individuals. As Paul said, "So no one can find fault . . . we are making provision for what is honorable" (2 Cor. 8:20–21). Policies should have implementing procedures that ensure the gifts are accurately and efficiently accounted for. An example set of procedures for the counting team might include:

- Verify name and amount on envelopes.
- Count currency.
- Count/endorse checks. If there is a check in the offering without an envelope, create an envelope for that person and record the amount.
- Tally receipts.
- Prepare deposit slip.
- Place money in a locked bank bag.
- Deliver funds.

An example set of procedures for receipt of money during the week might include:

- The issuance of a cash receipt will always be made for cash received during the week.
- The issuance of a cash receipt will not be required for in-line sales such as tickets to concerts or events or for group-served meals.
- Program or ministry leaders who receive money for trips, training supplies, craft or recreation activities or the like will be required to issue a receipt to the individual. Where goods and services are rendered, receipts bearing such notation will be placed on the individual's copy as well on the record of receipt.
- No individual other than the church treasurer, church administrator, or financial secretary may retain funds received during any twenty-four-hour period. All receipts by program, activity, event, or ministry leaders must be turned in within twenty-four hours of the receipt of such funds. The financial secretary will issue a cash receipt for such funds received.

These example procedures demonstrate an important fiscal philosophy—receipts must be accounted for and secured immediately. Failure to do so will result in careless operations which will eventually lead to suggested or actual mismanagement of money.

3. *Recording funds.* Two key players are present in the recording of funds—the church treasurer and the financial secretary or clerk. Sometimes the CBA will substitute as one of these two. While processes will vary from church to church or organization to organization, certain standards should be followed:

- With the copy of the deposit slip left at the church, the CBA, treasurer, and/or the financial secretary go to the bank the next workday and recount and deposit the funds.
- Frequently banking officials will provide the second person for the final tabulation. You can be sure they will count it before allowing a deposit to the account. If this is the case, then ensure that the bank verifies that a certified teller has counted the funds.
- The financial secretary should record gifts to the individual giving records, using the offering envelopes as documents.
- The CBA, treasurer, or financial secretary should verify that any "designated" gifts are legal and appropriate.
- Funds are posted to a general ledger or designated gift ledger.
- Some churches will distribute funds proportionally; however, the wisest process for distributing funds is based on need and request for authorization.

4. *Disbursement of funds.* It should be a general policy that disbursement of funds for any reason should follow an established procedure.

(1) An individual should be designated as the authority to expend funds. That person or persons are designated by the church as the purchasing agent for the church, and all documents of payment should fall under their responsibility and authority.

(2) Expenditures should not exceed ability to pay the encumbrance. An interesting case happened in one church. The church had no centralized or designated purchasing authority. However, one of the staff was assigned as administrator as a collateral duty. This person did not understand common accounting practices. When a budget unit requestor came in and asked for an expenditure, he would look at the bank balance, and if money was there, he would authorize the purchase. Where he failed to look was the financial secretary's ledger. If he had looked here, he would have noted several obligations against that bank balance for purchases already made but not yet paid. In other words, he was double spending the money. The use of a controlled purchase agent who uses a purchase order system and posts the purchase request against a computerized management system will greatly reduce this problem.

(3) Expenditures should be approved in the church budget. Leaders go to the church with a proposed budget stating that this is how the funds you bring to the "storehouse" will be spent. After the church approves the budget, fiscal ethics demand that administrators honor that obligation.

(4) The use of a purchase order system will facilitate a "paper trail" for the expenditure. See the next item.

(5) Most churches will establish a spending limit without review. This prudent policy provides for the purchasing agent a "comfort" backup. Even if a major purchase is authorized in a budget proposal, a second evaluation often helps to ensure stewardship. For example, as administrator I was authorized to spend up to $1,000 without question for any budgeted item. Over that limit I was required to inform the finance committee of the impending expenditure.

(6) Disbursement should be by check or electronic transfer. Rarely in our modern society is cash a recognized method for conducting business that requires a track of the expenditure. Checks, electronic transfers, or other documented methods of making payment are becoming normative.

5. *Purchase orders.* The request to expend funds from any account should be made through a purchase order system. Methods of use vary from church to church and organization to organization. However, certain standard elements should be present:

- There should be only one (two at the most) individuals designated by the church as the purchasing agent who has the authority to obligate church funds through the approval of the purchase order submitted by a budget unit.
- The two-person rule must be followed in that the person who requests an item for purchase cannot be the same person who authorizes the purchase.
- The two-person rule also applies in that the same person authorizing purchase cannot be the same person who makes payment.
- Purchase orders should be in a printed format with the following information:
  — A sequential numbering/tracking system
  — Date of request
  — Space for name, address, e-mail/telephone of church
  — Space for specific identification of item required, amount, and estimated cost
  — Space for purchasing agent to enter name and address of supplier
  — Space for name of requestor/budget unit
  — Space for authorizing signature
  — Space to indicate receipt of delivery
- Some states require that tax-exempt status/number be noted.
- Purchase orders should be used for the authorization of any expenditure of funds; this includes a check request for reimbursement or personal authorized expenses to ministry personnel.

Line-Item Accounting. Whether the budget item is an ongoing, ministry program item that has been prioritized or an item of the budget that represents a contingency fund or unfunded challenge item, all elements must be assigned some accounting classification. That assignment is usually termed a line-item and is given some nomenclature that will allow the funds manager to access that item for transactions or reporting. For many years my dad was the treasurer of the church. As an accountant he would labor over books where entries would be penned into ledgers. Surprisingly, many organizations continue to use a manual ledger system of accounting today. But most have moved to one of the many computerized church management systems that are available. Such a system not only makes fund accounting much easier; it is faster and far more accurate.

One of the responsibilities of the administrator is to set up the accounting line-item system to be put in place. Sometimes that is mandated by the church management systems used; other times it must be entered into the system. Later in this book we will discuss church office operations and will go into greater detail about the selection of the church management system. However,

PURCHASE ORDER

PURCHASE ORDER
Example Church
100 Main Street
All America City 123456
A Religious Tax Exempt Organization of the State of Here

Telephone 123-456-7890

Email ExampleChurch.netorg

ORDERED FROM:

PURCHASE ORDER NUMBER _____
Please refer to this number on all
Invoice label, billing, and correspondence

DATE ORDERED	SHIP VIA	DELIVER BY	BUDGET CODE	ACCOUNT CODE	TERMS

Quantity	Description	Unit Price	Amount

Requesting Budget Unit Manager

Authority to Purchase
Purchasing Agent

Date Received

Received By

an important concept needs to be developed now. In selecting a church management system, determine what you want the system to do for you and then choose the system that best parallels your desires for a system. There are over three dozen major suppliers of church management systems in the marketplace; each has its commonalities, but each also has its own unique elements. In selecting a system for fiscal operations, look for one that will:

- Provide flexibility in defining the account codes.
- Integrate fund account codes for ease of fund acquisition.
- Provide a high level of security from illegal access.
- Offer a variety of formats for reports as well as built-in flags for variations.

In the office chapter we will generate a scheme for consistent and logical filing and correspondence identification measures. That system should be linked to the fiscal accounting system developed for fund accounting. An illustration of a fiscal accounting line-item system might be:

1000	Pastoral Ministries
2000	Program Ministries, Education
3000	Program Ministries, Music
4000	Personnel Administration
5000	Fiscal Administration
6000	Property Administration
7000	Church Office
8000	Debt Retirement
9000	Designated Accounts

As an example, a budget funding allocation for pulpit supply might have a fund line-item code of 1023, indicating the budget unit manager is the pastor (pastoral ministries) and has a priority assignment of 23, indicating that it is very important in the scheme of planning in pastoral ministries. (See the scheme for indicating priority importance earlier in this chapter.) A ski trip for the singles minister might be 2478, indicating that the line item is educational programming (2000) that it relates to the single minister (400—we will develop this in the office chapter) and has a priority of 78, meaning that it is a desirable item but has a lower priority and can be cut if necessary without seriously impacting the singles ministry.

Reports to the Church. Valid fiscal operations require the use of numerous reports. Church or organization bylaws or policies and procedures will normally dictate annual, monthly, or even weekly reports of fund transactions. Many states now are beginning to require churches to report their financial operations on an annual basis as part of the requirements for incorporation as a not-for-profit, religious organization. Nonchurch nonprofits will almost always be required by state comptrollers to report financial status.

1. *Local reports.* The church or organization should expect the treasurer, finance secretary, and/or the church administrator to be able to provide an accounting of funds at a moment's notice. In order to provide adequate accounting, the fund manager must:

- Maintain a current posting of all transactions. Do not allow funds or obligations to accumulate.
- Plan for reasonable reporting:
  — Survey staff to see what they need/want.
  — Survey committees/teams/councils to see what they need.
  — Survey the church to determine what they expect.
- As a minimum, at each scheduled business meeting, prepare a financial report detailing expenditures, obligations, balance, and budget status.
- Prepare a summary and projected expenditures for budget units during budget preparation time.
- Prepare an annual report detailing all receipts, expenditures, and balances.

Frequently I am asked if staff salaries should be part of reports given to the church or organization. Legally, members of an institution have a right to access the financial status of the church or organization. Legally, an individual has a right to have privacy of his financial condition, and revelation of that information cannot be made without his approval. So how does a church or nonprofit handle revealing budget decisions regarding salary? The easiest answer is to lump all salaries and benefit data (the privacy act-protected information) into one lump figure and post that as a line item for the budget. Then the administrator prepares a separate report of the specific salaries, benefit packages, and other personnel cost items by individual. Then, when an individual asks, "What are we paying the youth minister?" the administrator can say that if the person who is asking the question is a member of the organization/church, an analysis of that information is available upon request, but the information will not be disclosed as a matter of public record.

In the several years that this matter was handled in this manner when I was a church administrator, I had less than a handful of people ask for that information. I always cautioned the individuals who got the sheet that the information was personal information and they could be held liable if it was disclosed to an unauthorized person; in fact a statement to that effect was printed on the sheet.

An interesting dynamic occurs in any organization. While there will always be a few self-appointed auditors of the church funds, the vast majority of the members will not want to become involved in the finances. The reason for that is trust. When the leadership of an organization develops a comfortable level of trust, then the routine functions of administration, including fund accounting, are relegated to them without question. If, on the other hand, leadership does anything to challenge or question that trust level, the members will become sensitive to almost every operation. When, as a consultant, I go into a church to evaluate administrative processes and find very long and very detailed policies and procedures relating to the fiscal operations of the church, I almost always find upon research a church that had a major financial problem, which they attempted to solve by creating odious and overbearing policies and procedures.

Reports to the membership in a timely and understandable format will go a long way toward developing a strong level of confidence in the fiscal administrative affairs of the church leadership. Poorly written reports, infrequent reports, or reports that have major gaps in the information will cause question and suspicion and will lead to mistrust of the leadership's ability to handle the fiscal operations of the church or institution.

2. *Legal reports.* In addition to the periodic reports to the membership, several other types of reports may be applicable to church/organization fiscal accounting.

Many state governments require a report of church transaction as part of the process of incorporation as a nonprofit religious organization. Some governmental agencies now require churches and other nonprofits to explain how funds expended are directly related to the operations of the church and its ministries or tax-exempt organization and thus are not subject to local taxation.

Several federal reporting requirements are summarized in IRS publication 1828. These are detailed in such publications as IRS Publication 517, 525, 526, 533, 557, and 561. Unrelated business expenses as discussed in IRS Publication

598 are reported on Form 990T. If the church gains funds into its general revenue that come from profit-making activities, then taxes must be paid on that revenue. An example might be the revenue gained by a downtown church that rents parking spaces in their church parking lot during the week. If that revenue exceeds a specified amount, the church will pay an unrelated business tax on the receipts.

Employee tax returns are given on IRS W2 and W4 documents. While churches are permitted to opt out of the federal tax system, most do not. If the church is opposed for religious reasons to the payment of employer Social Security and Medicare taxes, then IRS document 8274 will assist them in making this determination. Clergy who determine their religious conviction prevents them from submitting clerical earnings to Social Security taxes may opt out of the system through the provisions defined in IRS 4361 series. (Remember that ordained, licensed, or commissioned clergy will pay the entire Social Security tax payment as defined in the Self-Employment Contributions Act (SECA).) Clergy are responsible for ensuring their federal taxes are paid, but they may allow the church or organization to withhold those taxes and make payments for them.

Donor information reporting disposition of donated property is discussed in publications such as IRS 526 and 561 series as well as instructions on forms 8282 and 8283, which describe the reporting requirements for noncash donations. Depending on the value and type of property, the church or organization will have certain disposition reporting responsibilities to both the government and the individual.

IRS Publication 526 discusses the various criteria by which a contribution to a church or other qualified nonprofit organization may be considered a tax-deductible gift. Numerous provisions are discussed; for example, quid-pro-quo statements that no goods or services were provided for charitable contributions of $250 or greater on quarterly and annual giving records provided to the member before January 31. Another example would be the report of gifts of cash of $10,000 or greater reported on Form 8300.

A word of summary about legal reports of fiscal responsibilities by churches and the personnel who serve them. Each year changes occur to the tax code that will affect churches and clergy. It is nearly impossible for individuals to keep up with these changes. Most administrative publications such as *Church Business, Your Church, The Clergy Journal, The Church Law and Tax Report,* and the *NACBA Ledger* have sections that discuss these changes. Additionally, numerous online resources will assist the church administrator. An exceptional resource is the Web site at IRS.gov.

3. *Audits.* Each year the fiscal activities of the church should be audited. An audit not only considers the financial transactions but examines the policies

and procedures for financial operations. Audits contribute to the confidence in fiscal operations of churches and protect the individuals who handle the funds of the church. Every church should conduct two types of audits:

(1) A local audit by a church-appointed audit team, frequently termed an internal audit. During this audit not only are the policies and procedures relating to fiscal operations reviewed, but the actual financial statements and documents are reconciled with accounts, balances, and funds on hand. These types of audits can only be performed by persons who are familiar with standard criteria for fiscal operations that are normally used by a certified public accountant.

(2) Every second or third year, a comprehensive audit by a team of auditors not affiliated with the church. This is termed the independent audit and provides a certification of compliance or reports areas of discovery. Independent audits go beyond the internal audit in that they will inspect the policies and procedures established for fiscal operations, the experience level of the personnel who are assigned to carry out those processes, the equipment and inventory to carry out the activities, and the actual reconciliation of the fund accounts of the church or organization. This audit is time-consuming (and frequently expensive) but will provide to the church or organization either a comprehensive audit review—analysis and comment based on inspection of books and procedures—or an audit compilation—a presentation of fiscal statement without review or comment of processes.

Remember that audits provide a statement of "reasonable assurance" that the church or organization's fiscal posture ascribes to generally accepted auditing and accounting principles. While audits cannot ensure complete and total affirmation of fiscal operations that are appropriate, they can go a long way toward protecting the integrity of the personnel involved in the fiscal operations as well as ensuring that the financial status of the church or organization is safe and protected.

Assistance in Church Financial Operations

Where does one turn to seek assistance in the day-to-day financial operations of the church? Many churches have recognized the need to provide professional direction for the business needs of the church and have called a church business administrator. Others have employed at least a full-time or part-time financial officer. Some churches have turned their financial accounting operations over to a CPA or other financial management firm. In actuality, today the church has the resources to manage effectively the fiscal operations by virtue of the development of church management software that does all the needed activities legally and without bias, and the increased interest in authors who have provided excellent resource materials.

Church Management Software. Most churches today use some form of church management software for membership and fund accounting. These systems can run as simply as through a PC environment to a full mainframe hardware system. The cost can range between a couple of hundred dollars to thousands. There are actually some shareware programs a small church could use that are free. Church management software requires minimal training and understanding about fund operations since they are built into the software. In the chapter on church office operations, we will explore what types of systems are best suited for church or nonprofit applications.

Publications. Each year publications are revised and issued in a current tax-year format that provides for the church and nonprofit an up-to-date analysis of fiscal responsibility. Publications include Busby's *Zondervan's Church and Nonprofit Tax and Finance Guide, NACBA Annual Church Compensation Report,* and GuideStone Financial Resources of the Southern Baptist Convention's *Minister's Guide to Taxes,*[4] revised and issued annually.

Chapter Review

Fiscal operations in the church or nonprofit religious organization require a keen sense of attention to detail on the part of the administrator because of the double-edged sword of trust in the leadership that is inherent in the Christian community and because of the necessity for honest and accurate records which the responsibility demands. There are many areas in ministerial leadership where less than exceptional performance can be forgiven; but the administration of the fiscal resources is not one of them—either from the local parishioner's point of view or from the legal authorities who monitor the contributions to those entities. In reflecting upon the elements of this chapter, you should be able to:

- Define fund management and identify the personnel or organizational entities that will be entrusted with the fiscal resources.
- Describe appropriate areas of fiscal administration that will require the creation of formal policies and procedures to define local interpretation of reasonable accountability processes.
- Describe an appropriate format for developing a budget for a church or nonprofit organization.
- Discuss the two-man-rule and how it is applied throughout fiscal operations.
- Present an argument for the presence of appropriate reports and audits.

Administering Physical Resources

CHAPTER

7

We need church buildings to help us accomplish our mission: and church buildings will be kept in proper perspective if community is created and nurtured by the people who construct and maintain these structures.

JOE D. MARLOW, *SACRED SPACE: TOWARD A THEOLOGY OF CHURCH BUILDINGS*

The Biblical Foundation for a Structure

In Genesis 8:20 we find recorded that when Noah stepped off the ark and "built an altar to the LORD," his sacrifice was probably upon a mound formed of stones in the open countryside. We find Abram building a similar altar to the Lord between Bethel and Ai (Gen. 12:8; 13:4), and later God tested him as he built an altar on the mountain to offer Isaac (Gen. 22:9).

Archeological and historical data from the period of the Old Testament patriarchs indicates that other cultures built and used temples to worship their gods. Egyptian, Mesopotamian, and Babylonian cultures left records of structured temple worship. For the group of people that would come to be called the nation of Israel, their god was *the* God. He was the singular God of the universe—Creator, Sustainer, and sole focus of worship. He took no image, likened himself to no being, and was not confined to any place or time. Thus, for the Hebrews, there was no temple that could be erected to him because he was everywhere. The altar in the open allowed the aroma of the sacrifice to rise upward as a sweet-smelling offering by the worshipper.

This concept of worship changed with the exodus. While the Israelites were traveling to the promised land, God directed Moses to construct a "sanctuary for Me so that I may dwell among them" (Exod. 25:8). In the verses that follow God directed, "You must make it according to all that I show you—the design of the tabernacle as well as the design of all its furnishings" (Exod. 25:9). And after giving the construction details, the designation of priestly function and dress, and the instruments for worship, God provided a final commentary in

Exodus 29:42–43, 45–46: "This will be a regular burnt offering throughout your generations at the entrance to the tent of meeting before the LORD, where I will meet you to speak with you. I will also meet with the Israelites there, and that place will be consecrated by My glory . . . I will dwell among the Israelites and be their God. And they will know that I am the LORD their God, who brought them out of the land of Egypt, so that I might dwell among them. I am the LORD their God."

At this juncture in the life of his chosen people, God elected to tabernacle with them. Why he thought this a necessity after hundreds of years could be debated in theological circles for weeks on end. The fact is that God directed his worshippers to erect a physical structure where worshipping him could take place. No image of God was placed in the building—only the instruments that facilitated worship. God's presence was noted by the people as he filled the Holy of Holies with his cloud (Exod. 40:34).

David desired to convert the old tentlike facade of the tabernacle to a permanent structure (1 Chron. 28:2–3) but would be required by God to pass on to his son Solomon the task of building the first temple of worship to the Lord. Four hundred and eight years after the nation of Israel left Egypt, in the fourth year of Solomon's reign, work on a temple approximately ninety feet long, thirty feet wide, and fort-five feet high was begun. It would be a massive work involving over 200,000 workers and using the finest of building materials. When completed, it stood as an architectural marvel and the most splendid building of the day. In an appearance to Solomon, God promised, "I have consecrated this temple you have built, to put My name there forever; My eyes and My heart will be there at all times" (1 Kings 9:3). At the dedication of the temple, it "was filled with a cloud . . . for the glory of the LORD filled God's temple" (2 Chron. 5:13–14) as God had done before with the tabernacle.

This philosophy of God's presence in the temple pervaded through the time of Christ. It is no wonder that Jesus became enraged when he saw his Father's place of worship being used as a workplace by thieves. He drew to their remembrances the pronouncements of the prophets Isaiah (Isa. 56:6–7) and Jeremiah (Jer. 7:1–11) who cautioned the nation of Israel to reverence the temple as a house of worship and prayer. This event of cleansing the temple is recorded by all four Gospel writers (see Matt. 21:12–13; Mark 11:15–17; Luke 19:45–46; and John 2:13–16). Though Jesus reverenced the temple and used it many times for a platform for teaching, Jesus predicted the fall of the temple at a future date (see Matt. 24:1–2; Mark 13:1–2; Luke 21:5–6).

In A.D. 70 the Romans, under the direction of Titus, destroyed the temple. In the relief of the Arch of Titus in Rome can be seen the Roman troops sacking the temple of its furnishings. To this day this "house of the Lord" has not been rebuilt. Devout Jews worship at a portion of the structure commonly known as the Wailing Wall. Prophecy calls for the temple to be rebuilt by the nation of Israel.

Before leaving the Israelites' places of worship and turning to the New Testament Christian church, a discussion of another important Jewish place of meeting—the synagogue—is needful since the synagogue played an important role in the development of the Christian church. When the Southern Kingdom, which included Jerusalem and the temple Solomon built, was captured in 586 B.C. by the Babylonians, the temple was plundered and destroyed. The leadership was taken into captivity. As they joined their northern Jewish kinsmen who had been dispersed by Assyria some 130 years earlier, the Jews no longer had a place to meet God, to worship, offer sacrifice, or to receive instruction. They were slaves in a foreign land. Their leadership was decimated and their identity and culture threatened. Soon, however, groups of Jews banded together to meet for mutual support and to participate in the practices of remembrance of their God. Leaders and teachers were selected for these meeting (or assembly) places.

Up to this point the Scriptures had resided in the memory of the religious leaders; now it was a necessity to write these Scriptures—the law—the Torah, prophetical sayings, the history and poetry of the nation—in order to preserve it since many of those leaders were either killed or were not allowed to practice the faith.

Even with the end of the Exile and return to Jerusalem and a rebuilt temple, the synagogue continued to be an important structure in the life of the Jewish people. It was their "local" meeting place away from Jerusalem. Their teachers (rabbis) became the substitute for the priestly teachers of the temple. They now had copies of the holy Scriptures and could read and have interpreted for them the words of God. At the time of Christ, every township that had ten adult Jewish males had a synagogue. It was the place of study and preparation from which future Christian church leaders would spring.

Though some of the early followers of Jesus were not Jews, from the early inception of the Christian church, followers of the Way were of Jewish background or descent. Initially they did not abandon their former worship style since Jesus said that he had not come to set aside the Law but to fulfill it. They met in the temple and synagogue (Acts 2:46) and discussed Jesus. Their holy Scripture was the same as that used by the Jewish people.

Within a short time, however, it became apparent to both sides that the religion of the Christian was not the religion of the Jew. The early followers were asked to leave the synagogue and temple mount. Having no other place to go, the Christians began to meet in one another's homes. Because the homes of that era were small, these house churches were generally just a few individuals and were identified by the name of the individuals in whose home they were meeting. The house church filled the void of the common meeting place that had been taken away from them and satisfied the concept that wherever two or three believers were gathered in Jesus' name, he was with them (see Matt. 18:20).

As the writings of the apostolic and church fathers became known, the philosophy that the individual is the temple of God became prominent. Stephen declared that God does not live in a temple built by human hands (Acts 7:48). Paul told the churches at Corinth and Ephesus that the Christian is the body of the temple (1 Cor. 3:16; 6:19; and Eph. 2:21). Peter declared that the individual believer is the building stones of the church along with the priests who minister in the building (1 Pet. 2:4–5).

Several years ago while I was still on active duty with the U.S. Navy, we were scheduled to make a port visit in Sicily to the city of Syracuse. Information about a tour of the area aroused my interest because the tour included a visit to the "oldest known Christian church." Having toured ancient Syracuse and seen the various ruins there, we boarded the tour bus and headed out to the countryside. Some few miles into the island we came down into a valley filled with vineyards and groves of fruit trees. Off in the distance was a structure that resembled one of the many monasteries and ancient buildings I had seen throughout the Mediterranean.

As we approached the building, it appeared to be old—but not two thousand years old! I thought that maybe they had built the monastery around the old structure and inside we would find the oldest church. But we drove right by the building around to a much smaller, more modern building. We entered this building and found along one wall a gift shop where you could buy items from the monks. At the far end of the room was an opening with a set of stairs going down.

As we got to the bottom of the stairs, the space opened up to a cave or underground space that had been chiseled in the stone in the shape of a cross. It was about fifteen to twenty feet wide and maybe forty to fifty feet long. Where the cross arms of the side rooms met was what one would describe as a pulpit or lectern. Immediately in front of this pulpit was a pit carved also in the shape of a cross with steps going down at either end. The pit was about three feet deep, and the guide said this was where baptisms occurred. Two church leaders would stand in the arms of the cross, and the person would enter at the foot of the cross and exit at the head. Along the long walls were carved narrow shelves which we thought were pews, but the guide said that worshippers stood there. No one sat down. There was a very good reason for this because the church was a product of the persecution of Christians in the early years. At the place we entered was a replica of a large wooden door which was closed and bolted during services. At the other end of the cave at the top of the room was a narrow slit that led to an almost endless cave system which provided an escape route. The cave system had been transformed into a catacomb of martyrs because not all worshippers escaped.

I often ask my students, "Was this really the oldest Christian church?" in hope that they will realize that, while this might have been a structure that housed a body of believers, this was *not* the church. The early, persecuted church understood this, but the "Romanized" legal church would forget this concept.

The Roman basilica that was used as both a courthouse and a stock exchange became the model for the Roman Christian church. It was a rectangular hall with two rows of columns dividing it into three sections. A semicircular niche was at one end. A throne for the bishop was set up in the apse and benches for presbyters were placed on either side of this end. This bench area later became elongated to form the cross shape we see in many old cathedrals. The Lord's Supper table became a permanent part of the arrangement, and in later years the throne and the Lord's Supper table were physically separated from the rest of the building by an *iconostasis,* a massive solid screen adorned with icons or pictorial representations of the saints. With time the chancel (or room for the clergy) was separated from the nave (the room for the laity). The baptism font was at the back of the nave. When the importance of the clergy increased, side rooms were attached alongside the long sides of the nave to make up clergy offices.

As the church became wealthy and evolved into the dominant institution of the era, elaborate churches began to take form throughout both Western and Eastern Christendom. Many of these structures stand today as monuments of the philosophy of "nothing but the best for the Lord" in building and structures. Without question the Christian church, especially the Western or Roman church, would be the dominant influence in all areas of life from art and architecture to zoology and zoos.

With the Protestant Reformation a transformation of the church structure took place. The philosophy of worship was transformed from the importance of the place, process, and leaders, to the person being worshipped. The screen that separated the clergy from the laity was taken away, and the facility took on the shape of one large room. The pulpit for the proclamation of the Word remained prominent. The baptismal basin was moved to the front and given equal importance with the Lord's Supper table. The eighteenth-century elongated, crossshaped structure gave way to square and even circular patterns for the building design. Until the nineteenth century churches were monuments to the Lord. By the twentieth century the concept changed to a *meeting place* versus *house of the Lord.*

Today when you say, "I am a member of Such-and-So Church," a person responds with "Isn't that the church on the interstate loop," or "Isn't that church located downtown." While we embrace the philosophy that the church is made up of the people of the membership, we still tend to associate the church with its location in our conversation. This is a truism, especially to the nonchurch member. The structure, site, and sign identify the church. We can generally identify the type of church body or denomination by the architecture of the facility they worship in.

Is the church building nothing more than a shelter from the elements or is it "the Lord's house"? The answer is yes to both sentiments. Just as the cave of the early church in Sicily gave that church a sense of security and a place to carry out worship, our facilities today offer a place to carry out what we deem as our sacerdotal functions called church. In most of the world's societies the church building is considered a sacred place. God is worshipped there or attacked there. Parishioners flock there for worship, prayer, and Bible study. Zealots and infidels burn it. The church building is often seen as a sanctuary from the woes and ills of the world.

Christ stated that he would send his Holy Spirit to be with us (John 14:15–18) to provide counsel and serve as his representative to the world on his and his Father's behalf. Our hymns, anthems, and praise songs speak of the presence of the Spirit in our midst whenever we come together in the "Lord's house." While we know that we can meet God in any area of life, we formalize that meeting in our worship facility. Perhaps Solomon expressed our modern sentiment in his letter to Hiram, king of Tyre, when soliciting lumber for the building of the temple: "The temple that I am building will be great, for our God is greater than any of the gods. But who is able to build a temple for Him, since even heaven and the highest heaven cannot contain Him? Who am I then that I should build a house for Him except as a place to burn incense before Him?" (2 Chron. 2:5–6). Church facilities cannot contain God, but they can offer a place where we can meet and worship him.

The Concept of the Modern Church Facility

Rare is the church that has the wealth of Solomon to build its facility. In 1 Chronicles David told Solomon that he was to build the temple but that he, David, had already started collecting the materials for the structure: "Nearly four thousand tons of gold, nearly forty thousand tons of silver, and so much iron and bronze that it cannot be weighed. I have also gathered lumber and stone for the walls" (1 Chron. 22:14 NLT). In 1 Chronicles 29:2 NLT, David also identified "onyx, other precious stones, costly jewels, and all kinds of fine stone and marble." Over 180,600 paid laborers from Israel, Gebal, and Tyre worked on the temple (1 Kings 5:13–15; 2 Chron. 2:2).

In 538 B.C. Zerubbabel had a far smaller budget to reconstruct the temple after the return of the Jewish people from the Babylonian exile. Though he met with resistance, by 516 B.C. he had completed a spartan temple structure. While Herod the Great was a renowned builder of his day, his new temple at Jerusalem in 20 B.C. was modest in cost, compared to the first temple built by Solomon.

From the little white wooden church up the valley road to the large marble and steel church in midtown, Christians have spent literally trillions of dollars building worship centers they call their churches. Much to the chagrin of tax and municipal authorities, churches and other sacerdotal spaces consume large amounts of land. While we do understand the theology of the church, we still have difficulty with the practical structure.

Of all the topics addressed by Jesus, his discussions relating to personal and corporate stewardship stand out as significant topics. For instance, in Luke 12:35–40 Jesus describes how a faithful steward is to be prepared. In Luke 16:1–9 he discussed a shrewd yet dishonest steward. In Luke 16:10–13 and also in Luke 19:11–26, Jesus called for stewards to be faithful and responsible with the trust that has been given to them.

The early church fathers, in their letters of instruction to the first-century church, repeated the theme of the capable steward. Paul repeated the call to be faithful stewards (1 Cor. 4:12; Titus 1:7). Peter also repeated that call (1 Pet. 4:10). Paul told Timothy to require of church leaders a personal as well as corporate stewardship (1 Tim. 3:4–5). Paul admonished the church of Corinth to carry out their affairs in a responsible and orderly fashion (1 Cor. 14:40). That responsibility required them to bring the tithes and offerings to the church (1 Cor. 16:2). Peter reminded us that when we become stewards of the gifts of God, we glorify him in our obedience (1 Pet. 4:11). And the writer to the Hebrews reminded us that God will remember our diligence as stewards of the faith (Heb. 6:10).

Most church facilities are built with the blood, sweat, and sacrifices of the members of that church. Members have seen their gifts and contributions go into the mortar and bricks of that building. Many of them are aware of the costs involved in the construction and furnishings of the facility. Many times portions of the facility are dedicated to a loved one or a favorite leader of the church.

During the latter part of the twentieth century and moving into the twenty-first century, the construction and remodeling of church facilities is at a greater level than any period in the past. Riding on the affluence that exists from a strong stock market and low unemployment, billions of dollars for construction, remodeling and repair are going on in every area of church life. Parishioners are being asked to contribute at a rate higher than ever before.

Some interesting dynamics are surfacing with regard to this surge in building. First, the generation of "givers" is dying out. In many churches today, the principal contributors are the older generations that came out of the Depression and lived through World War II. They are classified by demographers as the "survivors." While they may not be the most affluent members of their churches, they are usually the most willing to contribute. They are the individuals who built the original church and are ready to do whatever it takes to upgrade and maintain it. These generations of givers are being replaced by generations that have more spendable income, but they are less prone to be regular contributors to the church.

Another interesting dynamic coming out of this era is the inflated costs for building and maintaining a church facility. A building that cost $80,000 to build a decade ago will cost the same to remodel today and cost three times that amount to rebuild. Many churches did not make plans for growth or upgrading when the original facility was built and are now paying high dollar per square foot to remodel to meet ministry needs and existing code requirements.

Another dynamic is that church facilities are taking on a form that does not relate to the pattern of architecture of the past. Traditional facilities are being blended with modern structures. Single-use worship/Bible study facilities are giving way to multiple-use buildings that can take on a variety of ministry requirements in a single container. Worship centers become classrooms which then become recreational facilities. Efficiency of space utilization parallels cost effectiveness in management decisions relating to facility construction and use.

The administrator needs to be aware that there is a personal sensitivity toward the facility on the part of the parishioner. Several years ago as I was leading a church through a building program as the chairman of the building committee, the decision had been made to relocate the facility to a new site. This decision had come after much study, research, and dialogue with town and neighborhood officials. It was a logical decision in the mind of many of us who had been involved with the study. It was the only viable decision from a financial point of view.

I remember one tense meeting with the congregation when our committee was presenting the results of a meeting with a regional telephone company that had expressed a strong interest in buying our facility to use as an employee training center after we had relocated. During that meeting one of our dear members stood up and said, "I don't care who you sell this church to. I have attended Sunday school for the past 25 years down in room 203. I am going to continue to come here every Sunday regardless of who is here." For her, worship and Bible study were linked to a place she revered.

I learned several lessons about people as a church administrator that I did not learn in the Navy. For example, you had better make sure the women's bathroom is clean and well stocked. The nursery had better be spotless and sweet smelling, even though the babies may not be. And another bitter lesson I learned is that you don't move a senior adult Sunday school class without their permission regardless of the necessity for space reallocation. That one came when I relocated the church library to make room for a larger nursery space. While the need for additional nursery space was real, and the relocated site of the library made it more accessible to the rest of the church, I didn't take into account the class of senior adult women that met there. The library was their project, and a portion of their Sunday morning time was devoted to straightening up the place. I had given them a study space; it just wasn't in the library. I was known as "that boy who moved our Sunday school class" by those women. Not until my mother visited us and attended that class for a month or so did the saints give me a break and realize that just possibly I was not the uncaring person they thought I was. Just for the record, I have repented of that sin and have never done it again!

In addition to the keen sensitivity to the cost of the worship, study, and ministry spaces, there is an unbelievable emotional allegiance by members to their church building. It is their church home, and they cherish it as dearly—and sometimes more so—as the home they sleep in. It is their Sunday school classroom, their spot on the pew, their locker in the recreation facility. In our dollars-and-cents, pragmatic society, ministers must never lose sight of the fact that a strong emotional link exists between many parishioners and the church facility. Managers struggle with how they can preserve that sense of allegiance while moving the church through the dynamics of ministry and growth at the same time.

There is also a keen sensitivity of the community toward the meeting house. In colonial America the church building was the local school during the week, a town meeting hall when needed, and a place of worship on Sunday. It was the focus of the community. The pastor was a community leader. As America grew, it grew about the local church. Located on the corner of First and Main, the church was the centerpiece of architecture for the community. It was a place where babies were dedicated, marriage vows were offered, and funerals for loved ones were conducted. It was where the Boy Scout troop met and where the community voted. In times of crisis it was a haven for the victim, a source of help for the needy. Whether the individual was a member of the church or not, the church facility was a respected fixture of the community.

Today the church still stands for that, and, many times, much more. While the social awareness of the Christian today is probably no greater than in former times, more and more the church body is becoming aware of their sensitivity to the social needs of the community about them. While the Boy Scout troop still meets there, an after-school program for latch-key kids may also exist there as well. The Tuesday morning Bible study circle may still meet, but the church may also be host to an abused wife, drug rehabilitation, or crisis pregnancy ministry. In many respects the church today is reaching its community with a cup of cold water with a vigor that was not evident in times past.

I became fully aware of this fact a few years ago as the church administrator of a church in Oklahoma just after the "oil bust." Not only did we have the "down-and-outer," but our community was riddled with the "up-and-outer." I learned that in times of crisis, people of all stations of life turned to the church for help. Later, as church administrator, I learned that even if a person never darkened the doorway of a church, he wanted his loved one's funeral at a church, or he wanted his daughter married at the church. Somehow that seemed to sanctify and make right the rites.

In neighborhoods across the nation church leaders are joining hands with community leaders and developing solutions to local issues that frequently involve the utilization of church spaces. Church buildings house schools, preschool day-care facilities, support groups, senior adult day care and retirement activities, and after-school programs. People in the community vote there, give blood there, and bring donations to the church to meet needs in times of calamity and crisis. Ministers cannot isolate their churches from the community, nor can they insulate the parish from involvement in the community. The tenuous line between providing worship and Bible study space for the member and contributing to the total community is a difficult management task. Pastors and other church leaders must be capable of responding to these dynamics.

In recent years the rules have changed in regard to the church facility. One of the unique ministries I have as a seminary professor is the opportunity to visit in the churches of former students to discuss issues with their various committees and leadership teams. I am often asked to come to validate what the former student has already informed the church about. Frequently I hear this expression, "Professor, we never had to do it like that before." And you know what, they are right. There was a time when, for the most part, the church was left alone, separated from the regulations imposed by federal, state, and local governments. But times have changed.

Today federal and state laws are being written that specifically include churches and religious organizations or which do not exclude them from applicability. Local ordinances include all elements of the community, including the church. What has happened is that church leaders have been violators of the rules. It doesn't make any difference whether this is from ignorance or stubbornness. The results are the same; the church is perceived as an outlaw by many community authorities.

Generally, churches want to be good members of the community, state, and nation. They want to avoid any embarrassment, or worse, penalty for failing to be good citizens. The problem that exists in many churches, however, is that there is no valid mechanism in place to keep the body informed of these changes. The pastor, as administrator of the church, is expected to keep up on these matters. We have already noted in the preface of this book that they generally do not have the training to manage the church, much less keep up with all the rules and regulations.

This chapter will assist the pastor, church administrator, or student of management to begin to grasp the complexities of church facility management. The ultimate objective is to provide a philosophical as well as a practical basis for conducting the work of the church.

Organizing to Do Facility Management

Earlier in the book we provided a sample church organizational chart in a simplified form:

THE SENIOR PASTOR			
ASSOCIATE PASTOR	MINISTER OF EDUCATION	MINISTER OF MUSIC	ADMINISTRATOR
Counseling personnel	Senior Adults	Choir Directors	Office Supervisor Secretaries Financial Clerk
Chaplains	Median Adults	Orchestra Director	
Nursing Home Ministry	Young Adults	Organist	Building Supervisor Janitors Maintenance Personnel
Family Life Ministry	Single Adults	Pianists	
	Youth		Church Hostess Cooks
	Children		
	Preschool		

Such an example organization represents a line organization in that it assigns specific levels of authority and assigns supervisory responsibilities. It is a matrix, however, in that the ministry areas are interrelated. Without education ministries, pastoral nursing home ministries would have little to support their work. In like fashion, without the programs of the church, why have a maintenance staff?

When considering the organization for property management, the CBA can conveniently divide his activities into two categories: (1) Management actions.

These are usually accomplished or directed by the CBA, and they are effective because of established policy and procedure directives. (2) Administrative activities. These are usually accomplished by support professionals. While it will be the responsibility of the CBA to carry out the majority of the management action activities, property maintenance per se is usually assigned to a custodial staff. In the vast majority of churches today, this task is accomplished by an in-house workforce.

In many respects the bottom line in property management is cost effectiveness. Most church governing boards today expect their staff administrators to practice good stewardship. When you consider that approximately 20 percent of the total church budget will be used in facility management operations, it is essential that the CBA be aware of efficient methods of plant operation.

From a random survey of churches with a total operation budget of $100,000 or more, the average costs per management area of the administrator's property maintenance budget looks like this:

ADMINISTRATOR'S FACILITY MAINTENANCE BUDGET

In a recent survey by the Cleaning Management Institute of various types of facility managers, it was noted that the churches which responded to their survey spent, on average, 12 cents per square foot of facility for maintenance supplies alone (*Cleaning Management and Maintenance,* May 2004, In-house Survey).[1]

In that same survey churches reported that in addition to routine housekeeping responsibilities they were responsible for accomplishing the following activities:

Grounds care	65%*
Miscellaneous building repairs	71%
Snow removal	53%

Masonry repairs	70%
Laundry operations	29%
Renovation/construction	47%
Exterior painting	64%
HVAC system maintenance	65%
Relamping	76%
Interior painting	71%
Pest control	65%
Other miscellaneous duties	35%

* percent respondents who did these additional jobs

The complexity and dynamics of maintaining a church facility are enormous. If the CBA is the senior pastor of the church, these responsibilities compound the already large task he has in leading the church. If the CBA has been assigned that role in addition to some other ministry position (in many churches the role of administrator is often linked with that of the minister of education), then facility management becomes a large detractor from what he perceives as his primary ministry. Only in the large church that can afford a dedicated CBA will the management of the facility become the focus of that person's work, but by then the task is so great that a suborganization will be required.

Let us propose some organizations to get the job done. We have already introduced the concept of the church business administrator (CBA), whether pastor or other assigned staff member or volunteer. As with the administration of personnel and finances, it is strongly recommended that a committee be assigned to become the property managers of the church. The charter for such a committee might look like the following:

CHURCH PROPERTIES COMMITTEE

CONSTITUTION. The church properties committee is responsible for the efficient, effective, and safe administration of all physical assets of the church. These will include buildings, internal and external maintenance, vehicles and other motorized equipment, and other plant account equipment. The church properties committee will be responsible for efficient space utilization and adequate provision of ministry furniture, hardware, and equipment. The church properties committee will ensure that the facility is safely and securely maintained and managed.

MEMBERSHIP. Nine to twelve members will be assigned annually by the committee on committees. One-third of the membership will be renewed annually with no member serving more than two successive terms (six years). The committee on committees will appoint annually a deacon chair. The chairman may serve as many successive terms as deemed appropriate by the committee on committees. The church business administrator will serve as the professional staff liaison. The building supervisor will serve as a permanent ad hoc committee member.

RESPONSIBILITIES.

1. Develop, recommend, and administer policies and procedures which apply to the following areas of church property management:
   a. Facility space allocation and use
   b. Facility maintenance and cleanliness
   c. Safety and security
   d. Insurance
   e. Food service
   f. Facility and equipment inspection
   g. Facility and equipment replacement schedules
   h. Transportation equipment
   i. Church parking
   j. Energy and energy conservation
   k. Coordination responsibilities with other committees and program groups
2. Conduct an annual inventory, inspection, and evaluation of all church property and equipment assets.
3. Evaluate space utilization needs and requirements. Effectuate space rearrangement to secure maximum use of the resources.
4. Evaluate and coordinate with the administrative committee adequate personnel resources to facilitate effective and efficient operation of the physical plant.
5. Schedule for adequate and appropriate maintenance, repair, and renovation of physical spaces and equipment.
6. Evaluate and coordinate with the administrative committee adequate budget resources to effectively and efficiently maintain the physical plant.
7. Provide administrative assistance in securing:
   a. Adequate parking
   b. Special equipment needs for special programs or activities of the church
   c. Special transportation needs
   d. Special program or ministry equipment or facilities
8. Appoint subcommittees as needed with the coordination of the committee on committees to effectively and efficiently carry out the responsibilities assigned.

REPORTS. Provide a narrative quarterly report that details elements of responsibility that are of interest to the church at large. Such items may include: special purchases, needs not yet met, future activities that may impact program, and so forth. Annually the church properties committee will report the inventory and status of facility equipment, significant purchases, and maintenance accomplishments, personnel status, any budget modifications, and future and planned property activities.

Again, as with the statement of the other committees discussed for personnel and finances, the church property committee is a polity organization of the church and is empowered by the church to act in its behalf in matters that relate to the property and management of the church facilities and equipment. Some types of organization that might exist are:

A Single Staff Member Church, The Pastor

A church properties committee is formed that will develop the policies and procedures for facility management. It will act as inspectors and evaluators of the program. The senior pastor will become a member of this committee. A janitor or custodian will be employed by the properties committee who will be responsible to the pastor for cleanliness and maintenance of the building.

Staff Member Assigned Additional CBA Duties

Again, a church properties committee is formed to develop policies for facility management. But it backs away from duties as procedure developer, allowing the CBA and employed staff of custodians to develop their own procedures. The church properties committee may still be involved in inspection and evaluation activities. The staff member who has been assigned CBA responsibilities will act as a staff liaison with the church properties committee and will become the committee's on-site maintenance administrator. The custodial staff will be organized under a lead custodian, who will directly supervise the activities of the maintenance staff. This maintenance supervisor will be directly responsible to the ministry staff member with CBA responsibilities.

This type of organization also lends itself well to maintenance operations that are carried out by volunteers or by contract housekeepers and maintenance personnel. The staff administrator is still responsible for task accomplishment, but the activities are inspected and supervised by a lead custodian.

Organizations That Have a Dedicated CBA

Churches that are large enough to warrant a professional staff member whose only responsibilities are the administration of the church often make the mistaken determination that committees relating to these issues are not necessary since they now have a professional who can do the work. The weakness to this logic is that the CBA must focus on three primary issues for church administration: personnel, finances, and facility. Policy comes from church decisions about how it wants the church to operate—not from an individual professional's conception. Thus, the logic for having church personnel, finance, and property committees is just as valid as before, and to some degree even more demanding because of the enormity of the task.

The CBA becomes a liaison member of the church properties committee, working with that group in the development of policy and management philosophy for the church facilities. Usually the CBA is expected to function as the resource source for these decisions. The CBA will be tasked by the church properties committee to develop procedures that will respond to management decisions made in committee. The CBA will also be assigned supervisory responsibilities for the workforce. Just as prudent CBAs delegate church office supervision to an office manager and delegate event, kitchen, and food service resonsibilities to a church hostess, the smart CBA will delegate supervision of maintenance and management to a lead custodian or the building supervisor.

The building supervisor is responsible directly to the CBA for the maintenance, repair, and housekeeping of the organization's facilities and properties. Later in the chapter we will discuss specific job descriptions of these various positions. This individual is usually one who has been employed not only because of skills in housekeeping but also because he or she will be able to maintain, either personally or through supervisions of contractors, the electrical, plumbing, and HVAC systems of the church; to paint and effect minor repairs and remodeling; and to maintain other equipment such as kitchen and grounds equipment.

Church Facility Manual

Personnel Assignments

Effective organization and management can reduce the degree of confusion and uncertainty that exists when no specific guidance is provided in the operation of the church. Church policies and procedures will have a definite impact on the working and personal relationships of the individuals in the church. If one is to consider the church as a team involved in the mission of the church, then every member must work together in a coordinated effort. We have already introduced the church business administrator and the church properties committee. Now let's consider two other important members of the church facility team—the building supervisor and a custodian.

BUILDING SUPERVISOR

PRINCIPAL FUNCTION. Responsible to the CBA for the maintenance and housekeeping of all church buildings, grounds, and equipment. Supervises maintenance and housekeeping personnel.

QUALIFICATIONS FOR THE POSITION. Training in the methodology of facility housekeeping and maintenance or equivalent experience. Familiar with general maintenance operations. Ability to plan, conduct, supervise, and evaluate a program of facility and equipment maintenance. Must display adequate literacy and physical ability to conduct maintenance operations. Individual must possess adequate interpersonal communication skills.

REQUIREMENTS OF THE POSITION.

1. Plan, conduct, supervise, and evaluate a program of systematic housekeeping; see that church buildings and grounds are safe, secure, and habitable at all times.
2. Plan, conduct, supervise, and evaluate a program of planned maintenance of facility, equipment, and transportation assets.
3. Make recommendations for employment and termination of all housekeeping personnel; supervise the work of all housekeeping personnel.
4. Conduct periodic safety and security inspections. Correct routine problems; recommend corrective action to church properties committee for major items.
5. Maintain custody of keys and securing devices.
6. Supervise all contract work on facilities and equipment.
7. Advise church properties committee of facility and equipment needs and budget requirements.
8. Develop and monitor a plan of energy efficiency use.
9. Assist the CBA and church properties committee in the conduct of an annual inventory and inspection of church facility assets.
10. Schedule housekeeping requirements in response to general and special church calendar events.
11. Perform other related duties as assigned by the CBA.

CUSTODIAN

PRINCIPAL FUNCTION. Responsible to the building supervisor for facility and grounds maintenance and habitability.

QUALIFICATIONS FOR THE POSITION. Training as a janitor or custodian or equivalent experience. General maintenance skills of painting, carpentry, plumbing, electrical, etc. General grounds and gardening skills. Individual should be sufficiently literate to carry out maintenance operations. Must display adequate physical health and strength to carry out maintenance and custodial activities, including the lifting of heavy weight, movement of furniture and equipment.

REQUIREMENTS OF THE POSITION.

1. Conduct scheduled daily, weekly, monthly, and annual facility cleaning operations.
2. Conduct routine maintenance operations without report; report major facility, equipment, or grounds maintenance problems to the building supervisor.
3. Operate heating and cooling equipment according to the schedule of the church calendar.
4. Open and secure the facility daily; secure facility at the end of special meetings or church events.
5. Move furniture, set up tables and chairs for special church activities and programs; set up assembly and classrooms for regular activities.
6. Prepare baptistry for use as directed and clean following use.
7. Set up for and clean up after weddings, funerals, and other social, community, and church events as directed.
8. Mow grass, trim shrubbery; maintain clean church entrances, sidewalks, and parking areas.
9. Perform other related duties as assigned by the building supervisor.

In many churches the lead or senior custodian will be assigned the role responsibility as the building supervisor. Other terms often used in facility maintenance include janitors and maids. Janitors and maids are individuals who have housekeeping responsibilities and will not be assigned routine maintenance operations. Because of the limited number of persons employed, most churches and nonprofits will seek custodians since they expect these individuals not only to keep the facility clean, safe, and habitable; but also they will be expected to complete light repairs, maintenance, and construction.

A church would not hire a pastor who couldn't preach; a school would not employee a teacher who could not teach; then why hire a custodian who can't clean or maintain the facility? Having gone to the trouble to determine the need for an employee, the considerations in personnel employment, writing a job description that determines who is qualified to hold the position, and then asking for applicants for the position, it is now time to consider the applicants in light of all that has gone before. In selecting an individual for maintenance, the selection process must ensure the criteria of the job qualifications are met.

For example, in the job description for a custodian given above, qualifications included craft skills, literacy, and adequate physical health. These become test points. You must have a specific test that you give to *each* of the individuals you have invited for an interview. For instance, ask specific questions about electrical problems—what is the minimum wire size for a 20-amp circuit? Have them read a manufacturer safety data sheet and explain what it says. Ask the interviewee to set up a Bible study classroom by moving desks and tables to demonstrate strength to do the job.

The Facility Space Plan

The space plan is nothing more than an assessment of the facility—the rooms, equipment, and so forth—and how these areas are used. The objective is to describe the space, how it is constructed and equipped, the unique features of the room, and what can be done with that space.

Several years ago as a church administrator, I went looking for the church's "as-built" drawings. When confronted with blank looks, I explained that I was looking for the blueprints the architect gave to the church after each of the buildings was built. On these drawings would be notations of any changes that were made during the construction. In other words, plans of the building that reflected the actual building that was finally built. Still blank looks. "I don't ever remember seeing anything like that" was the general response. So with tape measure and pad in hand, I set about to create a diagram of the church. This diagram eventually became an appendix to the church organization manual that was created for this church.

The objective of a diagram of the church is to show the square footage (ft^2) of the facility by room and space. If you don't know what you have, how will you know what you have to maintain? The blueprint I developed was in reality a footprint (a drawing showing walls, doors, windows, etc.) with certain designated features for each room. Below is how a room was identified on the drawing.

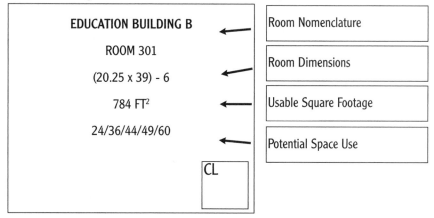

Each room on the footprint diagram was identified as above. Note some features of this designation. Both the dimensions and the total usable square footage were given. This allows the administrator to visualize the space for maintenance requirements and total space utilization for program needs. The space has a total of about 790 ft^2 for space to maintain. This includes a 6 ft^2 closet. For planning programs use, however, the administrator will count only on a space of 784 ft^2.

What can be done with that 784 ft^2 appears in the "potential space use" line. Various sources provide suggestions about space requirements for program needs in churches or program activities. For instance, the church architecture division of LifeWay Christian Resources of the Southern Baptist Convention has published a series of "rules of thumb" that have been gleaned over the years that suggest certain square footage provisions for various age groups of individuals. Using these suggestions for space size based on age division, the church then decided what provisions would be made for their particular situation.

LifeWay Suggestion		Church Designation	
Preschool	25–35 ft^2	Preschool	32 ft^2
Children	25 ft^2	Children	22 ft^2
Youth	20 ft^2	Youth	18 ft^2
Adults	15–20 ft^2	College	16 ft^2
		Adults	13 ft^2

Thus in the room on page 195, it would be possible to use it for programs for twenty-four preschoolers, thirty-six children, forty-four youth, forty-nine college students, or sixty adults at the designated space limitations the church had chosen. Note that in this particular church there was a significant college ministry. Since no rules of thumb existed, the church made up its own designation based upon suggestions of the college ministry council and the college minister. These rules of thumb are not rigid. Churches and organizations must consider their own particular ministry, the unique requirements of that ministry and then create their own space-use designations.

One other comment before moving on to explore how the space plan aids in the development of a maintenance schedule. When assigning rooms to program ministries, the administrator must be aware of several important factors. Building codes and fire safety regulations will restrict where you can designate rooms for preschoolers and children. Generally speaking, these rooms must be on ground level with immediate or near immediate exit of the building possible. Additionally, senior adult rooms will need to be placed on lower levels of multiple-storied buildings unless an elevator has been provided, and they should be near entrances and the worship center to reduce walking distance.

Another factor to consider in assigning rooms is the fact that while you may have a department of adults with an enrollment of one hundred, usually on any given meeting day only one-third to one-half will show up. The astute administrator often uses the 80 percent rule when assigning spaces. In the room above, the administrator can assign a department of 75 adults because 80 percent of 75 is 60 and the room will hold 60 adults at 13 ft² per person. Thus, using the suggested rule-of-thumb room-load designation and prudent use of the 80 percent rule, an administrator can make room assignments for program ministries or activities. This leads to the second element of the space utilization plan—frequency.

How often and what the space is used for are important to determine the maintenance requirements. As an example, a preschool classroom that is used on Sunday for a Sunday school classroom and then used other times during the week for a mother's-day-out program, a children's choir program, or a mission activity will have significantly higher cleaning requirements than a classroom that is used only on Sunday for a Sunday school classroom. On the other hand, a senior adult women's Sunday school classroom that is used during the week for a missionary circle meeting probably will have limited additional cleaning requirements simply because senior adults are generally less messy than preschoolers. One maintenance activity will probably take care of the senior adult classroom whereas the preschool classroom will need maintenance after each event.

Each room and space in the facility will need to have a frequency of routine use determination. Special and infrequent use criteria must be taken into consideration in the development of a formula to determine how many man hours it takes per week to maintain the facility. This is usually done by the assignment of a subjective fudge factor for "miscellaneous" maintenance activities, as we will see in a few paragraphs.

The final element in the formula of our space utilization plan is determining what we have to maintain. The time, cleaning products and equipment, and skills necessary for maintaining a vinyl floor in a preschool classroom are significantly different than caring for a commercial carpet in a youth activity room. How the room is composed is important.

In order to prepare maintenance schedules and determine maintenance needs, the composition of the construction elements, equipment, and ceiling/wall/floor textures must be known. This will require an analysis and recording of these facets in a format that is retrievable to compute maintenance schedules. A suggested form is given below that combines the room designation, space use, and space composition elements. A form such as this will be required for every space in the facility.

Let's take a moment to review before moving on. In determining our personnel needs to maintain the facility, we have first developed a space utilization plan. Elements of this plan included:

- Creating a footprint of the facility from blueprints or actual measurements.
- Calculating how much square footage will be required to be maintained.
- Determining how often spaces will be used.
- Assessing the type of construction materials used and equipment in the space.

Now it is time to take this information and determine what type of activities will be required to maintain the space. Not every room will need a thorough cleaning every time a custodian enters it. Various maintenance and housekeeping activities will be called for, depending on the condition of the room and schedules of maintenance that have been established. Facility maintenance can be categorized as (1) preventative maintenance, the planned servicing and repairs of equipment and facilities which result from inspections and systematic schedules; and (2) operational maintenance, or those activities and services which are continuous in order to provide physical resources which are clean, comfortable, attractive, and safe (see plan on the opposite page).

Certain standard terms describe maintenance activities, and these terms allow the administrator to define easily the events that will be accomplished (see table on p. 200).

At this point in the process, the facility manager determines what maintenance activities are necessary for each space based upon the type of space, the characteristics of the space, and the frequency of use of the space. For example:

Sanctuary:	Police Sunday afternoon
	Police early week
	Police and vacuum Saturday
	Clean and restore every other week
Offices:	Police and vacuum daily
	Clean and restore weekly
Washrooms:	Police daily
	Clean and restore twice weekly
Nursery	Clean and restore Sunday afternoon
	Clean and restore within twenty-four hours of use during week

And so forth until all spaces of the church have a determination of what action is required and how often that action should occur.

The next step is to determine how long each one of these maintenance actions will take. Through the years various tables have been developed that estimate time to accomplish certain maintenance activities. The tables, such as the one below, are useful only because they will provide the manager an estimate of the time to complete these tasks with an experienced, trained

EXAMPLE COMMUNITY CHURCH, ANYTOWNS, OKLAHOMA
SPACE UTILIZATION PLAN

TITLE OF SPACE _____ ROOM NO. _____

LOCATION OF SPACE _____

DIMENSIONS: _____ X _____ TOTAL FT² _____

SPACE UTILIZATION:

ACTIVITY	DAY	TIME	ACTIVITY	DAY	TIME

CONSTRUCTION/MAINTENANCE ELEMENTS:

Walls: Texture _____ Color _____

Nailing Surfaces _____

Special Coverings _____

Floor: Subfloor _____ Covering _____

Ceiling: Type _____

Openings: Doors _____ Type _____

Windows _____ Type _____

Lighting: Fixture Type _____ Number _____

Outlets: Type _____ Number _____

Heating: Type _____ Source Element _____

Thermostat _____

Cooling: Type _____ Source Element _____

Thermostat _____

Plumbing: Sink _____ Toilet _____

Floor Drain _____ Other _____

Hot Water Unit _____ Location _____

MAINTENANCE RECORD CROSS REFERENCE _____

FIXED EQUIPMENT:

Chalkboard ___ X _____ White Marker Board ____ X ___ Tackboard ___ X _____ Coat Racks

Cabinets _____

Shelving _____

Picture Rail _____ Pegboard _____

Window Coverings:

Type _____ Number _____

Other fixed _____

Special purpose fixed equipment _____

MOVEABLE EQUIPMENT

Educational Equipment:

Chairs Type _____ Special Purpose _____ Number _____ Storage Unit _____

Tables Type _____ Size ___ X ___ No. _____

Lectern _____ Easel _____ Piano _____

Special Moveable Equipment

Office Equipment:

Desks Type _____ Size _____ No. _____

Chairs _____ Number _____

Bookcase _____ File _____

Cabinets _____ Shelves _____

Storage Unit _____

Other _____

Machines

Word Processing _____

Copy/FAX/Scanner _____ Data System _____

Telephone _____

Special Use Equipment

SPECIAL DESIGN MATERIALS AND EQUIPMENT

_____

DATE OF LAST INSPECTION _____ BY _____

COMMENTS:

Activity	Actions
Police	Pick up all loose paper and trash. Empty trash cans and replace liners. Quickly put furnishings in order. Visually inspect area.
Clean	Spray/apply detergent and/or germicidal cleanser to fixture, wall, or other surfaces to remove dirt by wiping with clean rags or towels. Remove built-up scum, dirt, or grease.
Clean and Restore	Spray/apply detergent and/or germicidal cleanser to fixture, wall, or other surfaces to remove dirt by wiping with clean rags or towels. Remove scum, dirt, or grease. Replace consumable supplies like towels, soap, tissue, etc. Remove trash and replace disposable bags. Sanitize all surfaces.
Dust	Spray surfaces with cleanser/wax and wipe clean with cloth.
Push/dust mop	Use of wide, treated mop head over hard flooring to pick up dust, loose dirt, and debris.
Wet mop	Use of string mop and water to clean/rinse hard flooring. Handle pressure required to scrub floor thoroughly.
Damp mop/spot mop	Use of slightly wet string mop to lightly clean hard floors.
Buff	Use of low-speed floor machine and pad to remove scuff marks.
Spray buff	Use of diluted wax solution and buffer to add shine to hard flooring between stripping and wax applications.
Burnish	Use of high-speed floor machine to reconstitute floor finish and restore luster and shine.
Vacuum	Use of upright or backpack vacuum to remove dirt and debris from surfaces of floor, drapery, furniture, or fixtures.
Strip and wax	Removal of old floor finish by thoroughly scrubbing floor with floor machines and grit pads and then reapplying two or more coats of floor finish.
Top clean carpet	Vacuum and use bonnet pad, foam, or dry chemical to clean top portion of carpet.
Deep clean carpet	Use of water-based steam or pressure-penetrating cleanser to place in solution dirt and debris throughout the carpet and then removing the dirty solution by vacuum.
Routine preventative maintenance	Periodic realignment of equipment, replacing filters, oiling moving parts, tightening screws and bolts. Visually inspecting the equipment for unusual wear. Take meter readings when required.
Repair and restore	Replacing broken parts, restoring equipment and machinery to normal operational status. Performing such actions as painting, carpentry, plumbing, or electrical craftwork.

ACTIVITY	TIME*	ACTIVITY	TIME*
OFFICES		FLOORS	
Police light traffic	12m	STAIRWELLS	
Police medium traffic	13m	Sweep/mop/vacuum landings	25m
Police heavy traffic	15m	Treads	0.5m/tread
Vacuum avg. obstructions	20m	CARPETS	
Vacuum heavy obstructions	30m	Vacuuming few obstructions	20m
RESTROOMS		Vacuuming with obstructions	30m
Clean	60m	Bonnet cleaning	30m
Clean and restore	90m	Chemical cleaning	90m
Clean restroom and locker room	120m	Foam cleaning	45m
CLASSROOMS		Hot water extraction	60m
Police heavy use	10m	Spot cleaning	10m/spot
Police light use	5m	RESILIENT FLOORS	
Police and vacuum	15m	General broom sweeping	15m
Clean white/chalk boards	30m	Dust mop few obstructions	6m
Piano dust and wax	5m each	Dust mop obstructions	10m
WALLS		Damp mop few obstructions	25m
Hand wipe painted walls	200m	Damp mop with obstructions	45m
Hand wipe vinyl/textured	120m	Wet mop/rinse few obstructions	35m
Machine clean	100m	Wet mop/rinse obstructed	50m
Clean/polish marble/stone	100m	Machine scrub 12-in. disk	48m
WINDOWS		Machine scrub 20-in. disk	18m
Interior spray/wipe small pane	90m	Machine stripping 20-in. 175rpm	120m
Interior squeegee large pane	75m	Machine stripping 20-in. 300rpm	80m
Exterior spray/wipe	120m	Apply finish, liquid	45m
Exterior squeegee	30m	Apply finish, paste	60m

Resilient floor finishing operations using 20-inch disk*

ACTIVITY	175-RPM Machine	300-RPM Machine	1000/1600-RPM Machine	2000-RPM Electric Machine	2000-RPM Non-electric Machine
BUFF	25M	15M			
SPRAY BUFF	45M	30M	15M		
BURNISHING			6M	4M	3.5M

*Unless otherwise indicated, time for operation is given in minutes per 1,000 ft^2

maintenance staff. For the purpose of determining staff needs, the tables on page 201 will be useful.

It might be useful to give some examples using the above calculations. Suppose a church that operates a Christian school as part of its ministry uses the recreation facility of the church. There is a 70 ft x 120 ft gym with vinyl floor, two 30 ft x 40 ft locker rooms/toilets, and a 15 ft x 15 ft office. It is decided that every day the gym floor needs to be dust mopped. On Wednesday night the gym floor needs to be wet mopped after the evening meal. On Friday the gym floor will be burnished using a 1,000-rpm electric machine. The toilets and locker rooms will be cleaned and restored daily. The office area will be policed and vacuumed on Friday.

GYM FLOOR 70 x 120 = 8,400 ft²
Dust mop 5 times weekly at 6 minutes per 1,000 ft²
    5 x 6 x 8.4   = 252 minutes
Wet mop 1 time weekly at 35 minutes per 1,000 ft²
    1 x 35 x 8.4   = 294 minutes
Burnishing 1 time weekly with 1,000 rpm burnisher
at 6 minutes per 1,000 ft²
         1 x 6 x 8.4   = 252 minutes
Total   798 minutes
                           13.3 hours

LOCKER ROOMS/TOILETS two at 30 x 40 = 2,400 ft²
Clean and restock 5 times weekly at 120 minutes
per 1,000 ft²
        5 x 120 x 2.4   = 1,440 minutes
                        24 hours

OFFICE one 15 x 15 = 225 ft²
Police 1 time weekly at 13 minutes per 1,000 ft²
        1 x 13 x 0.225   = 2.9 minutes
Vacuum 1 time weekly at 20 minutes per 1,000 ft²
        1 x 20 x 0.225   = 4.5 minutes
Total   7.4 minutes
                        .12 hours

Total maintenance responsibility   37.42 hours

This means that it will require the employment of one full-time custodian just to maintain the recreation building for the week!

The above analysis must be accomplished for each area/space in the church or facility. Below is an example of an analysis of an entire church facility by major space groups.

HOUSEKEEPING SURVEY NEEDS PROJECTION
SUMMARY

Area/Task	Hours/Week
Sanctuary	10.58 hours
Church offices	17.66
Toilets	8.02
Halls and walkways	29.98
Education building A	32.00
Education building B	26.87
Recreation facility	37.42
Kitchen/fellowship hall	16.03
Child care center	17.89
Total routine maintenance	196.45 hours

The above analysis represents the direct computation of the estimates for task accomplishment for each space in the church. It is reported in summarized blocks as we did in the example that was titled *recreation facility.* That complex had two locker rooms/toilets, a gym, and an office. In the subspaces above, the sanctuary might have the auditorium, choir room, baptistry and dressing rooms, a welcome center, and an electronics sound booth. The church offices might be made up of five executive office suites, four secretarial stations, a waiting room, finance office, a workroom, and a storage facility. Toilets may include three men, three women, and one general restroom. And so forth. Each space must be counted.

Just a word of encouragement before you close the book and say that this is too hard. What we are doing in computing this estimate of work is to establish justification for the hiring of custodial staff to maintain the facility. You go to a personnel or finance committee and say you need five custodians to keep the building clean, safe, and habitable, and you may or may not get them. Go with the above analysis in hand, and you have justified the five employees. This is a one-time computation. You do not have to do this every week. It is good to review your computations every once in a while, but for the most part this task in its entirety will not have to be repeated.

We are not through with the above computation yet. What about the weekly bonnet cleaning of the hall carpets, the twice-a-year stripping of the gym floor, and refinishing it. How about the once-a-year window cleaning or twice-a-year deep cleaning of all carpets. Those items will take time. They will not be scheduled to occur all at the same time, but the time must be accounted for.

Suppose you determine the following special maintenance actions will occur during the year:

Weekly bonnet cleaning of 12,000 ft^2 hall carpet

Twice year deep cleaning of 52,000 ft^2 carpet throughout the facility

Annual cleaning of 4,600 ft^2 exterior windows; 5,700 ft^2 interior windows/glass

Twice-a-year stripping of 8,400 ft^2 gym floor and refinishing

Twice-a-year stripping and refinishing 14,700 ft^2 of vinyl/tile floor

How much time will this take? This computation must also be made and then converted to a weekly requirement format.

Weekly bonnet cleaning of 12,000 ft^2 hall carpet
  52 x 30 min/1,000 x 12.0 = 18,720 min   =312 hours/year
Twice-a-year deep cleaning of 52,000 ft^2 carpet throughout the facility
  2 x 60 min/1,000 x 52.0 = 6,240 min   =104 hours/year
Annual cleaning of 4,600 ft^2 exterior windows; 5,700 ft^2 interior windows/glass
  1 x 120 min/1,000 x 4.6 = 552 min   =9.2 hours/year
                                          exterior windows
  1 x 90 min/1,000 x 5.7 = 513 min   =8.6 hours/year
                                          interior windows
Twice-a-year stripping of 8,400 ft^2 gym floor and refinishing
  2 x 80 min/300rpm machine/
      1,000 x 8.4 = 1344 min   = 22.4 hours strip
  2 x 45 min liquid finish/
      1,000 x 8.4 = 756 min   =12.6 hours new finish
Twice-a-year stripping and refinishing 14,700 ft^2 of vinyl/tile floor
  2 x 80 min/300rpm machine/
      1,000 x 14.7 = 2352 min   =39.2 hours strip
  2 x 45 min liquid finish/
      1,000 x 14.7 = 1323 min   =22.05 hours new finish

  Total special maintenance operations   530.05 hours/year
                                            10.19 hours/week

We need to add this figure to our projection of maintenance needs:

HOUSEKEEPING SURVEY NEEDS PROJECTION
SUMMARY

Area/Task	Hours/Week
Sanctuary	10.58 hours
Church offices	17.66
Toilets	8.02
Halls and walkways	29.98
Education building A	32.00
Education building B	26.87
Recreation facility	37.42
Kitchen/fellowship hall	16.03
Child care center	17.89
Total routine maintenance	196.45 hours
Total special maintenance operations	10.19 hours
Subtotal	206.64 hours

We are not through yet! What happens when a delivery truck pulls up with twenty-two cases of new folding chairs? Who unloads them? Who sets up a Bible study room when the Tuesday morning women's Bible study group needs to meet at the church since Aunt Maude is sick and they need a place to meet? Who sets up the sanctuary for a funeral? What about the set-up time for getting ready to do work? Who changes the lightbulbs? What about routine preventative maintenance and the infrequent repair and restore jobs that need to be done. And finally, what about the urgent need to go to the post office and deliver a package, or to run to the office supply store to get several reams of special paper? In Texas, we have a name for this person—the "gofer." You know, go-fer-this, go-fer-that. Research has indicated that 5 to 10 percent of maintenance time is taken up with these operations. Using a 5 percent figure for the 206.64 hours/week of routine and special maintenance operations above, we discover that the computation will require us to add 10.33 hours to the formula.

One final computation is needed before we draw a double line to the computations that determine how many hours per week it will require us to schedule to maintain the facility. Frequently maintenance personnel will be assigned routine, special operations that do not necessarily pertain to maintenance. An example of such scheduled time is opening and securing the facility or time to bring online heating or cooling equipment. Filling the baptistry each Sunday morning could be another. Placing parking and welcome center signs and getting out supplies for greeters and ushers might be additional nonmaintenance operations. Delivering or picking up mail might also be assigned to the maintenance staff. The amount of time carried out in these special custodial operations needs to be added to the bottom line. For the sake of numbers, let's assume that these responsibilities will consume eight hours of custodial time per week.

Now our computations are complete; let's summarize:

HOUSEKEEPING SURVEY NEEDS PROJECTION SUMMARY

Area/Task	Hours/Week
Sanctuary	10.58 hours
Church offices	17.66
Toilets	8.02
Halls and walkways	29.98
Education building A	32.00
Education building B	26.87
Recreation facility	37.42
Kitchen/fellowship hall	16.03
Child care center	17.89
Total routine maintenance	196.45 hours
Total special maintenance operations	10.19 hours
5 percent for unscheduled operations	0.33 hours
Scheduled special custodial operations	8.00 hours
Total custodial requirements	224.97 hours
Number of custodians required 224.97 hours / 40 hours/week	5.62 custodians

Let's review what we have done so far. We established a space utilization plan that discovered how many square feet of facility we had and what the construction and equipment composition of those spaces were. We then analyzed the use of these spaces. From this analysis we determined what maintenance actions were required on a weekly basis for each space in the space utilization plan. We then computed any special scheduled maintenance operations that were accomplished infrequently and divided that total time across the year. We added in a "fudge factor" for contingencies and unexpected operations as well as adding in a figure that described any nonmaintenance operations the custodians would be responsible for. Adding those figures we now have an estimate of how many man-hours will be required to maintain the facility.

What management tools do we now have?

1. We have a system that describes each space in the facility; its composition, equipment, and special requirements.

2. We have a system that provides a basis for scheduling routine maintenance and recording that maintenance.
3. We have a system that describes how and when a space is used, thus allowing scheduling to be consolidated.
4. We have a system that describes routine as well as nonroutine maintenance actions that are required to maintain that space in a clean, safe, and habitable condition.
5. We have a system that describes routine as well as nonroutine maintenance actions that will assist in the scheduling of maintenance activities by custodial personnel.
6. We have justified the personnel maintenance requirements to maintain the facility in a clean, safe, and habitable condition.
7. We have established a baseline for estimating costs for maintaining the facility.

Determining Maintenance Mix

When the question is asked, "How many custodians does it take . . . ?" the answer will always be at least one. Why one? Why not two, three, or six? This section will deal with the issue of contract maintenance personnel and other non-in-house maintenance personnel.

Contractor versus in-house maintenance crew. Several years ago as the CBA of a large church that had a recreation facility as part of the ministry program, I would have to close down the gym for a couple weeks each year for floor maintenance. The manufacturer of the floor had recommended that we strip the old finish from the wood-product floor every six months and then apply a new three-coat finish. The floor really required that type of maintenance, since the gym area was used as a six-day-a-week recreational area, a dining area for five to six hundred on Wednesday night, and a college Sunday school meeting area for four to five hundred students.

The problem with stripping and refinishing twice yearly was that a major ministry of the church was shut down for two to three weeks a year! The odor was terrible since we were using a phenolic/oil-base chemical. If the temperature or humidity was not just right, drying time for the finish would extend into the next week. In discussing this problem with a person who was responsible for the maintenance of gym floors for the local school system, he suggested that I consider contracting this service. He told me that for a long time he had a crew that went from school to school doing the floor maintenance. The cost of equipment, supplies, and manpower was what caused him to investigate the use of a floor-maintenance contractor.

I contacted his contractor and made some interesting discoveries. First, the state-of-the-art in floor maintenance had changed dramatically since the initial floor installation and instructions from the supplier. Second, he said that using water-based chemicals would eliminate the odor that permeated the church for weeks after floor refinishing. And finally, he said that his crew could come in and do the operation in a night and a day since he would be using machinery and dryers. The facility would be ready for use within two days. From then on I contracted out the stripping and refinishing of the gym floor.

The decision to contract for maintenance services or to do the work with an in-house employed crew is a decision the manager must make. That decision should be made with a full assessment of the advantages and disadvantages of using contract personnel.

Here are the advantages of using contractors:

1. It eliminates personnel problems. The contractor is responsible for employment decisions: recruitment, hiring, and firing. If you specify a person with a background check, the contractor will be responsible for that action. You will not have to make salary decisions or make tax-reporting decisions. Benefits such as medical insurance are the contractor's responsibility. Probably the greatest personnel advantage is the fact that a steady workforce to maintain the facility will be provided by the contractor; you do not have to account for vacation, sick leave, or other employee time off.

2. It eliminates the need to purchase expensive equipment. Sophisticated cleaning equipment is expensive. The purchase of such equipment will significantly impact the capital funds available for ministry equipment. By using a contractor, you will expect that contractor to be responsible for providing his own equipment. You will not have to worry about downtime, equipment repair or replacement, or depreciation.

3. You are not responsible for the consumable cleaning supplies. The contractor will select the best cleaning chemicals that are appropriate for his equipment and the task. You have no ordering or storage responsibilities. The contractor assumes the responsibility for product decisions.

4. The responsibility for providing trained personnel becomes the contractor's. The contractor will ensure that his or her employees know how to use the equipment and products efficiently to accomplish the task. Specialized training becomes the responsibility of the contractor.

Here are the disadvantages of using contractors:

1. A greater degree of planning is required on the part of the church manager. Specific schedules must be established to allow the contractor access to the space. Variations to these schedules must be coordinated with the contractor. In some instances, flexibility of planning church/organization events is dictated by maintenance schedules.

2. Inspection of work accomplished becomes more difficult. Whether the maintenance is accomplished by a contractor or an in-house crew, the

cleanliness and habitability of the facility still must be supervised. With a contract maintenance crew, this evaluation process is more difficult.

3. Immediate custodial problems are more difficult to handle. When events such as spills or other cleanliness problems, called meetings, funerals, and weddings occur, it is often impossible to accommodate these situations with a contract maintenance scheme.

4. The loss of the "gofer" for handling delivery/pickups, special program setups, hauling and unloading could present some difficulties with normal routine.

5. Security of the facility may be compromised. A contractor will have to have access to the facility. That will translate into a cleaning supervisor with a key to the facility. Access is thus passed to a second-party controller. A second security issue is that it is usually a custodian who opens and closes the church for services or program events. That service will probably not be available with a contract service.

The wise facility manager will conduct an evaluation of his or her own situation and weigh the real costs of an in-house maintenance operation against the costs for a contracted maintenance program. The real costs include equipment needs, cleaning products and supplies, storage requirements, waste, training in use of equipment, repair and downtime of equipment, depreciation, and the inability of the equipment purchased to clean difficult or unusual problems.

Regardless of your decision, the answer to the basic question remains the same. How many custodians? The answer is still one. You still need a gofer, a person to make an emergency setup, or to respond to an unscheduled need. And most important, you need someone to inspect the work of a contractor. You don't want to assume that responsibility; you have enough to do.

A suggested balance is offered. Employ at least one in-house custodian. Assess the maintenance responsibilities of the facility. Consider contracting out major tasks or tasks that require specialized equipment. For instance, in the example we discussed above in the computation of required maintenance time, these special operations could be considered contract items:

- Weekly bonnet cleaning of 12,000 ft^2 hall carpet: **312 hours/year**
- Twice-a-year deep cleaning of 52,000 ft^2 carpet throughout the facility: **104 hours/year**
- Annual cleaning of 4,600 ft^2 exterior windows; 5,700 ft^2 interior windows/glass: **9.2 hours/year exterior windows and 8.6 hours/year interior windows**
- Twice-a-year stripping of 8,400 ft^2 gym floor and refinishing: **22.4 hours strip and 12.6 hours new finish**
- Twice-a-year stripping and refinishing 14,700 ft^2 of vinyl/tile floor: **39.2 hours strip and 22.05 hours new finish**

This translates to 530 hours per year or 10.19 hours of maintenance per week that could be contracted.

Beyond special maintenance contracts, the church or organization may contract with a cleaning service to place an individual or individuals in the church as a full-time assignment. This is an attractive option because it provides continuity of service while at the same time enjoying the benefits of not having to make employment, training, or replacement decisions. In most cases when this option is explored, the contractor will expect the church to provide equipment, supplies, and the space to store these items.

Contractors will bid a church or organization's job in one of several ways. The administrator needs to be aware of how the contract price is derived.

1. *Hourly unit method.* This method is the most commonly used by cleaning maintenance contractors. It involves a determination of the square footage to be cleaned and the degree of difficulty in the cleaning operations. A series of rules-of-thumb exist:

Type of environment to be cleaned	Average ft² cleaned per person per hour
Open, no obstructions	3,250
Light soil, some obstructions	2,750
Normal soil, average obstructions	2,500
Heavy soil or numerous obstructions	2,250
Heavy soil and traffic/congestion present	1,750

An example: Suppose your 25,000 ft² needs to be cleaned five times per week. The job is to occur after hours. The contractor determines a normal soil/average obstruction environment. The contract includes two special floor cleaning requirements: deep clean carpet and strip and wax resilient flooring twice a year. The contractor pays her employees $7.10 per hour.

Normal weekly operations:

25,000 ft² / 2,500 ft²/person/hour	= 10 hours per day
10 hours/day x 22 days/month	= 220 hours/month
220 hours/month x $7.10	= $1,562 labor cost/month

Special maintenance operations:

Extractor cleaning of 20,000 ft² carpet

2 x 60 min/1,000 ft² x 20,000	= 20 hours

Strip/refinish 5,000 ft² resilient flooring using 20 inch 300 rpm machine

2 x 80 min/1,000 ft² x 5,000	= 13.3 hours
2 x 45 min/1,000 ft² x 5,000	= 7.5 hours
20 + 13.3 + 7.5 hours	= 40.8 hours x $7.10
	= $289 68 labor cost $289.68 / 12 months
	= $24.14 costs per month

Expect a bid of ($1562 + $24.14) x 2 = $3,172.28 cost/month

Where did the "x 2" come from? That is the contractor's overhead and profit.

2. *Work unit method.* This system relies on an estimation of the capability of the worker. These tables are similar to those given earlier in this chapter, but rather than time in minutes per 1,000 square feet, the work unit tables are expressed in work units to completion format. An example problem will not be useful at this time since the tables are not available to us, and the capability of a worker is a function of the determination of the supervisor. Some employees can produce more work units per hour than others. As a general rule, contracts that are bid using the work unit method are 15 to 20 percent higher than using the other two methods discussed in this section.

3. *Fixed unit pricing method.* This method is similar to the square footage method in that it relies upon a determination of the total square footage to be cleaned and the environment that surrounds that space. The estimate is based, however, on the average costs to clean such a space given the current market and economy. For instance, estimates in the south central part of the U.S. were:

$0.054/ft^2 cleaned for large, open spaces with light work/flooring

.064/ft^2 cleaning at the "average" rate. Large buildings (5,000 ft+) with average service. This rate equates to minimum wage plus overhead.

.074/ft^2 cleaning rate used for some congestion or specialized cleaning tasks

.084/ft^2 heavy cleaning required, high impact areas, congestion. The rate is used for small jobs.

For example, suppose you wanted only to have the contractor clean 1,000 ft^2 of offices every evening during the week. Offices are considered "average" cleaning, but in this instance since you are only contracting for 1,000 ft^2, you will pay the higher price of $.084. Thus, $0.084 x 1,000 x 2 = $168/month. If you contracted your 25,000 ft^2 church using this method, you would get the lower "average" cleaning rate of $0.064/ft^2, and the bid would probably be: $0.064 x 25,000 x 2 = $3,200/month.

Compare this bid of $3,200 to the hourly unit method bid of $3,172. They are nearly the same. Therefore, you will be able to use either the fixed unit or hourly unit scheme in determining what to expect from a contractor in the bidding process. A word of caution: The cost per hour or cost per square foot will vary from region to region and over time as the economy fluctuates. Annually the Cleaning Management Institute produces a report of the industry in which they report average cost per region. If you do not have access to this periodical, check your local library. Possibly the maintenance manager of a local hospital, school system, or university may be a subscriber/member.

Why would an administrator want to do these computations? In the first place, they give you an estimate of what it would cost you to contract out the work. You already know how to calculate the cost for an in-house crew—time x salary + benefits. You must now add what it will take in equipment and supplies to get the job done, and you now have a comparative figure. Another reason the administrator might want to do this computation is to determine if there are any portions of the housekeeping task that might be contracted out in a cost-efficient move. For example, if carpet cleaning does not really take an inordinate amount of employee time but the cost of the equipment makes it a cost-prohibitive in-house operation, then the decision may be to contract out carpet cleaning and reassign personnel to other areas and at the same time not purchase expensive equipment.

Working with Volunteers

Suppose on a Saturday morning a group of twenty-five individuals come together for coffee, juice, and doughnuts and after a brief time of fellowship and prayer, they work at cleaning and fixing up the church from eight to noon. The four hours each volunteer gave you added up to one hundred hours for the entire crew. Suppose that you pay your janitors $8.10 per hour. That Saturday morning you got one hundred man-hours of work accomplished, and that equated to $810 in janitorial work for free.

There are several good reasons to consider the use of volunteers as part (notice I said part) of your maintenance plan.

1. It provides a sense of belonging. Members meet others with like gifts and sense of church responsibility. They form fellowship bonds as they work together. And they feel part of the larger group, the church. An appropriate philosophy of the use of spiritual gifts might be that some are called to serve the church in such a manner.

2. It fosters a sense of ownership. Members are working on "their" church. Frequently assignments are made in the area or program they work in on Sunday or Wednesday night. By working "on" the church, individuals see "in" the church. They discover areas of the church they probably seldom see on a routine basis.

3. It develops a sense of stewardship. Members feel they are contributing to the church, not only their time but their talents and skills. It provides a mechanism where members can see their stewardship in action. While administrators will enjoy the money saved, so will the members.

Successful use of volunteer labor requires a plan. You should:
- Have a specific activity or activities in mind. List the jobs to be done.
- Have a range of skill-ability. Some people will be able to do only housekeeping; others will have craft skills like electricians, plumbers, carpenters.

- Provide the necessary materials. Don't expect them to bring cleaning supplies or equipment. Gather these items beforehand.
- Provide unique equipment. If you are going to clean windows, obtain scaffolding. If it is building a classroom, get power tools.
- Motivate the participants. Move through the group and encourage them.
- Thank them, not only on the job that day, but follow up the next week with a personal note. Tell them what they accomplished and what it meant to the church—both in monetary terms and program ministry. Recognize them in bulletins and from the pulpit.

A word of caution: You cannot give credit on a giving record for time spent as a volunteer. Check IRS Publication 526 *Charitable Contributions* for specific information if your parishioners disagree.

The use of ministry teams can be an important element of the maintenance strategy that includes the use of volunteers. One year the youth minister came to me and asked if the youth could take on the task of mowing the lawn for the summer. I had serious reservations about the prospect because the church for the past several years had used a contractor to maintain the church grounds. The youth minister's rationale was that the youth were searching for ways that they could feel a part of the body. They wanted to contribute to the church! I met with the youth council and youth minister and agreed that the youth would take on the task. They would use their own (actually their parent's) equipment, and the adults of the youth council would provide the supervision.

That summer was the beginning of an exciting facet of the youth ministry at the church. They met each Saturday morning for a light breakfast, a period of Bible study and prayer, and then received assignments. They were usually done by ten to eleven o'clock that morning. The grounds looked great! They took great pride in what they were doing. We made sure the church body knew that the exceptional looking grounds were the efforts of the youth ministry division. They had so many volunteers they had to form teams that rotated through the month.

When the youth council asked if they could continue next year with the project, I was more than willing to have the youth as part of the volunteer maintenance team. I budgeted for equipment and purchased all they needed so their parents' lawn equipment would not have to be used. It was a great team ministry relationship. I kept them in good equipment. I purchased T-shirts one year, hats another. The youth minister used the Saturday mornings as another touch point to get close to the individuals in his ministry.

Volunteer team ministries were started in a variety of areas that relieved maintenance requirements. The flower ministry team not only ensured the plant decorations in the facility were watered and healthy; they took responsibility for the garden and flower areas of the outdoor landscaping. The church was a 1950s construction church and required many modifications to the facility to meet modern concepts of program ministry. A young men's Bible study group became my "wrecking crew" ministry team. They volunteered to assist in minor renovations to the church, tearing out partition walls to enlarge spaces and then refurbishing and painting the space.

Volunteers in the church are vital. They cannot replace the routine maintenance operations of maintaining the church facility, but they can become an essential supplemental source of maintenance and housekeeping personnel. When they spend ten hours cleaning out closets or bookshelves, you have just freed up ten hours of custodial time to do tasks that only they are trained to accomplish.

Personnel Training

The effectiveness of any maintenance program is a function of the expertise of the people who are employed to accomplish the custodial and housekeeping tasks. Earlier in the discussion of employment, we stated that you should seek to employ the most qualified person. Implied in that admonition was the principle of hiring a person who was capable of doing the job as the result of training, experience, or both. Because most church or nonprofit organizations offer an attractive work environment and because churches usually pay a salary that is above the national average for janitorial personnel, it is usually easy to employ qualified maintenance personnel.

Once they are employed, it is the responsibility of the church to continue to upgrade the level of expertise of the maintenance personnel. There are three general areas of additional training.

1. *On-the-job-training.* For on-the-job training to be effective, you must first have someone on the maintenance staff who can train the employee. If the supervisor is to do the training, it must be part of the job description; time must be allowed in the computation of workload; and specific time must be set aside weekly or monthly for training.

2. *Vendors and product distributors.* I would not buy a cleaning product or piece of equipment that a vendor or salesperson was not willing to demonstrate and to train my maintenance personnel in its proper use. We will talk about products later in the text, but if the vendor will not stand behind his product, the product is not worth buying.

Frequently in the larger metropolitan areas, product distributors will invite the product manufacturing representatives to conduct a clinic or workshop for their products. These training opportunities not only introduce new product lines but also provide training in existing or base products of the manufacturer.

Organizations like the National Association of Church Business Administration and National Association of Church Facility Managers conduct day long workshops where they invite product distributors to introduce and train maintenance personnel in the proper use of the equipment or product.

3. *Schools and training programs.* Many regional trade schools and community colleges offer courses that focus on facility management that would be appropriate for you or your building supervisor to attend. A few local schools are available for training in custodial operations. An excellent training program for the supervisor and custodian as well exists with the Cleaning Management Institute. In addition to the courses, the institute provides several texts that assist in facility maintenance operations. Trade publications like *Cleaning Management* of the Cleaning Management Institute and *Executive Housekeeping* offer articles that assist in facility management.

One of the most useful facets of the trade publications is the presence of advertiser links to ask for information about products. Many manufacturers will provide instruction books and pamphlets about their product lines. Since the number and types of training opportunities will change over time, only a representative sample is given to assist the facility manager. A search of the Internet will provide numerous opportunities for training.

Training is an important ongoing activity that every facility manager must take seriously if the church or organization's physical assets are to be maintained efficiently and adequately. One should never overlook the literature about maintenance which vendors/suppliers provide. The products they sell have brochures and guidance manuals that are available for your use. It is easy to obtain these materials, and, once you begin to use products and equipment with the supplier, they will ensure you are thoroughly informed about their products—present and future. Product information is also available on Web sites of providers of the cleaning products and equipment.

Scheduling for Maintenance

One of the first tasks any administrator is willing to delegate is that of scheduling. It is a tedious, laborious, and often thankless job. But somebody has to do it. As we noted in chapter 2, scheduling is putting plans on a calendar. It is the process of saying when certain activities will occur. Scheduling is preceded by determining what is to be done, setting established parameters for how it is to be done, and determining who will do it. Scheduling is a process. Management leadership will establish the parameters and conditions for task accomplishment and then delegate to administrative supervisors to get the job done.

I learned an interesting fact about delegation while in the Navy. If the commanding officer tells you to do something, he will expect you to do it, even if you delegate to one of your subordinates some or all of the task. When the commanding officer wants to know the status of an assignment, he comes to you, not to the subordinate to whom you delegated the task.

If church leadership, whether the pastor or the properties committee, said they wanted the church to be clean, safe, and habitable for the various programs, then as CBA I became fully responsible for accomplishing the task. But make no bones about it, I delegated the maintenance operations to the building supervisor, who scheduled getting the work accomplished. Does this mean I had nothing to do with scheduling? I was still involved in establishing the type of schedule to be used, monitoring the effectiveness of the schedule, and evaluating whether the schedule that had been established was accomplishing the assignment to the expectation of my leaders.

Why is scheduling important? There are four basic reasons scheduling is critical for the effective facility management.

1. Scheduling ensures all areas of the facility are cleaned. Schedules are comprehensive, and they consider all the tasks. Some tasks will be routine, weekly maintenance, and housekeeping actions. Other tasks will be periodic or as scheduled. The administrator's task is to make sure all maintenance actions that are planned throughout the year are scheduled for accomplishment.

2. Scheduling distributes the work appropriately and equally. Schedulers visualize the job with knowledge of what the task entails and the expectations of time to accomplishment. Prorata assignments become important to ensure completion of the maintenance activity.

3. Scheduling takes into account nonroutine activities. Preventative maintenance actions often occur infrequently and would not normally be part of a daily routine schedule. But they are necessary and planned actions and must be placed on a maintenance schedule.

4. Scheduling is necessary so you can modify planned maintenance activities to accommodate unplanned or unexpected activities. If a maintenance activity has to be replaced or a schedule altered, an established schedule will allow the administrator to make the necessary revisions to ensure completion at a later time.

Formats for Scheduling

Whether scheduling for maintenance actions is a responsibility that is delegated, it will be the manager's responsibility to establish the parameters and philosophy for the process and the administrator's responsibility to see that it gets done. Schedules may appear in a variety of formats, each with advantages and disadvantages. Additionally, some schedules will be more appropriate for different types and sizes of churches.

1. Daily Schedules. Probably the easiest maintenance schedule to make is when you have one custodian who is responsible for doing everything. In actuality

TUESDAY 6 JUNE/158

SHIFT ONE	Vacuum all office spaces
Unlock doors and turn on lights	Extraction Clean Education wing 2 carpets
Police and vacuum office area	Remove all trash kitchen/recreation building
Vacuum Chapel	Clean and disinfect nursery area
Police and vacuum Education wing 2	Turn off all lights in facility
Police and vacuum Worship Center	Lock all building and set alarm
SHIFT TWO	
Clean and re-stock Education building toilets	
Dust mop gym floor	
Clean and restock Recreation building toilets	
Wet mop showers, disinfect floors and walls	
Police Music suite for Sr Adult Choir	
Bonnet Clean Sanctuary Foyer	
SHIFT THREE	
Secure offices	

Shift Two will provide for morning mail run
Shift Three will provide for afternoon mail run

you and the custodian become partners in developing the schedule. Your primary responsibility is to inform him of the program schedule of the church or organization and then allow him to develop a maintenance scheme to get the job done.

The task becomes more difficult in a larger organization. We have determined what maintenance tasks need to be accomplished in each space and how frequently those tasks must be completed. Additionally, the maintenance administrator knows what types of special operations need to be scheduled daily, weekly, monthly, and annually. Schedules that list maintenance operations then can be developed for each day. For example, on this page is a maintenance schedule for Tuesday June 6, or the 158th maintenance day of the year.

A schedule chart similar to the one above must be completed for each maintenance day of the year. These charts list the tasks that must be accomplished for that day. Personnel assignments are made the week that the maintenance action is scheduled, since the supervisor must account for vacation, sickness, etc.

While this is a big task, remember that it is an administrative function that should not require constant adjustment. If additional maintenance responsibilities or new facility is added, then new items may be added. This type of schedule is easily maintained using a computer-based management system.

2. Shift Scheduling. Suppose your church begins the day with a men's Bible study group that meets at 6:00 A.M. and ends with a recreation program that closes down at 10:00 P.M. that evening. The church has decided to assign to the custodial staff the responsibility to open and secure the facility daily. For a single custodian that would be a sixteen-hour workday. Probably a church with such an expansive ministry as this will have more than one janitor on staff. By staggering shifts, the entire sixteen-hour period is covered.

For larger churches or churches with extensive programs, preschool care programs, or with a school or academy attached, the use of staggered personnel assignments may be the way to schedule maintenance. The preliminary steps are the same as daily schedules. Determine facility maintenance needs per space based on schedule and maintenance actions required, determine personnel requirements, and develop a daily maintenance scheme that accounts for all routine, special, and unscheduled events.

Each shift must have a supervisor who will make personnel maintenance assignments. Shifts will normally be staggered throughout the day to provide both continuity and overlap. For instance, shift 1 may begin at 5:30 A.M. and go to 1:00 P.M. with a half-hour mid-morning break. Shift 2 would begin at 11:00 A.M. and go to 7:30 P.M. with a half-hour mid-afternoon break. Shift 3 would begin at 5:00 P.M. and end at 1:30 A.M. with a mid-evening thirty-minute break. If personnel are scheduled through the weekend, the manager may choose to have shorter work periods during the day to extend the forty-hour workweek into the weekend.

The dynamics of shift scheduling are numerous. Some personnel will want to remain on the same shift assignment on a permanent basis. Others will want to rotate so they will not always be working late in the evening. Some individuals will want to work the weekend schedule; others will want to avoid weekend assignments. Shift scheduling will require a building supervisor who will not only administer the scheme but who will also be the inspector and evaluator of work assignments.

3. Task Assignment. This form of scheduling is usually reserved for facilities with extensive maintenance requirements. It takes on two formats.

Individual specific task assignments. Suppose in your computation of maintenance requirements you discover that maintenance of the kitchen area, the dining rooms, and all bathroom facilities took thirty-seven man-hours of labor each week. Then you could conceivably assign one person these tasks. The only scheduling would be ensuring that specific areas were cleaned before they were needed for use. For instance, cleaning the kitchen would have to occur on two specific occasions: immediately before and after its use. Before—it would need to be wiped down, mopped, and sanitized. After—thoroughly cleaned, trash removed, equipment cleaned, and floors and walls cleaned.

Another individual could be assigned vacuuming responsibilities all day, every day, while another individual may have room cleaning and straightening responsibilities.

Assignment by specific task makes it easy to hold the appropriate person accountable. It causes scheduling problems, however, when that person is absent and no one can take his place because all other janitors have specific assignments that will take their entire workday.

Individual task area assignments. Another form of assigning work is to assign a person a specific task area on a daily basis. This scheme takes advantage of the varying capabilities of the maintenance personnel. Each task has an assignment card made up that describes the task, the equipment and supply requirements, a step-by-step procedure for completing the task, and an estimate of the time for completion. At the beginning of the workday, the building supervisor meets with janitorial and custodial personnel and makes assignments of the maintenance actions that his or her schedule indicates must be accomplished that day. An example of such an assignment card is on page 220.

This scheme will require a card to be prepared for each maintenance action; routine, special, or unscheduled.

4. Crew Assignment. The final format is similar to the individual task assignment in that it assigns a specific set of recurring tasks; however, this time the assignment is made to a group of individuals. This format is usually used only in large facilities. In this format you will have a crew of individuals that performs a specific function on a continuing basis. For instance, you may have two or three individuals who will clean washrooms, toilets, and dressing areas every day. Another crew will perform carpet cleaning while another crew will care for resilient floors. Another crew will be assigned "bright work," or the polishing of pews, furniture, and other wooden fixtures. You may have a glass crew, a yard crew, or a routine preventative maintenance crew.

You cannot hand a crew of janitors a vacuum and say "here, go forth and vacuum." To use this format the manager must still go through the process of determining what maintenance actions need to be accomplished, when these actions should be done, and how much time it will take. You will want to make sure that all areas of the facility are adequately cleaned and that the appropriate number of personnel is assigned to the project to get the job done adequately.

An example assignment schedule for a carpet cleaning crew is on page 220.

A schedule card will have to be made up for each crew that outlines their maintenance responsibilities. Maintenance tasks may be combined. For example, the "bright work" wood polishers might also have glass-polishing responsibilities.

MAINTENANCE ASSIGNMENT
Carpet Cleaning Crew

MONDAY
Shifts 1 & 2
Vacuum all halls
Vacuum interior of sanctuary
Shift 3
Vacuum office area
Extraction clean

TUESDAY
Shifts 1 & 2
Vacuum classrooms Bldg. A
Bonnet clean halls Bldg. A
Shift 3
Vacuum office area
Extraction clean

WEDNESDAY
Shifts 1 & 2
Vacuum music suite
Vacuum classrooms Bldg. B
Bonnet clean halls Bldg. B
Shift 3
Vacuum office area
Vacuum chapel
Vacuum dining room

THRUSDAY
Shifts 1 & 2
Vacuum all halls
Bonnet clean foyer
Shift 3
Vacuum office area
Spot clean all reported areas

FRIDAY
Shift 1 & 2
Vacuum classrooms Bldg. C
Bonnet clean halls Bldg. C
Shift 3
Vacuum office area
Bonnet clean sanctuary as needed

SATURDAY
Shifts 1 & 2
Vacuum all halls
Shift 3
Vacuum sanctuary and surrounding
worship center areas

EXTRACTION CLEANING SCHEDULE

1/26	Classrooms Bldg. C, level 1	14/39	Classrooms Bldg. A, level 1
2/27	Classrooms Bldg. C level 2	15/40	Classrooms Bldg. A, level 2
3/28	Classrooms Bldg. C level 3	16/41	Classrooms Bldg. A, level 3
4/29	Parlor	17/42	Library/Media Center
5/30	Fellowship Hall	18/43	Halls Bldg. C, level 1
6/31	Classrooms Bldg. B, level 1	19/44	Halls Bldg. C, level 2
7/32	Classrooms Bldg. B, level 2	20/45	Halls Bldg. C, level 3
8/33	Sanctuary foyer	21/46	Halls Bldg. B, level 1
9/34	Sanctuary	22/47	Halls Bldg. B, level 2
10/35	Staff Offices	23/48	Halls Bldg. A, level 1
11/36	Executive Offices	24/49	Halls Bldg. A, level 2
12/37	Music Suite	25/50	Halls Bldg. A, level 3
13/38	Music Suite	26/51	As needed

Preventative Maintenance Schedules

The heart of a preventative maintenance program is the inspection and inventory of facility assets in a timely and systematic manner. The plant account, the stationary and movable equipment in the church facility, represents a significant investment of funds. Anywhere from 20 to 30 percent of the value of a facility will be made up of these items. Like the fixed assets, the buildings and all that is nailed down, attention must be paid to their care and maintenance on a routine basis.

Earlier in this chapter we discussed the fact that attention must be paid to the stewardship of the resources of the church since they represent not only the tangible representation of tithes and offerings but also because God expects us to be stewards in every area of life and ministry. The development of a formal system of inventory control, inspection, and maintenance is suggested as the best way to accomplish this.

1. Inventory. It would be ridiculous to expect a facility manager to keep up with every item of stationary and movable equipment in the church. But certain equipment and furnishings should be accounted for. Some churches or

EQUIPMENT INVENTORY AND MAINTENANCE RECORD
Data Sheet

Equipment nomenclature _____

Location _____ Inventory Number _____

Manufacturers description _____

Model number _____ Serial Number _____

Supplier _____ Date Purchased _____

Cost Data:

      Equipment cost   _____

      Shipping charges   _____

      Installation charges _____

      Trade-in/discount   _____

      Total cost   _____

Warranty

      Manufacturer's _____ Supplier's_____

      Terms_____

      _____

      Certificate filed in:

Service Contract

      Supplier_____

      Period _____ to _____

      Cost per period _____

      Terms_____

EQUIPMENT INVENTORY AND MAINTENANCE RECORD
Record of Inventory, Inspection, and Maintenance

DATE	INSPECTION INVENTORY MAINTENANCE (Indicate which)	ACTION TAKEN	BY

Repair		
Date	**Action**	**By Whom**

organizations require the CBA to know the condition and position of every chair, table, and lectern. Others establish a value limit of those items that need to be accounted for. The development of a format for knowing what is present in the plant account must be the administrator's first task. An example format for such an inventory and maintenance record form is given above. This form may become a paper record, but it is apparent that by using a data field format, the form can be computerized for electronic record and entry. The objective is to have in a single form the equipment recorded, its nomenclature identified, the location of the equipment specified, and maintenance and repair data tabulated.

The church or organization should specify in its policy and procedures what is to be recorded. For example, a church may state that all tables, chairs, and other classroom equipment; office equipment; electronic and sound equipment; and any fixed item that costs $100 or greater will be recorded. Two rules of thumb: (1) An item that could be pilfered or raises security concerns should should be accounted for on a regular basis. (2) An item that requires routine (monthly, annual, etc.) maintenance should be placed in inventory.

Accountability may be accomplished in several fashions. Sometimes the inventory control record sheet/card similar to the one below will be all that is necessary to list the items that are to be accounted for. This system will work with single items such as a sound system amplifier or an office computer. Where this scheme breaks down is if the church or organization chooses to account for many items of the same category. For example, folding chairs. These items will be scattered throughout the facility and will be difficult to account for.

Another way to account for equipment is to use the space utilization plan sheet that was created for each room of the facility. In this document is listed all equipment that should be in place for that particular room or space. So a classroom will have all chairs, tables, sound equipment, etc. listed. By taking the sheet into the room, the inspector can verify the presence of these items.

Probably the most useful and the most frequently used method is to tag each accountable item with an identification number. In the equipment inventory and maintenance record above, note the line item on the second line—inventory number. Office supply or stationary supply sources sell a small metal foil tag that can be affixed to the piece of equipment. Here's an example:

Example Community Church

Inventory Control No. 0000023

It is strongly suggested that the tag have the organization name as part of the inventory control scheme. Look for tags that are durable. An important facet of a good inventory control tag will be the use of a strong adhesive to affix the tag. Place the tag in a conspicuous place without making it unsightly or a distraction. For identification of several similar items (such as folding chairs), place the identification tag in the same place on each item. That way the inventory team will not have to search for the tag. This same admonition can be made about other inventoried materials.

2. Inspection. The second step in the formation of an effective preventive maintenance schedule is the development of a system of inspection. This process should be part of the facility section of a church organization manual and will ensure that the facility is evaluated on a routine, scheduled basis. Here's an example of such a policy and procedures:

In response to the biblical admonition to be stewards of the resources of the church, it will be the policy of Example Church to inspect the properties, furnishings, fixtures, and equipment on an annual basis. The following procedures will apply:

• In April of each calendar year the CBA, building supervisor, chairman of the church properties committee, and at least two members of the church properties committee will inspect the grounds and facilities of the church. The inspection will be accomplished using the facility and space inspection and maintenance record ECC Form 0708/yr and the property and grounds inspection and maintenance record ECC Form 0709/yr. A record of these inspections will be filed with the space utilization ECC Form 0701/yr that pertains to each space inspected. The following will be noted:

— Any repairs or modifications to the space
— The presence of any wear or deterioration
— Absence of designated equipment or fixtures
— Items that impact safety, habitability, or appropriate convince

• In June of each calendar year the CBA, building supervisor, chairman of the church properties committee (or designated representative) and employed professional trade contractors for HVAC, electrical, and plumbing will inspect the facility to determine the condition of the mechanical and electrical systems of the church. Report of the condition will be made on the facility and space inspection and maintenance record ECC Form 0708/yr and the equipment inventory and maintenance record ECC Form 0703/yr. The CBA will schedule immediate repair or replacement of any items that impact safety or security of the facility. Other recommend repairs will be placed on maintenance schedules.

• In October of each calendar year, the CBA, building supervisor, chairman of the church properties committee (or designated representative) and officials representing the fire marshall's office and the church insurance carrier will inspect the facility for safety, fire hazards, and other items that may

INSPECTION AND MAINTENANCE RECORD

Title of Space _____ Room No. _____
Inspected by _____ Date _____

ITEM/AREA	CONDITION	RECOMMENDATION FOR MAINTENANCE OR REPAIR	CBA ACTION
Walls			
Ceiling			
Floor			
Doors			
Windows			
Lighting			
Electrical			
Plumbing			
Heating			
Cooling			
Fixed Equipment			
Moveable Equipment			
Special Equipment			
Other items of notation			

Comments:

File with Appropriate Space Utilization Plan

imperil the safety or security of individuals who use or are present in the facilities. A narrative report of this inspection and the actions taken to correct deficiencies will be made part of the annual church report of December of each calendar year.

• In January of each calendar year the CBA, building supervisor, church hostess, and representatives from the state and county health departments will inspect the food-service facilities for the purpose of rectification. A report of that inspection will be made part of the quarterly business meeting report to the church in April of the same year.

While the above policy and procedures statement may not be all-inclusive, it is sufficient to demonstrate the thought process that must transpire when developing a scheme to evaluate the facility and equipment. The scheme identifies when the inspection will occur, who will do it, what they are to look for, and to whom/or how they are to report their findings. Note the inclusion of forms. We have already seen the space utilization plan sheet and the equipment inventory and maintenance record sheets. The development of an inspection guide should respond to items that appear in those types of documents. An example format for recording an inspection is on the previous page.

A form created for an exterior inspection might include consideration of the roof condition, gutters, vents and portals, windows and doors, light fixtures, wall structure and any decorative trim, the parking lots, and any items like shrubbery and trees.

Before closing a discussion of inspections, a couple of other types of inspection schemes should be discussed since they lend themselves well to church or nonprofit organization type facilities.

The first is a cleaning checklist type inspection. You have seen these in washrooms and toilets at McDonald's or Burger King. Theoretically once every hour an employee comes in and polices the restroom and then signs off that it has been accomplished. A church probably does not need an hourly schedule, but a daily schedule may be appropriate. These types of inspections accomplish several things.

- They remind the employee that the maintenance action is due.
- They prompt the maintenance person to the action required.
- They assure the clientele that the facility has been cleaned.
- They indicate a responsible employee.

This scheme provides a method for evaluating the work of the janitorial personnel. The comment section can be used by a supervisor to correct any problems if a system or reporting maintenance action is not in place.

A simplified format for a restroom inspection might look like this:

DAILY TOILET CLEANING CHECKLIST

Month _____

Restroom location _____

Day of Week	Tissue refilled	Towels refilled	Lavatory cleaned	Sinks cleaned	Mirror cleaned	Deodorizer checked	Walls cleaned	Surfaces sanitized	Floor mopped	Electrical mechanical	Work done by	Comments
1												
2												
3												
4												
5												
6												

Another scheme to provide an evaluation of the facility takes as its impetus the old admonition, "If you don't inspect and correct, your parishioners will inspect and report." Nothing is more embarrassing to a facility manager than to have someone say, "Why don't you fix the hole in the wall in our classroom?" Whenever someone came in with comments about their ministry spaces,

I would ask them to help me. "I appreciate your telling me about the hole in your classroom," I would say. "Since I am not in your room everyday and you are," I would continue, "Why don't you help me by evaluating your area so I can make out work orders and get your area repaired." Then I would hand them an inspection form that looked like this example:

Room Inspection Report

Room Description _____Room # _____

Describe the condition of the room:

Report any problems:

What would you like to see have done to correct the problem:

Person making the report:_____ Date _____

A word of warning: if you choose to use this type of evaluation by parishioners, you should be prepared to act on their suggestions. That does not necessarily mean that you make major modifications to the room. What it does mean is that if they report a deterioration of room cleanliness, safety, or habitability, then you should go about correcting it. If a structural or major maintenance problem exists, investigate and plan for appropriate action. Regardless of what you do, report your completed or planned action to the person who completed the report. Experience has proved that:

- Using such a format adds eyes to your evaluation program.
- Taking action often prevents future maintenance problems.
- Respecting the reporting parishioner's suggestion strengthens the bond between the church and your position as administrator.
- Responding to their report increases the likelihood of their support in future maintenance endeavors. They are now part of the team.

Computerized Maintenance Systems

Before leaving the section dealing with schedules, formats for inventory and control, and inspections, a discussion of computer-assisted operations might be in order. At the present time, computer-assisted management schemes for maintenance, housekeeping, and facility management are expensive and specifically designed for large installations like hospitals, universities, or large office complexes. The smaller user, such as a church, does not have a market provider. This does not mean that computerized management is not available to the church facility manager. Computers are a vital part of an efficient and effective facility management operation.

Here are some of the advantages provided by computers.

- Computer operations decrease labor costs by increasing efficiency and productivity through programmed activities. That is, there will be efficient use of the available personnel and a prioritization of maintenance activities when manpower limitations occur.
- Computer systems improve cost control by ensuring that planned inventory and maintenance operations are carried out. By using prompt signals, the manager will not miss the occasional or nonroutine maintenance activity.
- Computer data systems provide a format for standardizing inventory and inspection schedules.
- Data files may be used to recall maintenance activities and assign personnel.
- Reports document personnel activities such as inspection, repair, maintenance, and warranty activity.
- Computer management systems provide an electronic medium for the use of energy management systems, fire and intrusion security systems, alarm systems, and digital communication networks.
- Integrated management systems allow a variety of managers to access data files and actions simultaneously.

The admonition for providing a computer system for facility management is the same for any computerized management system. (1) Determine what you want from the system. (2) Select the software that will do what you want. (3) Purchase the hardware to run the software.

Unless the church or nonprofit organization has several thousand dollars to spend for a facility management system, the CBA has two options available: (1) Adapt an event scheduling software to schedule maintenance action. (2) Create a maintenance management system from a database software.

Adapt an event scheduler. Most church management system software packages will have an event scheduler as a part of the package the church or nonprofit organization may purchase. These are usually designed like a calendar/scheduling software. The manager will create a file for each room or space in the facility. A calendar and event schedule will be created for each entry. Then, using the analysis of maintenance requirement actions created earlier, the manager will schedule maintenance activities for those spaces.

This scheme will take some time to set up, but its use will be rather simple. The manager will be able to ask the computer to search for all rooms/spaces that require policing on Tuesday, day 158, and make a list of those areas. Then ask the computer to search for all rooms/spaces that require vacuuming for Tuesday, day 158, and make a list of those spaces. You get the idea. With these lists of work activities, the manager can assign the work to the maintenance crew by using one of the systems discussed earlier in the chapter.

As church management systems evolve and become more useful to the church facility manager, one of them will eventually have a built-in house-keeping scheduler.

Create a facility management system from a database. Most every office software package has a database element by which you create documents with specified fields that may be recalled, compiled, and collated. Creation of such a system is not that difficult. However, the development of flowcharts that determine how data is assessed, computed, compiled, and reported requires some forethought. An example flow might look like:

- Compile a list of rooms to be policed and vacuumed for day 158.
- Determine the square footage of this listing.
- Using a predetermined time for maintenance activity of 13 minutes/1,000 ft² for policing and 30 minutes/1,000 ft² for vacuuming, compute how much time this maintenance activity will take.
- Report by listing rooms and time for completion of each room.

One other example of using this database system might be:

- Search and compile a list of all rooms that are carpeted that have not had extraction cleaning in 180 days or longer.
- Determine square footage of this listing.
- Using the predetermined time for completion of extraction cleaning of 60 minutes/1,000 ft², compute time for this maintenance action.
- Using summary data for maintenance actions computed for days 157 to 162, determine which rooms may be scheduled for extraction cleaning during this period.
- Report rooms that should be scheduled for extraction cleaning.

Database systems allow the user to make computations. Therefore, the activities of computing how much time to carry out certain maintenance or housekeeping activities can be assigned to computer development. The manager will still have to provide the base data of estimated time of activity and the square footage of the space to be maintained. But the computer system can be written to allow a manager to ask the computer to determine the best time for the activity, based on a preestablished facility use schedule, the amount of personnel time based on available custodians/janitors, and to integrate any special or unscheduled activities. Again, as with using an event scheduler program, the assignment of personnel to accomplish the job will usually have to reside with the facility manager. The computer can tell you how much time the jobs will take, but the exact assignment will have to be manually developed.

Chapter Review

This chapter has demonstrated that the construct of a building for worship is a historical and biblical concept. While not a necessity, it is an element of corporate worship that enhances the ministry and worship experience. The reader should be able to respond to the following important facets of the church facility:

- How does the church facility relate to the admonition to worship God and at the same time respond to the teachings of Scripture that call for us to be stewards of the ministry and gifts provided?
- How does the contemporary church structure assist the community in carrying out the biblical mandate for evangelism, fellowship, discipleship, ministry, and worship?
- Describe an organization that will sufficiently care for the church facility.
- Describe the process for assessing the housekeeping and maintenance needs to maintain the church facility. Outline a process for scheduling such activities and maintaining the plant equipment.
- What are some activities that the administrator should consider in developing policies and procedures to maintain the church facility?

Administering the Office

CHAPTER 8

Many have undertaken to compile a narrative about the events that have been fulfilled among us, just as the original eyewitnesses and servants of the word handed them down to us. It also seemed good to me, since I have carefully investigated everything from the very first, to write to you in orderly sequence, most honorable Theophilus, so that you may know the certainty of the things about which you have been instructed.

LUKE 1:1–4

We have already seen in chapter 3 the importance of creating a written document to detail how the church accomplishes its mission and purpose. We called that document the church organization manual because it gave a complete and composite analysis of all polity and function of the church or organization. One of the portions of that document was the office procedures manual.

In many churches after the Sunday Bible study time and worship, the lights of the church are extinguished and the doors are locked, not to be reopened until the next Sunday. But in many other churches, the doors are open periodically during the week and church ministry continues in the section of the church office. In moderate- to larger-sized churches, the functions of the church continue throughout the week—even on Saturday. In fact, when you stop to think about it, more hours of ministry are conducted in the church office than anywhere else in the facility. This is because that is where the offices of the pastor and other ministers are located as well as the support personnel that ensure the functions of the church are carried out.

Through the years authors have described the church office as the hub of activity or the center of ministry. It has been called the source of inspiration, consultation, conference, and development. It is the place where ministry comes together; where ministry is distributed. The modern office serves several functions:

1. *It is a place where organization comes together.* The church office is where the senior pastor and other ministers conduct business, study, meet needs, prepare, counsel, and interact with the body. It is the centralized location where support personnel can be gathered to carry out the administrative, clerical, and physical support of the organization or church. While few people in the community know where the home of a minister is, they know where the

church facility is; there they can find the individuals who represent the church. Members and visitors alike identify the office as the place where the officials can be found and the official functions of the institution are carried out.

2. *The church office is the communication hub of the church or organization.* Coming from the "all business" environment of a government office, it bothered me that our church office receptionist was often spending an inordinate amount of time during each morning to "chat" on the phone. Usually she was a very responsible and efficient person, but the unofficial talking on the phone seemed out of place. I asked the office manager to check into this problem. Soon she reported back that our receptionist was talking to some of the older members of our church. These people called the church office because they knew they could talk to someone. It was almost like they were saying; "I want someone to know I am alive today." They were crying out to the church to meet a need—a need for communicating with people. Many of them would sit alone all day in their homes without contact with the world, and this scared them. Our solution was to meet with the senior adult council and create a phone tree. Each morning our receptionist would call two or three different senior adults and give them a verse of Scripture and a bit of church news and then ask that person to contact a couple of others, who would in turn call a couple of others and so forth. It is unbelievable the impact this simple action had on our senior members.

Whether the communication is the placement or receipt of a call, the updating of a Web site, the creation of bulletins, newsletters, or fliers, the church office is responsible for the disbursement of critical information to the community it serves. Offices must have the necessary tools and personnel to communicate.

3. *The plans of the church or nonprofit organization are formalized in the arena of an office structure.* Where do you go to find out what is happening next week in the church? In our church the best place is to call the church office, visit our Web site, or stop by the office and look at the church calendar that is posted for the entire year. Ministers, officers, committees, councils, and ministry teams report their activities and plans to the church office. There the plans are consolidated and posted for coordination and action.

4. *The church office is a place of counseling and where needs are met.* In our office, if the receptionist was on the phone, a designated second (and third, forth, etc.) secretary was to pick up the phone and respond to the caller. Our objective was to have every call received before the third ring. One morning one of the back-up secretaries responded to a call. She was on the line for a long time. From time to time I noted that she was involved in an intense conversation. My mind pictured several things going on—all of them bad. Soon she hung up and just sat for a moment in shock. After she regained her composure, we asked her if anything was wrong.

"I just talked to a person who called to say that he is about to commit suicide and wanted to know how God would view his actions; would he let him into heaven?" she replied. She went on to relate elements of the conversation. By that time all of the office staff and ministerial staff were listening to her relate this conversation. Her concern was that she did not know how to handle the call since the person would not let her pass him off to a minister.

All the office staff agreed that day that most of them were poorly equipped to handle such a situation. Our solution was to obtain one of the many excellent books written for phone counselors and to train everyone how to use it. Each week in our training time we would go through a new topic.

Whether it is the pastor conducting a counseling session, a phone conversation, or just a meeting of people who have a need, the church or nonprofit office is a place for life-changing dialogue and interaction. The office staff must be prepared for this.

5. *The church office is a gathering place, a place for fellowship.* Don't you just love it when one of your office staff loves to bake! A word of caution, however: too much coffee fellowship is not good for your belt line. Seriously, because of the proximity of the persons involved, office staff must be friends; they must be able to fellowship with one another. There is a tenuous line between the decorum of a formal office and the friendliness of the warm relationships. Administrators must pay close attention between getting the job done and enjoying the work and people you work with. In a humorous article in *Church Administration* magazine, Elizabeth Ballard described three types of organization that define inefficient offices:

- A *catchall* office is one in disarray with piles of paper, curriculum, sacks of food and lost articles, last weekend-youth retreat leftovers, and so forth. There just doesn't seem to be any order.
- A *catch-up* office is one that seems always to be behind. They are fire-fighters, solving the "immediate" problem—stamping out problems. There is no consideration to planning or organization. Time management is a philosophy that escapes the staff in such an office.
- A *catch-me-if-you-can* office is a catch-up office gone bad. People are running around like chickens with their heads cut off. A lot of time is expended in trying to find out what they should be doing next and in how to do it. This is an office that would like to be effective, but it does not have the time to become so.
- To this list I would add the *catch-as-catch-can* office. This is the social club where people inside and outside the office group congregate to "fellowship." Little is accomplished because of the inordinate amount of time spent "visiting."[1]

How does an administrator go about creating an effective church office? Let me offer four suggestions.

1. Staff the office adequately.
2. Establish an organizational scheme (policy and procedures) for office management functions.
3. Create a desk manual for each office position.
4. Provide efficient equipment.

The remainder of this chapter will address these four issues.

Staff the Office Adequately

I am frequently asked, "How many staff should we have?" My answer is always the same: "It depends."

- It depends on the polity of the church. Often the documents of the church will define how the staff is organized and supported.
- It depends on the ministry needs. While all churches will need a senior pastor, teaching pastor—or whatever term you feel comfortable with—not all will need a minister of education, youth, children's, or whatever. Not every church has a family life center requiring an activities minister. Support personnel for the office will follow the form and function of the ministerial staff.
- It depends on the organization of the ministry and program staff. Some churches will organize leadership around the functional areas. Support staff will then be required to meet the needs of functional areas.
- It depends on the philosophy of staff support that the church leadership has accepted. Some churches will assign a specific support individual to a specific minister; other churches will assign office support personnel to a group of ministers, while other churches will establish an office pool and assign work as required.
- It depends on the configuration of the church office. For an office that has the ministerial and program staff centralized in one area, consolidating and pooling support staff may be an option. For churches with a dispersed campus complex, more individuals will be required.

Marvin Judy in *Multiple Staff Ministry* says the secretarial support staff is a function of church size. He would not provide a paid office person until the church has reached four hundred members.[2] Lyle Schaller in *The Multiple Staff* links it to the ministerial staff and provides office staff to each major minister (senior pastor, education and music ministers) and a half office person for each other minister. The administrative officer would receive a financial records clerk.[3] Charles Tidwell in *Church Administration* links support staff to both size of church and numbers of professional staff that requires office support.[4]

Depending upon the size and type of organization, several positions can be identified:

OFFICE ADMINISTRATOR

PRINCIPAL FUNCTION. Responsible for the proper operation and conduct of the church office and the supervision of support personnel in the church office. Acts as administrative assistant to the church business administrator.

QUALIFICATIONS FOR THE POSITION. Formal training in office and personnel management or equivalent experience. Ability to function as secretary. Computer literate. Personal demeanor to interact with member and nonmember in a professional and Christian manner.

REQUIREMENTS FOR THE POSITION.

1.   Assist in the development and ongoing review and modification of an office procedures manual; implement provisions of the office procedures manual.

2.   Direct the development of a desk manual for each functional position in the church office structure; periodically review for accuracy of description of position activities.

3.   Supervise the administration of the church office, including the personnel assigned and equipment used.

4.   Act as direct representative of the CBA as delegated.

5.   Coordinate the output of office products: set priorities for accomplishment, review time allowances, and designate personnel to accomplish the task.

6.   Maintain a record of all church administrative activities.

7.   Supervise the ordering of church office literature, supplies, and equipment.

8.   Administrate the office change fund and stamp distribution.

9.   Plan, organize, supervise, and evaluate a program of volunteer office personnel.

10. Perform other duties as assigned by the CBA.

In most churches or nonprofit organizations, the office administrator is generally one of the functional secretaries who has been assigned additional duties as the coordinator of the work environment of the church. In some organizations the role of office administrator is assumed by the church administrator or business officer of the organization. In the larger support organization, however, it is essential to have a functionary in the chain of command to whom the administrator can delegate the responsibilities for the general administration of the office and its personnel.

RECEPTIONIST

PRINCIPAL FUNCTION. Responsible for receiving all telephone calls, visitors, mail and deliveries to the church office.

QUALIFICATIONS FOR THE POSITION. General office and communication skills. Pleasing phone voice and personal demeanor. Computer literate.

REQUIREMENTS OF THE POSITION.

1. Answer and process all telephone calls and messages.
2. Receive all visitors to the church office.
3. Maintain church calendar of activities, events, and programs.
4. Prepare mail for mailing, deliver, or arrange for delivery of outgoing mail; receive, sort, classify, and deliver all incoming mail.
5. Provide telephone notification of meetings, conferences, and so forth as directed.
6. Type miscellaneous items as directed by the office administrator.
7. Conduct all business in a Christian manner, exhibiting an excellent first impression to member and visitor alike.
8. Perform other duties as assigned by the office administrator.

Again, as with the office supervisor/administrator, often the role of receptionist is assigned to one of the other functioning secretaries. Whether this is the case or not, the individual designated as the receptionist needs to be chosen carefully since this is the person who makes an initial impression upon visitors and members alike. Note in the qualifications section you ask for a "pleasing phone voice and personal demeanor." This will require some degree of assessment upon application.

SECRETARY

PRINCIPAL FUNCTION. Responsible to the office administrator to prepare, mail, and file correspondence as directed by assigned ministry supervisor. When assigned to a specific professional staff member, function as the receptionist for that staff member.

QUALIFICATIONS FOR THE POSITION. Computer literate. Familiar with general office procedures and equipment.

REQUIREMENTS OF THE POSITION.

1. Type and prepare correspondence for mailing.
2. File correspondence and other assigned materials.
3. Transcribe dictation as required.
4. Type or develop manuscript as directed by supervising staff member.
5. Perform specific duties related to the particular program or activity organization assigned as designated by the supervising staff member.
6. Train and supervise assigned volunteer or part-time office personnel.
7. Perform other duties as assigned by the office administrator.

The term *secretary* is being replaced in some quarters by nomenclature such as administrative assistant or ministry assistant. This gives greater recognition to the professionalism of the position that many individuals hold. While this term may be more appropriate for a church or nonprofit organization, the functions remain the same. As discussed earlier in the chapter, a secretary may be assigned to one particular professional staff member and thus in truth becomes an assistant to that one person. In smaller organizations, or in organizations which have chosen to use an office pool concept for clerical and office support, the individual is in truth a clerk or secretary.

FINANCIAL SECRETARY

PRINCIPAL FUNCTION. Responsible to the CBA for maintaining the church financial records, for receipt and disbursement of church funds, and for preparing periodical financial reports.

QUALIFICATIONS FOR THE POSITION. Ability to type 40 CWPM. Computer literate. Familiarity with general ledger and bookkeeping procedures either through formal training or equivalent experience. Must be able to be bonded, a certified notary of the state.

REQUIREMENTS OF THE POSITION.

1. Receive, count, and deposit all church offerings according to church policy.

2. Post receipts and disbursements of all accounts according to church financial procedures.

3. Post offerings weekly to individual accounts; file envelopes.

4. Prepare bank reconciliation statements monthly.

5. Prepare monthly, quarterly, and annual budget financial reports for the administrative committee.

6. Receive and answer queries about financial matters from authorized staff and committee personnel; maintain a file of invoices, correspondence, and reports.

7. Check and total all invoices when approved; inform responsible persons of their budget status.

8. Prepare and issue checks in accordance with church policy.

9. Check and compute weekly time cards of hourly paid workers; issue checks; issue checks to salaried full-time and part-time personnel according to church policy.

RECORDS SECRETARY

PRINCIPAL FUNCTION. Responsible to the CBA for maintaining and distributing general church and program organization records of membership and operations. Responsible for the production of the church directory. Assists the church librarian in maintaining a historical record of the church.

QUALIFICATIONS FOR THE POSITION. Ability to type 30 CWPM. Computer literate. Training in routine clerical skills or equivalent experience.

REQUIREMENTS OF THE POSITION.

1. Maintains church rolls, keeping all vital information up-to-date.

2. Maintains program organization records.

3. Requests and forwards church letters, compiles and types lists of members lettered out, maintains and produces the monthly report of membership.

4. Coordinates the preparation of the annual church report.

5. Maintains and files pertinent historical documents and records; maintains a file of all minutes of quarterly church business meetings and other specially called business sessions.

6. Performs other record responsibilities as assigned by the CBA.

The above two office positions are unique or focused positions. Many medium-sized churches will choose to divide the responsibilities of one of the regular ministry assistant personnel to include the responsibilities of the above two positions. This is a valid choice since in those size churches the job does not necessarily require a full-time position. In larger churches, however, data entry and financial accountability are full-time requirements and must have dedicated personnel assigned to that responsibility.

Establish a Church Office Procedures Manual

The church office procedures manual is an integral part of the administrative section of the church organization manual. Sections of the manual will vary from church to church depending on the nature and makeup of that church. However, certain sections should be in all manuals:

General Office Expectations
- Hours of operation
- Work periods
- Lunch and rest break periods
- Personal appearance
- Presence of desk or work area
- Visitors to the church office
- Confidentiality

Standardized Operations
- Preparation of correspondence
- Filing procedures
- Forms management
- Cost reimbursable work
- Use of church equipment
- Computer operations
- Personal sales
- Telephone procedures
- Electronic mail
- Literature

Many of these topics will be discussed in this chapter.

Create a Desk Manual for Each Office Position

Let's review. Earlier in this book we established the concept of designing a manual for doing church. We called it the church organization manual. The manual was divided into three parts:

1. A section that describes what the Holy Spirit has called the church to do—the constitution and bylaws and history of the church.
2. A section that describes how the church is organized to accomplish the mission and purpose of the church—the committee/council/ministry team structure and job descriptions.
3. A section that describes in detail how the church implements its mission and purpose—the administrative policies and procedures that get it done.

We have just described a manual that makes up part of the third section above that describes the policies and procedures related to the church office—the office policy and procedure manual. Within the office policy and procedure manual is another manual, the desk manual. The basic concept of the desk manual is to provide workers in the office a document that describes in detail what they do each day. It is a time management tool developed by each employee under the supervision of an office supervisor or manager. Several significant advantages exist for the use of a desk manual:

- It aids in the training of new employees.
- It prevents employees from having to come to their supervisor to answer questions.
- It standardizes procedures across several individuals/functions in the church office structure.
- It allows temporary personnel to carry on the functions of the position without extensive training.
- It provides a reference to measure time allocation and use on the part of the employee.

An important part of the desk manual is a time-management tool that we will call the daily work planner. It is nothing more than a listing of the work that is expected to be accomplished during each workday. It comes about by assessing what the individual does and then recording it in a diagrammatic format.

1. Begin with a one- to two-week listing of what the individuals in the position do every day. This will require the person to stop periodically and make a record of activities and the time it took to do them.
2. Group activities into three categories: (1) Everyday, routine events, (2) weekly activities, and (3) infrequent activities.

3. Create a work planner for each day that will list these activities. The description should be adequate so that a person newly hired or filling in temporarily could accomplish the job.
An example planning sheet might look like this:

Secretary to the Senior Pastor
DAILY WORK PLANNER—MONDAY

To Be Done	Details	Time Given
Check pastor's desk	Check and change calendar, note appointments, turn on computer, empty outgoing mail basket, fill water pitcher	10 min.
Correspondence	Sort and distribute internal mail, prepare pastor's outgoing weekend mail	20 min.
Type visitor letters	Obtain list of Sunday school and church visitors and prepare the pastor's welcome letter	15 min.
Set up for morning staff meeting	Climatize the conference room, make coffee, verify agenda, collect notepads and pencils, post updated schedule	30 min.
Arrange for the		
Collect pastor's article for weekly newsletter	Obtain letter from pastor, proof and deliver corrected and approved copy to office supervisor by end of day	15 min.
Order materials	When requested, order materials requested by the pastor	30 min.

In addition to this daily planner, information relating to the following should be provided:

- Location of files and records. If passwords are used to access files or records, a copy of the current password should be given to the office supervisor.

- Key persons whom the individual corresponds with in the routine activities of the position.
- Any fiscal operations; source of supplies, purchase order processes, etc.
- Unique or specialized equipment the individual is responsible for.
- Standardized activities such as correspondence preparation, record entry, etc.

An example of a standardized activity document is given above. Note that it is given in sufficient detail to allow any competent secretary to prepare the correspondence.

SUBJECT: CORRESPONDENCE PREPARATION
FREQUENCY: AS NEEDED
RESPONSIBILITY: SENIOR PASTOR'S SECRETARY

POLICY

1. The preparation of staff correspondence is a priority task. Correspondence preparation will not be delayed more than one day after it is given to the secretary.
2. All correspondence that will be signed by the pastor or any ministerial staff member will be typed or printed on letterhead stationary, single-spaced. (Note: if the body of the letter is less than five lines, the letter will be double-spaced.)
3. Letters are to be typed in full block style—no indentation.
4. All correspondence will be proofed for grammar, spelling, and style by the preparer and reviewed by one other person before signature.
5. File at least one hard copy of the correspondence in addition to the hard disk file and the routine electronic backups. The hard copy will be filed by sequence file number and date in the lower file drawer under "Pastor's Correspondence."

PROCEDURE

1. Materials needed: Letterhead stationary
   (in upper right desk drawer)
   Letterhead envelopes
   (in upper right desk drawer)
2. Settings will be: Times New Roman, 10 point
   One-inch margin left and right
3. Insert date 2 inches from top (line 14).
4. Triple space from date and type inside address at the left margin.
5. Double-space and type salutation. Use comma ending.
6. Double-space between salutation and body of the letter.
7. Double-space between body and complimentary close.

8. Leave four blank lines for signature; type the pastor's name.
9. Single-space and type *Senior Pastor.*
10. Double-space and type complimentary, reference, or copy to information in the format:

    cc. Frank Raymond, Minister of Education
11. Proofread by running Grammatik or by having a coworker proofread.
12. Give proofed letter ready for signature to the senior pastor for final proofing
13. If necessary, make changes and obtain pastor's signature.
14. Prepare envelope. Add four-digit zip code address router to address. Print envelope with barcode.
15. Insert the signed letter and all enclosures into the envelope and seal.
16. Place the letter ready to be mailed in the receptionist's Mail-Outgoing box for postal stamping.
17. Save document by using sequence number and date format.
18. File hard copy of correspondence along with any rough or hand-prepared drafts. (Note: drafts will be discarded at the end of the first year of file assessment and reduction.)

Office Correspondence

Scripture indicates that because of Moses' position in the Egyptian pharaoh's court, he was probably well educated in both Egyptian and Sumerian languages. His forty years in the desert taught him the Hebrew language. Thus while giving the Law in Exodus 34:27 when God said, "Write down these words, for I have made a covenant with you and with Israel based on these words," Moses was fully capable of writing what God said. In addition to that, because of his background and education, he was able to compose that portion of Scripture attributed to him—Scripture that became the basis of the Hebrew educational system. Note that God also had Moses record the history of the nation in Exodus 17:14: "Write this down on a scroll as a reminder." God also commanded a song to be written in Deuteronomy 31:19: "Write down this song for yourselves."

Recording God's events became a commonplace activity for the Jewish community. Joshua would write about the renewal of the law in Joshua 24:26. Samuel wrote about the renewed law in 1 Samuel 10:25. David recorded his songs and praises. The prophets Isaiah, Ezra, Jeremiah, and a host of other prophetic writers recorded their visions and calls from God. On the island of Patmos the angel of the Lord commanded John to "write on a scroll what you see and send it to the seven churches: Ephesus, Smyrna, Pergamum, Thyatira, Sardis, Philadelphia, and Laodicea. . . . Therefore write what you have seen, what is, and what will take place after this" (Rev. 1:11,19). The apostle Paul's greatest teaching came from his letters and epistles to the various churches of the first century.

Document Preparation

Over hundreds of years God called on inspired and Spirit-filled authors to create a manual of history, poetry, prophecy, philosophy, theology, dogma and doctrine, and revelation. Without a managing hand by the Holy Spirit, the manual we call the Bible would never have come into existence. God chose a learned man like Moses, a sensitive musician like David, a strong leader like Isaiah, a religious scholar like Paul, a scientist like Luke, and a close associate of Jesus like John to record his revelation to mankind.

Good correspondence becomes the hallmark of an effective organization. If an organization cannot communicate with the people whom it serves, it is not an efficient and proficient entity. Earlier we learned that the church office is a communicator for the church. What makes up good communication?

Six Elements of Good Correspondence

If the written word is to be mightier than the sword, certain elements of appropriate presentation should be present:

- Communicative. Good correspondence gives important information to the reader. It tells them what they need and want to know.
- Clear. The writer must use language that can be understood by the reader. This calls for a recognition that their vocabulary may differ from yours.
- Concise. Good correspondence gets to the point; it takes the least amount of time possible to convey your message.
- Complete. Provide all the information needed to understand what you are trying to say. While conciseness is to be sought, cryptology is not a virtue. Say what needs to be said in an understandable and complete manner.
- Correct. Verify that all the major and minor points are correct. Ensure the correspondence has no errors in punctuation, vocabulary, spelling, or grammar. Is the correspondence neat and attractive?
- Courteous. Do not insult the reader's intelligence or demean any belief. Seek to enhance goodwill and reader self-esteem.

Composing an Effective Letter or Memorandum

1. Begin the letter with a short opening statement. "Thank you, Ms. Jones, for your comments about last Sunday's bulletin." Or "MEMORANDUM Staff Retreat, Saturday, 14 September at 9 a.m."

2. The first paragraph should contain the principal point of the correspondence. "The enclosed book, *Sunday School for a New Century* by Bill Taylor and Louis Hanks, will help you understand our new Sunday school plans for the next year."

3. Be positive. Make your correspondence read in such a way that the reader will agree, want to participate, and do what you ask.

4. Ask for action in a clear and definite way. Do not make a mystery of what you want the reader to do.

5. Write a brief but courteous "good-bye." Do not be overly flowery or familiar, but convey the attitude of the desire for a continued correspondence. "If there is any way that my office can assist you in the future, please do not hesitate to call on us."

6. Review the letter; did it say what you wanted to say and in the fewest number of words for clarity? Ask someone else to read the letter for both content (grammar, spelling, punctuation, etc.) and context (ask this person questions about what you wanted to convey).

Good correspondence includes short sentences as well as long sentences. Most good writers prefer a lean, simplified letter. One that:

- Breaks sentences to ensure only one idea is communicated per sentence.
- Avoids filler, or words that fail to contribute to what is being said.
- Moves in an orderly, logical sequence of statements.
- Is concise but not cryptic; not a mystery.

There are a variety of types of correspondence in use in the church. The selection of the style of writing is often a determination by the writer. Many church offices are choosing to designate a specific style for consistency.

1. Official style correspondence is used by many executives and professionals for personal letters.
2. Semiblock correspondence is less official; it combines attractive appearance with utility.
3. Block style is the most widely used business/government letter form. It includes preparation notation and filing instructions on the letter.
4. Full block correspondence is a quick-and-easy business letter style for offices that do not use filing instructions as part of the correspondence format.
5. A simplified letter or memorandum format is a quick-and-easy style for internal and external memorandum-type correspondence. It eliminates the traditional salutations and closings.

For examples and description of styles of writing, see *A Manual of Style* by Donna Gandy, part of the Church Secretaries Desk Reference series by Convention Press, now LifeWay Press of the SBC, and *The Little Style Guide* to *Great Christian Writing and Publishing* by Leonard and Carolyn Goss, Broadman & Holman Publishers, 2004.

Document Management

Once a document has been prepared, the church office must do something with it. Document management involves (1) procedures for transmitting the document, (2) procedures for filing and retrieving the document, and (3) procedures for disposition after retention.

With the advent of the modern computer and electronic communication, transmission of correspondence has taken on a form beyond the written letter. While the posted letter is still the most common form of transmission of correspondence, information providers are using a variety of formats for sending the message. For the written letter a serial file scheme using numbers or letters for filing and retrieval is the most common form of identifying a letter. This letter is usually forwarded to its receiver either by a postal service or transmitted by an electronic system such as a fax or an e-mail attachment.

Electronic mail (e-mail) is becoming popular. It is fast, inexpensive, and allows for a much faster turnaround. The correspondence may be either typed into the message itself, or a document may be an attached file—using e-mail as a form of fax. Care must be taken with attachments because the receiver must have the same software system as the producer. Often it is better to make the communication within the body of the text of the e-mail rather than giving it as an attachment that must be opened.

Documents should be filed in some format that will assist the office personnel to retrieve it readily for future use. Whether the document is a paper copy or electronic file, the office manager must have an established format. Donna Gandy in her Convention Press booklet, *Fundamentals of Filing,* lists several types of filing systems:

1. A serial or correspondence file that is created with some systematic retrieval system. This may be by date, a sequence number, folder title, or whatever.

2. A forms management filing system that establishes some scheme for organizing the various forms and printed material of the office.

3. A church action file—or more appropriately termed—a *church polity* file. This file includes policy and procedure documents, minutes of business and committee meetings, decisions by polity organizations, and the reviews of polity documents such as the annual review of the constitution and bylaws.

4. Church confidential files. These documents may be part of one of any document mentioned in this section—letter, employment form, financial report, etc.

5. Church historical files are documents that do not fit the category of church action file items. These include significant events in the life of the

church, directories, copies of documents such as budgets, special programs, or events.

6. Church membership files are biographic records of the membership of the church.

7. Vertical files are folders of documents such as catalogs, pamphlets, promotional materials, and correspondence from outside the organization. These filing systems usually appear as manila folders, hanging files, and are placed in vertical (or horizontal) filing cabinets—thus the name. An important facet of this file management system is the process of keeping this file from becoming too large.

8. Other filing systems such as prospect, sermon, clip art, etc. can be established as needed.

With today's modern computer systems, many of the file records listed above can be retained on magnetic disc or CD. Membership, stewardship, financial, attendance, and inventory systems are available on typical computer office systems.

A document disposition management system must be in place to cut down the clutter. One of the members of our church was an assistant fire chief. As a member of the properties committee of the church, he suggested that we have the city fire marshall inspect our facility. I had just had the building inspector for our new insurance company come and look over our facility and make suggestions—many of which saved us considerable money on our policy. So I felt comfortable having the fire marshall inspect our church. That was good—he was able to help us justify expenditures for safety and fire protection; and that was bad—once they come to your facility, they come back every year for an annual inspection.

On one of these subsequent inspection tours, he called me to an upstairs air-handling room and pointed out a serious fire hazard. In this room (that contained electrical and mechanical equipment) were dozens of boxes or papers. When we dragged them out and started going through them, we found offering envelopes, files, giving records, pastoral correspondence, and so forth from nearly twenty years ago. Apparently someone needed more space in his storage closet and moved the files to this space. I had the records secretary go through the boxes (this took a full afternoon) and we wound up keeping less than a folder full of documents. The rest went into the dumpster.

The church needs a method of assessing the value of retained information on an annual basis. A specific individual or office should be designated as the file maintenance custodian. Retention of records is often dictated by insurance companies, the IRS, federal and state regulations, and the statute of limitations.

Every church or organization should conduct an administrative audit annually to validate the records and files that have been produced during the

FILES TO BE KEPT INDEFINITELY OR PERMANENTLY

Record	Type
Audit reports	Financial
Balance sheets	Financial
Records of original entry	Financial
Annual budget and revisions	Financial
Check register	Financial
Financial statements/reports	Financial
Minutes of church business meetings	Administrative
Minutes of meetings of boards or trustees or officers	Administrative
Policy and procedure manuals	Administrative
Articles of Incorporation	Corporate
Building permits, easements, engineering reports	Legal
Constitution and bylaws	Corporate and Legal
Federal employer identification EIN	Corporate
Legal opinions or other litigation documents	Legal
Deeds, surveys, appraisals, and property documents	Corporate
Tax-exempt status documents	Legal
Accident reports, injury claims, settlements	Legal
Terminations for cause, adverse personnel actions	Legal

FILES TO BE KEPT 7 YEARS

Record	Type
Cancelled checks	Financial
Cash disbursement records	Financial
Cash receipt, payroll, and purchase records	Financial
Church member/non-member record of giving	Financial
Records relating to investment, Keogh, pension plans	Financial
Payroll records	Personnel

FILES TO BE KEPT 3 YEARS

Record	Type
Accounts payable	Financial
Bank transaction documents	Financial
Budget worksheets	Financial
Credit-debit memo	Financial
Reimbursable expense reports and backup data	Financial
Periodic financial reports	Financial
Member's individual giving envelope	Financial
Petty cash vouchers	Financial
Vendor invoices and statements	Financial
General correspondence	Administration
Non-contestable tax records	Personnel

FILES TO BE KEPT CURRENT AND RETAINED AS LONG AS THE RECORD IS APPLICABLE AND IN USE	
Record	Type
Church publications: bulletins, mail-outs, etc	Administration
Equipment purchase-service/warranty and manuals	Administration
Inventory records	Administration
Membership listings	Administration
Insurance policies	Administration
Personnel records	Personnel

year. Some records should be disposed of at the end of the annual audit; others will be placed in files for future review. And still other files will be designated as permanent. The tables above may assist you in establishing a retention scheme.

Internal Communication Procedures

Mail Procedures

Let me be honest and tell you that there are no standardized mail-handling procedures for the church or nonprofit organization. What can be given are some suggestions to make sure that mail is handled in an organized fashion. The wise administrator will take ideas such as those given below to the office and determine what his organization wants or needs.

Incoming Mail. Mail should be accepted in a central location. The post office carrier will almost always insist on this. You must have a box or a person to receive the mail. It is strongly recommended that this be the same person all the time.

By federal law, personally addressed mail must go to the person addressed. The individual may designate someone else to open the mail if he or she wishes. For example, the pastor may tell his secretary to open his mail to make sure a disgruntled parishioner has not sent a bomb because of last Sunday's sermon (just kidding!). But this should be an established, documented request. An excellent place for a copy of this directive would be his secretary's desk manual.

Mail addressed directly to an office should be forwarded directly to that office. That office (for instance the minister of education—education office) may designate a person to open and distribute mail for that office. Bills, invoices, and documents of record should be forwarded to the financial office or secretary. In some churches this material is forwarded to the administrative (CBA) office.

Mail addressed to the church should be directed to a specific individual to open for determination of the proper receiving/action office. In most churches this is the administrative/church office supervisor or the CBA. Establish a routing system so individuals who have a need to see the mail will do so. Establish a procedure in the office that will ensure that routed mail is moved along. Often the use of a routing stamp or routing sheet with designated readers will suffice.

Outgoing Mail. This should be handled by one person. Most organizations will designate the receptionist or the office manager as the responsible individual to stamp/frank mail and forward it. Since money (postage) is involved, an established procedure for accountability must be in place and routinely audited.

- Provide this person with a cash fund to pay for returned mail.
- Provide for training with the postal service to ensure mail is properly prepared. The U.S. Postal Service provides booklets, materials, etc. as well as training and a local community relations official to help customers prepare their mail properly.
- Establish a direct liaison with the bulk mail supervisor or consider using a bulk mail service.
- Establish a standard time for mail delivery or pick up to ensure the correspondence preparer will know when mail will leave the church or organization.

Telephone Procedures

Modern telephone systems are remarkable, sophisticated instruments. They can be a significant tool in helping the church carry out its mission or an unbelievable hindrance. A couple of weeks ago I wanted to call a friend at a church in a distant state. I dialed his church number and got a recorded message with nine choices. For the next few minutes—while my long-distance clock was running—I tried to contact my friend. All I kept getting were recorded messages. Never was I given the option of talking to a human for assistance. I sent him an e-mail and told him to call me—on his dime.

Phone-answering systems are great, but they must be user-friendly. Your member will call the church and possibly will know an extension, but a nonmember won't. Church offices are supposed to be friendly, open, communicative, helpful places. If people can't get to you, how can you be user-friendly?

When establishing telephone procedures:

- Purchase a system that allows a person to go directly to a telephone station.
- Ensure an alternative for "human" assistance is always there.
- Look for systems that allow for such features as call forwarding, call waiting, etc.
- Look for systems that integrate emergency links—alarm and panic systems.

- Ensure that all telephone calls are receipted for or a record of the call is made. This may be as simple as a voice-mail box to a receptionist completing a call message slip and placing it in the minister's or employee's box.
- Consider providing mobile phones, pagers, or other remote communication devices.

Electronic and PDA Communications

With the advent of the computer office and devices like the Palm Pilot, message pagers, and wireless communication links, the employees of the church office are linked in a communication network that is becoming remarkably efficient, fast, and complex. The following are some considerations the administrator can use to become electronically accessible:

- Develop a Web site that provides general church information with links to additional information about the topics, but also develop links to ministerial offices at the home page of the church Web site.
- Network computers so offices can exchange, share, and communicate information and material.
- Link office and personal calendars through networks and personal data systems.
- Subscribe to or contract an electronic management contractor/ facilitator to maintain and upgrade systems and procedures as well as provide necessary security and system virus protection.
- Include electronic addressing in church or organization directories and personnel information products.

Computer Management Systems

"Intelligent people are always open to new ideas. In fact, they look for them" (Prov. 18:15 NLT). Nothing has impacted our society in the past quarter century like the digital computer. In the 1980s I attended a seminar in which the presenter stated that unless the church becomes computer adaptive and proficient by the year 2000, the church will fall so far behind the technology continuum that it will never regain relevancy in the community. Today children become computer literate in elementary school. Most states in the nation that evaluate the academic proficiency of high school graduates require them to demonstrate computer literacy.

There was a time when a church could claim that the computer was too expensive, or was designed for the larger church, or that to hire someone to operate the computer would be too costly. This is no longer a valid statement. Personal and office computer systems are less expensive than the twentieth-century electric typewriter and have far more significant and useful capability.

In the church office the computer will take on two configurations: (1) a stand-alone, one-person (personal) use, computer or (2) a network system with a variety of workstations all using a common database and server. The type of configuration that is the most effective for the church office will be a function of the size of the office, the number of users, and the necessity to link information files. If you have one or two user stations, the wise administrator would probably purchase personal/stand-alone systems. Beyond that, network systems are so inexpensive now that it would be foolish not to consider this alternative.

Rather than encumbering every PC hard drive with data files such as membership, education, or activities, the administrative office will provide to one server an extensive storage system and backup resource that can be accessed by all network users. This allows, for instance, the music minister to access membership files, while at the same having an extensive music file on his or her own hard-drive storage system. The network scheme also facilitates centralized CD or zip back-up maintenance systems as well as electrical surge protection and battery back-up systems for emergencies.

When evaluating the computer management needs of the church office, the administrator will ask three questions: (1) What are the needs of the church with regard to electronic data processing? (2) What software applications are available that will address those needs? (3) What hardware and equipment will be required to operate and support the software?

Assessing Needs

A variety of church office operations are facilitated by using computerized church management systems:

- Membership database, including pictures files.
- Word processing.
- Desktop publishing of bulletins, newsletters, literature.
- Educational presentations.
- Financial records.
- Inventory and management control systems.
- Prospect files and visitation.
- Calendar and scheduling.

The administrator should provide the leadership in selecting applications that will make the church office more efficient while enhancing the product and process of office procedures. The determination to move from flannel graph and overhead transparency to PowerPoint presentations will require, for instance, a coordination of education materials producers and media personnel who will provide the projection equipment. This administrative coordination of the education and media personnel is best facilitated by an individual who is familiar with the software products available as well as the hardware and corollary equipment that is needed—the administrator. Thus the church office becomes the central repository of expertise in these product areas.

In the past computer management systems were a mystery to most church members. But in the last decade, most businesses and institutions have computerized their operations, and many people in the church today are computer literate. The wise administrator will call upon the expertise that exists in the church and form study groups to determine computerized processes throughout the church. A computer ministry team, similar to a media ministry team, that investigates, recommends, and even maintains media systems in the church could be set up to aid the administrator in this process. Additionally, numerous professional companies exist to provide audit, evaluation, and recommendation for office management systems. While these experts come with a price tag, often the cost of such a professional analysis is worthwhile since they will bring to the church or institution concepts of modern technology and practical, tested systems.

Assessing Software Applications

There probably exists a software application for anything you can think of. If it can be computerized, someone will try it. Software today will do the simple to the complex. There probably is a software package for every church, large or small, and there is an appropriate price for every size church.

The process for selecting software applications for the church should include the following:

1. A detailed analysis of types of administrative operations that have been computerized—in both the present configuration and other examples of church/institution systems.

2. An assessment of what administrative operations the church or organization conducts that would be facilitated by having a computer management system carry them out.

3. A determination of what administrative processes need to be shared or networked.

4. An evaluation of the potential software suppliers:

- How long has the developer/supplier been in business? Remember, the computer software business is a highly transient and fluid business. Companies are being bought out every day, so one system developer many now be under a different name.
- Is the software system an integrated system? Will it interface with common word processing, training, spreadsheet, etc. programs?
- How long has the system been in use? Are the bugs out of the program?

- Does the system come with training? Are online or integrated helps available?
- What type of literature/support is provided?
- Does the system come with follow-on support by the developer or supplier?
- Does the system include future upgrades?
- Is the system guaranteed or warranted?

In larger churches (five hundred members or more) it probably will be wise to consider two separate software systems: (1) a general office and membership file management system and (2) a financial records and membership giving file management system. While there may be allowance for some link between the two systems by selected users, because of the security of financial operations as well as the confidential nature of membership financial records, by having two separate systems, the need for a complex password security systems is avoided.

Assessing Hardware Needs

There is a sixfold rule of thumb about the purchase of computer hardware: (1) Buy the most expensive computer system you can afford. (2) Make sure it has the largest available memory possible. (3) Get plenty of RAM. (4) Get all the bells and whistles you can jam into the chassis. (5) Make sure the "board" has room to grow. (6) Get the fastest critter out there.

There is a good reason for these admonitions: the moment you walk out the door with your computer system, it is obsolete! If your computer plays the national anthem (or "Amazing Grace") when you start up, then you are on the right track. My son works for a major computer chip manufacturer. His development group is working on the processor chips of the next generations of computers. It is unbelievable how the capability of the computer of this day will change in just a decade. Reflect how quickly the computer you are familiar with has evolved in the past five years. That development rate is exponential and will continue to grow faster than we can imagine. Thus the admonition, *buy the best possible.*

The church or organization's hardware needs will often be dictated by:
1. The software application system requirements that are being used or planning to be used.
2. The degree of integration and networking available or desired.
3. The requirements of the end products of the processes. Will the systems integrate with a desktop publishing system, an integrated communication system, a record/retrieval system?
4. The speed, complexity, and sophistication of the end-user requirements.

5. The number and types of peripheral equipment that will integrate with the systems.

The administrator may go about acquiring hardware by a variety of means:

- Get a shopping cart and a few thousand dollars and go to the local computer or electronic supplier.
- Ask church members to donate their old computers to the church.
- Form a consulting computer ministry team to carry out the assessment above in concert with you, the administrator, and the office personnel who will be using the systems.
- Hire a consultant or systems provider to recommend equipment and applications.
- Hire a firm that will investigate, report, purchase, install, and train personnel in the system.

I vote for one of the latter three choices.

Compliance Issues

Churches and nonprofit organizations across America are in danger of violating a law that protects the copyright of computer software manufacturers. Many people think that when they purchase software, it can be installed on numerous computers in the facility. What leaders need to understand is that computer software can be either an asset or a liability. When computer software is purchased, properly installed, and learned, it can be an invaluable asset to an effective ministry. It can aid research and development of staff and members. It can be used to develop study aids for teaching and preaching. However, if it is copied or obtained by less than honorable means, it becomes a liability.

The Copyright Act, Title 17 of the U.S. Code, was amended in 1980 to include computer programs. According to Title 17, it is illegal to purchase a single set of original software to load on more than one computer, or to lend, copy, or distribute purchased software for any reason without prior written consent of the software manufacturer. According to "Software Piracy and the Law," a pamphlet of the Business Software Alliance, Washington D.C., it is estimated that nearly 35 percent of the business software in America is obtained illegally. The major violations are (1) making copies of software to place on more than one computer, and (2) making copies to use at home.

Administrators must be familiar with the terms and conditions of each software system. If a church management software package is purchased for the church or institution, the vendor will designate how many units or users the system allows before incurring additional fees. Additionally, upgrades to systems must be to a specified license purchase.

Most major software manufacturers are now packaging the software in groups of applications called suites. MacIntosh, Microsoft, and other application providers have married their products for ease of integration (and cost). For example, Microsoft's Office© contains such applications as MS Word, Excel, PowerPoint, Outlook Publisher, and so forth. When purchased as such, there is one license, and the applications cannot be broken up between a variety of users in the church office. Some software providers are beginning to allow a purchaser to place a software package on a dual system if the same person uses that system. For instance, the pastor may have a laptop computer at the office and a PC at home. Some licenses will allow him to place the same suite on the two systems if he is the only end user. You must confirm this and not assume that contingency exists with the software purchased.

Church Management Software Systems

From the beginning of the advent of using computers in churches and other nonprofit religious organizations, a software product has been developed and marketed as a church management software. Through the years software developers have come and gone. Today *Christian Computing Magazine,* one of the longest-tenured such magazines, lists about twenty-five reliable system providers. These software systems are unique since they are tailored to the needs of the church and church-oriented organizations. Depending on the supplier, they will integrate membership records, organizational structure, giving, budget and financial management, scheduling and calendaring, pictorial directories, alarm systems, and just about every function that goes on in the church. Additionally, the systems integrate with most common word processing, database, analysis, and music systems sold today.

When selecting a church management software provider, you should ask some of the same questions asked earlier about software systems. However, there are a few additional things to consider.

- Ask how long the supplier has been in business and how long the particular software has been in existence?
- You will want to know who else uses the system and talk to them to get the user's opinion of the product. The supplier will say that their system is the best thing since sliced bread. Who else thinks it is that good?
- Compare the capabilities of the various systems. Biggest is not always best. You want a system© that meets your current and future needs.
- Ask for a demonstration of the system. Arrange for that demonstration to occur at a site other than your workstations. View the system that is installed in a user site. That way you can ask questions of the user. Do not let the vendor install it on your computer to demonstrate it; it

will take up memory space, remove one or more stations from being used, and if you choose not to purchase the software, it will take time to remove it from your system. Also built into these systems are links to other software and Internet packages that will be established and may affect your operating systems when the system is removed.

- Is the system capable of growing with the church or organization's needs? You may not have an immediate need for all the bells and whistles now, but in the future you might. How easy is it to modify or add to the system, and what are the costs involved?
- Finally, ascertain what technical support and training are available. How is it received, and for how long will it be provided? In the future, what will be the ongoing costs for system support?

Office Procedures

Before ending the chapter, a comment or two about office decorum. This chapter has discussed numerous topics about developing the techniques of office activity. The presence of the office, however, is a critical element of how well it is perceived and received by the community it supports. By looking at the office, can you tell that it is a well-organized, efficient office; or are things just happening—without rhyme or reason? It is like the mother who walks into the church nursery with her little bundle of joy. The area is clean, it smells good, it is bright and airy, the personnel are professional, and there is a sense of security and confidence. She leaves her child without a care in her mind.

Often I am invited into churches to evaluate their facility or operation. I have been in church offices where you could not find the workstation for the clutter of pictures, flowers, knickknacks, and food. If the phone rang, it would take ten rings before someone found the receiver. I have also been in church offices that looked as stark as the ones I saw at the Pentagon in Washington, where everyone had to clear their desks completely, turn over their in/out boxes to show they were empty, lock their computers in a secure cabinet, and place the phone in the center of the desk facing outward so the Marine could verify that it was not being used. There needs to be a balance. Consider the following suggestions about office space decorum.

1. Arrange your office area so the visitor is readily acknowledged and can be attended to. This is often taken care of with a receptionist position with a suitable waiting area.

2. Provide appropriate and adequate equipment and furniture. Some spaces will require seating other than the workstation. Others will require file cabinets and storage units. Be sensitive to the employee's needs without cluttering the space.

3. Agree to a reasonable degree of personalization of the office space. For ministerial staff, the space becomes an extension of their presence. However, in an office the secretary/ministry assistant is a functionary of the organization. Yet, since they spend nearly a third of their day there, they should be able to express their personality there. Whatever level of personalization is granted, it should be standardized, clearly expressed, and enforced.

4. The office space should be located near a major entrance to the church or facility, it should be entered through a main hallway or artery, and it should be secure. The use of signs, large sections of windows, or glass doorways will assist in locating the office. The office should telegraph a welcome environment within. Decorations, floral and greenery arrangements, lighting, reception areas, and appropriate pictures and wall hangings will assist in creating that atmosphere.

5. When a person comes to the church office, he or she should be greeted. We will address security of the office in the next chapter. Office hours should be posted and honored. If the office closes for lunch, then tell the public. Otherwise, have someone at the receptionist desk during that period. Because of the program needs of many churches today, office hours are often extended beyond the usual eight-to-five time frame. Nothing prevents a church or organization from having office hours that extend into the evening, occur on Saturday or Sunday, or other unusual times. The key to such variety is ensuring employment regulations regarding the workweek are not violated.

We have discussed nonexempt employee status already. One of the regulations regarding the hourly waged nonexempt employee is that their workweek is limited to forty hours. Those forty hours can occur as you designate, but they cannot be exceeded without paying time and a half overtime wages. Thus, nothing prevents an employer from hiring an office worker who works Sunday through Thursday, or from Tuesday through Saturday, just as long as employment law is not violated.

6. Be considerate of the employee. The workday should include periods for breaks in the morning and afternoon. An appropriate period should be given for lunch if the workday extends to the afternoon. Decisions about food or drink at the work space should take into account the needs of the individual in addition to the desire to have a professional-looking office. Provide a break room and locate restrooms within a reasonable distance from the office area. Allow an occasional call from home, but regulate its frequency. Allow visitors, but monitor timeliness. Provide for opportunities for personal days off, sick leave, and family emergency time. The bottom line is taken from a tenet of human resource management which states that if you treat your employees like people, they will act like the God-created individuals they are. Treat them poorly, and they will respond likewise. They will do their job but little else.

Chapter Review

Regardless of the size of the church or organization, office procedures are a necessary part of the activities that sustain the viability and energy of the membership while providing an essential link to the community at the same time. Whether the church office is in the home of the pastor or occupies numerous rooms in a large facility, the dynamics of the office will carry out essential operations that define who the church is and what it does. The church office is, thus, the lifeblood of the organization from Sunday to Sunday. In developing an understanding of the essential nature of the church/organization office, the reader should be able to:

- Articulate at least five functions of the office.
- Describe the staff organization for an office.
- Identify the need for office and desk manuals.
- Describe how an effective piece of correspondence is communicated to the members.
- Outline internal and external communication procedures.
- Identify essential elements of a computer-managed office.

Administering
Risk Management

A prudent man foresees the difficulties ahead and prepares for them; the simpleton goes blindly on and suffers the consequences.
PROVERBS 22:3 TLB

Risk management is the scheme the prudent administrator takes to foresee dangers in the environment of the church or organization and the actions taken to prevent them or to address the consequences in case they occur. In America today, and throughout the world for that matter, activities of preparedness are becoming essential elements of every organization, both religious and otherwise.

On a pleasant Wednesday night in September 1999, as I was driving home, I was passed by a speeding police car with its lights flashing and siren blasting. Within a block I was passed by another police car headed in the same direction. And before I could turn the corner to the subdivision I lived in, an ambulance screamed by headed in the direction of the two police cars. As I was pulling into my driveway, an announcer on the Christian radio station I was tuned into reported that a shooting had occurred in a Fort Worth prayer service and that we should be in prayer for that situation. As I got out of my vehicle, I looked to the north toward the interstate and noted a police helicopter as well as a news media helicopter hovering. My initial thought was that an accident had happened on the interstate. When I got inside, my wife told me that a news flash on the TV had said that a gunman had attacked some youth at Wedgwood Church. As we listened to the TV and the Christian radio station, it became apparent that a serious, deadly event had happened.

Wedgwood Baptist Church was a popular church in our community. Many of the students I taught at the seminary in Fort Worth, Texas, were members of this church or were on staff there. I received a call in about an hour from one of my doctoral students who said that he and his family were safe but that he knew of at least a couple of our students who had been shot but did not know of their condition. The news media mentioned some names that evening. One in particular interested me since he would have been in my class that next morning. Others were staff members who were in the doctoral program I headed. We prayed all evening and stayed glued to the television set to gather what information we could. I received calls from time to time from individuals and had determined that Jeff, my student, and others who were students had been shot. Some eyewitnesses reported seeing them dead; others said they had been taken to a hospital.

The next morning at my eight o'clock class, Jeff was not in his usual seat. I told the class we needed to pray. I told them I had heard that he was dead; but that some other person had reported he had been taken by ambulance to the hospital. We prayed. The next hour in another class, I continued the prayer time for the situation and families involved at Wedgwood. I remember looking out into the classroom at one of my favorite students. She was just staring straight ahead, just as though she was not there. I will never forget that look. I learned later that she had been sitting on a couch in the entrance talking with her best friend when a gunman walked up and shot her friend dead, right before her eyes.

The rest of this book could be filled with the stories of Wedgwood. My student Jeff was the first shot. As a church staff member, he had gone up to the gunman to ask him to put out his cigarette before entering the church. Another student, Kevin, the church counselor, was shot in the back as he ran to call the police. What happened at Wedgwood was not supposed to happen! Not in America, not in a church—a sanctuary of peace and safety. And yet it did, and it has happened before and has happened since. Today pastors, administrators, elders and deacons, committees, and other leaders in the organization must consider the facets of risk management and take the precautions necessary to address these issues. Gone are the days of the open church with no locks, no barriers, and no restrictions. And yet the church or religious non-profit organization must wrestle with the desire to be open to the community they wish to serve while at the same time demonstrating caution.

One is reminded of the story of the rebuilding of Jerusalem as told in the book of Nehemiah. The threat of an attack is given in the enemy's words in 4:11: "They won't know or see anything until we're among them and can kill them and stop the work." Nehemiah's immediate response is found in verse 13; "So I stationed people behind the lowest sections of the wall, at the vulnerable areas. I stationed them by families with their swords, spears, and bows." The long-term solution is found in verses 16–18: "From that day on, half of my men did the work while the other half held spears, shields, bows, and armor. The officers supported all the people of Judah, who were rebuilding the wall. The laborers who carried the loads worked with one hand and held a weapon with the other. Each of the builders had his sword strapped around his waist while he was building."

While we must continue to do our God-ordained work, we have entered a day when we must develop the vigilance of Nehemiah. In the past churches were not robbed or vandalized. Religious structures were considered sanctuaries of peace, and the values of the religious group were respected. Churches were generally given latitude with regard to tort action and lawsuits when accidents or unfortunate events occurred. Churches were not bound by many laws ascribed to other elements of the public. Those days are gone.

For the past decade the most popular seminars at national bar association meetings has been how to win cases against churches and nonprofit organizations. Numerous law schools across the nation have courses in tort action against religious or nonprofit organizations. Laws have included the church and nonprofit in compliance provisions. Many state and local municipal governments demand inspections and validation of compliance in the areas of safety, security, and common protection. In addition to that, most insurance carriers that provide coverage to churches and nonprofit organizations require their clients to comply with a litany of issues to prevent the carrier from having to pay costly claims.

This chapter will deal with risk management in three areas: safety, security, and insurance. Additionally, in subsequent chapters that deal with administrative issues that must be considered in the program ministries and activities of the church or organization, comments will be included for each that relates protection that the risk management program will provide.

Safety

Safety in its foundational sense is "common horse sense." A person wouldn't stick his hand in a fire. Why? Because he knows it will burn him. So if you know fire burns, avoid fires. It's that simple.

In many respects a church is an accident waiting to happen. A few years ago when I was administrator in a church in Oklahoma, an incident happened in the church that brought this fact to my attention. One morning after the worship service, as we were closing down, we tried to hurry along a few members who were still in the front foyer talking. Their children were with them. One of the youngsters, also impatiently waiting for his parents, was in the doorway of the church. He was using his fanny to swing open the glass doors. He would hit it, and it would swing open. Then as it closed, he would catch it again and send it back on its way.

Suddenly there was a loud pop, and the child was lying on the floor in a pile of glass slivers with a long shard planted deeply in his back. We called emergency response personnel, and the child was taken to the emergency room.

Fortunately, the glass sliver had missed organs and major arteries. Upon investigating the accident we discovered the glass doors were plate glass but not safety glass. Building code required safety glass because it shatters into tiny, nonhazardous pieces.

Fortunately the child recovered. But it could have been worse. With the assistance of our insurance agent, the properties committee surveyed all the doors and ground-floor windows of the church. We found that over half did not meet code by having safety or laminated glass. Over time we replaced all those doors and windows.

In the church facility many people pass in and out each week; our job is to make that passage safe for them. From nonskid surfaces to removal of trip hazards, from repairing electrical cords to installing ground-fault outlets, from ice removal to germ removal, we must be vigilant to provide a safe environment. This is your job as church administrator. Let's consider some safety issues.

Code Compliance

When plans are drawn for a church facility, the architect or engineer must be aware of building codes for structural and engineering safety. He must also comply with safety codes. All municipalities use the National Fire Protection Agency's Life Safety Code NFPA 101. This code defines how doors are to open, how many feet from a doorway to exterior entrance for children during an escape, how many people can safely occupy a room, how many and where fire exit signs should be placed, what spaces need to have sprinkler systems, and a myriad of other safety issues. Copies of the publication may be found in a public library or at the local fire inspector's office. The church will be bound by code requirements by both fire marshals and municipal building inspectors.

Many church facilities do not meet safety code requirements. A term that is often used is that the facility is grandfathered under older code provisions, and it does not have to meet the current restrictions. This is the same stupid logic as having a tire on your car that has bald spots and not replacing it because other parts of the tire still have some rubber. For example, in a part of your church building, you have an electrical service that is not up to code. In another part of your church your electrical service is up to code. Guess how much of your church burns down when the old service shorts out and causes a fire. The entire building! Now when you install the newer service in the newer part of the building, you choose not to upgrade the older service because it was grandfathered in under an older code that allowed a less-than-adequate service. You choose poorly. Most municipal building codes will prevent you from having contiguous inadequate code compliance. That same protection is often not afforded to rural areas where codes do not exist.

How do you find out about these codes and restrictions? Your local municipal, county, or state code enforcement section will have a world of information that will provide you assistance. But unless you are a builder or some other tradesman, reading these code requirements is arduous and often confusing. There are other sources. Your architect or builder must know these codes in order to be licensed. They should not allow you to build an unsafe facility. Another valuable resource is your insurance agent. Most major insurance companies provide a service to their clients that assist them in ensuring their facility is safe and secure. After all, they want to help you not to have claims because claims cost them money. Sometimes the assistance comes from the agent themselves or an underwriter. And some larger groups provide inspectors. These individuals are trained to identify and suggest corrections to unsafe conditions in a facility.

One other option is to allow municipal inspectors to evaluate your facility. These types of inspections have been alluded to in this book so far. Fire marshal inspectors, code compliance officers, and professional safety inspectors are available in most areas of the country. But if they find something wrong, you are obligated to correct the problem. Some types of violations could shut your facility down until corrected. For example, a leaking gas line, exposed wiring systems, and building portions that are ready to collapse are things that an inspector would deem as too hazardous to continue to use the space until corrected. He has the authority to close you down until your building meets code requirements.

OSHA Safe Working Environment Law of 1986

This law requires employers to provide a safe working environment for their employees. It also requires manufacturers of products that pose a potential hazard to identify that hazard, provide instructions to prevent danger in use, and how to react in the event the hazard occurs. It requires posting of safety and warning information. This requirement covers everything from climbing to chemicals, from lighting to ladders. Churches are not exempt from the law.

But what if your church does not hire sufficient numbers of employees to be covered under the law? The intent of the law is that an employer should provide a safe working environment for their employees. And that is how the law is being interpreted. For example, I learned about one small church that had a small janitorial staff. One day one of the janitors was overcome by chemical fumes in the cleaning closet and passed out. When he was found, he had died from the concentration of fumes in the closet. The family of the janitor sued the church for not providing a safe working environment. The defense lawyer argued that the church did not have sufficient numbers of employees for the OSHA law to apply. But even if it did, the church had posted the necessary manufacturer's safety data sheets for the chemicals in the closet. The church lost the case because the individual hired was Hispanic and could not read the safety data sheets that were in English only. The civil court held that the church was obligated to provide a safe working environment for its employees. This case has been a precedent case for numerous other lawsuits against churches and other nonprofit organizations.

Thus, if the safety data sheet says wear gloves and eye protection when handling this type of chemical, the employer has to provide—and should enforce the use of—the safety equipment. The same requirement relates to equipment the employees use. Kitchen equipment, lawn and gardening tools and implements, ladders, and office equipment should be of the quality and should be maintained in such a way that they can be used safely as well as effectively.

Lighting

While one does not usually think of lighting as a safety feature of a facility, it is certainly an enhancer of safety. Who has not walked into a door frame or a wall or stumbled over an object in a darkened room or hall? But the space does not have to be dark for it to be an unsafe space. Insurance companies are beginning to assess premium increases for clients who do not provide a safe lighting environment. For example, they have deemed that a minimum of two candle power in parking lots is necessary for people to move from their vehicle to the facility. They will designate a ten-candle power light level at entrances exterior to the building and the same intensity just inside a foyer. Inside, safety code compliance will require that battery-powered emergency lighting and exit lighting systems be in place for all large community spaces, hallways, and stairwells. Architects should provide, and code compliance inspectors will insist upon, either ambient or artificial lighting in all enclosed spaces where personnel movement is expected. This includes hallways, foyers, toilets, and other common spaces. Here's a rule of thumb: take your Bible into a space or out into the parking lot. If you can read it at normal reading distance, then you have adequate light for safe movement.

Responding to Emergencies

In the wake of the events at Wedgwood Baptist Church and through the experience of accidents on the premises, churches are beginning to form emergency reaction teams. These are ministry teams made up of volunteers who are trained to respond to emergency situations—from intrusion to accident, from health emergency to crises. These teams provide immediate assistance until professional, municipal emergency response personnel (police, fire, and ambulance) can respond.

One evening my wife and I were visiting a church where I was providing consultant services. We noted a small commotion in the left side of the sanctuary. The pastor asked the church to pause and be in prayer for the situation. In a brief time a person was carried out of the sanctuary on a stretcher and the service resumed. I discovered later that the person whom they removed had experienced a heart attack, and the church's emergency response team had taken care of the situation. They had a signal for summoning them, a meeting place where supplies were provided, and a system of communication with responding emergency personnel. On that team were a nurse and also a fire department paramedic. They had administered local assistance and taken the person to a designated entrance where an ambulance took the person to the local hospital emergency room. Because of their quick action, the person survived. I was impressed!

Some guidelines need to be observed if the church or organization plans to provide this service.

1. This needs to be a ministry team activity. The church cannot require such a team; it must be volunteer. As an administrator, approach an individual or individuals about their organizing and servicing this activity as a ministry. Their talents and gifts are being used for the good of the body. This is biblical. This group must be trained or willing to have the training to do this ministry. That will take a lot of dedication and interest on their part. But they will sense that they are serving the church or organization.

2. This must be a trained group of individuals. Nothing is more dangerous than a poorly executed act of assistance. If for no other reason than the group is acting in the church on behalf of the church, the church is liable for poorly provided emergency care. Training must be inherent and must be ongoing. A church or organization should not consider the provision of this group unless two or more individuals are trained to carry out the necessary functions.

3. There needs to be close coordination with local emergency providers. These groups become trainers, support personnel, and sometimes potential members. Additionally, just as important as the fire department knowing where the readout board for a fire alarm system is located, a municipal rescue squad, paramedic, or ambulance service needs to know where to respond when called. Sometimes this can be standardized by working with small community groups. In most cases it needs to be part of the reporting system.

4. There needs to be an organization, a process, and a procedure for mobilizing the group. An announcing or paging system needs to be provided. This may be as simple as a Sunday school ending time bell to providing a pager. A meeting place from which to respond to the emergency needs to be established. That meeting place should have certain equipment and communication devices provided. There should be a delegated person who will establish and carry

out the dialogue with a 911 or other emergency dispatcher. With the popularity of the mobile telephone, this person should carry a checklist to ensure the dispatcher is receiving all necessary information. And some form of record of the event should be provided that can be carried to a hospital or other care facility to assist triage personnel in determining what has happened up to that moment.

5. There should be necessary equipment provided to carry out the emergency. A couple of words of warning: First, the emergency response team is a mediatory source of assistance; it should not be considered a terminal assistance provider. Second, no equipment should be provided unless the personnel to use it have been trained to use it safely. Defibrillators, respirators, and other emergency equipments are popular today but can be dangerous to the person if not used properly. Provide equipment only to the level of training of the personnel who will respond and use it.

A final word about safety: Safety should be the concern of the church or organization administrator, a designated committee or group, or someone. Too often safety is an issue only when it is needed—usually after the fact. It should be included as a responsibility of the job description of an administrator; it should be included in the responsibilities of a facilities committee. Some designated person or persons should be inspecting for and responding to safety issues in the church or institution.

Security

In an article in *Your Church* magazine in March 2000, I asked a rhetorical question about the events that had just happened the year before at Wedgwood Baptist Church. "Must we train ushers to watch for armed intruders? Should attendants who patrol the parking lot to prevent vandalism also watch for unsavory characters who shouldn't be allowed into the church?"[1] Like the events of the tragedy of the World Trade Center attack on September 11 shattered confidence in the security of America, the attack on youth at Wedgwood a year earlier shattered confidence in security of houses of worship. Even before Wedgwood, however, churches were beginning to become aware of the need to provide a secure working and worship environment.

Many people in my generation grew up in a community where people rarely locked their doors. The churches we attended were always open, even at night. A half century later, we now live in a lockdown society. That same hometown church now has an electronic latch and intercom system to gain entrance; all other doors are locked. Security specialists tell us that churches are security risks because of the inherent nature of openness of the church facility. But the most vulnerable time for a church facility is Sunday afternoon. It's open, but nobody's home. Following are some security issues that the church administrator should consider.

Lighting

Evil loves darkness. The Bible says that the thief comes in the darkness of night. While we can't keep the sun up for twenty-four hours, we can make it light. We have already mentioned exterior lighting from a safety perspective. From a security perspective, it is just as critical.

A few years back the church my family and I attended was having trouble with transients breaking into the church and setting up housekeeping. They would raid the kitchen and then choose a ground-floor room, often one of our children's department rooms, and spend the night. As a member of the church's building committee, I mentioned this problem to my son who was a K-9 officer for the local law enforcement agency. He suggested that we open up the church one evening and let Breaston (the 140-pound police dog) wander through the building. Imagine the surprise of our visitors when Breaston walked in on their card party! It cost the church a window because they jumped out without bothering to open the window. But the word apparently got around because we didn't have that trouble for a long time after that.

Time passed, and I became the administrator of this same church. One evening one of our ministers was working late, and he heard sounds of people moving about in the building. My son no longer had his dog, so I told this minister that the next time he heard these sounds he should call the police. He did. The police came. But unlike their four-footed officer earlier, they were reluctant to venture into the building in the dark. They did not know where the light switches were and did not want to move through the building in the dark. From this experience we came up with two innovative solutions.

Access points to the church (doors, windows, parking lots, foyers, etc.) had lights on them twenty-four hours a day. Sometimes God provided the light with sunlight; other times we provided artificial light. At every doorway entrance to the church, we had low-voltage fluorescent lighting to a minimum of twenty candle power. Over every exterior window at ground level, we provided ten candle power of lighting, also on a low-voltage system. We then placed these lighting systems on a photocell energize mechanism that one of the church's electricians rigged up. In our parking lots the photocell system was preceded by a timer. Thus, from the moment people left the church to the time they arrived at their vehicles in the parking lot, they were in light. Here's an illustration of the scheme for the parking lot:

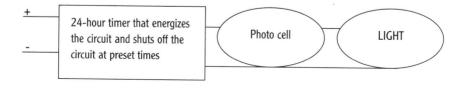

You can set the timer to come on at any time you want, say at four in the afternoon. This energizes the photocell. When it gets dark, the photocell turns on the parking lot lights. At a predetermined time in the evening, when all church activities are completed, the timer turns off the parking lot lights. This type of system not only saves money in electricity costs, but it also removes the need to remember to reset the timer. Obviously, the system you install for doorways that will remain on all evening will not have the timer installed.

A second installation we made was to the interior of the building by providing lighting on a continuous basis for the hallways and stairwells. We replaced every exit sign with a system that was connected to a low-voltage power source and then connected that to a back-up battery power system. Then as part of that circuit, we placed a low-wattage, low-voltage light source in the center of every hallway. For hallways that exceeded thirty feet, a light was provided every fifteen feet. We located that light source in the ceiling fixture of that hallway. These lights remained on twenty-four hours a day and provided a minimum of two candle power of light in the hallway regardless of whether primary power was on.

We then connected the 120-volt hallway lights to a motion sensor. For longer hallways we placed additional sensors to ensure that whenever anyone entered the hallway, regardless of whether it was at the hall entrance or from one of the side rooms, the lights would be on in the hallway. Stairwell lighting systems had motion sensors placed at every landing. This system allowed anyone to move throughout the church without having to turn on a hall or stairwell switch. And obviously, if someone was not supposed to be there, the lights would come on, and they couldn't turn them off. Here's a rough diagram of this system:

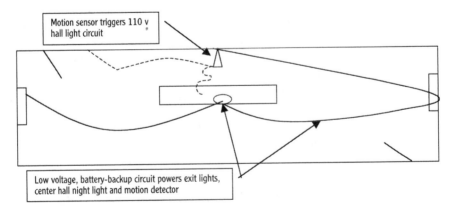

Motion sensor triggers 110 v hall light circuit

Low voltage, battery-backup circuit powers exit lights, center hall night light and motion detector

Alarm Systems

In addition to fire-alarm systems to provide for the safety of people in the church or institution facility, the church should have a security system that protects the most valuable assets of the church (electronics, files, media, offices, etc.). Alarm systems are useless unless there is an active response— whether the local police or a security agency. When assessing the need for an alarm system, consider what you want to protect. Global alarm systems, while cheaper, are not always the most effective.

A rural church installed a system that used a central motion detector in the sanctuary and the hallway leading to the office and classrooms. It was hooked up to the local county sheriff's department for response. Each time the alarm went off, the pastor joined the deputy who responded to search the building. They never found anyone, and the alarm was reset. They thought that when the deputy drove up, whoever was in the building left. In a couple of months the church got a bill from the sheriff's department for "excessive" responses. The church discovered that the county commissioners limited the responses to a false alarm to only two a month; after that a fee was charged.

One evening the pastor was working late and heard a sound in the hall. He stuck his head out the door to come eyeball to eyeball with a large raccoon that had found an entrance in to the church. The pastor chased him back through the hole he had entered by. The next day a couple of men nailed a piece of sheet metal over the hole, and the false alarms (and excess response charges) stopped.

Determine what is of value in the church or organization facility that needs security protection and then alarm that, for example, storage closets that have expensive electronic sound and video equipment. Office spaces, especially those with computer and computer system equipment, should be alarmed. Rooms that have secure files such as the finance office or records office should have not only a security system alarm but maybe also a security lock system for entry.

Whether the system is local or silent is another consideration. Visual or noisemaking alarm systems inhibit or deter theft. Silent alarm systems try to catch the thief in the act. Neither alarm system will prevent theft; they just slow it down. If the decision is to go with a cheaper local alarm system (one that is not responded to by an outside source), make your deterrence obnoxious—loud alarms, bright lights. If your objective is to get a lower insurance rate, you will have to go with a silent, outside-monitored response system that will probably cost you as much as the insurance premium you save.

While alarm systems are usually thought of as systems that are installed to detect intrusion or violation when no one is around, daytime security systems for occupied work spaces are becoming a necessity in many regions of the country. These alarm systems become necessary when certain conditions exist.

For example, if an academy, school, or child care program is in the facility; when large unused spaces exist that cannot or are not monitored by sight or locked to prevent entry; or when office spaces are so separated from one another that for security of the individuals who occupy those spaces an alarm system is a must. These alarms could include monitored TV and video systems as well as sensors and detectors.

Panic buttons should be installed at critical points in the church—nursery, offices, welcome centers, etc. These switches are connected to the alarm system of the church and provide an immediate local response to an emergency or danger. Place these switches where personnel are usually located or working so they may activate them without drawing attention to the fact that they are summoning help. During the workday these alarms may be terminated in a manned space such as the space that has TV security monitors that are being observed by a central employee. If the church or organization does not have a monitored space, then the alarm should sound at the centrally monitored location for the general alarm system. In most communities the panic alarm can be connected directly to a local security provider or law enforcement agency.

A penny saved is often a penny burned. In many respects security is just being careful. For centuries security was not a matter of concern for the church or ministry organization. No one would dare steal from God. I remember my mother telling me that I should be careful of what I do and say in church because it was "God's house," implying that God was watching. Not enough mothers are telling their children to be careful of what they do. That attitude of disrespect for places of ministry is coupled with a church or ministry organization that "trusts" people and has caused a significant increase in the breach of security.

A few years ago we were visiting my son in Virginia. We were staying in an upstairs bedroom. My wife had left her purse on a table downstairs—in full view of anyone who looked in a window. Someone broke in the house and stole her purse. Today my wife does not leave her purse out in open view; she takes it to her bedroom and secures it. Why? Because of the hassle she had to go through to cancel checks and credit cards, get her driver's license renewed, and obtain another military ID. It was a hard lesson, but she learned from it. Remember, risk management is closing the barn door before the horse gets out. This means that churches and other organizations should take steps to be proactive in developing a security scheme. Here are some practical suggestions.

1. Place metal-clad or solid doors at locations where security is an issue— or alarm the door. If glass is used, it should be security glass—glass of sufficient thickness to prevent entry by a blow or have an imbedded security mesh or grid.

2. Lock windows and doors. Law enforcement agencies state that criminals walk through open doors in many cases of vandalism or theft. Either the

facility was not locked, or they gained entry before closing and carried out their vandalism or theft after hours. All areas of a facility that are not monitored should be secured.

3. Place valuable equipment out of the sight of people who may pass by. Use cabinets and consoles for electronic equipment. Computer systems should be in a locked and monitored or alarmed space.

4. Never keep money on the premises. We have already addressed this issue in the financial chapter. Kitty funds and office funds should always be counted at the end of the day and placed in a secure, locked location.

5. Double- and triple-lock spaces. Fire safety codes will require you to have emergency exit through certain doors to your facility. In many doorways that are adjacent to unmonitored spaces but where doors exist for safety reasons, have door hardware only on the inside. Entry from the outside would be only through a keyed deadbolt. Doors with panic bars that secure can also have deadbolts if those locks have a turn latch exit on the inside. (Never place chains and padlocks on these types of doors. A slide bar double security could be purchased that can be quickly lifted to gain emergency exit.) Place your financial and membership records behind a triple security system: keyed lock to the area, numeric or card key secondary lock to enter the room, and a locked cabinet for the equipment or files.

Numerous aids assist administrators to become security smart. Probably the best resource you have is the community relations representative of your local law enforcement agency. These men and women want to help you prevent crime. Through the years I have had several law enforcement officers in the churches I served, and I frequently asked them to assist me in identifying and correcting problems. In addition to law enforcement personnel, your insurance agent is also interested in your church or organization being proactive to prevent security breaches. Most have brochures, videos, and other training aids. Some will visit your facility and walk through it with a security or properties committee to help identify problem areas and make suggestions to prevent problems.

Establish Key Control.

I told the story earlier about an inspector finding several paper and other consumable items stored in one of our heating/cooling rooms. The following Sunday I took a group of the properties committee up to the room to show them the problem. When we arrived, I remembered I had left the keys to the space in my desk drawer. "Never mind, Bob, I have a master key," one of the committee members responded. As it turned out, more than one master key was held by the group members.

Who has a master key to your church? Probably more people than you think. When the problem was discussed with the leadership of the church, it was determined that the church would budget for and change our lock system. A professional locksmith was employed. He worked out a strategic system of grouping similar entry needs into sets of locks, and we dramatically reduced the number of master keys that were issued. The church or nonprofit organization must establish a system by which a person is issued a key by signature and a policy that states they are accountable for its use. Issue keys only to spaces where people need access. When you can afford it, use electronic keys that can be changed when the space is compromised.

Develop a Sense of Security

For decades the mind-set of most Americans has been one of a sense of security. Recent events such as those cited at Wedgwood and the World Trade Center of 9-11 has changed all that. It is very easy, however, to be lulled into a false sense of security, especially if the organization or institution has taken steps to ensure good security. But security will not happen in the church or institution unless someone or a group of individuals makes it their responsibility to ensure that it happens. This is generally the individual or group who is designated as the administrators of the church or organization.

In addition to an emergency reaction team, train staff, ushers, greeters, and others to be sensitive to needs of individuals during worship services. When I talked to my former student, Jeff Lasiter—the first person shot in the Wedgwood shooting, he said that in retrospect he should have known that the shooter was trouble. People have a sixth sense that tells them when something is wrong.

How do leaders or administrators develop a sense of security in the organization? Consider these ideas:

1. The parking lot welcome ministry team should also become a parking lot patrol to provide not only security to vehicles but also protection to people. They should be trained to observe unusual activity. With a portable communication device, they can relay observations to a central reporting point.

2. Deacons and other adults who roam the halls during services can provide protection to children and workers alike. They should be trained to observe who is in the area and to identify their reasons for being there.

3. Openness and visibility reduce opportunity for the individual who attempts to carry out clandestine activity. Windows into counseling rooms and rooms with children and youth provide visual protection for the client, parishioner, and leader.

4. Develop an attitude of security by instructing people to lock spaces when they are not in use. Provide security screens for computers. Require the use of

passwords and change them often. Allow only authorized individuals into areas of sensitive information or where valuable commodities are stored. Develop a system of inventory control and accountability.

In many respects security is a state of mind. The Scripture cited at the beginning states that the careless person pays for his indifference. If a thief wants to steal from you, no security system will prevent it. It will slow down the process and become a hindrance, but it will not prevent it. So security in the church or organization is placing roadblocks to illegal and inappropriate acts. The more cautious we are in protecting the individuals we serve, the greater their sense of security for your church or organization.

Insurance

One Sunday evening about a half hour before the evening service, storm clouds gathered over the church where I was the administrator. In central Oklahoma that was a common occurrence, but on this evening the warning sirens sounded. We went to the areas where Sunday evening programs were being held and requested that everybody go to the lower level of the educational building. My son and I arrived in the sanctuary about the time hail the size of baseballs started coming through the windows. Glass was flying everywhere. Hail came through with enough velocity to fire the ice across the sanctuary and bounce it back into the center.

We rushed to put pew pads on the new grand piano, then retreated to safety just about the time the tornado passed overhead—sucking out stained-glass windows from the pressure. Then came the heavy rain and floods that filled the entire lower level of our 52,000 ft^2 facility. When our insurance agent had finished the tally the next week, we had over $97,000 in damage.

About the same time I received a check from the insurance company, we received a notification that our insurance had been cancelled. I was surprised, so I contacted our agent. I had done my homework, and I had figured that our premiums for the last dozen years more than paid for the check they had just written. "It's not the amount of the claim that has caused the national office to order the cancellation," he said. "It's the number of claims in the past five years you have had. You have filed over a dozen claims for stolen electronic equipment." It was then that I learned that state insurance regulators allowed insurance companies to cancel the policy of a client if they have greater than an average of one claim per year for a three-year period—regardless of premiums paid and claims paid. To my surprise and dismay, I discovered that our media committee had filed a claim every time a piece of equipment had been stolen, regardless of value. We paid a $200 deductible and the insurance company forked over the rest—usually not even the amount of the monthly premium.

What began as a bad experience, however, turned out to be a great learning activity. I found a national insurance agency that concentrated on insuring churches, and who provided their clients assistance in making the facility safe, secure, and protected. Scott and I became good friends. He was an unusual insurance agent in that he set out to assist the church to understand the dynamics of insurance and how a client could dramatically reduce the costs for insurance, while at the same time increasing the level of protection and coverage.

Churches and nonprofit organizations should consider several types of insurance. Depending upon the programs and ministries that are carried out, these usually fall into one of four categories:

Liability

This is coverage that focuses on protection against lawsuits that allege the church or organization has caused some form of personal or property injury through its actions. As mentioned in chapter 3, one of the advantages of incorporating the church or organization is that in instances of tort action, the corporation, not the individuals or officers, bear the burden of the suit. Thus, liability insurance that is purchased by the institution protects the entity, its officers and members alike. Liability insurance comes in many forms. Depending on the need of the church or organization, protection should be provided for the following needs.

Commercial general liability. This provides for protection whenever the church or organization is alleged to have caused bodily or property damage to a person, a group of persons, or an entity in the course of its programs or activities.

Vehicle. Often termed automobile insurance, this coverage is necessary even if the church or organization does not own or operate vehicles since the policy covers rented vehicles and volunteers when their private vehicle is used for church or organization activities.

Liability for the Actions of Officers and Leaders. This type of liability includes malpractice and/or omissions of service for individuals who provide professional services such as counseling. Another form of this insurance involves the financial activities of those who are involved in the fiscal management of the organization's resources. Included in this insurance are directors and officers to protect them in the event of lawsuits from within the organization for failure to make proper and required decisions, or, for making decisions that were deemed detrimental to the organization.

Property

This is coverage that protects the church or organization's physical assets. This includes the structures, equipment, and fixtures. The church or organization will be required to select from a list of causes of loss to determine their specific coverage. This format replaces the all-risk categories that existed in many coverage policies and has been provided to allow the client to select from types of coverage those elements that are applicable to their situation. These policies usually are categorized as follows:

1. *Basic cause of loss.* This includes damage from "acts of nature" such as fire, lightning, wind, hail, smoke. It will also include causes of man which include riot, civil violence, vandalism, malicious mischief, and vehicle or aircraft damage. Most basic cause of loss policies will include damage such as sinkhole collapse, volcanic action (but not earthquake), and sprinkler damage.

2. *Broad cause of loss.* This is a policy that includes the basic features but will also include physical loss for such items as limited glass breakage, snow or ice damage, falling objects and collapse, and water damage that is not flood related.

3. *Special cause of loss.* This is issued to provide the most comprehensive coverage possible. Formerly termed an all-risk policy, this policy will cover anything that happens unless specifically excluded. And that is the key issue the administrator must consider in this policy—what is excluded? Examples of common exclusions include war, radiation, insect infestation, biological infestation, movement of earth, and flood. Additionally, some states have allowed companies to limit the level of coverage to such action by nature as hail or storm.

4. *Additional specific cause of loss.* This coverage is added to one of the three types of policies described above and provides loss protection for items that have been specifically eliminated or not covered by the policy. For example, earthquake and earth movement, major glass, antiquities, or historical elements such as stained-glass windows. By federal law, flood insurance is only available through the national flood insurance program administered by the Federal Emergency Management Agency.

Administrators must ensure that the insurance selected adequately covers the loss incurred. Protection is provided to insurance companies by requiring clients to provide a minimum of coinsurance to the level of 20 percent of the loss. This will require a choice between purchasing insurance that provides actual cash value (replacement cost less depreciation) or replacement cost basis, which provides complete replacement without considering the depreciation that may have occurred or appreciation in cost of materials to rebuild the structure.

Suppose, for example, the church has a facility worth one million dollars. They choose to insure it for $750,000. The sanctuary burns down—total loss of $500,000. The church has replacement-cost insurance. The company will provide to the church only $468,750 of the one-half million dollar loss because the church failed to insure to a minimum of 80 percent ($800,000) and, therefore, the insurance company is only obligated to provide 75 to 80 percent of the claim. If the church had selected an actual cash-value policy, it would have been paid significantly less because depreciation would have been computed based upon age and condition of the sanctuary at the time of the loss. If the church had paid attention to the administration of the policy and increased the coverage by only $50,000 more to meet the 80 percent minimum, the company would have paid the entire replacement costs.

The astute administrator will pay close attention to any coinsurance clause in a property policy and make sure that the facility is covered to a minimum of that requirement. Most smart administrators will usually insure to a minimum of 10 percent over value or purchase an inflation guard clause for the policy to ensure the facility is always to the minimum of the coinsurance requirement of the policy.

Before leaving property insurance, a couple of other items need to be mentioned. Administrators should determine if temporary use, new construction structures, remodeling, and other types of changes or facility use considerations are included in the insurance. Second, administrators should determine how the policy premiums are calculated and how deductibles will affect the premium. In a section later in this chapter, we will discuss numerous activities that the church or organization can undertake that will significantly lower premium costs by altering or modifying their structures.

Fiduciary Bonds

A third type of insurance is that which protects the fiscal assets of the church or organization. Often called fidelity bonds or employee dishonest bonds, these insurance policies indemnify the church or nonprofit from loss of property or assets through fraud, employee dishonesty, theft, or embezzlement. They may be focused on an individual or individuals such as a financial secretary, treasurer, or administrator; or they may be general in scope, providing blanket coverage to cover all employees or individuals who have access to the finances of the church or organization. While most bonds will be applicable to the employees or officers of an organization, specified board members, volunteers, or volunteer groups can be added as a rider to the policy.

The amount of the bond should be carefully assessed since the premium for the insurance is based on the amount of the bond. Usually the amount of the bond will be limited to the maximum amount the individual or group may have access to through the course of normal business and between intervals of audit and/or report. Astute administrators will be aware that exclusion provisions that may exist in the policy such as necessity of proof of loss via bonded individual, the level of investigation required for background investigation of individuals who have fiduciary responsibility, and numbers of individuals who may be insured under the bond provision as well as the statute of limitations for discovery of loss.

Workman's Compensation

A final category of insurance the church or organization may have to consider is that which is required by employment agencies in most states. While the provisions and requirements vary from state to state, for all practical purposes employers must provide compensation for all injuries to employed personnel. This requirement applies regardless of the status (full-time, part-time) and the hours worked. This is a no-fault insurance provision whereby the employee does not have to prove liability of the employer, only that they were injured on the job. Benefits include payment of all medical costs as well as compensation to the employee for wages lost during the time they are out of work because of the injury.

Since workman's compensation applies only to employees of the church or organization, volunteers are eliminated from the provisions of the process. A volunteer who is injured on the job as a volunteer may sue the church or organization if negligence on the part of the employer is proved. This suit will fall under the provisions of the employer's liability insurance.

You have heard the adage that an ounce of prevention is worth a pound of cure. For many years I served in the U.S. Navy. While America during those years was involved in some sort of strife in various parts of the world, for the most part our fleet would "show the flag." This was a term we used to let the world know that the U.S. had a strong military force and the rationale for that force was to serve as a deterrent to any attacker. National political policy is that if you attack America, you will be dealt with in the severest terms.

Wise risk management administrators are proactive—shutting the barn door before the horse gets out. While seminars, organizations, and aids abound, it is only through a considered, common-sense approach to risk management activities that results will be achieved. Below are some suggestions that may spur some creative activity in your organization or church:

1. *Consolidate insurance.* In the story related earlier about having to obtain new property (called hazard then) insurance after the storm, the insurance agent's first suggestion was a business suggestion. Through the years the church had several insurance policies—hazard, workman's compensation, transportation, counseling, etc. He suggested to the church that his company could handle all the policies in a consolidated package. The rationale was attractive: it would save money. The reason is simple. When an insurance company writes a policy, a portion of the premium paid goes into a holding fund in which the company pays claims. A portion of the premium paid covers the

administrative costs to the company to issue the policy. If you consolidate the policies into a single holder, the administrative costs are reduced dramatically. Most major insurance carriers that deal routinely with churches and other nonprofit organizations provide such service. Our church consolidated and cut premium cost by nearly 15 percent.

2. *Evaluate add-on riders.* Insurance for antiques, the pastor's/ministerial library, or other unique items are usually not in a general cause-of-loss policy and must be added. Some companies require additional riders to be written for counseling abuse, sexual abuse, child molestation, and other sensitive issues. Wise administrators will seriously consider who needs this protection and the limit of coverage to those individuals. Not all ministers have a valuable library, not all areas of the church have stained-glass windows, not all pastors counsel, not everyone has access to children.

3. *Insure to replace.* Unless otherwise specified, an item is insured for its value—which can be significantly less than what it would take to replace it. The church or organization will have to insure to within the required coinsurance limit required of the value of the total property. For churches that have a campus complex, the church should work with the insurance company and insure to the limit of an anticipated loss. For example, if the education building and sanctuary are separate buildings, then it might be advisable to insure only to the 80 percent limit of the total value of both properties, assuming both buildings will not be totally destroyed simultaneously. On the other hand, if the buildings are contiguous and the potential for a full wipeout exists, insure to the coinsurance minimum to ensure the facilities will have 100 percent replacement. Additionally, since property insurance covers only the facility and the fixed portions of the building, always insure to replace fixtures, equipment, and other items that will allow the ministry to continue. And always insure valuables and antiquities to the extent of the appraised value.

4. *Cover the mess with an umbrella.* Umbrella policies provide an insurer blanket coverage that extends beyond the limit of one or more policies. For instance, if your multielement insurance coverage provides a one-million-dollar limit for liability in case of an auto accident, an umbrella policy of two million dollars will provide additional coverage in case a judgment exceeds the one million dollars of the auto policy. What an umbrella allows the church or organization to do is to have reasonable policy limits and yet at the same time provide coverage in the event of a major disaster or judgment. Even though this will mean another policy, in the long run the agent will be able to demonstrate how such a strategy is a significant cost-reduction action.

5. *Improve your chances for a premium reduction.* In the months following the tornado that destroyed portions of our church and the reconstruction that followed, I became a hero in our church—well, at least with the finance

committee. As our new insurance agent was assessing the church for insurability, he told me that he would have to write the policy based on the risk to the company in certain areas. He gave me an example. When we went into one of the heating/furnace rooms, the room had several items of storage—past musical dramas, some literature that was not used, and so forth. "That is a fire hazard and increases your risk for fire in this area," he said. "Therefore I will have to evaluate you at a 'high' risk for this area. Get rid of the flammable stuff and storage and your risk is lowered, and thus your premium will reflect a lowered risk." We did that and saved money. Here are some other things we did to reduce our level of risk—and saved a bundle of money.

- Remove flammable materials from stairwells and other places that do not have fire-protected (sprinkler) storage.
- Add fire extinguishers so a person does not have to move more than twenty-five feet to grab one. Make sure fire extinguishers are tested annually. Make sure you have the right kind of fire extinguisher for the space.
- Provide a fire or smoke detector in each room that will house children. Make sure there is a fire detector in the hallway.
- Remove or trim bushes from near windows and doors. Add lighting that will illuminate all access points to the interior of the church.
- Place windows in the doors to rooms that will be occupied by people seventeen years old or less. In rooms where staff and volunteer counselors will meet in counseling or ministry, and in areas where an individual may work alone, provide visual access at all times. This may be plate windows or all glass doors.
- Provide double-secured doors to all critical papers and documents. Make back-up copies and store off-site, preferably in a bank vault. The second lock on a space of the finance office or records office should be an electronic combination lock that can be changed at regular intervals.
- Make sure fire doors to hallways and stairwells are in operating condition and cannot be blocked open. Remove door stops from these doors. Make sure the heat sensitive links in door opening devices are functional.
- Make sure all interior escape routes are marked and lighted with an emergency lighting system.
- Have a "response" alarm system.
- Ensure that all personnel who have access to children and youth areas have background checks, have received child abuse or molestation training, and comply with the "two-man rule."
- Remove, repair, or replace all trip or fall hazards such as handrails, carpet bumps, and hidden steps or ramps.

- Test for the presence of lead and have certification of such testing in all areas where children are present.
- Institute a system for inspection and maintenance of equipment and fixtures of the church.

6. *Control Claims.* This section started with my sad story of insurance cancellation because we had filed too many claims over a three-year period. The new insurance agent made an interesting suggestion. He said that we should increase our deductible for a claim. He would allow us to set deductibles for different sections of the policy. For instance, for fire, wind, rain, etc. we could set that at $2,500 but have a deductible of $500 for electronic or office equipment. He then suggested that we add a budget item for insurance claims of say $5,000 from which we would pay any deductible amounts. If we didn't have claims during the year, we didn't spend the $5,000. To control claims, we set up a review board in our properties committee that had to approve any claim. Once this policy was instituted, we often found that it would be the decision of the sub-committee not to file a claim with the insurance company, but instead to make the replacement from the $5,000 insurance fund. After many years since that tornado event, the church is still with the same insurance carrier and still saving money.

Chapter Review

Competent administrators must be attuned to the dynamics of risk management that addresses the safety and security of the people who participate in the activities of the church or organization. Additionally, the resources—physical as well as fiscal—must be afforded the level of protection to ensure the mission and purpose of the church or organization are sustained. While the reader was introduced to topics in this chapter on the three separate discussions of safety, security, and insurance, the fact is that elements of risk management merge into a consistent pattern of concern and action. The reader should be able to:

- Articulate the requirements to provide a safe environment for both the employee or visitor to the church or organization.
- Identify the elements of a security system that provides proactive actions to prevent breaches of security as well as actions that respond to emergencies or other situations requiring concerted action to protect property or sustain life.
- Describe a program of insurance that addresses the principal areas of liability, property damage, and fiscal and employee protection.

Administering
Planning Activities

Where there is no vision, the people perish:
but he that keepeth the law, happy is he.
PROVERBS 29:18 KJV

Addressing the crowd on the day of Pentecost in Jerusalem, Peter declared that the prophecy of the prophets Joel, Isaiah, and Ezekiel was now before them in the body of Christ and in the form of the new covenant as expressed through the church. Peter declared that their "young men will see visions, and your old men will dream dreams" (Acts 2:17).

Several years ago as a deacon in a small church, I was placed on a committee to rewrite our constitution and bylaws. We had discovered that our current document had been written in 1934, and the latest revision was done in 1956. It was over twenty years old and woefully out of date. Our pastor admonished us first to determine what the mission statement of the church was before we began since all that we wrote to describe the church's polity and operation had to flow out of what we were about theologically and doctrinally. Thus began a long odyssey that defined the character of the church for which we were about to create beliefs, doctrine, and polity.

The Mission and Purpose Statement

In their book *Leading the Congregation*, Norman Shawchuck and Roger Heuser state that a vision is a mystical happening dreamed in the hearts of God's servants by the Holy Spirit; it is not planned, and it is God's vision. Vision has dimensions that call for inward evaluation, outward consideration, and practical application.[1] The practical application of a vision by a church or religious organization is expressed in a mission statement. Therefore, God, speaking through the Holy Spirit to the leaders of the church, places a vision of ministry that needs to be accomplished. The leadership then sets out to assist the church or group in an interpretation of that vision and the establishment of goals and objectives that will implement that vision—the mission of the church.

Translating a vision from God into a practical ministry becomes the primary responsibility of the leadership of the organization. It becomes the foundation from which all actions spring, whether administrative or ministry. The mission or purpose statement of the church or organization comes as the result of several actions.

1. Determining What Scripture Defines as Appropriate Activity

Throughout Scripture the character and work of the Christian individual and institution is clearly defined. For example, the Great Commission of Matthew 28:19–20 calls for a continual, worldwide sharing of the gospel, the integration of new converts into a body of believers (the church) and the teaching and discipling of those individuals. Other passages speak about caring for the needy, sick, and helpless. And other verses speak of mission activities in the local community and the extended community of the world. Scripture calls us to worship God both individually and in a corporate community of believers.

2. Determining What the Christian Community Defines as Appropriate Activity

Historically the Christian church has been responsible for caring, ministering, and benevolent activities. Most hospitals sprang from church or denominational actions. Universities, colleges, and schools emerged from the church and denomination leadership. And in like manner, orphanages, retirement communities, and similar support agencies were the product of concerned Christian churches and organizations.

3. Determining How the Church Defines Its Mission

This is like a visionary leader casting a net into the water of the membership and gathering in the many ideas and expressions the congregation makes about how they are to implement their perceived spiritual gifts. If we are to agree with the notion that the Holy Spirit will not call a church or organization to accomplish a task that he has not already empowered someone to carry out, then leaders must listen to the hearts of the members as they express that call. And leaders must be quick to assist the member in understanding and defining that "gifted" call.

Creating the actual document that states the mission or purpose of the church or organization comes about in a variety of methods. The key element in developing such a statement is the inclusion of the people who must "buy into" the declaration. If the pastor creates a statement, it is deemed as the pastor's, not the church's. If it comes from the deacons, elders, or even a committee without the input of the people who must implement the mission statement, ownership of the sense of direction and the strategies to achieve them is not attained.

Whether creating a mission and purpose statement where none exists or modifying or reviewing an existing statement, a suggested process includes the following actions.

1. Assign to an organization within the church or organizational polity the task of creating the document statement. This may be an existing polity organization such as a board, elders, deacons, or it may be a specially formed group such as a temporary committee.

2. Ensure the ministerial and staff professional leaders are included. Ensure the committee or development body has as members those people in the church or institution who have the spiritual attentiveness to allow the Holy Spirit to work through them.

3. Cast the vision. Allow the group to dream dreams, to visualize where the church or organization should be headed to meet the expectations of the Holy Spirit. Provide an opportunity for the congregation or membership to express their dreams and communicate their wishes.

4. Write down the vision as perceived at this time. Place in words the dreams, the desires, and the potential that describe the vision of the group.

5. Research how Scripture, the historical church, and the Christian culture have interpreted visionary mandates in the past. Answer the questions: What must we do from a scriptural perspective? What must we do from a historical perspective? What must we do to meet the unique call to ministry we perceive the Holy Spirit has directed us to do? In other words, what should our church or organization be doing in this place, at this time, with the resources we have been given?

6. Formulate a mission statement and allow it to be discussed before adoption. Make the statement simple, direct, concise, and inclusive at the same time. It should be complete enough to say what you want but simple enough to learn and repeat. For example, "It is the mission of ABC Church to lead in Christian worship, discipleship, and ministry outreach to the OK community and to support and participate in evangelistic missions locally and throughout the world."

7. Promulgate the final version of the mission statement. The pastor may want to preach a series of sermons about how Scripture interprets the elements of the mission statement. Discussion groups may be formed to speak of ways that the church or organization can implement the document.

Plans to Implement the Mission Statement

Once the church or organization has a statement that will focus activities, ministries, programs, and events, plans need to be made to create goals and strategies that address mission objectives. In chapter 2 we introduced the process of administration that began with the planning process. There we identified seven activities that need to be considered in each plan: forecasting, establishing objectives, setting policy and procedures, outlining programming and establishing schedules, and then creating budgets that will meet those plans. We discussed the fact that planning begins the administrative process and the activities established therein are prevalent throughout the remainder of the administrative process.

Planning and planning groups occur in different situations in the life of the church or organization. They may be identified, however, in three specific areas:

Long-Range Planning

Every church or organization should have an entity identified to conduct long-range planning. Some group should be assigned the responsibility to develop and maintain the mission and purpose statement, provide review of the statement in view of changing contingencies, and suggest strategies that implement the mission statement. In many churches or organizations, this is the same group of people who went through the development of the mission statement. They are the vision casters. Whether they are a board, council, staff, or an independent committee, this group should represent the same spiritual foresight, recognized organizational leadership, and proactive vision that existed when the mission and purpose statements were formalized.

The formal development of a mission statement is the first activity of this group. An important follow-on action is the creation of potential actions that will address each of the elements of the mission statement. Often called long-range goals, these activities become the basis from which other plans are developed by the various elements of the church or organizational structure. For instance, in the example mission statement above, the church felt that a primary mission activity was the teaching and discipleship function. That may be implemented in several ways: through a Sunday school, weekday discipleship training programs, individual Bible study, small group and mentor studies, and so forth. It may be conducted at the church facility, via Internet, video, in homes, in offices, and so the ideas continue.

While most communities would support a Sunday school program in the church, not all are capable of weekday studies in homes. Discipleship training programs abound. However, the Holy Spirit may direct one church to focus on studies in homes, another church will be assigned a focus on college students on campus, and another church will be led to focus on a discipleship program to the elderly at a nursing home. So while all churches will probably have an element of discipleship in the mission statement, it is during the long-range planning that it is fleshed out into the various settings that are directed by the Holy Spirit for implementation.

The long-range planning group, therefore, will cast the vision for a discipleship ministry at the local college campus as one of the long-term strategies that the church will take in responding to the mission statement for conducting *Christian discipleship*. When and how this is implemented becomes a function of the activities that are carried out by professional staff ministers, education councils, and/or student ministry directors in their various program plans.

One final activity of the long-range planning group is the evaluation of the plans and actions that are or have been initiated to carry out the mission of the church or organization. "Are we moving forward in accomplishing our stated mission?" would be the question asked by the group. Thus, they become the lightning rod by which the long-term success of the mission of the church is measured. The church or organization has one measuring stick by which all programs, ministries, and activities are evaluated: What have we accomplished and what more is the Spirit leading us to do? From this assessment of the developed strategies to implement the mission statement, new or revised strategies can be envisioned.

Short-Range Planning

Short-range plans are usually termed annual plans because they are developed to be implemented within the time frame of a program year. They obtain their impetus from the long-range strategies that have been developed by the long-range planning group. Some institutions will schedule their program year to coincide with the projected budget year, while other groups—specifically churches—will schedule the program year around some other cycle, usually the academic year of the local school system. There are advantages to both cycles.

For example, a program cycle coincident with a budget year allows for easier tracking and reporting of resource needs and utilization. On the other hand, a program year that parallels the academic year of the local school system merges well with a Sunday school program that uses age grading as its basis for the school-age attendees. Its principal disadvantage is that it generally does not parallel the budget cycle of the church, which is usually keyed to a calendar, tax-year format. Thus budget considerations must bridge two program years or an annual program year must be considered in two budget cycles. The sequencing of the program cycle is an important decision that must be made in the development of short-range plans.

The development of a short-range or annual plan is the venue of the various programs, ministries, or activity units of the church or organization. In chapter 6 we introduced the concept of a budget unit. There we defined a budget unit as an entity of the church or organization that has been authorized to request budget allocations and granted permission to expend funds from the budget in response to the allocation made in the budget. These budget units include the professional and lay staff, committees, councils, ministry team program directors, and any other unit of the organization that meets the budget criteria. Every budget unit manager should develop an annual plan for program expenditures. How else can a budget request be made, and how can a funding authority grant permission for the expenditure?

Job descriptions for personnel holding leadership positions in the church will have as part of the responsibilities assigned, the development and sustenance of plans to implement the specific ministries they are called to perform. Additionally, the charter of every committee, council, and ministry team has designated activities and reports that allude to the creation of annual plans for carrying out their particular ministry, program, or activity. One of the quickest ways to ascertain who or what group should be creating annual plans is to consider the organizational chart of the church or institution that delineates the leadership elements which define what is being accomplished to meet the mission of the church or organization.

Short-range, annual plans are birthed from the strategies that are developed to implement the mission of the church or organization. Thus, a necessary starting point for all groups that create such plans is the review of the mission statement and the declared strategies that implement that plan. Let's return to the example of a discipleship/training mission statement and the development of a strategy to meet the needs of discipling on the college campus. This strategy may first call for the church to consider developing a ministry area for the college student. This may come in the form of a college/single ministry council, the assignment of the responsibility to another staff person—for example, the minister of education—or even the consideration by the personnel committee to call a professional staff member who will relate to college students.

Having assigned the long-range strategy to a leadership office, the next step is for that entity to begin the formulation of a plan that will implement the strategy. The strategy calls for a discipleship program to college students on campus. In developing the strategy, the short-range plan may be first to begin a Bible study program for students as part of an ongoing religious ministry—such as a denominational campus ministry or one of the many parachurch college ministries. A follow-on plan may be to obtain permission to use one of the college's meeting spaces to hold a discipling program. Or the plan may be to use the dorm room of one of the college student church members. The plan may call for meeting in a local restaurant, at the church, or in an individual's home.

As the where-to-meet issue is settled, what to study may be the next topic in the plan development. Numerous discipling publications, manuscripts, and programs exist that may be adopted. Plans must be made about which one to use, the costs involved, and the logistics to acquire them. Thus, an annual ministry action plan for an on-campus college discipleship program may be outlined as follows.

ANNUAL PLAN: On-campus discipleship program

LONG-RANGE STRATEGY: Discipleship program to the local college population

IMPLEMENTING MINISTRY: College/Single Ministry Council

RESOURCE REQUIREMENTS:

> LEADERSHIP: Volunteer personnel from council
>
> STAFF LIAISON/COORDINATOR: Minister of education
>
> MEETING PLACE: Rented room in the campus student union building
>
> FREQUENCY: Weekly during fall and spring semesters (32 weeks)
>
> TEACHING MATERIAL: CrossSeeker materials of LifeWay Christian Resources
>
> BUDGET REQUEST:

Building rental—32 weeks @ $20/week	$640
Publications—15 students with 4 books ea.	
45 books @ approx. $8 ea	$360
Refreshments—for 15 students	$400
Total budget submission	$1,400

The outline above is sufficient to take the annual plan to a coordinating leadership or church council for integration into the total annual plan for the church or agency. Of course, there are many details that must be developed to actually carry out the annual plan submission; that type of planning will occur in the next planning phase.

Once all budget units and program entities have developed their annual plans, these plans must be brought together to ensure that a coordinated annual plan exists for the entire church or organization. A church council or leadership team is the proper forum for this, since it is usually made up of all the key leaders of the organization. This group integrates the annual plan goals of each of the entities and ensures they do not interfere but interact within the complete annual plan that moves the church or organization forward to meet the mission statement. A published short-range, annual plan does several things for the church or organization:

- It recognizes the input and plans of the elements of the church or institution.
- It provides a composite picture of how the church or organization is moving toward achieving the strategies and goals of the mission statement and long-range plan.
- It provides a visible demonstration of organized leaders to meet the needs and objectives of the total body.
- The written document provides a basis for scheduling implementing strategies.
- The composite organizational annual plan provides a basis for evaluating the success of the church or organization in meeting strategies, objectives, and goals.

Strategic Planning

The detailed planning each program, ministry, or element of the church or organization engages in to carry out the objectives and goals of the long-range and short-range plans are called strategic plans. These are not to be confused with the long-range strategies that are developed to provide a broad, overarching concept for carrying out the mission of the church or organization. Strategic plans are the detailed plans that actually implement the broader plans. Every objective set in the annual plan should have a detailed implementing plan.

Returning once again to the long-range strategy of developing a discipleship training program on the college campus, the annual plan given in the annual planning section above now needs to be fleshed out.

ANNUAL PLAN: On-campus discipleship program

LONG-RANGE STRATEGY: Discipleship program to the local college population

IMPLEMENTING MINISTRY: College/Single Ministry Council

RESOURCE REQUIREMENTS:

LEADERSHIP: Charles and Iris Woods

STAFF LIAISON/COORDINATOR: Minister of education

MEETING PLACE: Student Center room 211

FREQUENCY: Weekly during fall and spring semesters
August 17-December 20; January 11-May 16

TEACHING MATERIAL: CrossSeeker materials of
LifeWay Christian Resources
Unit 1—Fall Semester,
The College Student and Personal Development

Unit 2—Spring Semester
Preparing for a Christian Lifestyle
BUDGET REQUEST:

Building rental—32 weeks @ $20/week	$640
Publications—15 students with 4 books ea.	
45 books @ approx. $8 ea	$360
Refreshments—for 15 students	$400
Total budget submission	$1,400

Plans now need to be made to identify leaders for each of the thirty-two sessions that will be conducted. Who will be in charge of the program—that is, who is the contact person? Who will be in charge of the refreshments? Of the twelve books in the CrossSeeker series, which three will be taught? The group leading the ministry needs to discuss how the training session will be conducted. What time? What day? Someone needs to make arrangements for a room in the student center and ensure that it is set up. How are the students contacted, and will there be publicity about the study? What if more than fifteen students attend? Will there be a contingency to increase the size this year? These and a myriad of other questions need to be resolved by the implementing ministry leadership (the college/single ministry council) and the designated staff liaison member (the minister of education). Strategic planning sessions need to be conducted to create the implementation plan for this discipleship ministry to college students.

While the ministry or program leadership has overall responsibility for the plan to be developed and implemented, the strategic plans for actual accomplishment need to follow certain guidelines:

- Any strategic plans must be within the bounds of the objectives and goals of the long-range and annual plans that call for them.
- Implementing activities must be established within the guidelines of existing church or organization polity and policy.
- Budget restrictions must be honored.
- The people who will actually implement the planned activity should be involved in the details of the plan.
- A system of monitoring the plan and a process for developing a report of accomplishments should be included.

Strategic plans are the multiple activities that go on in the life of a church or organization that give it identity as an institution with a purpose. Contemporary demographers who have studied the characteristics of modern population groups indicate an interesting factor that drives individuals in the consideration of whether they participate in a program or ministry. These individuals want to see activities that are worthwhile, thought out, and productive. Ministries and programs must be perceived by people to have produced results that are worthwhile and objective. An important element in this perception is well thought out plans that the individual has had a part in developing.

Planning for Building and Expansion

In Matthew's record of Jesus' early teaching that occurred on the mountain, Jesus admonished the listeners with this analogy, "Therefore, everyone who hears these words of Mine and acts on them will be like a sensible man who built his house on the rock. The rain fell, the rivers rose, and the winds blew and pounded that house. Yet it didn't collapse, because its foundation was on the rock" (Matt. 7:24–25). Christ calls the builder a "sensible" man. Other translations refer to this person as "wise," "prudent," or "practical." Each of these descriptions indicates that the builder is careful, cautious, and contemplative. He does not enter into the building process without due thought and consideration.

Such was the attitude of David, who was the architect of the first house of God. Turn to 1 Chronicles 28 and the chapters following to discover the process for the design of the temple. David had recognized that the tabernacle of the wilderness needed to be replaced with a newer facility. Note in verse 1 that he summoned all the national leadership to Jerusalem. In verse 2 he reported the vision the Spirit had provided him: "It was in my heart to build a house as a resting place for the ark of the LORD's covenant and as a footstool for our God. I had made preparations to build." Note in verse 6 that he identified the builder: "He said to me: 'Your son Solomon is the one who is to build My house and My courts.'"

Then in verses 11–13 David outlined the plans: "Then David gave his son Solomon the plans for the vestibule of the temple and its buildings, treasuries, upper rooms, inner rooms, and the room for the place of atonement. The plans contained everything he had in mind for the courts of the LORD's house . . . all the articles of service of the LORD's house." Then David pointed out in verse 19 that architectural plans had been drawn up: "By the LORD's hand on me, He enabled me to understand everything in writing, all the details of the plan."

And as a final act of leadership responsibility, David launched a stewardship campaign to pay for the temple structure:

> Then King David said to all the assembly, "My son Solomon—God has chosen him alone—is young and inexperienced. The task is great, for the temple will not be for man, but for the LORD God. So to the best of my ability I've made provision for the house of my God . . . Moreover, because of my delight in the house of my God, I now give my personal treasures of gold and silver for the house of my God over and above all that I've provided . . . Now, who will volunteer to consecrate himself to the LORD today?" Then the leaders of the

households, the leaders of the tribes of Israel, the commanders of thousands and of hundreds, and the officials in charge of the king's work gave willingly. For the service of God's house they gave (1 Chron. 29:1–3, 5–7).

The beginning of 2 Chronicles discusses the actual process of gathering workmen and materials and the task of completing and ultimately dedicating the temple structure.

Note some interesting facets of this passage of Scripture:

- The Holy Spirit imparted to David the need for a temple structure and described the design.
- David began stewardship preparations for the structure long before it was actually built.
- David relayed the vision to his son, the actual builder, in the form of a narrative and visual (written down) format.
- Solomon waited until the right time to begin the building.
- Solomon built the temple on the land that was designated by the Lord.
- Solomon used professional craftsmen as well as the people who would worship in the temple in the actual building process.
- The temple was built by using a variety of skills, each led by competent supervisors.
- Throughout the building process and upon its dedication, the purpose and focus of the temple was always held before the people; it was God's house.

Each year hundreds of millions of dollars are poured into building and renovation programs in religious and charitable organizations. The value of land and the structures on those lands are counted in the trillions of dollars in the United States. In the past in America, communities came together to build the meeting house because it often was used, in addition to the Sunday service, as the place for community business, often the schoolhouse for the children's education, where people were married and buried. As communities grew, denominationally supported buildings sprang up, supported by the parishioners of that particular belief system. Independent church groups and charitable organizations often sought out already existing structures as houses for their activities.

We have already discussed in chapter 7 the need for and the dynamics involved in the provision and use of a church facility. We need now to consider the plans necessary to bring to fruition the vision implanted in the hearts of leaders that will include the need for structures to house the ministry operations of the group.

The vision of the need to consider the physical facilities of the church often comes out of the annual reviews of the long-range plan for the church.

Often out of the evaluation of the mission statement of the church or organization will come the need to provide a "house" for the activity envisioned. The wise organization does not wait until the need is so apparent that they cannot meet that need in a timely fashion. What happens too often is that the church or organization waits until the need is critical. In their failure to meet the need, detriment to the impetus that brought them to the need occurs and the organization quits growing.

In the Chronicles, David foresaw that the temple project would be costly. Solomon realized that materials and craftsmen should be assembled before the project began. They had a plan. Churches and organizations need a growth plan that can be met when the need arises.

Frequently I am asked to visit churches that are in dire straits because of facility needs. They are in multiple services, extending their programming to days other than Sunday, and using small-group meetings in homes. All of these are excellent options before adding buildings, but these churches have come to the point that even these alternatives are not meeting their needs. One of the first questions I ask in such a visit is to see their master plan for growth. "Master plan, what is that?" the leaders sometimes ask. I want to scream at them: "The plan you should have begun the same month you added a second worship service, or moved your Sunday school to homes, or the moment you realized that someday in the future you would exceed the limits of your present facility if you continued to grow at the rate that caused you to move to an alternative program schedule." But in my polite, gentle way (don't laugh, former students), I address the issue of planning ahead for growth through the utilization of a master plan.

The Master Plan

Have you ever watched a home being built? Usually equipment is brought in to prepare the site for building. The soil is graded and stabilized, and engineers assess the need for foundation support. A foundation is laid, and the structure rises from the ground in stages—floors, walls, a roof. A siding finish is attached, and windows and doors are placed. Utility connections are made, and plumbing, electrical, heating/cooling systems are installed. Inside, the walls and ceilings are finished, and flooring is laid. Fixtures are installed, and the house is made ready for occupancy. During the home's construction workmen examine drawings and diagrams of what is to be built—the blueprints. A part of those blueprints is the specifications for wall type and texture, ceiling, and floor coverings, types of fixtures and their placement, colors, and finishes. These are the plans for the house. They began weeks ago in the mind of an architect and a client-owner. They were worked over in great detail long before construction began. It was the master plan for the construction of a house.

The process for developing a master plan for a church or institution follows much the same pattern. It occurs in phases, it builds upon the activities that go before, and it is a coordinated plan that has a terminal focus. While it is best to develop the plan from the very beginning, even long-established churches or institutions can develop a master plan. It basically asks these questions: (1) Where are we now? (2) Given the trends we can assess at this time, where could we go? (3) What resource planning is necessary to take us to that position? These are the same questions that were asked in the long-range planning process, but now they are couched in terms of facility needs. Thus the master plan gains its formulation from the work of the study group that considers the long-range plan of the church or organization, which in turn interprets the mission statement. The master plan is produced in four phases:

1. *Assessing of the Potential of the Church or Organization.* Recognition of the factors that would lead to growth or situations that would inhibit growth needs to be developed. What are community trends? What are ministry opportunities? What are the desires of the members? While the long-range planning group will always hold before it the prompting of the Holy Spirit, pragmatic elements must be considered. A church stuck in the middle of a city block, surrounded by tall buildings, and having no options for acquiring additional space will not grow in that location. They may increase programs by efficiently and effectively using the space they have, but they cannot add buildings to grow. I was a member of such a church. After the experts had made their determination that the church could not grow beyond sixteen hundred in a dual service/Bible study program, the church voted to accept that fact rather than consider relocating to a larger piece of property.

2. *Evaluatiing Current Assets.* The era of a single-use facility is fast becoming a thing of the past. Churches and organizations cannot afford to have buildings sit vacant for long periods during the week. The use of creative scheduling and space allocation is becoming a necessity. The master plan not only addresses the structure of the facility but the use of dynamics as well. How many times can the same space be used efficiently to meet the mission and program needs?

Numerous considerations must be made during this evaluation process:
- What is the age, history, and life expectancy of the structure?
- What facility value is assigned? Would it be cheaper to rebuild than remodel?
- Do facilities meet current building, safety, and accessibility codes?
- What configuration changes or additions need to be considered for multipurpose use of the space?
- What land use, easement, parking, and deed or other restrictions inhibit property use?

3. *Patterning the Growth Process.* What events, growth statistics, ministry expressions will cause the next phase to be operational? Given these criteria, what happens next? In other words, if growth reaches a certain level, what do we do next? The answer may be to move to a dual program use. Another response would be to consider the implementation of a building or remodeling process to enhance and continue the growth environment.

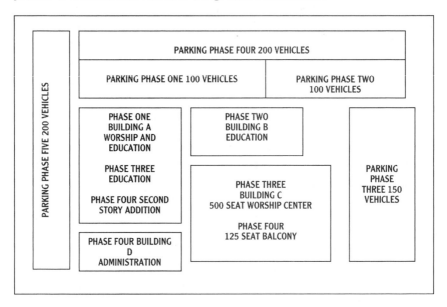

Patterning calls for the design of a method for accomplishing the goals of the long-range strategy. The actual design is not necessary, but an estimate of needs is required. This is often depicted in block format. An example might look like this:

Movement from one phase to the next occurs based on certain predetermined triggers. For example:

1. Phase 1 is the initial structure. A two-hundred-seat multipurpose auditorium and educational space for three age divisions—children, youth, and adults. This structure will function until education needs dictate the division by four age brackets (preschool, school-age children, secondary and college-age students, and adults).

2. Phase 2 is initiated when educational space calls for multiple classes and departments. The phase 1 worship center becomes a dual-use facility, serving a worship service before and after a Bible study program. Since the facility is now serving the needs for up to four-hundred people in worship, additional parking is required using the rule of thumb of one space per two individuals on site.

3. Phase 3 is triggered when the dual worship program of four-hundred people in worship is maximized. A worship facility of five-hundred will return the church to a single worship and call for the addition of education space where once a two-hundred-seat auditorium existed. This naturally calls for additional parking since we have the potential of additional people on site in excess of the parking available.

4. Phase 4 is triggered by educational growth that will call for additions to Building A and the potential for a balcony in Building C worship center. On-site parking is increased to allow for an expansion of up to eleven hundred individuals using the 2:1 ratio of persons to parking space.

5. Phase 5 is the addition of 200 more parking spaces as the church moves to a dual worship/Bible study format with the potential of 1,400 in simultaneous worship and education.

Given this master plan, the church would need to consider eight to nine acres of land to achieve the goals outlined. A rough rule of thumb is that it takes about one acre of land for every 125 people on site. If this site were maximized at phase 5, then potentially 1,400 people could be in worship and Bible study simultaneously.

Rules of thumb assist the planner in estimating global needs. Below is a table of some of the most commonly used estimators.

General estimate for site planning for worship, education, support, parking	1 acre per 100 to 125 in attendance	Education spaces Small church Large church	Per person 30-40 ft^2 45-55 ft^2
Worship center To 300 capacity Over 300 capacity Choir area Lobby	Per person 15-17 ft^2 12-18 ft^2 10% of WC 10-15% of WC	Education space by age Preschool Children Youth Adult	Per person 35 ft^2 25 ft^2 18-22 ft^2 18-22 ft^2
Administrative offices Pastor Staff General support	Per office 140-325 ft^2 120-200 ft^2 80 ft^2	Music offices Rehearsal room Robing and Library	Per space 10% larger than choir loft 5-8 ft^2/person
General Fellowship	1/3-1/2 of the education bldg	Greenbelts, roadways, sidewalks	8-10% of total acreage

Source: Church Architecture Division of LifeWay Christian Resources, Southern Baptist Convention at www.lifeway.com/churcharchitecture/resources.htm

4. Developing a Stewardship Plan. Just as King David realized that the construction of the temple would have a significant cost, a church or organization should plan to consider the costs for the master plan. This important step in the master plan recognizes the need to develop a scheme early on for paying for any building or remodeling project that will be undertaken. When or if a project is planned, significant advantage (as well as leverage) is held with the accumulation of funds to at least begin the project without reliance on outside resources for the completion. Lending agencies will require either collateral or at least the builder to have 20 percent of the cost in hand.

The stewardship plan should be part of the church's annual budget consideration. Either an ongoing line item or a designated fund account should be established for this purpose. Some churches or organizations may choose to enter into a building or remodeling program without borrowing. The early establishment of a stewardship plan becomes an absolute necessity if this is the philosophy for funding. If the church waits until the need is there, then a delay will have to occur as they collect the funds necessary to complete the project. Again, the problem is that the impetus that brought them to the growth need may dissipate as overcrowding and inconvenience drive people away.

Building or Remodeling Projects

When the time comes for a building or remodeling project, Gwenn McCormick in *Planning and Building Church Facilities* strongly recommends that the church or organization create a temporary committee to complete all phases of the project. He terms this group a steering committee.[2] In the charter establishing the committee, it should be granted complete authority to act in behalf of the church or organization to carry out all facets of the project. This includes:

- Evaluation of the scope of the project
- Assessment of current facilities and property
- Developing plans
- Acquiring funding
- Contract/construction management
- Promotion and publicity

In many situations the tendency is to place people on the project steering committee who have building or finance management skills. While individuals with those skills will be used in the process, they do not necessarily make the best people to be placed on this important committee. Project steering committee members should be individuals who:

- Are open to spiritual direction and guidance.
- Share the vision of the church or organization with the leaders.
- Understand the mission and the objectives and strategies that complement it.
- Are actively involved in the life and programs of the church or organization.
- Are not new Christians or new church members
- Possess the confidence of the members that they will represent them.

Out of this steering committee will be formed many subcommittees and work groups to carry out assigned portions of the plan. Before we continue with the development of a project plan, let's discuss the use of a subcommittee of the property committee to carry out small remodeling and repair projects. For example, the children's ministry leaders have asked the church to convert two small classrooms into a library and media center. The project was submitted as a budget item, and funding has been obtained from budget receipts and a significant gift of a member. The church may assign to the properties committee the responsibility to carry out the remodeling project. The justification may be both the size of the project and the fact the project was part of a larger plan for the educational spaces. The properties committee could form a subcommittee to accomplish the task, or they could manage it themselves. The decision to conduct the project within an already-established structure, to create a subgroup of the organization, or to develop a specified temporary committee to conduct the project should be a function of scope, complexity, and coordination among the elements of the church or organization.

The development of a building project has many stages. While they will be discussed individually below, the importance of recognizing that these stages interrelate cannot be overemphasized. That is why a central steering committee that controls all decisions is a necessity. In reality, many subcommittees and work groups will be formed that provide input for decisions that move the project toward completion. These subcommittees and work groups must be headed by a member of the steering committee, or a committee member must be assigned as liaison to the work/study group. Important subgroups of the project include the following.

1. *Site Evaluation and Acquisition.* The ideal situation would be for the leadership to have long ago developed a master plan that outlines the need for adequate land space and to have taken steps to acquire such land. Then they would have created a block diagram of the expansion on the property. In most instances, however, that is not the case; or it is not totally the case. The role of the site evaluation and acquisition subcommittee is to assess the current property usage and allocate space or acquire necessary additional space if needed. Following are things to consider with regard to selection of a site for the church or organization.

- *Location.* What is the target community and where do they live? Can they readily get to you?
- *Access.* Will the facility be located near major intersections or landmarks? Can the target audience move in and out of the space easily through access points that are located on separate streets or access points?

- *Visibility.* How will the target community know you are there? Can the facility be seen from major thoroughfares or roadways? Will your facility become a community landmark in itself?
- *Neighbors.* Who are the people around you? Avoid major industrial areas if you are asking parishioners to come to a community environment. How will the neighborhood accept you? What kind of neighbors will you be—ones that congest their streets or ones they will accept?
- *Contiguous.* What is adjacent to the property—an open field or a shopping mall? Is the property landlocked, meaning there is no potential for growth beyond the bounds of the property?
- *Topography.* What is the terrain like—hills or level, wooded or field? What soil conditions exist that impact building? What environmental conditions exist that may be restrictions to full use? What drainage issues will have to be resolved?
- *Utilities.* Are adequate services available? What costs will be involved in providing services to the site?

Following are things to consider with regard to position of the building on the site.

- *Visibility.* While a first-phase worship center may be toward the back of the property, the final phase sanctuary should be prominent on the property—the focus of the campus.
- *Parking Access.* Parking should be located near the access points from the street without having to use valuable land for roadways. Place parking areas so a person leaving his car can see the church facility he

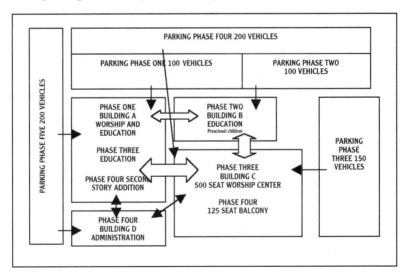

is moving toward. The largest number of spaces should be adjacent to the largest capacity building. Close, level movement ways is necessary for adequate handicap access.

- *Interior Traffic Flow.* Hallways and foyers should increase in size as you move from a lesser capacity area to spaces like the sanctuary or fellowship hall where larger numbers of people congregate. Locate activities such as senior adult ministry and preschool/children ministry areas closest to the facilities' primary room—the auditorium.

One of the easiest ways to visualize people flow management is to create diagrams of the buildings in the pattern of use.

Revisiting our master plan from above, we can draw arrows that indicate personnel flow in and around the buildings. In phase 1, traffic flow is in from the parking lot. In phase 2 the traffic flow comes from two parking lots to two buildings. The only interchange is the movement between buildings A and B. In phase 3 traffic patterns become more complex. There are three movement paths from the parking lots and three movement paths between the three buildings. The major traffic flow will be between buildings A and C with a lesser traffic flow between B and C, and even less traffic flow between buildings A and B. This assumes that adults and youth will have Bible study in building A and children will not leave building B during the worship and Bible study times.

The flow patterns into building B, thus, are parents delivering and picking up their children. When the administration building is added in phase 4, traffic between that and other buildings does not change the major traffic patterns between buildings A, B, and C. Minimum traffic flow will occur between A and D and C and D buildings as staff and other leaders move from offices to the ministry spaces. We now have added a fourth parking facility that feeds all areas. Notice the preschool/children's area is contiguous to the worship centers in all phases. The astute adult program leader will also ensure that the senior adults stay in building B. This will keep them contiguous to the worship center spaces.

2. *Building Design.* Another function of the project steering committee will be the selection of an architect, who will translate the dreams and desires of the church or organization into a functioning facility. This phase of the project is critical because changes or revision after the project is underway are more difficult and costly. Here the project committee is looking for a structural design that:

- Effectively uses space.
- Is designed for multiple activities.
- Allows for future expansion or modification.
- Is constructed with materials that lend to efficiency in maintenance.
- Are simplified, interlocking spaces which merge with the other facilities.

- Will be energy efficient.
- Meets all legal requirements for safety, security, and accessibility.

While the Religious Land Use and Institutionalized Persons Act of 2000 prevents local and municipal governments from imposing unreasonable demands on churches and nonprofit organizations, reasonable building and occupancy codes must be complied with.

Probably one of the most important activities the subgroup responsible for design will undertake will be the selection of an architect, who will put the desires of the church or organization on paper. In selecting an architect, keep three important considerations in mind.

1. Look for an architect who understands houses of worship and/or Christian education, or who understands the function of your particular organization or ministry.
2. Look for an architect who is licensed, an individual who knows the legal requirements for safety, habitability, and accessibility as well as one who is able to build a structurally sound facility.
3. Look for an architect who will develop a facility that is acceptable to your membership's taste. Look at examples of his or her work for compatibility to your needs; ask other clients about him or her.

An important statement needs to be made about the selection of an architect. Most architects are creative, artistic individuals who understand the mechanics of designing a structurally sound building that meets all building codes. What an architect is not is the dream caster for your organization. He does not dream your dreams, assess your programs, or define your mission statement. His or her job is to translate the church's or organization's dreams and desires into structural reality. The architect will listen to you and attempt to put on paper what he or she thinks you are saying. Therefore, the people who make up this subcommittee should be people who understand the desires of the church or organization and who are articulate in communicating those desires to the architect. Additionally, since architects tend to be expressive in their creativity, the subcommittee needs to remain focused on functionality, usability, and form rather than building a monumental expression that challenges the senses and the pocketbook.

The building design subcommittee can take several avenues in using the services of an architect. Many denominational offices have people on staff who assist churches in the development of plans for facilities. Even if they do not have an architect on staff, they have access to several architectural groups that meet the needs of the denomination. Another resource is the selection of one of many plan-design or design-build companies that have been established in the past couple of decades which focus their business on churches and religious nonprofit organizations. These companies advertise in the various religious trade magazines that focus on leadership and administration. Regardless of how or from what resource the architect is chosen, several elements of the contract for services should be discussed.

The fee structure. Usually the fee is based on a percentage of the total cost of the construction or remodeling project. The fee may vary, however. It may be established piecemeal; that is, for development of conceptual plans, for development of contract bidding, for monitoring the actual construction, for inspections, and for development of final as-built plans. Additionally, building models, scaled drawings for brochures, and the development of other types of artistic promotion and publicity may be additional costs. All of these costs and what they represent must be discussed before any contractual agreement is made.

The role of the architect in the contract development process, the role during construction, and the final acceptance requirements. Most churches and organizations will want to have the architect be their representative before zoning and code enforcement boards and inspectors. During construction, the church will want the architect to be an inspector for them to ensure that the structure is built as designed. If changes or modifications are necessary during construction, the church or organization will need the architect to create that change and to ensure it is accomplished to harmonize with the remainder of the plan.

Interaction with work groups. During the design phase the project steering committee and the design subcommittee want to integrate numerous elements of the church in obtaining their input in the project. These work groups may be existing committees, councils, or ministry teams, or they may be informal groups that are called together to provide input. For example, in phase 2 of our master plan above, the new education wing is designed for preschool and children's programs. It would be wise to include the input from work groups that are made up of the councils of those programs, the parents, and any other leaders of programs that relate to these areas. The concept is that the design reflects the expertise of the people who must use the space. A food service ministry team aids in designing a kitchen; an activities council helps design the recreation building; a work group of the office personnel and staff helps in the design of the administration building. The objective is to integrate as many ideas as feasible in order to create ownership in the project by the membership.

3. **Construction.** Several years ago I was the leader of a group of volunteers who responded to a call to modify the children's classroom area to meet the needs of a modernized teaching concept. The project involved the removal of several walls that divided the space into teaching cubicles. You may have seen these areas; they came out of the forties and fifties where there was an opening assembly. Then the classes were sent to these small rooms around the perimeter of the central department room. The new concept for children's ministry

called for the movement between activity areas all in one general space. The small rooms were deemed wasted space and needed to be included in the total room configuration.

One Saturday, sledgehammer in hand, several of us began to knock down walls to open the space up. One of our group was a construction type. About mid-morning he announced that maybe we should stop because he noted that we had just knocked down a load-bearing wall and the roof was in jeopardy. Looking through the ceiling, we saw a steel beam dangling in thin air, unsupported by any vertical element. We called an engineer, and he was able to help us modify our demolition by jacking the beam back in place and placing a post underneath for support. Know what you are doing before construction (or demolition in this case) begins. The design phase helps us understand what we want to get done; the construction phase gets it done.

The construction phase of a project may be accomplished in a variety of ways:

A design-build project. This is where the architectural firm becomes the contractor to carry out the design. They design it, then they build it. This process has great advantages in that if changes need to be made, they can be accomplished readily and usually with lesser costs. Additionally, a design-build contract will require less expense, since construction plans do not have to be mass-produced for a bidding process. The design-build concept takes advantage of focused experts, who channel their experience and expertise into producing church or similar facilities. A final advantage of this scheme is that the project designer knows what the project budget is and can design to those limitations. The major disadvantage in this scheme is that design-build companies are regionally organized and may not be geographically available.

A general contractor bidding project. This is where the architect designs the facility, obtains necessary permits and approvals for the project, and then develops plans that various building contractors bid upon. This scheme is advantageous when there is a competitive market for construction work. The contractor who is awarded the job has the responsibility for acquiring the necessary skills and trades to complete the job. The cost for the project is dependent upon the bids received being within the estimations of the architect and the excellence in the design documents that limit the additional costs of changes that are made after the bid has been received.

The construction manager and/or building superintendent process involves the church or organization assuming the role of a general contractor. The church then hires a person who will schedule the work of the various subcontractors and trades. The advantage to this system is that the owner remains in control. The major disadvantage is the additional administration and costs involved in the execution of this format. The church or organization assumes all legal and fiscal responsibility for the project.

Volunteers. Numerous organizations have been developed over the years that address the need to assist small congregations in erecting initial structures. Many denominational groups have also been commissioned to do the same. The use of volunteers can save significant labor costs. The use of volunteers requires an extraordinary degree of supervision and coordination.

The construction phase of any project is the most exciting and yet the most demanding. It has high visibility. Up to this point the project has moved along in the presence of small groups in meetings and through visual drawings and sketches. Now the project is taking form. Foundations are being poured, steel is being erected, and the project is taking on the appearance of the designed structure. This is the time the stewardship subcommittee has longed for because when people start to see the project underway, giving dramatically increases.

During this construction phase the project subcommittee needs to be alert to several issues:

Contract cost negotiation. Will the project cost be based on a fixed agreed-upon figure, or will it be based on actual cost plus a percentage? Will the contractor assume responsibility for payment of subcontractors, or will that be the responsibility of the church or organization?

Providing a performance bond. Most lending agencies will limit the loan amount to only 80 percent of the anticipated costs unless other collateral is provided. Both the owner and the lending agency should require a bond to insure the contractor actually performs the project as per requirements of the design.

Insurance must be carried. The contractor should provide general liability, building risk, and liquidated damage insurance to protect the project from loss due to suit or tort action. If the contractor is not required to have this insurance, who will provide this protection? In addition to insurance, a hold-harmless clause should be part of the contractor's agreement to protect the church or organization from actions against the contractor.

Changes or modifications to the design. Through the years I have come to know some really gifted architects, individuals who were trustworthy and competent. In the same time, I have rarely seen a project completed as drawn. Invariably changes have to be made. The focus should be to make the changes few and far between because they are usually costly and dramatically change the schedule for completion. To prevent these cost overruns from taking hold of the project, a specific method should be established for creating changes, and a designated group should be identified and given the authority to approve such changes.

The establishment of project completion procedures. As the project begins to end, how are punch-list items that have not been accomplished identified and subsequently completed? What process will be in place to obtain releases for payment of services for every subcontractor and vendor on the project? Who represents the church or organization for final building occupancy inspections by code enforcement personnel? What will be the extent of the warranty and guarantee of the project and the equipment installed? Who will witness the proper operation of equipment and materials that were installed? When will the as-built drawings be penned and submitted? How will the staff or management personnel be trained in the use of the facility?

These are key areas that must be addressed before the contractor hops in his pickup and drives off.

4. Promotion and Publicity. This subcommittee is an important facet of the project because it is responsible for selling the project and creating owner-ship by the members of the church or organization. This group will probably work in concert with the financial subcommittee. The promotion and publicity subcommittee begins its work at the moment of project conception and con-tinues through to the final open house reception at completion. This subcom-mittee creates the project title, the information materials about the project, the logo and the letterhead. They create models, brochures, fliers, and posters to keep the membership informed. And they are often called upon to assist the stewardship subgroup with the publicity involved in obtaining finances. Thus, the people on this subcommittee need to be creative, resourceful, and talented communicators.

This facet of the project may be conducted in-house or may be contracted. If the church or organization chooses to use one of the many stewardship cam-paign organizations that advertise their ability to increase membership giving, they will note that the major emphasis of these groups is the effective commu-nication of the project and the integration of members and others alike in the ownership of the project. Whether to choose an agency to assist the church in the promotion of the project is in reality a decision the leadership makes based on their understanding of the attitude of the target group to have an "outside" organization involved in this facet of the project. Elements in making this deci-sion include whether the church or organization has capable personnel to con-duct the promotion campaign, the attitude of the membership toward a group outside the organization being involved, the scope of the project, and time constraints.

5. Finance or Stewardship. This subcommittee is responsible for accumu-lating the necessary financing to complete the project. Few churches or organ-izations have the qualified personnel in their membership who can conduct a professional stewardship campaign. However if, as in the case of David in the passage cited earlier, the church or organization realizes that any future project will require adequate funding and that funding process begins long before the need arises, then adequate funds will be available to start and/or complete the project. Thus, the stewardship subcommittee builds upon the plan for financing that was established before conceptualization of the project.

This subcommittee asks three important questions:

- How much money do we have on hand?
- How much money can we raise in a short-term stewardship campaign?
- How much money will our budget support in long-term debt retirement?

Money on hand consists of those funds that have been accumulating as the result of an ongoing building fund collection. It will also include property, investments, and special gifts and contributions from budget overruns and excesses. Stewardship campaigns usually can create between one and one-half to three times a church or organization's annual budget, depending on the professionalism involved in the campaign and the attitude toward the project by the membership. These short-term campaigns usually occur in the form of special giving pledges for a period—usually three years—the sale of bonds, both closed to the membership and open to the general public, and one-time special offering opportunities.

Whether the church or organization chooses to incur debt is a matter that must be decided early in the project plan. If debt is not an option, the total funding for the project must be accumulated before the projects ends. On the other hand, if the decision is made to incur debt to fund all or portions of the project, the subcommittee must take into consideration certain elements:

1. Debt retirement capability will determine the amount a church can borrow. It is a function of size of church budget, existing debt, and loan history. Usually lenders allow a church or organization to assign no more than 25 to 30 percent of their annual budget to debt retirement.

2. Funds needed for construction completion will require additional funds by the church or organization. Usually lending agencies will allow no more than 75 to 80 percent of the total cost of the

---

Suppose your church wants to build a 1 million dollar sanctuary. Your annual budget is $360,000. You have additional buildings that allow you to ask the bank to lend you the $1,000,000 for 15 years at 7% interest. The repayment of this loan will require a monthly payment of $8,989 or $107,868 per year—about 30% of the annual budget. Over the life of the loan, the church will pay the bank a total of $1,618,020. That is $618,020 in interest or about 62% of the loan value.

Suppose the same church has been collecting money for a future building project and through the years has accumulated $300,000. It is now time to consider the new 1 million dollar sanctuary. Rather than considering borrowing money for the payment of the loan, the church seeks a short-term construction loan and commences a stewardship campaign. Nearly $900,000 is pledged to the campaign, to be paid in a three year period. In that three year period the church collects 90% of the pledge—$810,000. Through the cycle of the construction phase, the interest on the short-term 1 million dollar loan cost $102,800. The church collected a total of $810,000 and paid $102,800 in interest, which leaves a balance on the 1 million dollar loan of $292,800. Now since the church has accumulated $300,000; that is applied to the project and the church walks away with no debt. Or the church may choose to extend the stewardship campaign another 6 months and pay off the $292,800 remainder and leave the $300,000 alone. Or the church may choose to refinance the $292,800 balance of the loan for 15 years at 7% and in the life of the loan pay only about $118,000 in interest.

project to be allocated in a loan. This may increase only if the borrower has additional collateral.

3. In computing the funding required, the subcommittee must realize there will exist significant "additional" costs to the project. These costs include such things as land acquisition and site preparation, fees and permits to use the land and construct the facility, architectural fees that may range from 3 to 8 percent of the building cost, furnishings which usually add between 8 to 10 percent of the cost of construction, providing parking at an average cost of $600 to $800 per space, and landscaping which could add 0.5 to 1 percent of the project costs.

The value of planning ahead for a future building project cannot be overemphasized. Here are two examples to demonstrate the difference.

See the significant flexibility that having the $300,000 in the bank provides to the church in the second example. Even if it chooses to refinance and have an ongoing debt, it will only be about $2,300 per month or about $27,400 per year, which is only about 7.6 percent of the annual budget. That additional 22.5 percent in your budget can fund a lot of ministry.

Projects that involve building or remodeling require significant planning. They need to involve not only the significant leadership of the organization but also numerous other people who bring to the project their expertise and input. Small churches and organizations may take the five areas of the steering committee's responsibility and consolidate subcommittee responsibility. For example, the stewardship subcommittee may also be responsible for promotion and publicity. A single subcommittee may be designated for both design and construction. The entire steering committee may take on the task of site selection and location of the facility on the site.

In like manner, larger churches may have many more subcommittees and work groups that provide information and work to the steering committee. For example, with a larger project such as an educational building, the steering committee may designate a subcommittee to develop the plan for furnishings. This subcommittee in turn will create several work groups that provide age-group input, media and library, playground, safety and security, and so forth. A general concept is that the larger the organization or project, the greater the number of individuals who get to be involved in the planning and execution process.

Chapter Review

This chapter has discussed three essential planning processes that every church or organization needs to consider: development of the mission statement; the development of long-range, short-range, and strategic plans to implement the mission statement; and the development of a scheme for planning for facility growth. The reader should be able to:

- Articulate a scriptural foundation for planning.
- Describe the process for the development of a church or organization's mission statement.
- Describe how the long-range plan implements the strategies of the mission statement.
- Discuss the interrelationships that exist between the long-range, short-range, or annual plan, and the strategic planning that programs and ministries develop in response to the more general plans.
- Discuss the steps in a building or remodeling project. Include in this discussion the central role of the steering committee and the formation of subcommittees and work groups that carry out the different facets of a project.

Administering
Program Ministries

<table>
<tr>
<td>

CHAPTER

11

</td>
<td>

Now as we have many parts in one body, and all the parts do not have the same function, in the same way we who are many are one body in Christ and individually members of one another.

</td>
</tr>
</table>

members of one another. According to the grace given to us we have different gifts: if prophecy, use it according to the standard of faith; if service, in service; if teaching, in teaching; if exhorting, in exhortation; giving, with generosity; leading, with diligence; showing mercy, with cheerfulness.
ROMANS 12: 4–8

In the vision of the new temple, the prophet Ezekiel described the various roles of the priesthood where they are "responsible for the duties of the temple—for all its work and everything done in it" (Ezek. 44:14); they are to "approach Me to serve Me" (v. 15); they are to "teach My people the difference between the holy and the common, and explain to them the difference between the clean and the unclean" (v. 23); and in a dispute, they are to "officiate as judges and decide the case according to My ordinances" (v. 24). They are to lead in worship and sacrifice, teach, counsel, and direct. During the exile period that began about 721 B.C. for the Northern Kingdom and in 586 B.C. for the Southern Kingdom, an interesting phenomenon developed with regard to the relationship of the Hebrew culture and the God they worshipped. They were in captivity, in a distant land, and without a place to conduct worship. In response, the culture developed what is known as the synagogue system.

While the synagogue did not replace the requirement for sacrifice at the altar of God, it did serve an important function during this period. The synagogue was a fellowship hall for the oppressed Jews. They met, sang, ate, and studied God's Word. During this time a group of people were set apart to write down the Torah, the law. And other individuals were designated as the teachers of the law, the *rabboni*. They observed the feasts and festivals. They learned the law, history, and poetry of the culture. Soon the synagogue became the school, not only for the adult but also for the child and the rabbi, the principal teacher of the Hebrew culture. The interpretation of the Torah that related to the care of the child, widow, and aged became functions of the local synagogue.

Do you remember the discussion in chapter 6 of the book of Acts about the feeding of the widows? Some in the church were taking care of their widows, the Hebrew element, as an outgrowth of the tradition of the synagogue. The Gentile widows were being neglected. The solution offered by the apostles was to feed them, but this was to be a church ministry conducted by a selected group from the church body. The apostle's role would be to study and teach Scripture. The role of these selected individuals would be to carry out the benevolence ministry of caring for the widows.

While not implicitly defined in the New Testament, program ministries were implied. In Romans and Corinthians Paul described how the various gifts of service provided by the Holy Spirit are knit together to form a functioning body, and that the body should function in an orderly fashion in the support and uplifting of the membership. In Acts, Timothy, and Titus we see a church organized about leadership positions and functional activities. The many facets of worship are described. James challenged the church to be demonstrative of the faith they expressed in Christ by doing something that would show their transformed lives.

Throughout this text we have attempted to validate church administrative activities with biblical principals. While we may have stretched a point or two here and there, we have discovered that God's Word was always adequate and appropriate to provide guidance in administering the church. Such is the same when we come to the area of program administration. In recent years authors such as Rick Warren, Gene Mims, and Morlee Maynard have expressed the program functions of the church in a variety of ways. Warren and Mims focus around worship, discipleship, fellowship, evangelism, and ministry. Maynard adds missions to this listing of church functions. In describing the administration activities that relate to the programs of the church, let us consider these six general areas as the basis for discussion.[1]

Administering Programs of Worship

We may define worship as the recognition by the believer of God—who he is and what he has done for us. Worship is expressed in the experiences and service the Christian engages in through praise, adoration, celebration, confession, and thanksgiving. Throughout the history of the Bible, believers have worshipped God at the altar, in the tabernacle, in the temple, and the synagogue. With the Christian church, worship occurred in the temple and synagogue but quickly transferred to homes and then later to houses of worship constructed especially for that purpose. In Acts 2:42 worship involved teaching of the leaders, fellowship, communion, and prayer. In Ephesians 5:19 and Colossians 3:16 worship included the singing of psalms and songs. In 1 Corinthians 16:2 worship included the bringing of tithes and offerings. Also in 1 Corinthians 10:16–17 the observance of the Lord's Supper was part of the worship experience. In 1 Timothy 4:13 worship included public reading of Scripture, preaching, and teaching. While many people continued to reverence the Sabbath as God's day, the early church seemed to come together on the first day of the week, Sunday, for these observances (see Acts 20:7; 1 Cor. 16:2).

A few years ago I was serving in a small rural Texas church. One cold winter morning we were to have a baptismal service for a family who had come into the fellowship. The water had set overnight in the baptistry and had not been circulated through a hot water heater as was customarily done. In fact, the hot water heater was not turned on until just before the service and had just barely warmed the baptistry enough to melt the layer of ice on the surface of the water.

As the pastor stepped into the water, even with waders on, the bitter cold shot through his legs like knives. He looked shockingly at me sitting on the first row just as the father of the family being baptized stepped into the water. The father didn't have waders on, but since he had never been baptized before, I assume he wanted to set the example for the rest of the family, and he just "sucked it up." After the father hastily left the water, the mother stepped in. She also had a look of shock but probably figured this was the initiation rite she must endure, so she didn't let out a yip. Their teenage daughter was next. I figure she was worried about the fact that the other youth had told her that the white robe went transparent when it got wet and she was worried whether the T-shirt she had on underneath would protect her dignity and modesty. So the cold was not the major issue with her, but she didn't stay long in the water either.

Then came the eight-year-old. He entered the water with no preconceived notions. When his foot hit the ice cold water, he let out a yell. "This water is cold," he cried. A little chuckle came from the audience as he slowly entered the water. Chattering all the way, he was baptized and quickly left the baptistry loudly asking for a warm towel. We all learned a lesson that day: make sure the water in the baptistry is warm unless you want to freeze the candidates and have the pastor chatter through the sermon that follows.

Numerous administrative organizations need to be established, trained, and funded to carry out the worship programs of the church. Rather than forming a group of committees to carry out these functions, enlist and utilize the members into ministry teams. Remember from chapter 4 that ministry teams are groups of individuals who come together voluntarily to express their spiritual gift in service. They are not polity organizations; they are service organizations. They are budget units since most will require some funding to carry out their work. Let us look at some of these organizations that may be required to aid in administering worship.

Decorations Ministry Team

This group ensures that the worship spaces are appropriately appointed; they may also be involved in the general appearance of the church fixtures and furniture. They place flowers in the sanctuary, hang wall decorations in the foyer, provide seating in the vestibules and halls, and in general create an ambiance of pleasant surroundings. When called upon, they suggest color schemes, lighting needs, floor textures, and general habitability to ensure the worship center and church facility represents the sacred space the church deems it to be. Individuals on this ministry team are those with the gift of helps. They are creative, artistic individuals whose decorating taste should represent the general church membership. Leadership should recognize that the work of this ministry team sets the physical environment within which the congregation worships.

Greeters Ministry Team

This group of volunteers is given many names. Parking lot greeters, door openers, umbrella holders, shuttle bus drivers—you name it, they do it. This ministry team is critical for your church because they are the first impression many who visit the church get about the church. The principal responsibility of greeters is to move people from the outside of the church to the worship space. Their function should be readily apparent to any who come to your church. Parking lot greeters should be given colored traffic control vests. Door openers should have a name tag to assist the persons in identifying them. Umbrella holders should have an umbrella big enough for several people underneath. In other words, the members of this team need the necessary equipment and tools to do their job. I once asked a person what he did in the church. His response was, rather meekishly, "I am just a parking lot greeter." My response was an affirming, "Great, you have one of the most important jobs in the church. You set the tone for the rest of the day in the life of worshippers!"

Welcome Center Ministry Team

The welcome center is information central for the church. The greeters get worshipper into the building; the welcome center ministry team helps them get to the worship center, Bible study, nursery, or what have you. The welcome center must be physically located in a central part of the facility so it is easily visible to anyone who enters the church or organization. In larger facilities, it may be necessary to operate more than one welcome center. All programs and ministries should direct the dispensation of information to the church or organization through the welcome center. Information and publication racks, bulletin boards, directories and maps, notions and memorabilia gifts, as well as being a repository of equipment or aids for assisting the worshipper such as wheel chairs and listening devices should be provided. Neatness, orderliness, and taste should be evident. The ministry team members should be well versed and trained in every facet of the church or organization—or know where to quickly find the answer.

In chapter 9 we suggested that the welcome center serve as the meeting place for an emergency reaction team. Emergency equipment, supplies, and communication equipment would be placed there. While the welcome center is usually assigned to one staff member as liaison, in reality all program leaders provide the necessary input to make a welcome center an information center for the church or organization. In fact, it should be the standard policy of the church to use the welcome center as the information focal point of the church. That way members and visitors alike will receive the latest information about the activities and events of the church or organization.

Usher Ministry Team

We have already addressed in chapter 9 the critical importance the usher ministry team plays in providing safety and security to worshippers. Those activities are secondary, however, to the primary assignment of assisting the people in the act of worship. Ushers offer assistance in seating, provide an order of service of worship, receive the tithes and offerings, and other activities that make the worship experience focus on the God of worship. Like the other three ministry teams discussed so far, the usher ministry team is a primary influence in giving a good first impression of your church or organization. Training should assist the men and women who are ushers to be courteous, friendly, open, and outgoing. In addition to training, they should be identified. The use of a name tag is always useful. Some churches or organizations provide a small flower for the lapel. Regardless of the form of recognition, the worshipper should be able to quickly identify someone who can assist them in the act of worship. Ushers should express a sense of worship in their decorum and manner, speaking quietly and reverently. They should be quick to provide whatever aids are necessary to assist people in worship.

Ordinance Ministry Team

Depending on the beliefs of your particular church or organization, ministry teams should be developed to assist the leaders in carrying out the functions of the ordinances of the church. For instance, in our example at the beginning of this section, there may be a baptism ministry team that ensures the water is warm, to provide appropriate and clean robes, to provide towels and a private space to dress, and to be there to assist the individual through the rite. The same or another ministry team may be responsible for the preparation of the Lord's Supper. In smaller churches a single group may be responsible for these actions. In the larger church the formation of two or more teams may be appropriate. Adequate storage space and equipment must be provided. Usually the senior pastor will supervise these ministry teams.

Music Ministry Team

No other program in the church, other than the preaching, is associated with worship as closely as the music program. Many churches designate the music minister as the worship minister. In larger churches this individual works closely with the senior pastor in the development of the scheduled worship services. In larger congregations also this individual or group of individuals are paid employees of the church. These individuals—the worship leader, choir director, pianist, organist, or other instrumentalists—conduct the professional ministry function of worship. In the smaller church or organization, however, this function is often the responsibility of a volunteer song leader, pianist, or other such contributor. In this venue of the smaller church, a worship ministry team will provide the necessary administrative assistance to the senior pastor or teaching pastor to ensure the regularly scheduled and special event worship services have an appropriate mix of music, praise, and song. Adequate space cannot be devoted in this text to describe an appropriate music or worship ministry. However, it is appropriate to mention some administrative issues that must be considered in such a ministry.

Selection of Leadership Is Critical. The individual should be a competent musician. I used to sing in a choral group in college, played in the band in high school, and enjoyed and understood music. We were in a small church in the backwoods of Washington state, and our volunteer song leader moved on. The teaching pastor asked me if I would lead the singing. Sure, as long as I had a pianist who could transpose the songs into my key—bass—I could stand up there and wave my arms to the correct rhythm. I know that the very thought of me leading music with that mind-set kills a real music leader, but in some respects it is a truth. You don't have to have a professional voice to lead worship. It helps if you understand music and are familiar with the songs. What is needed is an adequate musician who has the desire to express the joy of worship through the music of the church. In a larger church that competency will have to be magnified, but the philosophy is the same. Choose a leader who has the ability to get the job done. The best musician may not be the best leader. Choose leadership based on calling, motivation, and ability to organize the ministry. Choose leadership based on their appropriate understanding of worship.

Choose appropriate music for worship. Currently churches and organizations are going through the trauma of having to deal with the "style" of worship they will have in the service. *Contemporary, traditional, praise,* and *blended* are terms that are being used to describe a worship style. The wise worship leader will match the style of worship with the desires and needs of the people they are attempting to lead in worship. Recognizing the differences in styles and the desires of the worshippers is essential. Music is expensive. A worship/music leader cannot afford to purchase copies of every type of music in hopes of finding something the membership will like. While the traditional hymnal may suffice for most worship situations, focus budget spending on building upon unique elements that enhance the worship experience while at the same time pleasing the desires of worship style of the worshippers. Not every church needs a pipe organ, but every church needs some form of instrument that provides the foundational melody for the worship song to be sung.

Organize for variety. Several years ago in a church I was serving in Oklahoma, the youth minister formed a youth singing group—four girls and four boys. My son was one of the guys. The music minister (worship leader) began to use the youth ensemble, first in the evening worship services and then later in the Sunday morning service. The group was good. Three of the girls went off to college at the same college in Arkansas. For a freshman talent night the three from Oklahoma and the roommate of one of the young ladies formed a quartet and sang a couple of songs. They were great! Soon they began singing in churches around the area as well as at chapel at school. Today that group is known as Point of Grace. These four young women have a tremendous ministry of song and development for women.

A good worship program takes advantage of the uniqueness of individuals, provides an opportunity for growth, and encourages a spirit of involvement among the members. Worship ministry team leadership should seek to express worship in a variety of formats—music, instruments, drama, media.

Budgets are essential. An appropriate worship ministry through music is not an inexpensive issue. Depending on the size of the program, elements of the ministry can be very expensive. Adequate and appropriate budgeting is essential. Obviously this will require the program to designate a budget unit manager. In larger churches this will be the music or worship minister. In the smaller situation with volunteer leadership, that person must be designated in the church organizational structure so that appropriate authority may be granted to expend funds from the church's or organization's budget allocation.

Administering Programs of Discipleship

Discipleship is a lifelong activity of transformation that begins when a person becomes a Christian and progresses as spiritual maturity is achieved through Bible study and Christian service and experience. Discipleship is personal Bible study and a group Sunday school class. It occurs in a one-on-one setting and in an auditorium of hundreds. Discipleship is the church's response to the third element of the Great Commission of Matthew 28:20 that calls for the "teaching them to observe everything I have commanded you" admonition of Christ. The very context of the name of the early follower, "disciple," translates a learning motif.

In 2 Peter 3:18 the apostle admonished the Christian to grow in grace and knowledge. Paul in Ephesians 4:11 pointed out that leaders were assigned by the Holy Spirit as teachers so the church could be built up, become mature, and attain the fullness of the knowledge of Christ. So while the individual Christian is responsible to mature in the knowledge and understanding of the teachings of Christ (2 Tim. 2:15), the church and other Christians are assigned the responsibility for effecting that growth through teaching, exhortation, encouragement, discipline, and prayer (Col. 3:15; Heb. 10:24; 1 Thess. 5:11; James 5:16).

Second only to the worship experience of the church, Bible study is the most important and most widely recognized program element of the church. As noted in the Scriptures cited, the early church took seriously the admonition to teach. The early believers came out of the learning motif of the temple and synagogue where the study of Scripture was an essential element of the religious experience. The early church studied the ancient scrolls where the writers of the Old Testament spoke of the God of creation and sustenance and the promise of the Messiah. Later they would read the letters of the apostles and church leaders. From the very beginning of the church, a training program for new believers was instituted. By the third century that training had formalized into bishop's schools for training leadership.

The monastic education of the Dark Ages continued the determination that not only was the church the repository of truth; it was the only place in which one could become learned. Schools were formed in each of the cathedrals of the church to train scholars who merged the knowledge of the world order with that which the Scripture (and church) authorized. Universities (guilds of scholars) were formed to study the religion of the age. A unique branch of the university that was formed about the time of the reformation was the theological seminary.

For nearly fourteen hundred years, religious study had been relegated to the church scholar. That changed dramatically with Martin Luther, John Calvin, and many others who protested the Roman Catholic Church's interpretation of Scripture. Out of that era came the notion that it was the Christian individual's responsibility to study Scripture and that the Bible alone contained the authoritative Word of God. Soon Bibles were available in the language of the common man, and individuals sought to study both individually and in groups. Today the Bible study program is the largest program entity in the vast majority of evangelical, Protestant churches.

Because the Bible study program is the largest, it has the largest organizational structure of any of the programs of the church. Consider, for example, the Sunday school program of a typical church. There will be a program director and usually an associate. There will be recording secretaries and financial officers. Each age group will have a divisional director, and those directors will organize their area of responsibility about departments that address the unique age-difference needs of the participants. In larger organizations these departments will be further divided into classes with teachers and other workers. Probably the best scriptural analogy is the Jethro principle of Exodus 18. Given in Sunday school terminology, it might be:

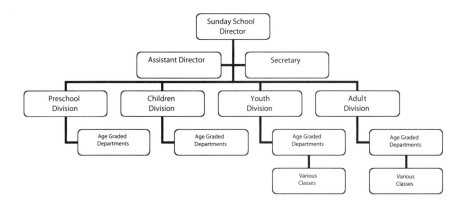

If the church has a professional education minister, that person will be the supervisor of the Sunday school director. In other churches supervision may be by an education council. Of course, this is just one of many different types of discipleship programming that might be going on in the church or organization. There may be weekday Bible studies, a new Christian training program, a leadership training program, and so forth. Possibly the church or organization operates an educational system such as a Christian academy or day school. Many churches and organizations operate weekday early education programs as part of the educational ministry. Thus, educational administration can call for many responses.

Some important administrative principles should be observed in the development of a discipleship program in the church or organization:

Develop an Organizational Chart That Describes the Structure of the Program

In chapter 4 we introduced the concept that an organization chart should be developed that interpreted the program and ministry entities that responded to the church or organization's mission statement. In that organization chart, leadership positions were defined for every program or ministry whether they existed then or not. In other words, the chart reflected the potential leadership requirements. The same type of chart should be developed for the discipleship program of the church. In the organizational chart we developed in chapter 4, the ministry functional area of education was identified with a minister of education as the professional leader. Within that ministry function were various programs: Sunday school, discipleship training, mission education, and so forth. Now it is necessary to refine the organizational chart for each of these program areas. We have already given a schematic chart for a Sunday school program above. What leadership must do now is flesh it out. How many preschool departments? And how will they be divided?

Through the years various educational publications have established certain rules of thumb that describe the size of room, the number of individuals that make up a department or class, and the pupils-to-teacher ratios. Below is a simple, easily remembered mnemonic that gives a rough rule of thumb for dividing a Bible study program that relies on an age division scheme.

Division	Max. Dept. Size	Max. Class Size	Number Workers Needed
Preschool	1 Dept/15	No Classes	1 Worker for Every 4
Children	1 Dept/30	No Classes	1 Worker for Every 6
Youth	1 Dept/60	1 Class/12	1 Worker for Every 8
Adults	1 Dept/120	1 Class/24	1 Worker for Every 5*

This assumes some workers are department and division workers such as secretaries, outreach, fellowship, etc.

For organizational structures that do not use an age-grade scheme, numbers of individuals participating will be dependent upon a variety of factors: size of the space, the type of material being presented, the degree of interaction between participant and leader and participant to participant. In most learning environments, the rule of thumb is that smaller is better. The small, intimate group allows for more interaction and personal attention. So, for example, in a new Christian discipleship group, the group should be limited to just a few people to ensure that personal interaction occurs. Therefore, the large church organizational chart may require more organizational units of new Christian training than a smaller church—or a dead church with no evangelism. The bottom line is that the form of the organization should follow the functional areas that have been designed to meet the mission of the church with regard to discipleship.

Ensure Leadership Is Adequately Trained

When we discussed the process of administration in chapter 2, we noted that several administrative activities were devoted to the selection and delegation of personnel to accomplish the job. The functional area of leading involved activities that called for the administrator to develop the worker.

Several years ago my wife and I were members of a Sunday school class that we really loved in the Charleston, South Carolina, area. The teacher was great. One Sunday she introduced an individual and said that he would be teaching as an intern in the class for the next month in preparation for his taking the class over the following month. She announced that next year was her sabbatical year and she would be leaving the class to prepare to work with the youth. I was concerned because we were losing a really good teacher, but I was also interested in this sabbatical and training program. I soon discovered that the church had an extensive leader preparation program. In fact it was so large that you had to be on a waiting list if you were not already one of the trained workers.

I discovered also that the training program came about when a member, who had been on the faculty of Furman University, heard the passionate pleas from the pulpit for workers in the children's area—almost every Sunday. Cooperating with the pastor, he instituted a teacher preparation class that included how to study the Bible, a study of the doctrines of the church, teaching methodology, and educational psychology. The training classes took off, and within a short period of time, trained leaders were available.

What the old professor recognized was that people are reluctant to attempt a teaching or leadership task if they feel they have not been adequately prepared for it. So by preparing them, they volunteered. By the time my wife and I left the church, the program had been expanded so that all leadership positions in the church would be filled only by graduates of that training program. The program lasted a year: six months of Bible, doctrine, teaching methodology, evangelism, and ministry studies and six months of internship and practice in a setting they were preparing for. The individual could only serve three years in that position before he had to take a sabbatical or leave the leadership totally. If the individual desired to return to the same leadership position area, he had to take a refresher course consisting of four months instruction in doctrine, methodology, and Bible study. During these four months they were given new skills and enhancements to do the job better.

If persons wanted to change leadership responsibilities, they had to complete an additional six-month internship in the area of the new service. The bottom line of operating a training program such as this in the church was that they had more leaders than they could use. In fact, the church had started a couple of mission churches with the overflow of leaders.

What program ministers must realize is that effectively trained people will want to work. If you recruit an individual for a discipleship ministry position, you should be able to guarantee to the person the training necessary to be effective and successful.

Provide the Necessary Resources for a Discipleship Program

For many years I have taught in the educational school at a seminary. Under their breath people used to refer to us as the "scissors and crayons" school. While it is true that we did some cutting and pasting, significantly more was going on. The days of flannel graphs and picture boards are fast disappearing. People in our discipleship programs, especially the children and youth, expect to see state-of-the-art training presentations. Video, computer generations and interactions, and Web-based systems are expected. Even most adults are sensitized to a sophisticated learning system that takes technology into the classroom and learning environment. Discipleship administrators must determine training resource needs and make budget provisions for them.

Develop Training Venues Outside the Walls

One of the greatest administrative issues churches and organizations are facing today is the provision of space to carry out their discipleship ministry. Growing churches are having to move to a concept of multiple use of space— two and three Bible study and worship programs each Sunday morning. Nonprofit organizations are finding that facilities are costly to acquire and use. The cost of providing spaces for the activities of the church or organization has exceeded its ability to budget. Therefore, innovative and new ways to package discipleship and training programs must be developed. The use of homes, office and school space, as well as the use of the Web and other electronic formats are becoming useful and necessary alternatives. Discipleship program administrators must budget for, acquire and train in the use of teaching technology that enhances the discipleship programs of the church or organization.

Administering Programs of Evangelism

Evangelism is the lifeblood of any organization. For the church, it is communication by believers of the good news of the gospel of Christ to a lost world and inviting people to become a part of the church fellowship. For the nonprofit religious organization it is the promulgation of the ministry focus and the invitation to become part of the group of people who have partnered to minister to that need.

While on earth, Christ called people to be partners in his mission. From the calling of the apostles along the seashore in Matthew 4:18–22 and Mark 1:16–20 to the calling of a tax collector in Luke 5:27–28 and the call of a persecutor of the early followers in Acts 9:15, Jesus' invitation was to become a disciple first, then an evangelist of the gospel. Jesus instructed his followers to proclaim the gospel: "Go, therefore, and make disciples of all nations" (Matt. 28:19). He called them to be witnesses "to the ends of the earth" (Acts 1:8). From the moment God empowered the church through the Holy Spirit (Acts 2:4–5) and throughout the remainder of the record of the Acts of the Apostles, Scripture records a church whose evangelistic spirit could not be quenched even in the face of persecution and death.

Evangelism is both individual in nature and corporate in formation. Each believer is called upon for a personal witness; and yet it is often through the programs of the church that this witness is expressed. Churches and organizations are classified as evangelical because they reach out to individuals outside their circle. Sermons are preached, lessons are taught, and ministry and outreach programs are carried out with the focus of delivering the message of Christ to an unbeliever with the objective of that person's acceptance of Christ as Savior.

Evangelism programs in the church or organization take on many forms and formats. Certain key administrative elements ensure that the program will be successful.

Know Your Constituency

In the first quarter of the twentieth century, denominational Sunday school administrator Arthur Flake postulated a five-step formula for growing the church through the Sunday school. The Flake Formula of (1) know your potential, (2) create an organization to grow, (3) recruit and train workers, (4) provide the space for growth, and (5) go after the people was and is the foundation of church growth plans for the past century.[2] Notice it begins with knowing the potential for growth and ends with an outreach visitation program. Flake says that evangelism (growth) occurs when you know where to evangelize. In recent years individuals have created focused target evangelism. From Bill Hybels and the seeker service orientation to the college campus focus of Bill Bright and Campus Crusade for Christ and the prison ministry of Chuck Colson and others, evangelistic efforts have concentrated on a group that needs to be receptive to the gospel of Christ. With the advent of computer collection of demographic and census data, numerous sources are available to the outreach evangelism administrator to assist in locating target groups. Denominational resources assist in categorizing prospects for outreach. And programs such as Andy Anderson's *Action Plan* and Bobby Welch's FAITH program help churches and organizations to identify potential evangelistic prospects.[3]

Go after the Prospects

Flake's Formula is bounded by two principles. The first we have already talked about—know the potential for evangelism. The second principle states that having developed a list of potential prospects, created an organization, staff, and space for them to gather, the growth circle is not complete until the church actually goes after the identified prospects. In the latter part of the last century, church developers were beginning to make an interesting point with regard to membership in the church—it was declining. Until that era the attitude of most churches was, "Here we are—Biggie Church located on First and Main. If you want to worship with us come on down." Students of the church growth phenomena began to state that this attitude must change if the church or organization is to survive. People aren't coming on down. We have to go out and get them and bring them in. Probably the flagship of this philosophy was the bus ministries that many churches and other nonprofits adopted to gather the people and bring them to their facility.

Outreach evangelism administrators must develop a program of visitation to go to prospects. Resources abound to aid in listing, assigning, and reporting on prospect and evangelism visitation. Numerous programs also exist for formalized evangelism training and conduct—from the *Evangelism Explosion* of Kennedy to the tract ministry of the *Four Spiritual Laws* of Campus Crusade.[4] There are four basic keys to a program of visitation.

1. It must be scheduled. To hand a person a prospect card and say, "If you have time this week, call on this person" will not work most of the time. The most successful outreach evangelism programs have a scheduled day and time for the visitation to occur.

2. It must involve training. Probably one of the most frightful experiences to a person who has never shared his faith is to do it the first time. To make the process easier and even commonplace, the administrator should provide training. Numerous programs and projects are available to choose from to assist in training for evangelistic visitation.

3. It must be facilitated. The administrator must provide the necessary resources to accomplish visitation. Maps, cards, and brochures must be provided.

4. There must be follow-up and accountability. Whether in a post visitation time, or the report on a card, the evangelistic visitation should be reported and evaluated.

Administering Programs of Ministry

Ministry is meeting needs. Ministry is an individual, church, or religious nonprofit carrying out specific actions that meet the needs of individuals or groups in the name of Jesus Christ. While some people are called on to be leaders, the purpose of leadership is clearly defined in Ephesians 4:12: "For the training of the saints in the work of ministry." Christians are called to be ministers—meeters of needs.

While the Old Testament called on the followers of the Torah to be benevolent to one another—meaning within the Hebrew culture—Jesus gave ministry a new definition with his call to meet the needs of all persons, Hebrew and Gentile alike. When Luke recorded in Acts 10:38 that Jesus "went about doing good," he did not relegate Jesus to healing only his followers. Luke was probably recalling the parable that was given to him during his research of Jesus' ministry describing the response Christ had made about being a good neighbor. In Luke 10:25–37 is the story of the good Samaritan who showed mercy and benevolent action to a total stranger.

No other writer in the New Testament was more interested in the healing and caring acts of Jesus than Luke, who was a physician. He recorded numerous instances where Jesus healed the blind, caused the deaf to hear, the lame to walk, and the demon-possessed to be mentally clear. Not all who were healed were identified by Luke as new followers of Christ. But it was the writer to the Jewish Christians—Matthew—who emphasized this attitude of ministry as he recorded the teachings of Jesus on his final week of earthly ministry. Speaking to his followers, Jesus gave the example that he was ministered to when food was provided him when he was hungry, a cup of cold water offered when he was thirsty, and clothing provided when he was cold. He said that when sick they cared for him and visited him when he was imprisoned. When queried by the followers about when they did this for him, Jesus responded, "I assure you: Whatever you did for one of the least of these brothers of Mine, you did for Me" (Matt. 25:40).

Throughout the history of the church, the call for benevolence in this passage from Matthew has been the basis for many acts of ministry, both within the structure of the church and the development of parachurch or nonprofit organizations that address these elements. Food kitchens and distributions are common ways of meeting hunger and thirst. Homeless shelters, orphanages, and homes for the widow and homeless are responses to taking the stranger in. Clothing distribution centers and work programs respond to clothing the needy. Hospitals, clinics, nursing homes, hospice care centers, and chaplaincy programs respond to the need to care for the ill. Prison and jail ministries abound in loving outreach to those whose lives have been captured by sin.

It is obvious from the examples given above that administration plays a key role in the development and management of such programs of ministry. Complete texts have been written that relate to hospital, nursing home, orphanage, and other institutionalized management. This text has focused on the church administrative processes, so let's continue that avenue of discussion and consider some administrative principles that need be considered when developing ministry actions.

Use Identified Leadership

In the local church four specific categories of individuals are identified either scripturally or through congregate recognition to carry out the role of focused ministry in the church.

The Paid, Professional Staff. Several years ago as our church was growing, the ability of the senior pastor to visit every person in the hospital from our membership consumed a lot of his time. So he devised a plan by which the other professional staff would take turns visiting the hospitals each day. As we would note the condition of the person visited, we were to report to the pas.tor, "Pastor, you better go visit him; he is in serious condition" or, "Fred is only in to have a wart removed. You could give him a call and wish him well." In other words we helped him focus his visits. For the most part this scheme worked. However, we soon found out that many people in the membership did not feel they had been visited by the "church" until the pastor showed up. After a while the church began to accept the fact that the "staff" represented the professional ministers, and in many cases having a different staff member show up each day was somewhat refreshing. Professional staff are, or should be, trained to carry out acts of ministry, benevolence, and care. Their role is to "equip the saints for works of ministry" so they must know how to do ministry before they can equip others.

The Deacons. By definition a deacon is a servant. In chapter 4 we visited the passage in Acts 6 about the seven who were chosen to serve. While often cited as the formation of the concept of deacon, this passage addresses the issue of servant ministry. Sheffield and Henry state that the deacon ministry of the church is a scripturally mandated office of ministry[5] (see Phil. 1:1; 1 Tim. 3:8). While the qualifications of the deacon generally mirror that given by Paul to bishops, overseers, and elders in 1 Timothy, the order and the use of the word *diakonos*—which is generally translated in the Greek as "servant," "server of tables," or "minister"—indicate that the role of the deacon is subservient to the others. That seems to be the case because early church history ascribes to the deacon the role of assistant to the leaders of the church.

So deacons are ministry servants. They carry out functions that assist and support the leadership of the church. While many church deacon groups function in similar roles as the overseers of the church, making rules, policy, and becoming the final decision-making body of the church, many other churches have properly interpreted the role of the deacon. They have active deacon ministries to the church and community that extend Christian care and concern.

A Chaplaincy Ministry. The definition of chaplain does not exist in Scripture but is found in the contemporary context of a minister who serves in a chapel, organization or assembly, or the military. In modern times we are most familiar with the military, fire or police, and hospital chaplains. Chaplains are usually associated with ministering to individuals in times of stress, trauma, or hurt. But chaplains abound in many situations—and not all are professionally trained ministers.

I mentioned earlier the need for the entire staff to carry out hospital visitation in our church. Within a few months of that process being instituted, we discovered a retired minister who had served in the military as a chaplain. He volunteered to begin a hospital chaplaincy program for the church. Since there were several hospitals in the metroplex area, his was a welcome relief. He recruited volunteers who would go to hospitals, nursing homes, rehabilitation centers, and hospice care centers to minister not only to those of the membership there, but to anyone who would be open to their ministry. Within a few short years the church had volunteer and paid hospital, jail, and nursing home chaplains integrated into the pastoral functions of the church (see the organizational chart in chapter 4).

Ministry Teams. Every church should have a benevolence ministry team, if for no other reason than to give opportunity for service to those individuals in the membership who have been gifted with the spiritual gift of helps, compassion, and ministry to those in need. Every group has these altruistic individuals who are spiritually compelled to meet other's needs. As mentioned in chapter 4, these groups need to be provided with the resources to carry out their ministry and the leadership to ensure they conform to the mission and objectives of the church. The ministry team could be a single organization that meets the multiplicity of needs of the community; or it may be divided into several groups.

For example, a team could operate a food and clothing closet, while another team would focus on meeting housing or emergency needs. Regardless of the format of the organization, each ministry team should be established with a specific charter that delineates the scope of the ministry and the assigned leadership and reporting responsibility.

Ensure Compliance with Local, State, and Federal Regulations

Ministry actions that are directed outside the membership of the church or organization are generally directed by specific laws relating to safety, security, and privacy. For example, a food kitchen may be regulated by local and state food service laws. A counseling ministry may require compliance with state licensure. The development of a federally funded day-care or after-school program will involve certain federal as well as state and local regulations. As a general rule of thumb, as long as the ministry action is carried out with and to the members of the organization, these external rules do not apply. But if the ministry activity extends beyond the membership, the regulations will need to be researched for compliance and met. It is imperative that some element of the church or organization leadership be assigned as a liaison staff officer to any ministry action, whether or not it involves action beyond the walls of the organization.

One area of compliance the church or organization must be particularly sensitive to is the regulations imposed by the IRS, the Immigration and Naturalization Service (INS), and other governing groups with regard to the aid and benefit to individuals. Numerous churches along the southern perimeter of the U.S. got in trouble with INS by employing illegal aliens. In an act of benevolence, the churches and organizations hired these individuals without certifying their employment as stipulated by law (review chapter 5). Not only did the church or organization lose an employee; many paid a hefty fine for their noncompliance.

In like manner, organizations and churches have received the ire of the IRS by inappropriately allowing funds to be used for the benefit of an individual. This scenario happens frequently. A member comes in and says that he is aware that another member is having a hard time, has lost his job and has medical bills. The individual wants to give the church a bunch of money to give to this person. So far, so good. It's great that the individual's Christian ethic prompts him to want to aid a fellowman. And the church administrator can certainly transmit the funds to the individual or family. But then comes the cruncher. The altruistic giver says, "Put this on my giving record." The legal and appropriate answer is, "I am sorry, federal law prevents me from doing this. I can give the money to the person, but I cannot give you credit for giving to the church." In other words, you cannot launder the money. The church or organization can get into serious trouble with the IRS for such action.

So how do individuals receive benefit from funds that have been collected by churches and nonprofits? By having an organization in place that manages the funds fairly. The two key words here are *manages* and *fairly*. There needs to be an authorized organizational entity chartered to accomplish benevolence activities for the membership. That is where the benevolence ministry team or some other formal organization and its instituting charter come in. The membership tells the group, "You create policy and procedure, you screen, you decide, and you carry out benevolence activities for us; we will provide the funds." Second, fairness. All members and others outside the membership, if the ministry is so targeted, must have fair access to the funds. There must be in place a procedure by which the ministry team evaluates need and establishes level of grant.

How does the church or organization effect this? One important activity would be to establish a line item for benevolence and actually fund it—make the activity part of the church-approved budget. If during the year funds fall short in this area, nothing prevents the church from going to the members and saying; "This Sunday we will take a special offering to meet some special needs that have taxed our benevolence fund, and we need to replenish the fund." You don't say, "The Welch family has fallen on hard times, and we need to take a special collection to help them." And what if someone comes in with a zillion dollars to give the Welch family? Tell them that you can accept the funds only with the understanding that the money will be credited to the benevolence account and that a determination for expenditure must be made only by the ministry team. If the giver influences the gift recipient, it cannot be credited. The key is openness, fairness, and compliance.

Require Accountability

Whether the action is directed within the organization or outside to a broader community, the individuals and groups that carry out ministry actions represent the total of the church or organization. They are elected or appointed by the church. They are chartered by the church or organization. They request and expend funds that are provided by the membership or congregation. They must report their activities to their authorizing agents. For example, each year your church has a ministry fair. On this Sunday evening each of the ministry groups of the church sets up a booth with pictures, charts, materials, and even examples of their ministry action the previous year. This is a wonderful way to report to the church what has happened. It is also a great opportunity to recruit new members to the ministry teams and organizations.

Administering Programs of Fellowship

The simplest definition of fellowship in the Christian context is spiritual bonding. It is those actions and activities that nurture and express care, concern, and love for one another. The early church was called a fellowship, a *koinonia*. It was the product of love that Christ calls us to in his "new" commandment: "Love one another as I have loved you" (John 15:12, 17). It is a self-sacrificing agape love that caused the early church to share their possessions (Acts 2:44; 4:32), bear one another's burdens (Gal. 6:2), be kind and compassionate (Eph. 4:32), carry out good deeds (Heb. 10:24), and pray for one another (James 5:16). The metaphors of the church as a body knit together or a building expertly fit together accurately describes the church of the first century. They were Christlike in their love for one another and for their fellowman. Their uniqueness caused others outside the fellowship to desire to be part of this spiritually bonded fellowship.

Fellowship in the local church or nonprofit organization is often thought of in the context of a group gathering, a party, or some other event that draws the membership together. While picnics, class parties, and other social occasions are an important part of fellowship, program administrators must be quick to recognize that the full expression of fellowship goes beyond these activities. Fellowship occurs in a Sunday evening service where members share a word of testimony or a passage of Scripture. It occurs in a Wednesday night prayer service where concerns and needs are lifted to the Father. It also occurs on a Saturday morning men's Bible study time, or on a Thursday evening singles recreation and Bible study gathering. The gathering of a committee in a member's home is a time of fellowship since hospitality is a true expression of Christian love. And believe it or not, a church business meeting can be a time of fellowship where members come together to resolve issues and celebrate the work of the church or organization.

Leadership should pay attention to certain administrative activities that will ensure the fellowship activity achieves its desired goal.

Provide Adequate and Appropriate Leadership

While some fellowship activities are spontaneous events, most are directive and planned. This demands leadership. A student came to me with an interesting dilemma. He was the pastor of a moderate-sized church. In this church a group of individuals had formed what was initially termed a home Bible study group, but the group's focus and activities had changed dramatically. One of this pastor's parishioners came to him to report that the leader, one of the church's deacons, was beginning to teach something that this person didn't believe and couldn't be supported in the Bible. In addition, most of their meeting time was spent putting down the leaders of the church and its activities. In my advice to the student, I suggested that he or the minister of education should have been aware of what was going on, but now he had to confront the issue. To make a long and hurtful story short: he did confront the group, they didn't like it, they argued, and eventually the group left and formed their own church, taking with them about 20 percent of the membership.

Calendar and Schedule Fellowship Events

Don't have activities in competition with one another. One winter one of my sons had to make a decision between attending a Valentine sweetheart banquet or a church league sports banquet—both scheduled the same night, one at the church and one at the local sports arena. I felt sorry for him because he had an interest in both and had worked hard in both situations. My fatherly advice was not to make the decision—let his girlfriend choose which she wanted to attend. (Aren't I a wise father, ladies?) The value of a church calendar, weekly staff and church leadership meetings, and a communication process are clearly evident. The conflicted schedule sent a message about an unorganized church and a disregard for the participant in the two programs.

Avoid Disruption, Confusion, and Conflict

The purpose of fellowship is the bringing together of people in love. A fine line exists between healthy discussion and disagreement and disruption in the meetings and activities of the church or organization. Both the individual who perpetrates dissention and the leader who allows dissention need to review how God in Scripture speaks to this issue. For example, in listing things God hates, the writer of Proverbs states that God hates anyone who sows discord among brethren (Prov. 6:19). It is interesting how the writer of Proverbs describes the one who causes dissention: hatred stirs up dissention (10:12); a hot-tempered man stirs up dissention (15:18); a perverse man stirs up dissention (16:28); a greedy man stirs up dissention (28:25); and an angry man stirs up dissention (29:22).

Paul chided the leaders of the Corinthian church for their lack of order and stated that "God is not a God of disorder but of peace" (1 Cor. 14:33). He also stated that "everything must be done decently and in order" (1 Cor. 14:40). Paul also said to "reject a divisive person after a first and second warning, knowing that such a person is perverted and sins, being self-condemned" (Titus 3:10–11). And James states that "where envy and selfish ambition exist, there is disorder and every kind of evil" (James 3:16).

Churches should adopt rules of business and function. Leaders should be quick to identify and challenge evil disorder. Allow Bible study groups to form, but have guidelines for their operation, leadership, and meeting. Conduct business sessions with an agenda and in conformance with a standard format such as Robert's Rules of Order. The wise pastor will allow another individual, usually the moderator, to conduct business sessions to demonstrate impartiality and fairness. This moderator will lead the sessions in an orderly, legal format.

Facilitate Fellowship

In the next chapter we will discuss support activities such as a recreation program, a food service program, and other similar support activities that, in many respects, foster the concept of fellowship in the church or organization. Each of these activities will require space, leadership, and funding. Facilitating fellowship activities can be as simple as a coffeepot and cups and as complex as a sit-down banquet. Program administrators need to make plans for such events, place those events in a church program calendar, and provide the resources to carry out those plans. Budgets, buildings, and beans are necessary elements of a successful fellowship program.

Administering Programs of Missions

The Great Commission of Christ in Matthew 28:19–20 was to "go . . . and make disciples." In actuality the Greek could better be understood as "as you are going." In another post-resurrection admonition, Jesus appointed us his witnesses in Jerusalem, Judea, Samaria, and the uttermost reaches of the world; in other words our city, our state, our neighboring states, and the entire world (Acts 1:8). God identified to Isaiah that his message of hope was for both Jew and Gentile (Isa. 49:6; 52:10). He sent Jonah to a neighboring country (Jon. 1:1–2; 3:1–2). Jesus sent his disciples into the local area (Matt. 9:35) and had the Father send the Holy Spirit on the day of Pentecost to allow foreign languages to be spoken to spread the good news of the gospel throughout the world (Acts 2:1–12). Philip went to Samaria and later encountered and discipled an Ethiopian leader in the same chapter (Acts 8:26–40). After his vision Peter became a missionary to the Gentile (Acts 10:17–48). Paul, upon his conversion, made missionary journeys into Asia Minor and ultimately into Europe. Paul told the church at Galatia that it was from the time he was in his mother's womb that God had appointed him to preach the gospel to the Gentiles (Gal. 1:15–16).

While individuals were the missionaries, the Christian churches were the commissioning agents. The churches at Jerusalem, Antioch, and Ephesus were often identified as the mother church of the first-century missionaries. Today as never before in the history of the Christian church, missionary outreach focus has become integral within the fabric and fiber of the church. Additionally, many religious not-for-profit organizations have focused their energies on sending missionaries and Christian workers throughout the world. Recent research has indicated that local churches devote about 15 percent of their annual budgets to missionary and outreach efforts.[6] Some denominational organizations such as the Southern Baptist Convention devote over half of their receipts from participating churches to missionary efforts.

With this significant emphasis on mission programs and the amount of funding that is being designated for this facet of Christian ministry, a few administrative admonitions are in order.

Organize for Mission Involvement

While most mission activities in the church will be voluntary, human nature is that people will not step forward without some sort of described or implied organization that will administer the activity. We all want the lost world to hear the gospel of Christ, right? How will that happen? Most people are willing to contribute funds for a mission project; others are willing to pray for missions. But to actually participate—"Don't we have career missionaries who do that?" And yet it is remarkable the number of mission projects that are happening as sponsored by the local church, a denomination, or a parachurch agency. Rather than allowing all these opportunities to inundate the membership, leaders need to plan and organize for a balanced mission effort, allowing some to participate by giving, others to support by prayer, while others actually go to the mission location. If the church or organization has not designated a professional staff member the responsibility for mission organization, the formation of a mission council or mission ministry team would be appropriate to act in that stead. The key is managed leadership.

Provide for a Variety of Mission Opportunities

There are two essentials with regard to this task: know what is out there, and know the potential for your church or organization. With the assortment of different mission opportunities that exist and the call for expenditures of funding and manpower for each, it is essential for the mission program administrator to become familiar with the elements of each in order to make recommendations for the disbursement of resources. Without this planning, resources will be stretched so thin that an effective mission ministry will not be possible. Providing variety:

- Allows the leadership to concentrate resources in selected mission venues that provide a diverse format for missions.
- Allows members to select from those opportunities for mission involvement those that they can be a part of.
- Reaches a broader spectrum of mission target groups.
- Concentrates funds into a few projects.

The key is to provide a mission program that every member could effectively be a part of, whether that is providing funds, prayer, or participating in the project.

Thoroughly Investigate the Project

Overseas mission projects will require coordination with various federal and national agencies. The types of projects are often dictated by the rules of the target community. Some countries will not allow open evangelism. Others will limit the equipment or materials brought into the country. Issues such as length of stay, amount of money brought, and transportation resources must be seriously considered. Even mission projects within the United States will require a high level of coordination. Ethnic, cultural, and relationship issues must be dealt with. Sponsorship and how the funding is allocated and spent must be firmly established. Safety and security issues are prevalent in all projects. The administrative key here is that it is better to be safe than sorry. Even the most minute detail should be thoroughly investigated and rehearsed.

Chapter Review

In many respects the programs of a church or organization define the character of the group. They become the manifestation of the interpretation that is placed upon the perceived mission and purpose the membership has developed. Programs become the lifeblood that flows through the church or organization by which the membership becomes integrated into the life of the church or organization. They become the active expressions of how the church goes about doing church—how the organization goes about doing what it has set as its rationale for existence. Thus a church worships, conducts Bible study, fellowships, and ministers to one another as well as those they are call to be missionaries to. Organizations feed, cloth, teach, care for, build, treat, and evangelize a target community through the agencies they create to accomplish their stated goals.

Historically, evaluators have cautioned churches and organizations not to allow the programs that implement the mission of the group to capture the focus and thus skew the interpretation of the true purpose behind the program. Many years ago my mother's church began a mission fair as a way to share with the church the various mission opportunities that existed in the denomination, state, and local area for missionary activity. The fair was successful and was repeated the next year, and the next, and the next, and so forth. Soon the mission fair became an all-consuming activity, taking up significant personnel resources as well as budget. Like a giant amoeba the fair had consumed the missions-oriented purpose of the fair. Booths got larger, games got more complex, handouts and trinkets got more expensive. Soon the mission fair overtook the mission program of the church.

I asked my mom one time as she was flustering about trying to get her booth completed: "What is the objective of the mission fair?" I thought that was a reasonable question given the effort she was expending. The answer I got was what many churches and organizations get when a program consumes the energy of the people involved. "I don't know. We have always had a mission fair. It is an important part of our church."

As a result of an understanding of the material in this chapter, the reader should be able to do the following:

- Describe how each program flows out of the Scriptural mandate and the church or organization's interpretation of the vision and mission statement that has been assigned by the Holy Spirit.

- List and define the six program categories that relate to the programs of the church or organization.
- Create organizational structure for the various programs of the church or organization and describe the critical nature of the leadership necessary for each.
- Relate program formation to the investigation and research of community needs and resources.
- Define the necessity for retaining administrative control of programs thorough the policies and procedures of the church or organization as well as the necessity for describing levels of accountability for their actions.

Administering
Support Activities

Now there are different gifts, but the same Spirit. There are different ministries, but the same Lord. And there are different activities, but the same God is active in everyone and everything. A manifestation of the Spirit is given to each person to produce what is beneficial.

1 CORINTHIANS 12: 4–7

Every book needs a catchall chapter, one in which the author has a bunch of things that do not fit neatly into other chapters and which are not topically long enough to be ascribed a chapter to itself. This is that chapter. The challenge will not only be in providing appropriate and important administrative information, but in presenting the material in some logical sequence so that the chapter does not look like a disorganized collection of afterthoughts.

In chapter 4 we delineated four principal functional areas of the church—pastoral, educational, music, and administrative support. We will divide this final chapter into those subtopic headings and discuss some important issues not previously covered or mentioned only briefly.

Pastoral Support Activities

A few years ago in the seminary I serve, we made the decision to survey the alumni on the opportunity of having hundreds of them on campus for a national meeting. We asked them, "In retrospect, how good a job did we do in preparing you for ministry? In particular, what should we have taught you that we didn't?" Since I was on the statistical analysis team, I had the opportunity to read and evaluate most of the reports and comments. The basics of the statistics I included in the preface to this book. What I did not mention was that there was a section where former students could write some comments they wished to convey that did not necessarily match the questions we had asked in the survey. I will always remember the comment of one of the alumni. "You didn't teach me how to baptize. I nearly drowned one of my parishioners!" Seminaries teach a lot of things, but some important facets of the ministry are learned in the school of experience. There are some things we can discuss, however, that will lessen the load of having to learn by the school of hard knocks. We will discuss at least five of those areas in this section.

Ordination

We will use the generic term *ordination* to describe the official designation of a minister or leader to accomplish his job. In the church, a minister will be ordained to be the senior pastor, minister of education, or whatever. In a religious organization an employee will be empowered through a job description and designation that gives to that person the sacerdotal authority to act on behalf of the organization. Ordination, commissioning, and licensure are terms that are officially recognized to designate a professional pastoral/ministerial leader. For the minister this recognized status brings with it certain rights for tax exemption or tax responsibility as we discovered in chapters 5 and 6. The designation is important in defining counseling responsibility. And the designation is important to groups such as your insurance agent to define the sacerdotal leadership in the organization. In recent years legal agencies of federal, state, and local governments have closely monitored the designation and activities of the persons in the church or organization with these titles.

To protect the church, organization, and individual, it is imperative that the procedure that defines how this designation comes about is formally adopted, promulgated, and followed. For example, how does an individual petition for or how is he selected for ordination? How is the qualifying group (ordination commission) selected, and by what criteria do they evaluate the applicant? How is the individual formally recognized and designated by the church or organization? These are critical issues since they impact the acceptability by agencies such as the IRS of that person's credentials. Can someone declare himself an ordained minister? No. Federal law says that has to be an activity of a church, denomination, or similar sacerdotal entity. In many states, for an individual to be licensed to ministry, he must demonstrate some level of training or preparation. To be commissioned as a jail chaplain, he will have to prove to municipal leaders that he has the professional training or experience to hold that position.

If the ordaining group makes specific exemptions or exclusions or establishes some criteria for designation based upon a theological or doctrinal position that defines their interpretation of Scripture or religious documents they ascribe to, then that must be part of the policy statement. Generally those exclusions or delimiting provisions will also be part of the constitution and bylaws of the church or organization. They must be stated in writing, openly ascribed to, and equally and uniformly applied in all the church or organization's dealings with individuals.

The Marriage Ceremony

As the administrator of a church in a college town, spring brought with it many headaches, principal of which was weddings and the various activities associated with them. From April through the summer, the church was used constantly for weddings, receptions, or the showers that preceded these events. The pastor and I learned quickly that unless we brought some order to this process, it would eat us alive. Administration was not only necessary; it was critical. Some key issues in developing a wedding policy manual include the following.

Establish a policy and write procedures. Make this document available. Many churches will publish a separate wedding brochure that is given to a bride describing all the steps necessary, the costs involved, and the expectations and limitations for conducting the marriage in the church facility.

Define who can use the facility. Many churches will presume that one of the community functions of the church is to open its doors to any bride who wants to have a wedding in the facility. Other churches will see the ceremony in their facilities open only to their members and families of their members. This attitude must be established in the policy and carried out fairly.

Define who is authorized to conduct the ceremony. Most churches will insist that one of their legally authorized pastors conduct the service. Some will allow an attendant minister possibly from outside the church. Others will just open their facility to anyone who has the legal authority to marry. Again, this must be established in the policy adopted by the church or organization.

Define when the ceremony can be conducted. While marriage ceremonies are usually defined as an integral part of the church's functions, they are generally relegated to a position of importance behind the normally scheduled events of the church. Many churches and institutions will insist that wedding ceremonies are subject to the availability of the facility only when programs or activities of the church are not scheduled—even a last-minute schedule. Other churches or organizational entities will honor a wedding date upon its being placed in the official schedule. Availability of the facilities is an important issue that requires clear establishment and is clearly communicated to the bride and groom.

Define any counseling requirements. Many pastors are moving to the contention that they will not conduct a wedding ceremony unless the bride and groom agree to a formal premarital program of counseling. This does not necessarily mean the pastor does all the counseling—only that the couple is subjected to counseling. In many churches and organizations where weddings occur, one of the first lay counseling ministries that is formed is a premarital counseling program to assist the pastoral staff in the responsibility of conducting a counseling program that spans several weeks.

Describe the format of the wedding. It is interesting to watch sensational TV where they show a bride and groom being married under water in SCUBA gear, or skydiving, or on horseback, or standing on the edge of a cliff, or on the edge of the ocean. In the Christian venue, the wedding ceremony is a religious event. It is scripturally inspired and calls for the participants to enter into the vow with the understanding that God instituted it as a life-time activity. (Maybe that is why so many oceanside marriages do not last—they build their marriage on sand.) Format includes the types of music played, the dress of the participants, the decorations and use of the facility (I never let the bride change the church environment atmosphere of the setting), and the importance that God plays in the union that is established. All this must be defined in policy and thoroughly discussed by the ministerial staff with the participants.

Establish restrictions and responsibilities. If smoking is not permitted; if the nursery is used, it must be manned by licensed care providers employed by the church, if the kitchen or fellowship hall is used, then the church hostess must be employed; if birdseed rather than rice is to be used; if plastic sheeting; must be placed beneath candles and flower holders; if loud music won't be permitted; if the . . . you get the idea. If there are contingencies on use or conduct, they should be described in the policy and procedures and communicated to the people involved. One important contingency should be who sets up and who takes down. Many facilities will require their own employees to function as wedding coordinators. Additionally, many will have strict rules for florists and caterers about the use and removal of their equipment. These are important issues to be defined and described.

Establish costs. Depending on the attitude of the church or organization toward the use of the facility as a wedding chapel, costs involved for conducting a wedding on site must be established. Many churches or organizations will only charge for extra expenses like the additional work of a custodian or hostess. Ministers and musicians will be given honorariums by the bride and groom. Other churches will have a fixed fee that includes the costs for heating/cooling, wear and tear, as well as personnel costs. The use of church utensils such as kitchen or hostess will be provided for a for-use fee.

To establish costs, first determine whether you want to charge for the wedding. Second, who will you charge: member, nonmember, both, or none? Third, determine what you will charge for. If it is personnel, you have the cost per hour for support personnel. Assume a wedding will take four hours to set up and take down. Then four x cost/hour = personnel cost. The same can be established for hostess and other personnel. If the church insists on its musicians being used, again you have a cost-per-hour wage for that person. Rental fees for linens, candleholders, kitchen implements, and such are purely subjective, and you can charge what you want. One way to see what these cost would be to ask a florist or caterer what they would charge the bride. When establishing costs, be fair, consistent, and reasonable. I am familiar with a church that does not want to put up with weddings in their facility by people outside the church. For the member, the cost is fifty dollars. For the nonmember, it is five thousand dollars! They get few outsiders wanting their wedding in that church.

Funerals

I discovered very quickly that even though I was the church administrator, my role as a minister in funerals was expected—a role I was ill prepared for initially. The first summer on staff after leaving the Navy, while I was the only staff member available to the congregation for a particular week, five people in our church had heart attacks and three died. In the military I had served as a CACO, casualty assistance calls officer, the person who delivers the news to a spouse or family that their loved one in the military had died. That was relatively easy since I usually didn't know the people involved and, after the funeral and delivery of the flag, did not see them again. This week was different. These were church members and the families of church members I knew.

God, in his infinite wisdom, knowing without his help I would bumble through the week, sent me Mrs. Lou. Every church or organization has a Mrs. Lou—a sweet, unpretentious person who through her Christian character and walk influences the lives of everyone about them. Mrs. Lou had taught just about every kid—many who were now adults—in the church. She was dearly loved. And I learned why. Though she had lost her mate, the father of her adult son, she was mature enough in her Christian faith that she looked beyond the events of the next few days. What she provided was the Christian interpretation of death, that it was a phase in the eternal life of an individual. She realized how stressed I was with two other funerals to help arrange while at the same time visiting daily to minister to the two who survived their heart attack. Rather than me ministering to her, Mrs. Lou ministered to me.

Death is a stress point in the life of a family, and it is a stress point in the life of the minister. Astute pastors will have in place a process for administering the many events and activities that surround a funeral. Some churches will assign to the deacon ministry the responsibility for assisting the pastor in this area. Others will create a bereavement ministry team to assist the pastor. Whatever the assignment, the focus and activity of the group should be to relieve the pastor from having to make administrative decisions so he may focus his entire effort on the comfort and compassion needed by the family.

Certain policies and procedures should be developed that describe the activities in this administrative plan.

Develop a centralized communication point. This may be the church receptionist, a chairman of a bereavement team or deacon. There should be one central point where information is gathered and transmitted to those who need it.

Develop a communication network. Quick and accurate dissemination of the pertinent facts is necessary for individuals who need to respond with Christian concern and compassion. This may be a Sunday school class, a Bible study group, or an aerobics group. People close to the individual and family need to know.

Establish who on the staff will take responsibility for the physical arrangements for the funeral. Usually this will be the administrator. But if the church or organization has not designated someone, this needs to be done so the pastor or organization leader does not have to devote energy to get it done.

Establish liaison with funeral homes and florists. Like the adage says, the two inevitable events in life are death and taxes. You know people are going to die, that usually the state will require some sort of legal internment, and that this function is usually carried out by the local funeral home. So discover their routine for conducting a service—what they provide and what the church or organization is expected to do. Who does what with whom? It is like a pre-arranged funeral for yourself. Everybody knows what to do; you are just waiting on the Lord's timing. In the church or organization, you know what needs to be done. All you need to know is to whom it will be done. You and the funeral home are ready.

Counseling

We have already discovered in this book that through wise counsel effective decisions are made. Scripture is full of instances where leaders as well as the common man sought the counsel of the wise, the mentor, the spiritually empowered individual. Throughout the history of the Christian church parishioners have turned to the pastor for guidance. In recent years that counseling has spread the breadth of issues from personal, public, political, and private. "Pastor, is it OK if we borrow money to buy a house. You know Scripture teaches us not to be debtor to anyone." "Pastor, my son is into drugs; what am I to do?" "Pastor I am really in love with this man, but he is not a Christian. I think I can convert him. Should I marry him?" "Pastor, I think my husband is seeing another woman. What should I do?" "Pastor, are you aware that your minister of music has pornographic material on his computer?" And the iceberg reveals itself.

Few ministers receive counseling skills as a routine part of their seminary curriculum. In recent years some seminaries and religious schools have developed Christian counseling programs that prepare men and women to deal with the issues that parishioners face. Churches and organizations that provide counseling need to be aware of issues relating to providing counseling services.

1. In general, if a minister provides counseling to a member of his congregation, whether that counseling is a doctrinal issue, and if that minister cites biblical principals as the foundation for resolution, that type of counseling is termed *ministerial counseling.* This form of counseling is usually not controlled by state regulations and has insurance regulations that are less stringent that those imposed on staff who do professional counseling.

2. Counseling provided to people who are not members of the congregation or organization is considered *professional counseling.* Also, in certain states, there are issues that have been deemed beyond the scope of ministerial counseling and must be addressed by professional counselors. This type of counseling usually requires compliance with state licensure regulations, so additional appropriate liability insurance for this activity must be carried.

3. A third issue that causes significant misunderstanding is ministerial confidence. In most counseling situations, those issues and discussions that are made with ministers and professional counselors are a confidential communication and are protected by federal and state law. But certain topics are not universally protected. For example, child molestation revealed to any individual in whatever capacity and in whatever level of confidence must be reported to appropriate, designated authorities. That is the state law in all states and territories of the nation. The person who does not report these situations is just as culpable as the perpetrator and can be prosecuted in criminal court. In most states spousal abuse must be reported. In others the revelation of intent to harm must be reported. And as our society becomes more aware of the tendency of terrorist acts on the part of others toward an individual or individuals, the confident communication shared in counseling may be open to required revelation.

In developing an administrative plan for counseling, certain issues need to be addressed:

Designate an individual in charge of the entire program. Most pastors who develop a counseling ministry will either designate one of the pastoral staff as the lead counseling administrator or assume this job himself. As an administrator, I would advise the delegation of the job. But in some churches that will not be possible, and the pastor or organizational leader must assume that role responsibility.

Create policies and procedures that define the program. Most established programs will produce a booklet that describes the services available. This will delineate fees if charged and outline procedures for the counseling sessions which include the amount of time and frequency that will be appropriated for the sessions.

Provide for security for the sessions. This administrative activity must be understood in the context of security from blame. That is, protect the counselor from being accused of inappropriate activity and protect the counselee from the potential of counselor's abuse. The best way to do this is the use of soundproof glass, the observation by a second party, and the recording of sessions. Policy should dictate that counseling should not occur behind closed doors, between parties of the opposite sex without a third party present, or private counseling that is being conducted under the provisions of the church or organizations purview where the counseling occurs in a site other than the church or organizational facilities.

Provide for confidentiality. Whether the counseling sessions are conducted in a licensed environment or as a function of ministerial counseling, the privacy of the client is to be observed except as noted in the provisions of required reporting above. This means that administrators must provide a secure location for notes and diary entries. If electronic sources are used, secure passwords must be created. By the federal privacy act law, these documents are to be open only to the counselor, the counselee, and in some cases court-appointed authorities. Pastors and other leaders must develop an attitude of respect for the confidentiality of the client.

For the parachurch organization counseling will usually be targeted to a specific client base. For example, counseling in a crisis pregnancy center will focus on those who are pregnant. In a shelter for the homeless, counseling will help people to assess their living conditions and develop skills that provide employment and thus be able to afford a living arrangement. In the church, counseling can often take on a hydra-headed format. With Scripture as the body, various heads could represent premarital counseling, marriage counseling, teen and childhood development counseling, drug addiction, sexual abuse, financial mismanagement, and so the counseling heads bob and weave. How does the concerned pastor or organization leader react?

The key is to focus on what you can do and delegate or refer to another professional counselor the rest. The religious nonprofit organization usually already does that. The difficulty resides with the church environment where the parishioner expects the pastor to be a fount of all wisdom and guidance. The church counseling program must be organized about two objectives: (1) Listen to all who come but screen the need. If church resources cannot address the need, these cases should be referred to other counseling programs. Therefore, the director of the counseling program must be aware of the counseling resources within the community to which he or she may refer the parishioner. (2) The second objective is to establish counseling programs to meet those needs with the in-house resources. Obviously the pastor or counseling director will assume some counseling situations, but without an infrastructure to support them these ministers will quickly burn out. Train and establish helpers.

An example is premarital counseling. Most churches will have couples who have established godly, biblically based marriages. Recruit these individuals to counsel the bride and groom. The pastor may want to reserve one or two sessions for himself, but the couples could conduct most of the sessions. Other counseling groups could be formed and trained to meet other needs. The key is selection and training.

Family Life and Recreation

In the 1970s many churches, capitalizing on the fitness craze that hit the nation, added to their facilities structures known as family life centers. In many respects this was a misnomer because they were actually churchified fitness centers. Weight rooms, gyms, aerobic rooms, handball and racketball courts, steam rooms and even swimming pools could be found in some of these complexes. Every once in a while a game room would be added to the waiting area, and in some a snack area was provided. A few had craft areas. Many churches and organizations soon discovered that these structures were not meeting their intended purpose and in many respects were like an albatross around their necks. These facilities became the cute puppy that grew up and ate more, took up needed space, and for all practical purposes did not have much of a function any more since cuteness disappeared.

Churches and organizations with these facilities were forced to make a critical decision. Do we continue under the present environment where a limited portion of our membership uses these ministry resources? Or do we change the form and format to meet other needs? What happened in the last part of the twentieth century was a revision of the programs that went on in those buildings. Gyms became more than a court for ten people to play ball on. They became skating rinks for entire youth groups, dining rooms for an entire church family on Wednesday night, meeting spaces for large discipleship and Bible study groups. The racketball court was configured to become a wally ball court where an entire singles group could play rather than an arena for only two to four racketball players. In other words, churches and organizations developed programs that would convert these spaces into multiple-use and multiple-program facilities.

While a church or organization does not have to have a dedicated facility for fellowship, there needs to be a mind-set and preparation for it to occur. As we learned in the previous chapter, the program function of fellowship in the church is not necessarily a game, meal, or activity. In fact, it is a recognition of a spiritual activity in the life of the believer. While the early church had a strong spiritual bonding, they did come together for a meal, to share, and to be with one another. They met in the synagogue, in homes, and on a hillside. Some of these activities may have been a spontaneous activity, but many more were probably planned.

I am a Baptist. It is a recognized fact of history that the Roman army and the Baptist church move forward on their bellies. The mention of *food* and *Baptist* in the same sentence is more commonplace than we want to admit. In a later section of this chapter, we will speak of food service in the church. Food service is a great way to facilitate fellowship in the church. After all, Luke records it as an early activity of the church in Acts, and Paul addresses the issue of the common meal and the Lord's Supper in 1 Corinthians.

Several years ago while I was a seminary student, for one of my administration classes, I had to plan and carry out an event in the church. At the same time, I was enrolled in a biblical background class and became interested in the life and times of the first-century church member. I proposed to the pastor the possibility of serving a "common meal" as it would have been eaten in the early church in Israel. The meal was to be served using the same éntrées and prepared in the same way as they were in the humble church of that day. We would follow the meal with an observance of the Lord's Supper. He thought it was a great idea as long as I did all the work. I involved my young adult Sunday school class in the research of foods, how they were prepared and served. We announced to the church the meal would be on a Maundy Thursday and that it was by reservation only since we had to buy the figs from Outer Slobovia.

One evening about 250 members of the church assembled in our gymnasium for a meal of unleavened bread, various raw vegetables and fruits, dried meat and fish, and grape juice. No knives, forks, spoons, or plates. We had napkins and tablecloths. And we did have a rough cup to drink from. For the sake of comfort, we did allow the people to sit in a folding chair. The meal was a hoot. Everyone thoroughly enjoyed eating the various kinds of foods. Toward the end of the meal, our pastor, dressed as Paul in complete costume and makeup, appeared and told us the story of the early church, how the meal became the glue that bonded them together in fellowship, how Christ on the night of his last meal with his apostles instituted a special observance that came out of the Passover meal they had just eaten. The pastor then led us in a communion service. We had placed on each table under a linen napkin a cruet with grape juice and enough small cups for each person at the table and a piece of unleavened bread. A deacon at each table served the communion. The meaning of the Lord's Supper was realized in the lives of those 250 people like no other time in their lives!

The next year we had more than eight hundred people sign up for this event. The word had gotten out. The next year we served more than fifteen hundred people in two sittings. And it continued to grow and continued to be an important part of the Passover week observance. In subsequent years other groups volunteered to participate. The drama team expanded the teaching. The ceramics classes provided first-century oil lamps for the tables as well as a souvenir mug crafted in the simple style of that day. An activity of fellowship was uniquely combined with a spiritual activity that developed the members. A distinctive first-century meal, a gymnasium dining hall, and drama combined to create fellowship.

We have placed the discussion of family life or recreation in the area of pastoral ministries for a specific reason: they are pastoral activities that build the body. That is the biblical responsibility of the pastor (review Eph. 4:11–16). Activities of family life and fellowship must spring out of the plans that develop members and nonmembers spiritually. Certain administrative activities must be considered by the pastoral staff as they develop family life and recreation activities.

Plan activities that grow the body. As with any program activity, the question must be asked whether the mission and purpose of the church are moved forward with what is planned. Specific questions about what strategy is achieved by the inclusion of the program or event must be asked and fully explored.

Plan fellowship and recreation activities that create outreach and evangelism opportunities. Most churches and organizations of the past century initially viewed their facilities as an outreach tool. But they quickly became a private recreation facility for a few. They failed because there was no intentional plan for outreach. While it is good to surround a lost basketball teammate with Christians, unless the Christians share their faith, nothing will be achieved. Build in Bible study, train leaders to evangelize, provide materials, be prepared to counsel.

Provide for the broadest participation. The name *family life center* implies that events will be planned and provided for the entire family—both genders, all ages. Contemporary philosophy calls for the creation of intergenerational and full family events. Though you will not eliminate individual activities and small team sports, they should be the exception rather than the rule for planning events.

Adequately fund such a program. If you think fees and charges in a family life center will pay for the events, you should buy a padlock now. It just will not happen. Just as with any quality program of ministry, a family life/recreation ministry takes planning, leadership, and funding. The initial costs of the facility and equipment should be considered just the beginning of a commitment that will sustain the program.

Ensure that adequate leadership is provided. Few churches and organizations can afford a full-time professional staff member dedicated to such a ministry. This is an excellent place for the pastor to develop an advisory council to provide the necessary leadership. To provide the many people it will take to carry out the program, create a ministry team of individuals who feel their spiritual gift targets this ministry. Allow them to function as the workers you will need to carry out this ministry.

Educational Support Activities

Second only to the worship experience, educational programming will garner the largest number of participants of any other program in the local church. In most religious nonprofit organizations, it will be the focus of the ministry. By the time of the first-century church, the educational fabric had been woven into the life of the Christian. From the historical background of the Hebrew culture, adults were being taught the law at the temple, the Old Testament documents had been canonized and were regularly studied in the synagogue. From earliest times the child was taught first in the home and then in the rabbinic schools in most synagogues throughout the world. From the admonition of the Great Commission, the early church took seriously the requirement to teach them "everything I have commanded you" (Matt. 28:20). Early schools were established to disciple the new convert and train leadership. By the time of the Renaissance, the church had in place a vast university system that provided instruction in virtually every discipline and profession. And by the time of the Reformation, the church had created specialized schools for theological study and preparation for ministry.

From the time of the Protestant Reformation, education became an important element of the motif of what the church was about. Luther, Zwingli, Calvin, Tyndale, and many others out of the sixteenth-century Reformation preached that the individual needed the tools to read and interpret the Bible not only for salvation but also for a proper understanding of what it means to be a Christian.

The establishment of a formalized religious education would not be the reformers' forte, however. It was the counterreformation of the Roman Catholic Church, principally through the Jesuit order founded by Ignatius of Loyola, that established a three-prong work that focused on education, missionary expansion—especially in the New World—and the counteracting of Protestant gains in Europe. It was this group that coined the phrase, "Give me a child until he is seven, and he will remain a Catholic the rest of his life." Together with the

Dominican, Franciscan, and Augustinian orders, they formed mission school-houses throughout the world.

Soon, however, Protestant educators such as Melanchthon, Beza, and Calvin began to focus on the necessity for the formation of educational motifs that taught reformation theology. During the period of the awakening of the seventeenth and eighteenth centuries, great evangelists such as Edwards, Whitefield, and the Wesleys began to couple the Christian message with the requirement to teach the Christian ethic. As the New England colonies were being established under the purely Calvinistic philosophy of the Puritans, they required each colony to have not only teachers but schoolhouses. In many instances this task was assigned to the parson or his wife. In the middle colonies schools were formed by denominational groups to teach their children a trade and to inculcate the beliefs of their particular group.

Many look to Robert Raikes and Thomas Stork, rector of St. John the Baptist Church, as the founders of the modern Sunday school movement. As editor of the *Gloucester Journal* in Gloucester, England, Raikes was familiar with the deplorable condition of the children of the city. Stork was equally concerned with their spiritual condition. Together they created a noble experiment to teach children of all ages and both genders to read, principally from the Bible. Raikes wrote some corollary curriculum. His school was distinguished from all other educational schemes in that rather than a catechism, creed, or confession, Raikes's Sunday school scholars were taught to read directly from the Bible. The program was not endorsed by the Anglican Church but was a secular movement to teach children to become rational, moral, and responsible citizens. In less than half a decade, the movement spread in England to over a quarter million students.

In the late 1700s, most children in America were in public school systems that incorporated an element of religious training based upon reformation Christianity. But as the new nation began to grow, certain leaders urged that the teaching of Christianity be separated from the public school and that it take place in the churches and homes. The church was ill prepared for this new responsibility. When the Raikes model of Sunday school came to America with its Bible-focused curriculum, the movement took root in the local churches as a means for providing Bible study for the child. Ultimately, the Sunday school program in the American culture became a child evangelism movement.

It was the philosophy of John Wesley and his Methodism that brought character to the teaching environment we find in the local church today. His pedagogical methods were succinct and important:

- Get the student's attention before teaching.
- Use words that can be understood.
- Use illustrations from everyday life.

- Establish a relationship of love.
- Be patient.
- Repeat yourself.
- Have within yourself the spirit of true religion.

Wesley did not relegate his teaching to the child only. His philosophy was that all people from the time of understanding needed to be discipled.

We have already looked at Arthur Flake and his Flake Formula of knowing the potential for learners, creating and expanding the organization, acquiring and training teachers, providing space for instruction, and an outreach visitation program as an early model for establishing education programs in the church or organization. In our contemporary culture, the educator must be an innovator, technician, curriculum developer, demographic analyst, space manager, and electronics genius.

It is interesting that in the description of the church leader, the overseer, in the listing of qualifications in 1 Timothy 3, all are character traits except one—the ability to teach well. This theme is mirrored in Ephesians 4:11 when Paul couples the words *pastor* and *teacher* into a single responsibility of the office. Pastors are the headmasters (teachers) of their congregations. And yet they are not expected to carry this responsibility alone. Others in the church have been gifted by the Holy Spirit with the ability to teach, exhort, and lead. Some important issues that impact a well-administered education ministry in the church or organization include the following.

The Curriculum

The thing that distinguished Robert Raikes's Sunday school movement of the eighteenth and nineteenth centuries was his use of the Bible as the main curriculum. When asked what the curriculum for the church is, the proper answer should be "the Bible." Unfortunately that is not always the answer. In our modern culture-sensitive society, many times the Bible is replaced with thematic or topical studies that relate only remotely to the Scripture. Are they important issues and topics? Certainly. But they should not be the focus of a Bible study period.

A phenomenon that has happened in the last quarter of the twentieth century is that people of all ages want to come to church to study the Bible. There is a trend toward conservatism. Even the national polls demonstrate a religious-oriented society. How the church as well as the religious nonprofit and the leadership of these entities respond to the responsibility of being the teachers of the parishioner is critical. In selecting curriculum certain considerations should be carefully evaluated:

- Is the proposed curriculum based on sound theology? Does it explore the truth and reality of the Christian faith?

- Is the philosophy that of assisting persons to become aware of God as revealed in Christ in order to have a personal commitment of faith and a zeal to live a Christ-centered life that produces a mature Christian?
- Does the curriculum use the Bible, both as source and focus?
- Does the curriculum relate to and build on the mission and purpose of the church or organization?
- Is the content comprehensive, properly balanced, sequential, and presented in an age-appropriate fashion?
- Does the curriculum meet the needs of the learners and elicit their response?
- Does the curriculum build the leadership, calling for their continued development?
- Are appropriate media resources available to support and build upon the content of the curriculum?
- Does the curriculum allow for appropriate and adequate administration by the leadership?

Media Center

The church in which I grew up in eastern Tennessee is unique in that it has a church library that rivals many public and private collections. Over a half century ago, a member of the church who was also involved in the public school library system began the library. Her objective was to provide to those teachers who could not afford the cost of reference materials a repository of resources that would allow them to be adequately prepared for their lessons. Additionally, she carefully selected books of general interest, Christian perspective, and leisure reading that became the periodic lifeblood of readers of all ages throughout the church.

Today church and organization libraries are becoming a multifunction element in the educational ministries of the church. While the printed book and manuscript still remains an essential element, many more forms of communication are available to the user. The term *media center* focuses on the essential element of providing to the educational elements of the church or organization the tools by which the curriculum can be presented, understood, and applied.

Of all the education organization elements, the media center lends itself perfectly to be administered by a ministry team. Though a professional staff member will have liaison responsibility to the team, because of the diversity of this area, a variety of people with different skills, interests, and desires for service are needed. Needed in a ministry team will be librarians and catalogers, audio and video technicians, and other forms of curriculum managers. Basic administrative issues that should be dealt with include the following.

Ensure there is a leader. Any committee, ministry team, or council needs a leader. While we are suggesting a volunteer ministry team organization, it needs someone who is designated the leader and to whom the pastor, education minister, or council can look to as coordinator.

Provide an accurate inventory of resources. Nothing is more frustrating than to think you have a resource but you are not sure. Card or online catalog systems exist to account for books and periodicals. Nearly every computer church management system has an inventory subroutine.

Develop and enforce an accountability system for checkout and return of resources. It does no good to have something if you don't know where it is. Again, most computer church management systems will have a checkout scheme with the inventory.

Develop sections of the media center to allow for uninterrupted material use. The audio section should have headphones; the video section should be placed so as not to distract others who are reading or studying. Computer systems should allow freedom of access while being monitored at the same time. A noisy checkout area should be separate from a quiet reading/listening/viewing area. Work areas for materials and classroom preparation should be shielded from the remainder of the study areas.

Provide a realistic budget for the media center. One of the commodities that has risen the fastest and greatest in recent years is paper products. Books, especially limited-edition books such as the theological reference books found in church libraries, are very expensive. And while the cost of electronic media equipment has fallen as new technology is brought online, it also is expensive. One of the best ways to prepare for these expenditures is to have a realistic annual assessment of budget needs based on the curriculum, the expectations of the members, and the usefulness of the technology to enhance the mission and purpose of the church. The key is to ensure the media materials are cost-effective investments. They are long-lasting, they serve the needs of the many, and they are selected with a balance toward ministry requirements.

Child Care Issues

One of the most critical areas of ministry administration that will require adroit and knowledgeable emphasis is ministry to children. In the past most churches and religious not-for-profits did not have a keen sensitivity to this issue. Aunt Maude, who loved children and who had worked in this area for free for a zillion years, was the single source of expertise in many child care programs. In recent decades, however, Aunt Maude is being rapidly replaced with qualified, trained individuals; many of whom have degrees from seminaries or colleges in childhood ministry. And there is an important reason administrators need to pay attention to this change.

You are familiar with the church growth adage about facilities that goes like this: the three important things an organization must pay attention to are parking, the women's restrooms, and the nursery. Parking is understandable. If people can't park, they won't stay. The women's restroom is an issue that discusses the adequacy of numbers of spaces as well as the appropriateness of the space. But why the nursery? I learned that lesson the hard way.

Our church nursery was located on the lower level of a first-unit building. Actually the rooms were below grade and infrequently we would have high water that would cause the drain lines to back up and even flood the spaces. Even though we quickly drained the space and vacuumed up the water, the moisture that remained in the walls caused mildew and odor. You cannot believe the number of "concerned" calls we received from mothers who were concerned about leaving their wonderful bundles of joy in a smelly nursery area. To correct the problem took lots of money and even a relocation of the nursery to "higher ground." But it was a necessary move because failure to do so impacted our ability to attract families with young children.

Our society expects clean, safe, and appropriate facilities for their children. In an environment where the sanctity of the church is not considered and the preeminence of the child is denigrated, it is critical for the church or organization to pay close attention to the administrative details of child care. Some important issues need to be addressed:

1. Be aware that there are regulations and guidelines that churches and religious nonprofits must abide by that have been established by state, local, and in many instances, denominational groups. For example; an after-school program, or a preschool day care system will probably be regulated and specific criteria must be met that inspects, authorizes, and licenses that entity. When dealing with children, ignorance of the law is no excuse.

2. Be aware also that insurance and other governance groups will require that certain safeguards, training, and physical conditions be met to ensure the safety and security of the child. While these regulations are outside political statutes, they are significant and binding nevertheless. Certain denominational groups that invoke compliance with decisions by leadership will require the compliance. Non-profits are often managed by a board or other group of directors that will require consideration and compliance. And in recent years, major insurance entities have placed significant requirements on their clients in the area of liability insurance with regard to children. The bottom line is to verify whether these guideline exist.

3. Select qualified leadership. In the past the argument has been that few churches could afford a full-time professional minister to children. Now the thinking is that churches and organizations cannot afford not to have a professional minister. The problem is that there are few seminary-trained, qualified

ministers available. In 2003, for the first time ever, the salary offered to a children's minister equaled that of the youth minister. The fact is that in some larger organizations and churches, the competition to acquire leadership is such that the position is well paid. The bottom line is that you will have to look hard and long for a minister to children and be prepared to pay well.

4. Ensure that all levels of leadership are screened. If the church or organization does nothing else to ensure the safety of the children under its care, the screening of every adult who will have contact with children is a must. If the care facility is a municipal- or state-licensed unit, there will be no option. If the church or organization is insured by one of the major carriers, there will be no option unless the group wants to pay an extremely high premium. The wise administrator will ensure that policy and procedures are in place which will ensure that all adults with access to children seventeen years and younger will be screened before allowing them to serve and that the level of screening will be as extensive as necessary to ensure the background of both the professional and lay worker is known before they are allowed access to the children. Whether the church or organization conducts the screening themselves through the many state and federal agencies that provide this data or they use a professional agency that will conduct the screening, the screening must be thorough, reported, and made a matter of record.

5. Ensure the two-man rule is observed at all times. In chapter 6 we discussed the two-man rule as it related to the finances of the church. We stated that funds should always be managed through the auspices of two independent and unrelated people. The same is true in the children's ministry. At no time should a child (or youth) be left in the care or responsibility of only one person. The arguments for such an arrangement are many. The core of the policy is to protect the child from molestation and the worker from being falsely accused.

6. Child care spaces should be open and in full view of leaders, yet closed and blocked from the view of an outsider. Place a window in the door of a classroom. Have no space within the facility blocked from the view of leaders. This includes storage areas and restrooms. A screening fence between a playground and the street prevents a pedophile from viewing the children. Well-designed spaces will have wide, open halls with no areas hidden from view; they will have adult eye-level windows and sight ports; and they will have security access points closely controlled to prevent unauthorized persons from entering the area.

7. The presence of a check-in/check-out procedure must be in place and understood by everyone. In conducting research for a book on security, I ran across a humorous cartoon showing parents checking in their baby. The church nursery had a bar code reader panel similar to a grocery store checkout counter. The child had a bar code stamped across its bottom and was being

"swiped" in. Less than a year later I was in a church and saw this happen. The child and parent had been issued a bar code bracelet similar to what you receive when you go to the hospital. The two bar codes had to match when swiped, or you couldn't check out the child. The methodology for carrying out this mandate varies widely from cards to bracelets to pagers. The key is to have a scheme that works and provides the necessary security to prevent an unauthorized person from gaining access to the child. If they don't have the key to unlock the door to let the child out, the child stays in your care until the proper key holder arrives. No exceptions.

8. Gather information about the child. Policy and procedures should be in place to gather important information about the child. This goes for members and visitors alike. Of course, every mother thinks her child is different—more wonderful than the rest—and the fact is they are different. In addition to general demographic data like name, age, address, etc., other data should also be collected. For instance, any special diet, allergy conditions, or medical issues that workers should be aware of. Find out about certain habits—she bites when angry—and mannerisms that will impact their sociability. Of course, venues like after-school programs, day cares, schools, and other long-term care units will seek a broader database that will include emergency numbers, physician information, and parents' work data. But the one piece of information that is absolutely critical to obtain—and possibly this needs to be verified upon every occasions of child care—is the location of the parents or guardian who is authorized to pick up the child during the time the child is under the church or organization's care. This includes the Sunday school classroom and where they sit in the sanctuary.

9. Develop an infectious disease and sick child policy. Another area of particular sensitivity by parents that has been developed in the past few years is an aversion to subjecting their children unnecessarily to illness. This writer is not qualified to provide a listing of illnesses that should be considered severe enough to tell a parent that the child must be removed from the presence of the other children. There are, however, numerous people who can—school nurses, doctors, and child care inspectors. What the church or organization must do is ascertain what level of introduction they will allow, post those conditions that will prevent a child from being part of the program, and then stick by the policy. Additionally, the policy should describe how a child is cared for until a parent is summoned when the child becomes ill when in the care of the church or organization. A sick room, isolated from other children, should be created. It can serve other functions when not used as such, but it is there to insulate the other children from illness.

10. Provide for the exceptional child. Demographers state that approximately 14 to 15 percent of the population has some sort of handicap—a

learning disability, movement disability, sight or hearing impairment, and so forth. No church or religious organization would intentionally turn away 15 percent of a potential membership pool, but we do when we disqualify a child from attending our programs. Someone who is trained or is capable of meeting the needs of the special child should be available. Programs do not have to be dramatically altered. Simple accommodations can be made to alleviate the particular challenge a child may have. Sometimes this is as simple as an additional worker in a classroom. Other times it may mean some special piece of equipment. If your church or organization does not have access to a volunteer or professional leader in this area of need, form a ministry team of parents and others who are sensitive to these needs and who have the resources to meet the challenge.

Training

In the previous chapter I related to you a program of potential leadership training in a church in South Carolina that I have always viewed as optimal. While few churches will experience the luxury of having an abundance of trained leaders, most have the resources available to them to prepare and sustain a competency in educational leadership. When Arthur Flake was formulating his formula decades ago, he recognized the necessity of recruiting and training leadership in order for the Sunday school to grow. Every interpreter of that formula and every deviser of a scheme to grow a church or organization has recognized the necessity of having qualified, trained leadership. You would not want a person who has never driven a nail to build your house or a mechanic who has never seen the inside of an engine to repair your car. Why would you want someone to teach a Sunday school class who has not learned to study the Bible? Or someone who has no idea about a library catalog system to serve as your media center director?

Certain administrative activities must be considered when developing training programs:

Training activities require planning. The development of a comprehensive church training plan is necessary to ensure the integration of events to provide an all-encompassing approach as well as to make sure that all essential elements of the church program are addressed. The annual church training plan should be considered at the same time as certain other major planning events occur—the annual budget, the annual program schedule, etc.—since many of the training events will require coordination on a schedule as well as funding.

Designate a coordinator for all leadership training. In most churches this will be a minister of education, associate pastor for discipleship, education council, or some other individual or group responsible for the education programs in the church or organization. This coordinator is not responsible for conducting the training. His or her principal function will be (1) to ensure that training occurs in all venues of the church; (2) to ensure that instruction and training is appropriate, in conformance with church or organization doctrine or dogma, and that it enhances the mission and purpose of the church or institution; and (3) to a resource or facilitator of the training plans. This coordinator becomes the central point of acquisition of common resource materials, the producer of churchwide or total organization products, and the manager of the repository of materials that will become the resource tools for future training programs.

Budget for Training. It would be wise to allow each program entity to list as a prioritized line item in their budget submission the request for training. By doing so, program and budget unit managers will be free to assess their training needs as well as the importance placed upon each training activity. This will allow you as administrator to query the total budget records to find out how much funding has been requested, allocated, and expended for training. At the same time, leadership can evaluate the training and preparation that is being conducted in each program or budget unit area.

Establish a scheme for ongoing training. Frequently I am invited to visit in person or by phone with church leaders whose education program is in the doldrums—dying or dead. "What can I do?" is often their query. My first point of analysis is to look at their annual training plan. (Usually they do not have one.) I look for three things: (1) A regularly scheduled—once or twice a year—potential leader training program. You need newly trained leaders to provide leadership for new work as well as to replace the attrition of workers. (2) I look for some form of event training that sensitizes the church or organization to the concept that leaders desire for the members to be trained. This event may be churchwide or organizationwide, it may focus on a program or ministry, or it may be thematic, concentrating on a particular issue. (3) And finally, I look to see if there is ongoing, periodic training for the existing leadership—a weekly workers meeting, a ministry team training meeting that includes skill training, a weekly program activity that includes direction from leadership. Ongoing training enhances skill, motivates workers, and builds the program to excellence.

The Venue for Instruction

When our Puritan fathers (and mothers) came to worship, they came to the "church house"—the assembly building that often was the church on Sunday, the schoolhouse during the week, and the town forum whenever needed. As the Sunday school movement became popular in America, children were often separated from the adults into rooms for their Bible study and activity. Through the years, until the last quarter of the twentieth century, the church house was the venue for worship, study and Christian activity. As the twenty-first century dawned, this changed dramatically.

In past years the affordability of facilities was within the range of most churches and organizations. And these facilities met the needs of worship, education, or program activity. (For those churches and institutions that are dying and have locked major portions of their facilities tighter than a drumhead, skip the remainder of this paragraph.) In many churches and growing organizations, facility management has become a great concern. In chapter 7 we addressed several issues of facility management, and we also introduced the concept of the multiple use of space. In the early 1980s the cost of church construction was approximately $55 per square foot. Twenty years later it is $155 per square foot. Churches and organizations simply cannot afford to build large complexes for their parishioners and, therefore, are having to turn to alternative and innovative use of the facility. Additionally, different venues outside the walls of the church or facility for the carrying out of a program of education are being explored and utilized.

Whether scheduling for multiple use of a facility or the development of an off-campus ministry approach, certain administrative elements should be considered:

Provide adequate space for the educational activity. Both in chapter 7 and in chapter 10, a discussion was presented about the appropriate space allocation for a variety of programs. These rule-of-thumb guidelines assist church planners and administrators alike in providing an appropriate space allowance that will ensure comfort while meeting the particular activity needs of the program. For example, if you have 100 adults in a Bible study program, they will require (100 x 15ft^2/person) = 1500 ft^2. You are going to have to look for ten rooms of about 10 x 15 feet. And of course if you expect the Bible study group to grow, you will have to use the 80 percent rule which means that the space will have to be 1800 ft^2 or ten rooms of 12 x 15 feet.

Where those ten rooms occur is an administrative program decision that will have to be made by the church or organization. Traditionally the answer would be to build Sunday school classrooms in an educational facility. That option may not be feasible. It could be that the answer is to use five rooms of this size twice—in a dual Sunday school program where half the membership worships while the other half are in a Bible study program, and then they exchange places. Another alternative would be to have some of the groups meeting in off-campus venues such as homes, rented spaces, or the like. Regardless of the venue, remember the axiom of the Flake Formula—provide space. It makes no difference if you have the best recruitment tool and teaching staff. If you do not have a place for these individuals to meet comfortably, the program will fail.

Provide physical resources for the program. Several years ago a growing church in Texas had the opportunity to acquire two or three used classroom facilities that the local public school system deemed cheaper to sell than to move and reuse. While the spaces were a valuable addition to the expanding Bible study program in the winter, when late spring and summer came, the church was faced with some unhappy members who were being asked to study in a non-airconditioned space. Since the elementary school did not hold classes during the summer months, the school board did not deem it necessary to install a climate control system that included air conditioning. Suddenly the church was faced with the added expense of purchasing three air-conditioning systems for the spaces.

Whether it is climate control systems, alarm and emergency systems, ramps and elevators, chalk or whiteboards, lighting, sinks and restrooms, or what have you, the educational space must come with appropriate equipment that will make it functional. The wise administrator will consider the use of an educational council, age group council, or ministry team to assist in the development of the necessary accoutrements that will make the space a useful and education-enhancing environment.

Ensure that the space meets fire safety and code requirements. One of the key responsibilities of the administration of any organization is the assurance of safety and security of the people they serve. While most buildings built in the last quarter century generally follow safety guidelines, older facilities may not have such safeguards. Numerous resources are available to assist administrators in determining whether their education facility meets these codes. One of the best is the National Fire Protection Association. This organization publishes resources that discuss access, alarms, limitations, etc. Another resource consists of the local building code requirements that can be obtained from the local code enforcement office. Some insurance companies provide brochures and will inspect your facility with safety in mind. And finally, local fire and police agencies will provide assistance through their community resource personnel to ensure the safety and security of the space.

If the church or organization authorizes the use of an off-campus site to carry out its program functions, this site becomes an extension of the main campus. A church rented a space in a strip mall for its youth ministry. The mall was adjacent to the main campus but owned by someone else. A gas leak occurred in one end of the building, and an explosion occurred in a room two doors down from where the youth were meeting. Fortunately no one was killed, but several were injured. In the litigation that followed, the courts held the owner of the mall *and* the church liable for the injuries. The ruling was that the church should have validated that the place was a safe place for children to meet. If you have a cell ministry meeting in homes or any off-site meetings, you need to be aware of the liability that exists.

Music Support Activities

In the previous chapter we discovered that music was an integral part of the worship experience. It has been in biblical history, in the past of the Christian church, and remains so in today's church. From the call to worship to the benediction, music provides the backdrop that creates the environment for spiritual worship. While the musical instrumentation may range from the upright piano to the grand multirank pipe organ, from the acoustic guitar to the string orchestra, the acquisition, care, and maintenance of the music ministry is an administrative detail that needs addressing. Whether the choir sings from a hymnal or from sheets of anthem music, attention to such factors of copyright as well as the actual music publications requires attention.

In recent years controversy has raged about worship styles—contemporary, traditional, blended, and so forth. This text will not address the pros or cons of any style of music in worship. What will be noted is that each style brings unique equipment and administrative challenges that require leadership to evaluate the processes to ensure effectiveness and excellence. These will require the administrator of the music programs to consider several issues.

The Organization for a Program of Music

As with any major program, an organizational scheme with attendant assignment of leadership must be created because the music ministry or program has many facets. Each of these require special and specific leadership. Several years ago I was in the choir of a large church that produced Christmas and Easter pageants. They were spectacular and were the rave of the community. After each of these productions however, the music minister was spent—usually physically sick. As the church administrator, I took note of the fact that the minister of music had assumed the total responsibility for the production. He was conductor, director, producer, recruiter, salesman—you name it, he was it. I asked him if I could assume the role of administrator for the next production and he gladly agreed.

I then set about to recruit people who would be set designers and builders, costume designers and creators, and individuals who would apply makeup and assist the cast in dressing. I got script writers and dramatists who created an attendant drama production. They were given the responsibility for recruiting and training the actors. Another group was responsible for acquiring the animals used—and cleaning up their mess! We organized lighting and sound crews to rent, create, install, and operate the equipment. In other words I created a production crew. Could the minister of music have done this? Probably, but why should he, when qualified and interested persons were available to do all these things for him.

Organization will be required based on the size of the church or institution and the programs of music ministry involved. Three organizational divisions are suggested:

An operational staff. This staff may include such individuals as an office secretary, music librarian, instrument custodian, sound technician, video technician, etc. based on the size of the organization. These are individuals, not groups of individuals. These are individuals the music minister can turn to in discussing a particular issue or problem and who then will be delegated the responsibility for carrying out the plans. For example, the entire sound/light board staff does not need to be present when the minister of music goes over the planned worship service and the various microphone and lighting requirements—just the leader. This operational staff may be paid or volunteer.

Staff Musicians. This organizational group will include such persons as the organist, pianists, and the orchestra/instrumentalist director. While infrequently these individuals are volunteer, generally these are hourly wage, paid employees of the music staff. In some larger churches these will include certain paid musicians who are vocalists and instrumentalists.

Program Leadership. The leader of the senior adult choir, the youth ensemble, the praise band, the children's graded choir program, the drama team—all these represent programs under the aegis of the music and worship ministry of the church. And all are leadership areas that will require designation and management in an organizational scheme.

A Process for Administering Resources

As part of a building committee, recently we were planning the addition of a new sanctuary. Our church had waited for a long time to come to this point, and there was a desire to ensure that everything was perfect. We discussed the instruments, the organ and piano, that existed in the old facility. It was the desire of many people that we begin a new worship center with a new piano and organ. Since the sanctuary would be much bigger, they thought the instruments should also be larger. "Have you any idea how much more that is going to add to the cost of the building program!" was my cry. After we investigated it, we discovered just how expensive these instruments would be. (We added them anyway.)

Of the equipment and materials to conduct a ministry program, probably the music program is the most expensive. And if the church or organization is committed to a quality program, it should be prepared to budget and expend funds to make it so. Since these are such valuable resources, administrative schemes must be created that ensure the assets.

Institute a policy and procedures for inventory control. While I am not advocating the accounting of every cymbal in the children's rhythm band, there should be a scheme in place to account for the assets of the ministry. Probably the policy should describe a value limit or identify inventory by type. For example, all electronic equipment, sheet and book music, and all other items of a value of $100 or greater will be cataloged and inventoried. Most computerized office management systems have built-in inventory programs. If not, any office computer database can be structured for such a management system.

Develop a policy and procedures for use. Until we finally got a handle on it, we were constantly running down the three portable sound systems we had. It seems like everyone knew where they were stored and would just go by and pick one up for an event or program. Finally we locked them up—that made a lot of people happy—and told them to plan ahead to use them and check them out with the music secretary. This accomplished two things. We knew where the pieces of equipment were, and we discovered that three units were not enough. The demand exceeded the supply. We got more. Who can use the $250,000 organ? What about the $40,000 grand piano; can it be wheeled into the gym? Does just anyone have a key to the soundboard in the auditorium? How are choir robes assigned and accounted for? Can another church use thirty copies of our sheet music that cost $4.95 a copy? What about our $300 each stage lights; where can they be used? Can another church or institution use them? These are just some of the many issues that require policies. Remember, a policy is a good thing. It answers a hard question before it is asked and represents thoughtful consideration and administration. But also remember, a policy broken or an exception granted invalidates the policy.

Develop Copyright Policy. Probably the most "attacked" institution in America today for copyright infringement is the local church. Ministers of music and other leaders must be fully acquainted with copyright laws and provisions that protect the originator of the music, drama, or production. Several organizations, including the music and drama industry itself, provide excellent free advice and information to churches and organizations with regard to legal use of the products. Of all the arenas of tort action in courts today, copyright infringement takes the dimmest view toward ignorance of the law than any venue.

Develop policy and procedures to maintain the resources. Pianos need periodic tuning; organs, sound boards, and other instruments need calibrating and repair; music and books need rebinding and taping; computer modules for lighting and video presentation need to be debugged. Equipment needs to be cared for. To wait until it fails is embarrassing as well as distracting. A failed spotlight in the midst of a dramatic point, a cracking microphone during a presentation, an annoying hum in a speaker system—these can destroy the mood as well as the message.

A Scheme for Integrating with Other Ministries

It is obvious that the music ministry integrates with the worship ministry. But what about the pastoral and educational ministry? Where do the arts such as music and drama fit in the activities of the church such as recreation, age group, missions, and discipleship? I have already mentioned earlier that my son was part of a youth ensemble in his high school years. I also mentioned that three of the young women in the group ultimately became three-fourths of the singing group Point of Grace. The neat thing about the youth ensemble group was that they were missionaries for the church. These young people often visited and sang in small churches that could not support a music ministry. When the youth made mission trips, the group performed concerts. When the youth group went to youth camps, they were the praise team for the vespers services.

The lifeblood of every adult music program is a graded choir program for the preschoolers and children of the church. There they get the basics for music and drama and their zeal for the use of the arts in worship. I love it when our children's choir sings a song and then uses sign language for the deaf to dramatize their words. Not every child can sing, but they can make a joyful noise to the Lord. Music ministry programs must nurture these innate desires by the children and youth. Of all periods in the history of the youth culture, music and drama now play a vital role in the life of the individual. The church or nonprofit must provide a venue for them to hear Christian music, see Christian video and drama, and participate in Christian art.

You are familiar with the titles Singing Saints, Joyful Singers, Senior Sangers, The Senior Chore (I spelled it correctly), and so forth. The senior adult choirs of many churches and groups are often a vibrant part of a senior adult ministry as well as a program of recreation and activity for the "mature" member. Not only do they sing in church; they sing also in nursing homes, hospitals, malls—just about anywhere they can get in. And they are well received ambassadors of the church or organization they represent.

All of these activities take planning. Not all of the activities of the arts are appropriate in every church or organization. The tenets for carrying out such programs must always be evaluated in light of these factors:

- Does it respond to, or enhance the mission of the church or organization?
- Does it contribute to the accomplishment of the goals of the program or organization that has planned the arts of music and drama?

- Do leaders understand the responsibility to make the music program Christian and growth producing and to integrate it with the other programs of the church?
- Is the program planned within the resources available for accomplishment?
- Is there a desire to produce a quality program? While performance excellence is not demanded, is the program worthwhile and culturally accepted?

Administration Support Activities

Then the Day of Unleavened Bread came when the Passover lamb had to be sacrificed. Jesus sent Peter and John, saying, "Go and prepare the Passover meal for us, so we can eat it." "Where do You want us to prepare it?" they asked Him. "Listen" He said to them, "when you've entered the city, a man carrying a water jug will meet you. Follow him into the house he enters. Tell the owner of the house, 'The Teacher asks you, "Where is the guest room where I can eat the Passover with My disciples?" Then he will show you a large, furnished room upstairs. Make the preparations there.' So they went and found it just as He had told them, and they prepared the Passover (Luke 22:7–13).

Throughout this final chapter we have discussed certain administrative activities that the principle programs rely upon to make them function. We have been following the basic division of organization given in chapter 4 of pastoral, educational, music, and support. Previously in chapter 11 we established that the programs of the church or organization flow out of the interpretation of the basic functions of worship, discipleship, evangelism, ministry, fellowship, and missions.

Before we discuss the final two topics relating to support activities, let me reiterate a philosophical stance that is a necessary element of administration in any organization, church, or religious nonprofit. That philosophy is built around the call to servanthood that Jesus called for and modeled. While Jesus delegated the task of finding a room for the Passover meal to some of his followers, the Gospel writers in unison record Jesus' act of washing the disciple's feet—an act relegated to the lowest servants or members of a household. Jesus told his followers that he did not come to be served but to serve (Matt. 20:28) and commanded that we follow his example of a servant attitude (John 13:15). While we all must enter into ministry with an attitude of a servant, the activities of administration empower the programs and organizations of the church or institution and enable them to function. Let me give you a personal example that will reveal my heart about how administrative support activities empower a ministry program.

My wife and I worked with the youth ministry of the church. Each summer our youth would attend a large Christian camp in Oklahoma. The first summer my wife went as one of the volunteers who did the cooking, counseling, and cleaning. The camp went well, and I did not pay attention to the detail that had gone into the preparation. The next summer, however, I became more aware of the many details required to make camp a success. My first introduction was that as a member of the properties committee we had to come up with transportation because the million-year-old church bus had broken down on the way to camp, and we needed to get them there—and tow the bus back.

What I took note of that summer was an overworked minister to youth. While he had training in Bible, discipleship, and youth ministry, he was not trained in the organizational art of delegation. He was doing all the work himself. The next year I was the lay church administrator, and I began to help him in these organizational activities by taking on some of the logistic responsibilities. Finally, when I was the full-time administrator, I went to him and requested permission to take on the administrative responsibility of youth camp. His responsibility would be to recruit and train his counselors and minister to the kids. I would do the rest.

You know me well enough by now to know that I did not do the work myself; I organized and delegated the work. I arranged for leased, safe transportation. We formed ministry teams which planned the meals, recruited the workers, and purchased the necessary food to feed the hungry hundreds. We had ministry teams that arranged for the financial activities that led up to the trip. We even arranged for the details like T-shirts, snacks, equipment, and the many other items that made the trip worthwhile.

Two important things happened that summer. First, they had a great summer camp and the youth minister loved the opportunity to spend time in ministry with the youth rather than tending to dozens of details. The second thing that happened was the youth minister learned he did not have to do everything himself. He learned some of the administrative skills I had used and was able himself to use them in future ministry opportunities. The key was that administration was an empowerment, not the ministry itself. It allowed the youth minister to give full attention to the program ministry at hand.

In this final section we want to discuss two important facets of support administration—transportation and food service.

Transportation Administration

"When they approached Jerusalem, at Bethphage and Bethany near the Mount of Olives, He sent two of His disciples and told them, 'Go into the village ahead of you. As soon as you enter it, you will find a young donkey tied there, on which no one has ever sat. Untie it and bring it here. If anyone says to you, "Why are you doing this?" say, "The Lord needs it and will send it back here right away"'" (Mark 11:1–3). We are familiar with the triumphal entry. While we understand it as a fulfillment of prophecy (2 Kings 9:13; Ps. 118:26; Isa. 62:11; Zech. 9:9; 14:4), it was facilitated with an unridden animal that was obtained by two of his disciples. Jesus needed transportation.

What I am about to say will be questioned by many of you who are reading this book. But if you will bear with me for a few more pages, maybe I can justify it. The statement is this: *If you can avoid it, do not buy your own transportation assets.* As an administrator I inherited a worn-out bus and two junk vans. When I departed I left the church with a panel van and a pickup truck, both of which were designed for work, not personnel transportation—and neither of which left the city limits. The three vehicles I inherited were money pits. They were in a constant state of repair. They knew when they were outside the city limits because they always developed mechanical problems or shut down completely.

You drive by any church or religious nonprofit and out front you will see parked rolling billboards—vehicles with the name of the institution on the side. Drive by the next day and they are still parked in the same place, and the next day, and the next. One wonders if the church or organization is so well off financially that it can have thousands of dollars in capital assets parked and not being used. And in this day of costly insurance premiums, can they really afford the yearly outlay of funds to have the privilege of owning the vehicle? Obviously I would not question the validity of ownership of church/institution vehicles without offering some alternatives.

Consider leasing contract or program use vehicles. With ownership comes responsibility for maintenance. With ownership comes capital investment. And with ownership comes the tendency to retain these assets longer than they can be safely used. If the church or organization operates a day school, after-school program, academy, etc. which requires the daily use of a vehicle, rather than investing capital in the purchase of a vehicle, consider the leasing or rental of the vehicles. Enter into an agreement that includes the provision of a maintenance contract that will keep the vehicles operational, safe, and secure.

Most vehicle manufacturers build vehicles that will last the time of the warranty period. You are familiar with this phenomenon. The moment your odometer passes the magic mileage, the car begins to have knocks, rattles, and problems. It is as if they built it into the odometer. Well, they did. They tested the vehicle and determined that under normal wear and tear, the critter would last this long. So that is where they set the warranty. They are playing the odds that the vast majority of their product will last this long, and they will have no repair obligation. Sometimes they lose, but they usually win. You don't want to keep a vehicle beyond the warranty period. Create your lease for that period. Then turn in the vehicle and get a new one under a new life expectancy.

Use transportation-for-hire resources for unique or one-time needs. Rather than having a bus sit out front waiting for a youth mission trip, a senior adult chautauqua, a children's visit to the zoo, or the weekly movement of the membership from a remote parking lot, arrange for a bus from a transportation supplier to do this for you. The advantage? They provide a clean, safe vehicle with driver. Legitimate, licensed companies provide insurance coverage. Their safety record is monitored by state licensing agencies as well as the National Transportation Agency. I advertised for bids and then negotiated a sole-source contract with a transportation supplier. They wanted our future business so they were Johnny on the spot, even when I came in with a request that was not part of the original planned contract for the year. Since the contract was a movement-of-people agreement and not a use-of-vehicle agreement, upon the very rare occasions when the vehicle broke down or had mechanical trouble, the company provided alternate transportation resources at no additional cost.

Provide a cost-reimbursable account for staff who use their private vehicles. Rather than buying the pastor a car, tell him that the church will provide a fund account that will reimburse him for the mileage he drives in church business. The same can be applied to other staff, case workers, and any person the organization authorizes to use their private vehicle for the business of the institution. There are processes to be followed. The church must first establish a cost-reimbursable account that meets the requirements of the IRS—delineation of who can use it, the call for receipts or records, and the limits of amounts per mile as established annually by the IRS. Such a plan allows for an officer or member to be reimbursed with tax exemption for business use of his vehicle. Publications like IRS Publication 463, "Travel, Entertainment, Gift and Car Expenses outline" the establishment of an accountable reimbursement travel account.

Ensure that transportation and liability insurance will cover the variety of transportation modes. If a church member is using his or her private vehicle for a church-authorized activity and an accident occurs, both the church and individual are liable. While most church insurance policies will state that the individual's insurance is primary in the case, many states are now adopting the position that both companies are equally culpable. So while your rented bus that takes your senior adults to Branson may have its insurance carrier, in the event of a mishap, your policy will be affected. This needs to be discussed with your insurance carrier. Do not assume anything. Make sure you are covered. It is suggested that this variance in liability coverage for transportation also be included in your umbrella policy.

Provide magnetic signs for the vehicles. If your church wants everybody to know that here comes the Shining Light Full Gospel Church of the Everlasting Forever and Forever of Wonderful Valley America, then have a sign company make up a magnetic sign that you can place on the side of the vehicle to say that. It is much cheaper than painting it on the side or back of the vehicle and a lot easier to remove. With permission of course, you can even slap it on the side of the rented bus that is taking the college ministry students on a ski trip. You get the identity you desire, the sign can be used on a variety of vehicles, and it can be transferred to a new lease when that time comes.

Establish a list of authorized drivers. The church or organization needs to establish policy and procedures that will define who is considered an authorized driver. Most insurance carriers will insist on this for their coverage. National and state law now requires certain classes of drivers for certain categories of vehicles. And in many instances throughout the country, there are limitations of ages of drivers as well as categories of vehicles that may be used for program transportation. Since these laws vary widely, it behooves the church or organization to investigate this matter thoroughly. Whether it is the responsibility of a properties committee, personnel committee, transportation ministry team, or risk management team, this issue must be addressed and followed without exception.

Food Service

"And every day they devoted themselves to meeting together in the temple complex, and broke bread from house to house. They ate their food with gladness and simplicity of heart, praising God and having favor with all the people" (Acts 2:46–47). From the time of the ancients, the custom of eating together has been respected as one of the most important cultural activities of any group of people. It was not so much the food that was eaten as the atmosphere and environment of eating. Providing an ample meal was an act of hospitality, celebration, and recognition. Using such descriptors as the killing of the fatted calf for the return of the prodigal son to the banquet feast of the son of the vineyard, Jesus taught that God's bounty was a blessing. Jesus dined in the midst of thousands on a mountainside and in the private home of his followers. He used the Passover meal as the springboard for instituting an ordinance of the church in the Lord's Supper.

I have already told you the story of the use of the Maundy Thursday meal as a time of great fellowship in our church. Let me relate another story to assist you in visualizing the food service program in your church. Our Wednesday night meal program was a wrecking ball to our budget. Even though we used volunteers to prepare, serve, and clean up, it still was an expensive operation. We had a good kitchen that had been included in the infamous family life center built in the 1970s. For a period while I was attending seminary, I commuted from central Oklahoma to Fort Worth and stayed in the men's dorm for a couple of nights every week. Those couple of nights included Wednesday night. Thus I was on the prowl to find the best Wednesday night food service I could find. And I found a great one.

After several months attending the church's meal program and Bible study, I talked to the church administrator about the meal. I told him how well I enjoyed it, especially the fact that it was reasonably priced. I commented that his budget for it must be high for such a quality program. His response knocked me off my feet. "Our Wednesday night meal is not a budget item. In fact, we make money on Wednesday night that we can apply to other areas of ministry, principally our outreach to the poor." A two-year-old could have pushed me over. How could a church food service make money? I learned. Soon our own food service was not only breaking even; we were also making money, so I could provide free coffee and doughnuts every Sunday to the adult Bible study programs, could provide all the plates/eating ware/cups for class parties, subsidize the youth's drink and vending machines, and so forth. Below are some issues we addressed to make the program work.

Determine how the food service program benefits the ministry. Paul had to address several issues with the Corinthian church. In 1 Corinthians we see him talking about eating food offered to idols in chapter 10 and then the violation of the common meal before the Lord's Supper in chapter 11. I like Paul's summary statement in 1 Corinthians 10:31: "Therefore, whether you eat or drink, or whatever you do, do everything for God's glory." The first criteria for establishing a food service is to recognize why the food service contributes to the mission or purpose of the church or organization.

Food service encourages fellowship. People gathered around a table talk to one another. They share a common bond. Meals are the universal glue that bonds cultures and people together. While the food, the format of eating, and even the style of eating vary widely, the very act is an act of hospitality and fellowship.

Food service supports the programs of the church. Wednesday night for us began with a family meal. However during that meal or immediately following the meal, meetings, events, programs, and so forth were carried out. We used food service to enhance ministries by providing for banquets. We had a Saturday morning men's Bible study that began with a breakfast. The singles came together on Thursday night for a meal, Bible study, and fellowship, and recreation time. On Sunday night the youth bridged youth choir and discipleship training with a short snack supper. To alleviate mothers from having to provide meals, programs of child care, day care, and school can provide a healthy noon meal.

Food service fosters involvement. A variety of groups become involved in the preparation of the meal event. We used volunteers as servers. We also used food preparers and clean-up personnel. Some families ate together, and at other times groups of friends ate together. Committees and ministry teams met.

Food service provides convenience. One of the most significant contributors to the food service program we had was the fact that mom did not have to fix a meal for her family and then rush to the church for a Wednesday night prayer meeting and choir practice. Nor did a wife have to get up on Saturday morning at 6:00 a.m. to feed her husband before he went to Bible study.

Food service develops spiritual growth. There are lots of examples, but here is the way we used it. Wednesday supper began serving at 5:30. At 6:30 many of the children and youth programs began and the adults remained around the table for a half hour Bible study. At 7:00 other programs began such as choir practice and some teams that chose not to have team meeting over supper. Those still in the fellowship hall at 7:00 were led in a prayer service by the pastoral staff. Usually by 7:30 most of the programs (except choir) were completed, and parents and children went home. It was during this time of Bible study and prayer that many people grew spiritually. We were opening the bread of life and giving others a cup of cold water in prayer.

Food service creates opportunities for ministry. Many groups will use food service as an outreach tool in their community. Whether a food kitchen serving meals or a food pantry giving staples to families in need, the food becomes the link for ministry and outreach.

Establish policies for food operation. Remember that policies are statements of how the organization will function. They attempt to respond to the contingencies and situations that may arise in the execution of a program. Food service operations are no less responsible for outlining how they will function. Briefly:

- Policies need to meet the mission and purpose of the church or organization.
- Policies and procedures should be fair and equally applicable.
- Responsibility for development and administration must be assigned.
- Accountability for compliance needs to be monitored.

Without effective guidelines for use, the food service areas of the church or organization can quickly become the most abused of all areas of ministry. A variety of issues must be addressed—from who can use the kitchen, its equipment and items to what charges, if any, will be applied. As you will see later in this section, these policies will be determined by the extent of the operation, the investment in capital equipment, and whether designated personnel are responsible for its operation.

Select personnel for effective operations. I appreciate the way Jesus handled Martha in the story of his visiting her and her sister Mary's home as recorded by Luke in Luke 10. In our churches we have Marys and we have Marthas. Jesus chided Martha for forgetting that the ministry purpose outweighs the actual hosting activity.

The selection of personnel to develop policies, carry out procedures, and ensure a palatable, healthy meal is critical to an efficient and successful food service operation. Whether you have a volunteer food handler or a food service director in charge of a large kitchen, individuals who represent the church or organization in the handling of food should have certain characteristics.

1. They should understand that food service is a support operation to the primary ministries of the church or organization.

2. They should be experienced in the area of required expertise. If a cook, they should be qualified and trained to cook for the numbers of people being served. If a bottle washer, they should know how to wash bottles.

3. They should meet qualifications for their job. Every individual in the food service operation from director, church host/hostess, cook, server, etc. should have job descriptions that describe what qualifies them to be in such positions. Part of those qualifications may be a state or local municipal food handler's license.

4. They should have mannerisms that will promote the environment of the meal. They should be outgoing, energetic, and seek harmony. They should be able to communicate. They themselves should be emotionally and spiritually mature.

5. They should be adequately paid if that is the decision of the church or organization. Preparing and serving is hard work. Try preparing a meal for three hundred people some day, and you will see what I mean. If there is to be pay, make it fair and equitable. Find out what the marketplace employees earn and match that.

Survey and select types of food service operations. I love covered-dish meals. My wife is a wonderful cook, but the opportunity to taste someone else's great cooking excites me. Food service opportunities abound: a potluck dinner, Wednesday night fellowship meal, a special event banquet, weddings and receptions, funeral luncheons, parties and gatherings, and meals for ongoing programs such as schools or care programs.

Here are the three basic types of food delivery service:

The potluck or covered dish meal. This is the easiest for the administrator. The people prepare it—in their own dishes—bring it and serve it and then take their excess as well as the dirty dishes home with them. This is the most popular form of food service and lends itself well to such events as class parties, picnics, funeral brunches, receptions, and luncheons. Usually the only responsibility of the administrator is to provide eating utensils, plates, and beverages.

The catered service. This is a covered dish but has only one supplier—the caterer. They prepare it, bring it in their own utensils, provide the service, clean up, and take it away. Depending upon caterer, they may bring the tables and chairs, the tableware and decorations—in other words, the whole shooting match. This service is great for off-site activities or large events that exceed the limits of the local church or organization. In recent years I am aware of many churches that contract with a caterer ongoing events such as the Wednesday night fellowship meal in order to prevent from having to purchase, store, and prepare and serve the meal.

The in-house service. This type of service requires the greatest administrative attention. It includes the acquisition of equipment, the purchase of supplies and food items, the employment of personnel, and the serving and cleanup of the mess. Without efficient operations, this form of food service could be the most expensive.

There are basically four styles of serving the food:

The buffet. This is where you put the food on a serving line and the people take what they want. The menu may be fixed, or you may provide a variety. While it may lower costs by reducing the number of service personnel, it is the most costly to serve since you have no control over the size of the portion.

Cafeteria style. This is a modified buffet where the individual chooses the food to be taken, but there is a level of control in that servers place portions on the plate or measured portions are already placed on serving dishes and cups. This has an advantage in that a variety is offered the individual and portion control is maintained. Its primary disadvantage is that in providing variety you will promote leftover food items and waste.

Plate service. Plate service occurs in two forms. The individual goes through a line and the items of food are placed on the plate and the person walks away with a "standard" meal. A second version is the table service where the individual sits down at a table and a server brings a plate with the food items already in place. This is usually termed banquet service. It has its advantages in portion control and selection of food items. Its principle disadvantage is the cost for providing the servers—and, depending on the size of the group, the delay in getting everyone served.

Family style. This is just like home. You sit down at a table and the food is in bowls and you serve yourself. While food items served are controlled, there is no portion control.

Create an efficient food service kitchen. The efficient kitchen begins with a vision, then a design. Too often churches will create a home-type kitchen in the

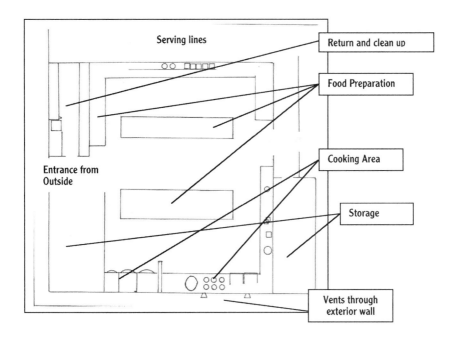

church, expecting it to meet the needs of food service to numerous families. If all a kitchen does is to keep warm preprepared food, then maybe a home-style range and oven will suffice. If food preparation will take place, however, professional, heavy-duty equipment is needed.

In the diagram above a simple kitchen is described. It is located on a ground floor for outside access. It will be adjacent to the serving and storage areas. Its location will allow for more than adequate utility (electricity, gas, water, and sewage) to be provided. Its size will be about one-fourth that of the eating space. It is zoned by task with cooking separated from preparation, from serving, and from return and cleanup. Ventilation is provided to remove heat and cooking gases as well as to circulate air in the entire room about every two to three minutes. The kitchen has hot water service to 120° F and a dishwasher that rinses at 180° F. Counter surfaces are either tile, metal, or other non-porous materials. Storage areas are dry and vermin proof. The equipment is heavy-duty, commercial kitchen grade. Safety features are built in like remote gas and electrical turnoffs; and fire suppression hoods are provided. Floor and wall surfaces are tile or another washable surface, and a drain is provided for wash-down cleaning of the entire space.

Provide quality food. Recently a restaurant chain opened a new restaurant in the local area. We had heard of this particular chain and its notoriety for a remarkable dining experience. So we visited. True to advertisement, the place was spectacularly appointed, the ambiance was remarkable, the wait help was well trained and gracious, the tables were exquisitely appointed, the menu was varied and well chosen—and the food? Well, the food was lousy. For several pages now we have been talking about a food service in the church or organization and all the administrative elements that will lead to success. But just as with the restaurant above, if the food isn't worth eating, people won't come back.

Food preparation takes planning. Food preparation takes people who understand how to prepare and produce food items. Food preparation requires the cook to be aware of the taste of the people who will eat the food. The key is menu planning. I began this section with the story of a church that had a successful food service. And I alluded to the fact that I was able to get there eventually. As Paul Harvey would say, now let's hear the rest of the story.

The leadership of the church decided that food service, especially the Wednesday evening meal, was an important part of our ministry. We thus created schedules for church committee/council/team meetings about that timeframe. Additionally, children and youth mission and music programs were scheduled during this time. We created an environment where the entire family would have activities and programs to attend as part of the family meal night. Then we recruited a leader. You should know by now that I wasn't going to do this. I was going to delegate to someone who could get it done. She was called the church hostess, and all social and food service events were her responsibility. She was given a budget and the authority to hire a staff. She employed a couple of cooks and a helper. She organized a ministry team to help with the service. An additional part-time janitor was employed for setup and cleanup.

We then set about to modify the kitchen to meet code, safety, and OSHA requirements. We were inspected by health safety personnel from the municipal inspection office. We replaced equipment that was not rated as commercial with commercial quality appliances and fixtures. We found used stainless steel tables and replaced the Formica-topped tables with these metal food preparation tables. The floors were already tile, but we added wall tile to five feet high. We ran electrical circuits to the serving areas so we would be able to use moveable, mobile serving carts and counters. We purchased an exterior, large walk-in freezer-refrigerator to store bulk purchases. And we had one of the interior freezers modified as a subzero quick freeze for leftovers. Commercial grade, large microwaves and convection ovens augmented the cooking appliances. A deep-fat fryer was purchased for quick cook items.

Then we were ready to plan for our service. We surveyed our congregation and determined what they liked to eat. We developed a cycle of six éntrées. We spaced the meals with an expensive meal followed by a less expensive meal. Sometimes we used a sequence format where leftovers of one meal became part of the ingredients of another.

Knowing our cycle, we were able to purchase in bulk, knowing that in a six-week cycle the item would be used. Our staple commodities were purchased in bulk. Since we had a dishwashing facility, we chose to use china plates, plastic glasses, and silverware for the basic utensils. We found cafeteria trays in a restaurant supply warehouse and were then able to offer preportioned salads, condiments, and deserts on disposable plates and bowls.

We knew we had to satisfy a variety of tastes and food needs. While the main entree was the six-meal cycle, we provided three alternative meals every time. First there was the alternative kid plate. We had hot dogs, hamburgers, corn dogs, and that type of food for children. We placed these items on a six-meal cycle also to make sure a variety was available. For the dieter, we had a refrigerated salad counter with a variety of condiments that could be added to a salad. And if the person wanted a little more, we had a soup bowl also. Prices varied by what the individual chose. Checkout was at the end of the line. We didn't require reservations because the meals were flexible enough that within a short time the hostess and cooks could estimate how much of what would be needed. On top of that, if it appeared that an item might run out, the efficient kitchen equipment allowed a quick cook so the serving basins never emptied. We kept close records of utilization and choice.

Within six months the Wednesday night meal was in the black. We were able actually to lower costs. We were able to establish a family cap for cost. We were able to contribute significantly to the ministry of the church through the food service. Because of the efficiency in this ministry, other areas of opportunity opened up for the church. Receptions, banquets, dinners, and luncheons were a few of the weekday events that contributed to the ministry effectiveness of the church.

Chapter Review

In this final chapter we have considered several administrative issues that relate to the basic core organizational areas of the church that we defined earlier in the book. The chapter is prompted by the notion that all ministry areas of a church or organization require attention to administrative activities in order to make the ministry successful. The chapter was not designed as a catchall for things forgotten in previous chapters. Neither did this chapter give an extensive treatise of the topics presented. But the chapter should prove to be a prompter of further administrative thought. "If this applies, then what about this" might be the questioning thought pattern of ministry professionals.

With regard to the four general areas of study, the reader should be able to make intelligent comments and responses to the following.

With regard to pastoral support activities:
- Define the nature and role that the designation that ordination brings.
- Discuss the critical issues that provide for the wedding service.
- Describe the sensitive issues relating to funerals.
- Be aware of the importance of the legal ramifications of a counseling ministry.
- Articulate how recreational and family activities build the ministry.

With regard to educational support activities:
- Relate the historical context of the ancient educational systems to modern Bible study programs.
- Describe important elements that relate to the creation of a curriculum of study.
- Discuss the many facets of the media center and how each contributes to the overall education program.
- Be aware of the many critical issues that relate to the safety and security of the child as they relate to childhood education programs.
- Create a training program for potential leadership.
- Describe alternative educational venues.

With regard to music support activities:
- Describe an appropriate program organization structure.
- Discuss how resources are administered.
- Relate how the music ministry builds and integrates with other program ministries of the church.

With regard to the administration support activities:
- Describe how a safe and reliable transportation program can be provided.
- Design and develop a program of food service that will support and enhance the other programs and ministries of the church or organization.

Notes

Preface

1. Robert Welch, "Called to Preach: Forced to Administer," *Your Church*, July/August 1996.

2. Three articles appeared in *Your Church* magazine written by John C. LaRue Jr., vice president of research and development for Christianity Today, Inc. "Pastor at Work: Where the Time Goes," July/August 1998; "Why Pastors Work Too Much," September/October 1998; and "Time Management for Hard-Working Pastors," November/December 1998.

3. Charles Willis, "Forced Termination of Pastors, Staff Leveling Off Survey Results Show," *Facts and Trends,* October 2001, 8–9.

Chapter 1

1. *Vine's Complete Expository Dictionary of Old and New Testament Words,* s.v. "Peace."

2. For an extensive treatment of the roles of the pastor and leadership in the function of the local church or Christian institution, see Kenneth Gangel, *Feeding and Leading: A Practical Handbook on Administration in Churches and Christian Organizations* (Wheaton, Ill.: Victor Books, 1994).

3. Fredrick W. Taylor, *Principles of Scientific Management,* 1967 rev. (New York: Norton, 1947).

4. Elton Mayo, *Human Problems of an Industrial Civilization* (New York: Macmillian, 1933). For a complete discussion of the Hawthorn studies see Henry Landsberger, "Hawthorne revisited: management and the worker, its critics and developments in human relations in industry" (Ithaca, N.Y.: New York School of Industrial and Labor Relations, Cornell University, 1967).

5. Douglas McGregor, *The Human Side of Enterprise* (New York: McGraw-Hill, 1960).

6. Henri Fayol, *General and Industrial Management* (Pitman Publishing, 1949). This is an English translation of the original 1916 work.

7. George R. Terry and Stephen G. Franklin, *Principles of Management* (Homewood, Ill.: Richard D. Irwin, Inc., 1962), 30–31.

8. Harold Koontz and Cyril O'Donnell, *Management: A Systems and Contingency Analysis of Managerial Functions* (New York: McGraw-Hill, 1976).

9. Paul Hersey, *The Situational Leader* (Escondido, Calif.: Center for Leadership Studies, 1992).

10. Ken Blanchard, *The One Minute Manager* (New York: William Morrow and Company, Inc., 1982).

11. Mary Walton, *The Deming Management Method* (New York: Dodd, Mead, 1986).

12. Definition used by the administration faculty of the School of Educational Ministries, Southwestern Baptist Theological Seminary and given in their unpublished syllabus, "Administrative Leadership for Ministry," 2000.

13. Franklin H. Littell, "The Radical Reformation," in Stephen C. Neill and Hans-Ruedi Weber, eds., *The Layman in Christian History* (Philadelphia: Westminister Press, 1963), 263.

14. Marvin T. Judy, *The Multiple Staff Ministry* (Nashville: Abingdon Press, 1969), 28–29.

Chapter 2

1. The material in this section is derived from the unpublished syllabus by the administration faculty of the School of Educational Ministries, Southwestern Baptist Theological Seminary, Fort Worth, Texas. It is the compilation and synthesis of the philosophy of Louis Allen's *The Management Profession* (McGraw-Hill, 1964), and Olan Hendrix's *Management for the Christian Leader* (Fenton, Mich.: Mott Media, 1981).

2. George Odiorne, *Management by Objectives* (New York: Pitman Publishing Corporation, 1965).

3. Vines, s.v. "elder."

4. Warren Bennis and Burt Nanus, *Leaders: The Strategies for Taking Charge* (Cambridge, Mass.: Harper and Row, 1985).

5. John P. Kotter, *What Leaders Really Do* (Cambridge, Mass.: Harvard Business School Press, 1999).

6. Norman Shawchuck and Roger Heuser, *Leading the Congregation* (Nashville: Abingdon Press, 1993).

7. Paul Hersey, *The Situational Leader* (New York: Warner Books, Inc., 1985). See also Kenneth Blanchard, Patricia Zigarmi, and Drea Zigarmi, *Leadership and the One Minute Manager* (New York: William Morrow and Company, Inc., 1985).

8. Douglas McGregor, *The Human Side of Enterprise* (New York: McGraw-Hill, 1960).

9. Kurt Lewin, *Field Theory in Social Sciences* (1951) and *Resolving Social Conflicts* (New York: Harper Trade Books, 1948).

10. Robert Blake and Jane Mouton, *Building a Dynamic Corporation through Grid Organization Development* (Reading, Mass.: Addison-Wesley, 1969).

11. Rensis Likert, *The Human Organization: Its Management and Value* (New York: McGraw-Hill, 1967).

12. Gary L. McIntosh and Samuel D. Rima Sr., *Overcoming the Dark Side of Leadership* (Grand Rapids, Mich.: Baker Books, 1997). This text has an excellent assessment tool that will aid in the discovery of dysfunctional leadership tendencies.

13. Shawchuck and Heuser, chapter 7.

14. Kenneth Blanchard and Norman Vincent Peale, *The Power of Ethical Management* (New York: Ballatine Books, 1988), 20.

15. Shawchuck and Heuser, 104–5.

Chapter 3

1. The 1988 version of *The Church Organization Manual* by this author was an exact duplicate of that original document developed by that church. Since that time the text has been used in seminary and Bible school classrooms in a revised and edited format. When it was adopted and published in 1992 by the National Association of Church Business Administration, agreement was made to "de-baptize" it and to add sections that would make the *Manual* current, legally defensible, and relevant to issues facing the church today. The latest revision was published by NACBA Press in 2002 and appears in both book and CD format.

2. The author has written a book titled *The Church Organization Manual,* which is an illustrated model of a complete church organization manual for a moderate-sized church. It is published by the National Church Business Administration Press, Richardson, Texas. It is usually updated every other year to ensure completeness and application to the local church. Nearly every topic discussed in this textbook is illustrated or exampled in the NACBA manual but without explanation or discussion.

Chapter 4

1. William Morris, ed., *The American Heritage Dictionary of the English Language* (New York: Houghton Mifflin Company), s.v. "polity."

2. Charles A. Tidwell, *The Educational Ministry of a Church,* rev. (Nashville: Broadman & Holman, 1996).

3. Gene Mims, *Kingdom Principles for Church Growth* (Nashville: Convention Press, 1994).

4. A. T. Robertson, *A Harmony of the Gospels for Students of the Life of Christ* (New York: Harper and Brothers, 1950).

5. Cliff Elkins, "Job Descriptions for Staff Members," *Church Administration,* April 1977, 20.

6. This author has a publication with the NACBA Press titled *The Church Organization Manual* that contains a comprehensive listing of over thirty job descriptions of professional, support staff, and lay leadership positions. Other publications with similar comprehensive examples of job descriptions exist. The church or institution is cautioned about going to such documents and copying wholesale the example job description. They may be used as examples, but the church or organization should work through the process of developing the job description that satisfies its needs rather than trying to force some example into their organizational scheme.

7. Jimmie Sheffield and Tim Holcomb, *Church Officer and Committee Guidebook,* rev. (Nashville: Convention Press, 1992).

8. *Robert's Rules of Order,* revised (Upper Saddle River, N.J.: Scott, Foresman, 1990).

Chapter 5

1. F. Hertzberg, B. Mausner, and B. Sauderman, *The Motivation to Work* (New York: John Wiley & Sons, 1959).

2. John C. LaRue Jr., "Pastor at Work: Where the Time Goes," *Your Church,* July/August 1998.

Chapter 6

1. Vines, s.v. "tithe."

2. The listing in this chapter comes from unpublished handout information provided to participants in the National Association of Church Business Administration certification courses that are conducted annually in various seminary and college/university settings nationwide. The list is not purported to be complete. In fact, the listing is validated each year by seminar coordinators. A list may be obtained from NACBA.net.

3. Vines, s.v. "servant."

4. Excellent resources are available to assist the church or organizational finance officer in the conduct of the institution's business. For example: Dan Busby, *Church and Nonprofit Tax & Finance Guide* and the *Minister's Tax and Financial Guide* (Grand Rapids, Mich.: Zondervan, published annually); Richard R. Hammar, et al, *Church Law & Tax Report* (Matthews, N.C.: Christian Ministry Resources, published periodically); Otto Crumroy, Stan Kukawka, and Frank Whitman, *Church Administration and Finance Guide* (Harrisburg, Pa.: Morehouse Publishing, 1998); David R. Pollock, *Business*

Management in the Local Church, rev. (Chicago: Moody Press, 1996); *NACBA National Church Staff Compensation Survey* (Richardson, Tex.: NACBA Press, published biannually).

Chapter 7

1. Cleaning Management Institute, "In-House Cleaning Operations Benchmarking Survey Report," *CM Cleaning & Maintenance Management,* May 2003, 35–42.

Chapter 8

1. Elizabeth S. Ballard, "Messages Communicated by Your Church Office," *Church Administration,* November 1987, 14–16.

2. Marvin Judy, *The Multiple Staff Ministry* (Nashville: Abingdon, 1967), 200–1.

3. Lyle Schaller, *The Multiple Staff and the Larger Church* (Nashville: Abingdon, 1980), 59–60.

4. Charles Tidwell, *Church Administration: Effective Leadership for Ministry* (Nashville: Broadman Press, 1985), 114–15.

Chapter 9

1. Robert Welch, "Lessons from Wedgewood Baptist," *Your Church,* March/April 2000.

Chapter 10

1. Norman Shawchuck and Roger Heuser, *Leading the Congregation* (Nashville: Abingdon Press, 1993), 69.

2. Gwenn E. McCormick, *Planning and Building Church Facilities* (Nashville: Broadman Press, 1992), 20.

Chapter 11

1. Rick Warren, *The Purpose Driven Church* (Grand Rapids, Mich.: Zondervan, Inc., 1995); Gene Mims, *Kingdom Principles for Church Growth* (Nashville: Convention Press, 1994); and Morlee H. Maynard, comp., *We're Here for the Churches,* rev. (Nashville: LifeWay Press, 2000).

2. Arthur Flake, *Building a Standard Sunday School* (Nashville: Sunday School Board of the Southern Baptist Convention, 1922).

3. Andy Anderson, *The Growth of Faith Spiral* (Nashville: Broadman & Holman, 1993); Bobby H. Welch, *Evangelism through the Sunday School—Journey in FAITH* (Nashville: LifeWay Press, 1998).

4. D. James Kennedy, *Evangelism Explosion: Equipping Churches for Friendship, Evangelism, Discipleship, and Healthy Growth* (Wheaton, Ill.:

Tyndale House Publisher, 1996). Campus Crusade for Christ's "Have You Heard of the Four Spiritual Laws?" as well as The Billy Graham Evangelistic Association's "Steps to Peace with God," and the American Tract Society's "Four Things God Wants You to Know" are all examples of efforts by groups to provide evangelistic helps through simple booklet ministries that any person can learn and use.

5. Robert Sheffield, comp., *Handbook for Planning Deacon Ministry* (Nashville LifeWay Press, 1999); and Jim Henry, *Deacons: Partners in Ministry and Growth* (Nashville: developed by Sampson Ministry Resources and distributed by LifeWay Christian Resources, 1997) are examples of the types of resources denominational groups make available to churches to provide leadership in deacon ministry.

6. John C. LaRue Jr., "Where Does the Church's Money Go?" *Your Church,* September/October 2002, 136.

Index